W9-BIQ-301

# WITHDRAWN

Perkins and Hemingway in Key West, 1935.

# THE ONLY THING THAT COUNTS

◆

THE
ERNEST HEMINGWAY/MAXWELL PERKINS
CORRESPONDENCE
1925–1947

*"the utterly real thing in writing is the only thing that counts"*
—MAXWELL PERKINS TO ERNEST HEMINGWAY, 1935

EDITED BY
## MATTHEW J. BRUCCOLI

WITH THE ASSISTANCE OF
### ROBERT W. TROGDON

SCRIBNER

SCRIBNER
1230 Avenue of the Americas
New York, NY 10020

DESIGNED BY ERICH HOBBING

Set in Sabon

Manufactured in the United States of America

1 3 5 7 9 10 8 6 4 2

Library of Congress Cataloging-in-Publication Data
Hemingway, Ernest, 1899–1961.
The only thing that counts : the Ernest Hemingway-Maxwell Perkins cor-
respondence 1925–1947 / edited by Matthew J. Bruccoli ; with the assis-
tance of Robert W. Trogdon.
p.   cm.
"The utterly real thing in writing is the only thing that counts."
1. Hemingway, Ernest, 1899–1961—Correspondence. 2. Novelists,
American—20th century—Correspondence. 3. Perkins, Maxwell E.
(Maxwell Evarts), 1884–1947—Correspondence. 4. Editors—United
States—Correspondence. 5. Hemingway, Ernest, 1899–1961—Friends
and associates. 6. Perkins, Maxwell E. (Maxwell Evarts), 1884–1947—
Friends and associates. 7. Authors and publishers—United States—His-
tory—20th century. 8. Hemingway, Ernest, 1899–1961—Editors.
I. Perkins, Maxwell E. (Maxwell Evarts), 1884–1947. II. Bruccoli,
Matthew Joseph, 1931– .
PS3515.E37Z492   1996
813'.52—dc20      96-25052
CIP

ISBN 0-684-81562-1

I'm glad you're going to write some stories. All You have to do is to follow your own judgement, or instinct, + disregard what is said, + convey the absolute bottom quality of each person, situation + thing. Isn't that simple!!—But it's what you have been doing. When you're ready do a novel. That's what they all must want. That's what they all tell me they want + want me to tell you. I don't think I can tell You anything. If what I have said should worry You + I knew it I'd beg you to disregard + forget it. I can get pretty depressed but even at worst I still believe—+ it's written in all the past—that the utterly real thing in writing is the only thing that counts, + the whole racket melts down before it. All you have to do is to trust Yourself. That's the truth.—I say all this mostly because I sometimes have thought that You thought I ought to advise You, or keep You advised. I do that for lots of people who write as a trade. With You it seems superfluous + absurd because those things that are important to that kind of writer + affect his fortunes, ought not to have anything to do with You,—+ so far You have not let them. I hope You never will, too.

—Perkins to Hemingway, 30 August 1935


Writing whether you want it or not is competitive—Most of the time you compete against time and dead men. . . .

—Hemingway to Perkins, 20 August 1928


If they feel disappointed and still want my "literary Credo" in a book on bull fighting they can run an insert saying "F-ck the whole god-damned lousy racket. . . ."

—Hemingway to Perkins, 28 June 1932


I find I know a lot more than when I used to write and think that is maybe what makes it easier in the end but it is still a very tough business.

—Hemingway to Perkins, 25 March 1939

The Editor Dedicates This Volume to

THE HOUSE OF SCRIBNER

In Its Sesquicentennial Year

and

In Memory of

CHARLES SCRIBNER, JR.

1921–1995

# ACKNOWLEDGMENTS

———————◆———————

Charles Scribner III conceived this volume with the editor and handled the arduous contractual chores. Patrick Hemingway provided much-appreciated encouragement.

Judith S. Baughman ran the office while this volume was in progress. Essential research aid was provided by these keepers of Hemingway collections: John Delaney and Alice V. Clark at the Princeton University Library; Megan Desnoyers and Stephen Plotkin at the John F. Kennedy Library; Timothy Murray and L. Rebecca Johnson-Melvin at the University of Delaware Library; Beth Alvarez and Deborah Volk at the University of Maryland Library. These graduate assistants at the University of South Carolina found the answers: Anthony Perrello, Robert Moss, Cy League, Park Bucker, and Justin Pittas-Giroux. Bert Dillon and Robert Newman provided chairmanly support. The splendid staff of the Thomas Cooper Library, University of South Carolina, was always helpful; but the Interlibrary Loan Department merits special recognition. Publication of this volume was eventually made possible by permission of the Ernest Hemingway Foundation and Society.

# PREFACE

It seems serendipitous that this rich volume of literary correspondence appear on the sesquicentennial of the Scribner publishing house. Both Hemingway and his editor Maxwell Perkins have become legends in American letters—and justifiably so. I cannot think of a twentieth-century author or editor who has left a deeper or more lasting imprint in modern literature than each of these two men. The letters they exchanged as professionals and friends for over two decades offer a rare glimpse into the creative relationship between writer and editor. This correspondence, selected and annotated by Matthew J. Bruccoli, who knows more about Fitzgerald, Hemingway, and Perkins than they ever knew about each other (and perhaps about themselves), needs no formal introduction. It tells a story as illuminating to Hemingway readers and students as it is salutary to prospective authors and editors—indeed to all who dwell in Shakespeare's "dukedom large enough," the world of books. Instead I should like to reflect, from both a personal and familial vantage point, on the writer who towers over our 150 years of publishing: Ernest Hemingway.

As I look back on my family's association with Hemingway I realize that I am only the *fourth* in the succession of Charles Scribners who have been involved in publishing Hemingway's works since he first debuted on our list in 1926—seventy years, a biblical life span ago. The Charles who presided at that auspicious moment was my great-grandfather, whose own father, the first CS, had founded Scribners in 1846. In 1932, my grandfather, yet another Charles (we are a redundant family), took over the helm and as Hemingway's contemporary proceeded to combine the roles of publisher and intimate friend to a degree unprecedented and perhaps unsurpassed in modern publishing. That relationship took on still greater significance after Perkins's death in 1947, which was a terrible blow to my grandfather as well as to Hemingway.

It is enough to say that Perkins had long since become my grandfather's inseparable friend: the two men had lunch together almost every working day. But Charles Scribner never attempted to assume the role of Perkins vis-à-vis Hemingway. The publisher's unique basis of friendship, and influence, was that he never presented himself as a *literary*—much less editorial—professional. In his tongue-in-cheek introduction to the 1946 edition of *A Farewell to Arms,* Hemingway wrote: "My publisher, Charles

Scribner, who knows a great deal about horses, as much as a man probably should be allowed to know about the publishing business, and, surprisingly, something about books, asked me to write about how I felt about illustrations and having a book illustrated." In short, Hemingway hated the illustrations. Yet my father's sobering first assignment at Scribners was to oversee the editing and production and to communicate with the unhappy author—without any prior publishing experience. His previous wartime assignment of breaking enemy codes must have seemed far less taxing in hindsight!

When my grandfather died at the age of sixty-two in 1952, the distraught author wrote to my grandmother: "Now my dear and good friend is gone and there is no one to confide in nor trust nor make rough jokes with and I feel so terribly about Charlie being gone that I can't write anymore. . . ." A week later he sent an equally heartfelt letter to my father, who was still on active duty in Washington as a naval lieutenant once again engaged in crypt-analysis during the Korean war:

> "I won't try to write to you how much he meant to me as a friend and as a publisher. He was the best and closest friend that I had and it seems impossible that I will never have another letter from him. It does not do any good to talk about it and there is nothing to say that makes it any easier. Since he had to die at least he has gotten it over with.
>
> If there is anything practical I can do please let me know. . . . I will try and not worry you about finances nor about anything else. You don't have to write me letters nor have me on your mind in any way. I know what a terribly tough job you have now with Navy, Estate and the House of Scribner to look after. They shouldn't do that to any human being. Please take it as easy as you can and feel free to call on me in any way that I can be of help. . . . This is not a good letter, Charlie. But I still feel too sad to write a good one.
>
> Your friend
> Ernest Hemingway"

(With typically Hemingwayesque precision, he then added this post-script: "Am sorry I don't know your rank so address this as a civilian. EH")

My father later commented in his book of essays, *In the Web of Ideas: The Education of a Publisher* (1993), that he could "not imagine a kinder expression of condolence or a more delicate assurance of loyalty. And in the lovely phrase of Dickens, he was better than his word. For the next nine years of his life, he was as easy to work with as any author I have ever known." Thrust into the presidency of Scribners at the age of thirty, Charles Scribner, Jr., was to be Hemingway's last publisher and personal editor. His relationship with our preeminent author was to prove no less fruitful (if more formal) than his father's had been.

After Hemingway's death in 1961, my father presided over the publication of the remaining works, beginning with *A Moveable Feast* and including the unfinished novels *Islands in the Stream* (for which he coined the title) and *The Garden of Eden*. His own account of these experiences with and without Hemingway is recorded in fascinating detail in his memoir *In the Company of Writers: A Life in Publishing* (1991). There he explains the reasons for his one act of disobedience ("for which I'll have to account to Ernest in the hereafter")—publishing a selection of Hemingway's letters in 1981.

Hemingway left strict instructions that his letters should not be published. But, with Mary's approval, I published them—and I think I did the right thing. To begin with, he had kidded my father about publishing his letters, so he had thought of such a thing. Second, I believe his letters show a side of him that nothing else in his work does, and it is a very nice side. I considered that I was justified. It is well known that Virgil left instructions for the *Aeneid* to be burned after his death. Fortunately not all literary executors obey such requests.

It seems only fitting that, of the four Charleses, my father be the one to assess Hemingway's significance as a writer and a man. The following text of a lecture he gave at the Princeton Club Library in New York in 1985 seems to me as sound and sensitive an appraisal as any I have read, and I therefore offer it in its full (and unedited) form.

### ERNEST HEMINGWAY: A PUBLISHER'S ASSESSMENT

I am delighted to have the opportunity to share a few thoughts about the writings of Ernest Hemingway and the character of the man. These are not neglected topics. In fact, in the course of the past several decades a huge scholarly industry has grown up around the life and works of Hemingway and virtually all the possible fields of Hemingway studies have been painstakingly gleaned. There is a Hemingway Society and a Hemingway Newsletter, and annual pilgrimages are made by enthusiasts to parts of the world featured in his books. Even a careless typo in a Hemingway book can become a subject for extended scholarly debate. Since I had the temerity to correct one of those passages I am painfully familiar with the passions that can be aroused. One is reminded of the prolonged iota subscript issue that rocked Christian theology for generations.

Given all this professional scholarship, I am reconciled to preserving my own amateur standing and accordingly have decided to confine myself here to remarks about Hemingway which may seem obvious. Obviousness does not deter me. In fact, I believe that in this and many other fields of study the obvious is nowadays neglected much too often.

One of the obvious facts about Hemingway is that virtually all his life, from the time he was a boy to the day he died, he thought of himself as a writer—nothing else. That image of himself created his ambition, directed his will, supplied his greatest satisfaction.

I think that from the start there was a kind of enchantment about his commitment to writing. Robert Louis Stevenson, in his autobiographical essay "The Lantern Bearers," describes the excitement he felt as a boy when he and his comrades would meet after dark, each of them carrying a bull's-eye lantern under his topcoat. All the lanterns were lit but kept covered for the greater part of the expedition. Then, at the end, they were uncovered and allowed to shine out full strength. But for those boys roaming the streets of Edinburgh, the bliss in the adventure lay in the knowledge that the lanterns were lit and burning brightly even in the dark under their topcoats.

Like all true artists, Hemingway carried from the start a bull's-eye lantern under his topcoat. Most of the time he kept it hidden from outsiders; he would talk about it tangentially, if at all. But it was there all the time, the most important thing in his life.

As early as his high school days he had come to think of himself as a writer. It was a reasonable pretension. Words came easily to him, and he had a natural sense of style for putting them together. One of the results of his years at the Oak Park and River Forest High School was to bring him to a realization of his talent. In his senior year he wrote lively reports for the weekly school paper and short stories for its literary magazine. That is not an unusual combination of genres for a schoolboy, but Hemingway never gave them up. Throughout his career he wrote stories and news reports.

The experience of seeing his work in print was as pleasing to him as it is to all writers, but in him it became an addiction. He was always on the lookout for material to use in a story; he was a magpie in that respect, industriously and almost by reflex action storing away in his memory colorful bits and pieces of life. His classmates had referred to him as "Our Ring Lardner," the highest compliment they could pay him, and at that time by no means inappropriate. When the time came for him to think about college, it could have been no great surprise to anyone that he chose instead a job as cub reporter on the Kansas City *Star*. He knew he had a bent for journalism and the job was in line with his ambition as a writer.

Hemingway's six-month stint on the *Star* has been described as an apprenticeship. Valuable in many ways, it provided him with material that he used for his later fiction. He learned how to dig out the facts of a story and he toiled to describe them simply and directly. He also learned to recognize a good story when he saw one. His image of himself as a writer had now developed into the reality of being a professional writer; status—and that particular status—was very important to him.

It is clear that as a writer Hemingway would develop still farther beyond the lessons he had learned in Kansas City. He would end up creating a style capable of representing events and truths that lie outside the scope of journalism, and to do that he had a certain amount of unlearning to do. His companions in journalism were impressed not only by his energy on the job but also by his interest in literature off the job. There was a bull's-eye lantern lighted under his coat.

Leaving the *Star* for wartime ambulance service in Italy interrupted writing, but the variety and vividness of the memories then stored up show that he was still seeing everything with the eye of the reporter.

The first crisis in his writing career occurred when he got back home. With his desire to be a "real" writer, an important writer, keen as ever, the stories he wrote then were rejected over and over for a whole year.

It must be startling for readers familiar with Hemingway's later work to read his productions of that period. In their stilted language these stories seem utterly unlike what we know he had it in him to write. He was clearly spinning his wheels. In the straits he was in at the time, it was providential that he managed to obtain a free-lance assignment on the Toronto *Star.* Almost a chance event, this was one of the most fortunate opportunities that ever came his way. For a writer, there is no substitute for being published and read. The *Star* gave him an appreciative readership and kept him writing on a regular basis. Between February 1920 and December 1924, he wrote over a hundred and fifty pieces for the *Star,* ranging from amusing sketches of everyday life close to home—medical fads, tips to campers, political satires, and the like—to firsthand observations as a foreign correspondent in postwar Europe.

This diversity of topics and styles raised his competence as a journalist to the top level of professionalism. It also gave him the opportunity to meet most of the literary masters who visited or lived in Paris in the twenties—Gertrude Stein, Scott Fitzgerald, Ford Madox Ford, James Joyce, Ezra Pound, and Archibald MacLeish.

One of Hemingway's most deeply rooted traits was his horror of being an outsider, let alone an also-ran. Once he had met writers of stature, it was inevitable that he would try to match or exceed their accomplishments. For a young newspaperman this might have proven a sin of envy deserving to be punished by the gods. But the gods would have been wrong, for they had already bestowed on him more than enough talent to fulfill his ambition.

It was in this period that Hemingway tried a number of experiments in the craft of fiction. One of his declared aims was to learn to write "one true sentence." The mini-stories that were privately published in *in our time* were the first fruits of this effort.

By stripping off virtually the entire context of an event and leaving a starkly isolated image in a timeless present, Hemingway found that the impact of the words on the reader could be greatly enhanced. Yet it is difficult to measure the success of that new style by means of the events that occur in that first series of sketches, because the description of executions or horrors on the battlefield or in the bull ring are able by themselves to elicit strong visceral effects in the reader—regardless of style.

But Hemingway did not stop there. He went on to apply the stripping technique to the mental states of individuals and to the relations between two or more characters. The stories "Up in Michigan" and "Cross-Country Snow" are early examples of that "subtractive" technique. The same principle dictated the use of laconic, allusive dialogue. The sparseness of detail forces the reader to pay close attention to whatever information is provided. As a result, the reader's imagination plays an active role and the narrative thereby acquires the convincing force of something worked for and lived through.

Hemingway later used the technique to describe certain events of his boyhood, for the clear purpose not so much of retelling as of reproducing the inner feeling of a character at a crucial moment in his life.

To what extent Hemingway was influenced by Joyce's method of revealing similar "epiphanies" in *Dubliners* is difficult to establish. I believe that he was so influenced but such perceptions can of course be neither proved nor disproved.

The important element in Hemingway's writings derives from his constant concern to convey powerful psychological states: despair and hope, fear and courage, anger and resignation. Like Conrad, he was primarily concerned with the soul. The story may deal with the body, that is, exciting action and vivid sensations; but the ultimate goal is the transformation of character.

Several years ago, in discussing her husband with me, Mary Hemingway told me about his extraordinary ability to walk into a room full of strangers and instantly divine the multiple relations and attitudes within the group. It is that gift that was responsible for the psychological subtlety of his fiction, a quality that has been overlooked by many readers and critics who take at face value his reputation as a writer concerned primarily with external action.

Let me conclude by telling about an incident that occurred at Scribners. I was a young man at the time, attempting to earn my spurs as a publisher. It was not long after our publication of *The Old Man and the Sea* when one of our college travelers discovered an embryonic version of the story that had been published in *Esquire* in 1936. For all I know, the man may have been told about this by one of the English professors he had called on. That young man is now a prominent literary agent—and what more can he desire from life? But it occurred to him that it would be an admirable thing to republish this *ur*-version of *The Old Man and the Sea* together with the novella itself in a special college edition.

We thought it was a pretty good idea too, and proposed it to the author. But Hemingway—Hemingway the *writer*—did not think it was a good idea at all. Nor was he open to any such good ideas at any time thereafter.

In the years that followed that episode, I often remembered Hemingway's fury at the suggestion. Why was he so put out? Until recently I ascribed this to his well-known resentment of scholars who ferreted out his sources or explored his life. In these matters, he was apt to express the combined disbelief and despair of a magician when someone in the audience keeps trying to explain his feats. Now I think I have a sharper understanding of that annoyance many years ago. For Hemingway his story had an outside and an inside. The outside might be the basis for a good yarn, and so it was in *Esquire*. But only the inside could be the basis for a work of literature.

CHARLES SCRIBNER, JR.

Upon publication of *The Old Man and the Sea* in the fall of 1952, Hemingway inscribed in his publisher's copy of the novella: "*Il faut (d'abord) durer.*" One must, first of all, endure. In a more comic vein he gave expression to the same idea in a letter written to my father on the eve of publication. Responding to a paternal report of how, at the age of fifteen months, I had taken to pulling books out of bookcases, Hemingway commented: "What young Charlie is probably trying to do is get the dead wood out of publishing. Make a note of it for his biographers." Four decades later, it is clear that Hemingway has endured, and *shall* endure, as the towering figure of twentieth-century American literature. There is no dead wood to be found here.

CHARLES SCRIBNER III

# Editorial Note

---

This volume does not publish the complete Hemingway/Perkins correspondence: it is a selection of the letters providing the most useful material about the two men, their editorial relationship, the House of Scribner, and the profession of authorship in America.[1]

The decision to cut Ernest Hemingway's letters was determined by production requirements; nonetheless, it is regrettable and challengeable. In a perfect publishing world it would be mandatory to include the complete texts of Hemingway's letters because everything he did connected with his writing. But in what is allegedly the real world, the choice had to be made between losing an entire letter or printing the most useful parts. Material dealing with Hemingway's work, his literary judgments, and the craft and trade of writing has been retained. Many of Hemingway's reports on hunting and fishing, as well as his news about friends (Waldo Peirce, Evan Shipman, Charles Sweeny) have been omitted. Word counts are stipulated for editorial cuts.

Hemingway's letters in this volume are printed without emendations; nonetheless these letters—whether handwritten or typed by him—cannot be accurately reproduced by typesetting. Hemingway's words can be transcribed; but the appearance of his words on the pages—which reinforces the messages—can be retained only in facsimile. Hemingway wrote letters in haste to catch a mail boat or a mail plane; he wrote in anger; and he wrote with alcohol in his bloodstream. Even under the best epistolary conditions he was not a tidy correspondent. These printed Hemingway letters convey an impression of neatness or finality that is often absent in the documents.

Hemingway's spellings and punctuation—or lack of punctuation—have been preserved; no punctuation has been supplied. His handwriting does not always make capital letters clear; in these instances the editors exercised best guesses based on experience with Hemingway manuscripts. Printing accommodations have been obligatory: editorial decisions have been made to differentiate Hemingway's hyphens and dashes. Dash lengths have been standardized, unless a long dash appears to be functional. Spaced hyphens in

---

[1]The Charles Scribner's Sons Archives at the Princeton University Library hold 472 letters from Hemingway to Perkins and 700 from Perkins to Hemingway. Additional letters are in the Hemingway Collection at the John F. Kennedy Library. This volume publishes 130 Hemingway letters and 108 Perkins letters.

typed letters have been treated as dashes unless used as hyphens (e.g., to form a compound adjective). The extra spacing between typed words and the spacing before or after punctuation marks has not been retained—except in a few instances where the word spacing appears to be meaningful. In almost every instance, the extra spacing was the unintentional result of Hemingway's habit of double-striking the space bar.

Maxwell Perkins's typed letters have been transcribed from the carbon copies in the Scribner's Archives. They are supplemented by his handwritten letters in the Kennedy Library. Perkins's letters have been excerpted, cutting purely business data and the editor's news about Hemingway's friends. Word counts are stipulated for editorial omissions. Perkins's typed letters were almost all dictated to his secretary; their consistent use of spaced hyphens and other punctuation characteristics has been retained. No editorial corrections have been made in Perkins's letters.

The footnoting provides the most necessary explanations—particularly for editorial matters. The more footnotes, the fewer letters.

The letter headings stipulate date and place of writing (if not provided in the letter) and a description of the document. ALS identifies an autograph letter signed; TLS identifies a typed letter signed; and CC is a carbon copy. Omissions at the beginning or end of a paragraph are designated by spaced periods. Omission of each complete paragraph is designated by a line of five spaced periods.

# THE ONLY THING
# THAT COUNTS

*adise* by stating that he would no longer feel comfortable at Scribners if it were rejected. Fitzgerald's first novel was a surprise literary and commercial success; and his loyalty to Perkins and Scribners prompted him to act as a volunteer literary scout for the firm. He brought his friend Ring Lardner to Perkins, and Lardner's reputation as a serious writer flourished under the Scribners imprint. Fitzgerald's greatest find was Hemingway. In 1924— before he had met Hemingway—Fitzgerald alerted Perkins to the work of a writer whose fiction had not yet appeared in America: "This is to tell you about a young man named Ernest Hemmingway, who lives in Paris, (an American) writes for the transatlantic Review + has a brilliant future. Ezra Pount published a collection of his short pieces in Paris, at some place like the Egotist Press. I havn't it hear now but its remarkable + I'd look him up right away. He's the real thing."[2] Perkins wrote to Hemingway, but the letter went astray; by the time Perkins made contact, Hemingway had signed with Horace Liveright. Fitzgerald's efforts as matchmaker succeeded after Hemingway became dissatisfied with Boni & Liveright.

Perkins's editorial technique was advisory and supportive—not collaborative. He did not revise or rewrite. He did not function as a line editor on typescripts and proofs. There is no evidence that he corrected grammar or punctuation; there are no extant Hemingway typescripts or proofs marked by Perkins. See his 14 August 1940 letter about *For Whom the Bell Tolls*. Perkins was concerned with the effect of the work as a whole. Novelist Caroline Gordon explained that "he steps into the author's place, and he is able to visualize the book almost exactly, I find, as the author visualizes it."[3]

When Fitzgerald protested against his advice to delete a passage ridiculing the Bible in *The Beautiful and Damned,* Perkins responded: "Don't ever <u>defer</u> to my judgment. You won't on any vital point, I know, and I should be ashamed, if it were possible to have made you; for a writer of any account must speak solely for himself."[4] Even Perkins's most intense editorial task, with Wolfe, was mainly precatory. When Wolfe left Scribners and Perkins in 1937 as a consequence of charges that he could not finish a novel without Perkins, the editor wrote: "But my impression was that you asked my help, that you wanted it. And it is my impression too that changes were not forced on you (you're not very forceable, Tom, nor am I very forceful), but were argued over, often for hours. . . . I believe the writer anyway, should always be the final judge, and I meant you to be so. I have always held to that position and have sometimes seen books hurt thereby, but at least as often helped. The book belongs to the author."[5]

[2]c. 10 October 1924; *F. Scott Fitzgerald: A Life in Letters,* ed. Matthew J. Bruccoli, with the assistance of Judith S. Baughman (New York: Scribners, 1994), p. 82.

[3]Malcolm Cowley, *Unshaken Friend* (Boulder, Colo.: Roberts Rinehart, 1985), p. 13.

[4]12 December 1921; *Dear Scott/Dear Max: The Fitzgerald-Perkins Correspondence,* ed. John Kuehl and Jackson R. Bryer (New York: Scribners, 1971), p. 47.

[5]A. Scott Berg, *Max Perkins: Editor of Genius* (New York: Congdon/Dutton, 1978), pp. 319–320.

Perkins did not write a critical manifesto, but his literary values can be extrapolated from the books by the writers he worked with most closely. He was a proponent of social realism: "the utterly real thing in writing is the only thing that counts." He admired well-structured novels with strong story content and believed that characters are the most memorable elements in fiction.

Hemingway and Perkins had eighteen definite meetings—including four fishing trips to Key West and one duck-shooting trip to Arkansas—some fifty days. Another fourteen probable meetings occurred when Hemingway was in New York.[6] Their relationship was perforce mainly epistolary as Hemingway lived in Key West or Cuba, traveled, and avoided the "angle-worm" literary life of New York. Perkins's seven-hundred-odd letters to Hemingway were mainly concerned with publishing business, as differentiated from literary matters. But Hemingway rarely wrote Perkins an impersonal letter; his nearly five hundred letters to Perkins are heavily dosed with reports of his activities and comments on his fields of expertise. The didactic and pedagogical impulses are manifest in all of Hemingway's correspondence. Perkins was not impervious to "the Hemingway treatment." The sedentary editor with a household full of women and a stable of female authors enjoyed his honorary membership in Hemingway's cult of masculinity. Perkins was a drinker and a military historian, but he was a sportsman only with or through Hemingway.

Hemingway's letters to Perkins did not provide keys to his fiction. He did not discuss his work in progress—apart from providing progress reports—or invite editorial advice while he was writing. As a consequence of Perkins's celebrated work with Wolfe that involved cutting and restructuring, students and teachers generally assume that he performed the same editorial services for all his authors. What transpired during the Hemingway/Perkins meetings remains unknown, but their correspondence establishes that Hemingway did not necessarily act on Perkins's written editorial suggestions. He disregarded Perkins's advice about revising the closing chapter of *A Farewell to Arms,* but he did accept Perkins's advice on dividing the novel into five sections. Hemingway disregarded Perkins's recommendation for cutting Chapter XVIII of *For Whom the Bell Tolls,* but he invited advice about ending the novel.

Commencing with *The Sun Also Rises,* Perkins's most perilous duty as Hemingway's editor was to persuade him to delete words that could not be printed by a respectable publisher—certainly not by Charles Scribner's Sons—and that the editor could not bring himself to write in letters or pronounce. The most widely repeated anecdote about Hemingway and Perkins—possibly apocryphal—has it that during one of their editorial meetings Hemingway persuaded Perkins to write on his desk calendar the words that the editor would not say. When Charles Scribner III noticed the calendar notations he remarked, "Don't you want to take the rest of the day off,

[6]See Chronology.

Max? You must be exhausted." Hemingway did not succeed in spelling out *fucking* until *To Have and Have Not* (1937). In certain cases Hemingway seemed to be testing Perkins: he surely knew that *c-cks-cker* or even *c-ks-r* was impossible to print in *A Farewell to Arms* (1929). The correspondence about heretofore-unprintable words supports Hemingway's claim that his intention was not to shock the guardians of decency or to derive publicity by using these words. His purpose was to provide a truthful impression of the language of his characters. Getting it right was always at the core of his technique. He insisted that particular words were integral to the total effect of a novel. As he told Perkins: "My point is that the operation of emasculation is a tiny one—It is very simple and easy to perform on men—animals and books—It is not a Major operation but, its effects are great—It is <u>never</u> performed <u>intentionally</u> on books—What we must both watch is that it should not be performed unintentionally—" (16 February 1929). Hemingway made it easier for the writers who came after him to write honestly.

The marked personality contrasts between Perkins and his star authors were largely negated by his commitment to good writing and his loyalty to his writers. While fulfilling his responsibilities to the House of Scribner he maintained his writers' confidence and trust—insofar as they were capable of trusting an editor or publisher. Fitzgerald was not difficult. Wolfe was chronically suspicious; no editor could have held him. Hemingway was less suspicious than Wolfe but required reassurances of Scribners' commitment to him. Like most authors, he was convinced that his books were inadequately advertised and that other authors were receiving more generous exposure. Perkins pacified Hemingway's rages and kept him on the Scribners list. Hemingway had three more wives after he became a Scribners author but only one editor during Perkins's lifetime.

Perkins endeavored to foster a clublike relationship among his authors, setting up meetings and relaying news about their activities. These efforts were not necessarily successful, for there was sibling rivalry. Perkins worried about Fitzgerald and shared his concern with Hemingway, who early assumed a big-brother attitude toward Fitzgerald—although Hemingway was the younger man.

Most of the business letters have been omitted, but the letters included here are frequently about money. Hemingway's commitment to the craft of literature is not diminished by the assertion that money made it possible for him to write. He made everything he did the material for literature—most obviously in *Death in the Afternoon* and *Green Hills of Africa*—and these activities were expensive. Hemingway's travels and avocations before *For Whom the Bell Tolls* were largely subvened by his first two wives. He did not write just for money and was uneasy about the corrupting effects of big-money deals. Nonetheless, he was a hard bargainer with Perkins because he needed large infusions of money to supplement the generosity of the Pfeiffer family and because he believed that Scribners was making more than he was from his work. Moreover, he did not have an agent. Maurice Speiser, his

New York lawyer, handled contractual details, and subsidiary rights, but Hemingway made his own deals.

The friendship between Hemingway and Perkins did not purge the author's permanent feeling that his relationship with Scribners was an employee-employer relationship. In 1933, he explained to Arnold Gingrich, the editor of *Esquire* with whom he was establishing a connection:

> I remember Max Perkins, of whom I am very fond, asking me, in a letter, when I would stop calling him Mr. Perkins. I am very fond of him, really, but wrote him that it would cost me at least $10,000 to stop calling him Mr.—(it has) and I did. In dealing with anyone in business when you become pals they can always invoke the necessities of business vs. your own needs while you must do things because you are a friend.[7]

Perkins instructed a publishing class in 1946: "An editor does not add to a book. At best he serves as a handmaiden to an author. Don't ever get to feeling important about yourself, because an editor at most releases energy. He writes nothing. . . . A writer's best work comes entirely from himself."[8] Ernest Hemingway would have written books and had them published without Maxwell Perkins. The editor influenced the writer's career and reputation by taking responsibility for the way the books and their author were presented—and by serving as a buffer between Hemingway and other personnel at the House of Scribner. Hemingway was not just famous before he was thirty: he was recognized as a master. The Cavalier's fame and stature were nurtured by the Puritan who worked on the fifth floor at 597 Fifth Avenue.

---

[7]*Ernest Hemingway: Selected Letters, 1917–1961,* ed. Carlos Baker (New York: Scribners, 1961), p. 390.

[8]As reported by Kenneth D. McCormack; Berg, *Max Perkins,* p. 6.

# HEMINGWAY/PERKINS CHRONOLOGY
## 1884–1926

◆

| | |
|---|---|
| 20 September 1884 | Maxwell Perkins is born in Manhattan. |
| 21 July 1899 | Ernest Hemingway is born in Oak Park, Illinois. |
| Spring 1907 | Perkins graduates from Harvard University. |
| Spring 1910 | Perkins joins the advertising department of Charles Scribner's Sons. |
| 1914 | Perkins becomes an editor at Scribners. |
| 8 July 1918 | Hemingway is wounded while serving with the Red Cross in Italy. |
| 26 March 1920 | Scribners publishes F. Scott Fitzgerald's first novel, *This Side of Paradise.* |
| 3 September 1920 | Hemingway marries Hadley Richardson. |
| 20 December 1920 | The Hemingways arrive in Paris. |
| 4 March 1922 | Scribners publishes Fitzgerald's second novel, *The Beautiful and Damned;* Perkins is one of the dedicatees. |
| 13 August 1923 | Robert McAlmon's Contact Press publishes Hemingway's *Three Stories and Ten Poems* in Paris. |
| Mid-March 1924 | William Bird's Three Mountains Press publishes Hemingway's *in our time* (vignettes) in Paris. |
| c. May 1924 | Fitzgerald recommends Hemingway to Perkins. |
| 21 February 1925 | Perkins writes to Hemingway for the first time, but the letter was not received. |
| 10 April 1925 | Scribners publishes Fitzgerald's third novel, *The Great Gatsby.* |
| 5 October 1925 | Boni & Liveright publishes Hemingway's first story collection, *In Our Time.* |
| 30 December 1925 | Boni & Liveright rejects Hemingway's *The Torrents of Spring,* his parody of Sherwood Anderson. |

9–17 February 1926    Hemingway comes to New York and meets Perkins for the first time on 11 February; Hemingway and Perkins sign a contract for the publication of *The Torrents of Spring* and Hemingway's first novel, *The Sun Also Rises,* on 17 February.

28 May 1926    Scribners publishes *The Torrents of Spring.*

22 October 1926    Scribners publishes *The Sun Also Rises.*

—R.W.T.

# THE TORRENTS OF SPRING

## A ROMANTIC NOVEL IN HONOR OF THE PASSING OF A GREAT RACE

—

## ERNEST HEMINGWAY

### AUTHOR OF "IN OUR TIME"

Front of the dust jacket for Hemingway's first Scribners book.

# THE SUN ALSO RISES

## ERNEST HEMINGWAY

**Author of**
**"IN OUR TIMES" and "THE TORRENTS OF SPRING"**

Front of the dust jacket by CLEON for the first Hemingway novel edited by Perkins.

*CC, 2 pp.*

Feb. 21, 1925

Dear Mr. Hemingway:

I have just read "in our time" published by the Three Mountains Press.[1] I had heard that you were doing very remarkable writing and was most anxious to see it and after a great deal of effort and correspondence, I finally did manage to get this book which seems not to be in circulation in this country. At all events I could not find it. I was greatly impressed by the power in the scenes and incidents pictured, and by the effectiveness of their relation to each other, and I am venturing to write to you to ask whether you have anything that you would allow us to consider as publishers. I am bound to say at the same time that I doubt if we could have seen a way to the publication of this book itself, on account of material considerations:- it is so small that it would give the booksellers no opportunity for substantial profit if issued at a price which custom would dictate. The trade would therefore not be interested in it. This is a pity because your method is obviously one which enables you to express what you have to say in very small compass, but a commercial publisher cannot disregard these factors. It occurred to me, however, that you might very well be writing something which would not have these practical objections and in any case, whatever you are writing, we should be most interested to consider.

Sincerely yours,

*ALS, 3pp.*

113 Rue Notre Dame des Champs,
Paris VI, France
April 15, 1925

Dear Mr. Perkins:

On returning from Austria I received your letter of February 26 inclosing a copy of a previous letter which unfortunately never reached me.[2] About ten days before your letter came I had a cabled offer from Boni and Liveright to bring out a book of my short stories in the fall. They asked me to reply by cable and I accepted.

I was very excited at getting your letter but did not see what I could do until I had seen the contract from Boni and Liveright. According to its terms they are to have an option on my next three books, they agreeing that unless they exercise this option to publish the second book within 60 days of the receipt of the manuscript their option shall lapse, and if they do

---

[1]Paris, 1924. F. Scott Fitzgerald had alerted MP to EH in October 1924. This letter initiated the correspondence.
[2]This is the first EH letter to MP.

not publish the second book they relinquish their option on the third book.

So that is how matters stand. I cannot tell you how pleased I was by your letter and you must know how gladly I would have sent Charles Scribner's Sons the manuscript of the book that is to come out this fall. It makes it seem almost worth while to get into Who's Who in order to have a known address.

I do want you to know how much I appreciated your letter and if I am ever in a position to send you anything to consider I shall certainly do so.

I hope some day to have a sort of Daughty's Arabia Deserta of the Bull Ring, a very big book with some wonderful pictures. But one has to save all winter to be able to bum in Spain in the summer and writing classics, I've always heard, takes some time. Somehow I don't care about writing a novel and I like to write short stories and I like to work at the bull fight book so I guess I'm a bad prospect for a publisher anyway. Somehow the novel seems to me to be an awfully artificial and worked out form but as some of the short stories now are stretching out to 8,000 to 12,000 words may be I'll get there yet.

The In Our Time is out of print and I've been trying to buy one to have myself now I hear it is valuable, so that probably explains your difficulty in getting it. I'm awfully glad you liked it and thank you again for writing me about a book.

|                        |                                                        |
|------------------------|--------------------------------------------------------|
| Very Sincerely,        | 113 Rue Notre Dame des Champs                          |
| Ernest Hemingway       | is a permanent address                                 |

\* \* \*

*EH and MP did not correspond between April 1925 and February 1926. In* Our Time *was published by Boni & Liveright in October 1925, and EH was still bound by contract to offer Boni & Liveright his next book.*

*CC, 4 pp., JFK*

Feb. 1, 1926

Dear Mr. Hemingway:

I, and we, think your "Fifty Grand" is a magnificent story. Scott sent it here,- I suppose with your authorization, and as I had just recently read "In Our Time" I naturally read this without a moment's delay.- And the magazine people read it immediately thereafter, and everyone here was roused up by it. It makes you see how poor most of the material is that is thought pretty good. Naturally we want to have it in the magazine[1] and we would pay two hundred and fifty dollars for it, which is more than we usually do pay for

---

[1]*Scribner's Magazine.* The story was published in *The Atlantic Monthly* 140 (July 1927): 1–15.

short stories. There is this one great obstacle: it is too long. If we run a story of over eight thousand words, we have to give it too much room; we are not like the large-page magazines, which run the text back into the advertisements. We have to hold the stories down, and we have lost some good ones on that account. But we have lost none as good as this one, I guess, if we must lose it. I had a hope that you might be able and willing to cut it by fifteen hundred words, for then it would fit. Could you do this, and if so have you a copy to do it from? It looks to me as if it would be difficult, but I do hope you can manage it, and will. I might as well say frankly that you would get more money—I suppose you know it—from Liberty, which Scott suggested I send this story to if we could not take it; but I do think that it might well be better to have it in Scribner's. Still, I won't urge this point for you will know the situation well enough. I am awfully sorry to hold up matters until you get this letter, and have written an answer, but we cannot bring ourselves to surrender the story without this attempt to get it. If the delay seems a bad one to you, and you feel that you cannot do as we want, wire me the one word "No" and I shall understand that I must send it on to Liberty. Address it simply Scribners, New York, and the message will come to me. You won't even have to sign it. If you wire "Yes" I shall know that it is all right, but that you must have the copy back, but if you have a carbon copy to cut, don't wire at all, but simply go ahead and send that to us. Certainly nobody else ought to attempt to cut the story by any possibility, even if you were willing to let them.

You would be pleased if you heard what people said of "In Our Time", those people who are quick to catch on to notable publications. It is vastly admired and this admiration is bound to spread. I think stories in Scribner's would help in that respect more than stories in Liberty, or the Post, or any of those more popular magazines, but as I am naturally prejudiced, it will hardly do for me to argue the point too much.

Reading "In Our Time" makes me even more disgusted with having failed to communicate with you more quickly last summer. I did not realize that you had so much material as that, by any means. I judged mainly by the Three Mountain Press book. I saw in one of the papers a note that you were writing a novel. It will certainly be awaited eagerly by a considerable number over here, including myself.

Sincerely yours,

*      *      *

*The Boni & Liveright contract for* IOT *stipulated that the publisher's option on EH's first three books would expire if any of them was declined. EH, who had become dissatisfied with Boni & Liveright after publication of* IOT, *submitted* The Torrents of Spring *as his second book under the contract. This parody of Sherwood Anderson's work was predictably declined by Boni & Liveright, which had a close publishing relationship with Anderson; therefore EH was free to publish with another house. EH denied it, but his decision to offer* TOS *to Boni & Liveright had the appearance of a scheme to break his contract, since he had a working draft of* The Sun Also Rises *that he did not offer to Boni & Liveright. F. Scott Fitzgerald, who was eager to bring EH to Scribners, cabled MP on 8 January 1926:* YOU CAN GET HEMINGWAYS FINISHED NOVEL PROVIDED YOU PUBLISH UNPROMISING SATIRE HARCOURT HAS MADE DEFINITE OFFER WIRE IMMEDIATELY WITHOUT QUALIFICATIONS. *MP replied:* PUBLISH NOVEL AT FIFTEEN PERCENT AND ADVANCE IF DESIRED ALSO SATIRE UNLESS OBJECTIONABLE OTHER THAN FINANCIALLY. *EH came to New York in February to meet with MP and other publishers; MP secured EH by accepting* TOS—*which he had probably read—and* SAR *sight unseen for a combined $1,500 advance. (For a full account of Fitzgerald's role in bringing EH to Scribners, see Bruccoli,* Fitzgerald and Hemingway *[New York: Carroll & Graf, 1994].)*

*ALS, 4 pp.*

113 Rue Notre Dame des Champs
Paris VI
April 24, 1926.

Dear Mr. Perkins:—

I am mailing you today The Sun Also Rises. It will probably be much better for you to have it so that you can go ahead on it and I can do additional working over in the proofs. There are plenty of small mistakes for the person who reads it in Mss. to catch before it goes to the printer—Mis spelled words, punctuation etc. I want the Mss. back with the proofs.

The three quotations in the front I'd like to see set up. May cut out the last one.[1]

Jonathan Cape is publishing In Our Time. Setting it up and printing it themselves. Mr. Liveright refused, Curtis Brown wrote me, to sell them sheets some months ago. I have the contract today. They get the British Empire rights not including Canada and pay me 10% royalty. 25 pounds advance.

Curtis Brown gave them the first refusal of both Torrents and The Sun A.R. Advances and terms for them to be arranged when and if published. This seemed just to me as they are setting up the In Our Time. Torrents would probably be useless in England and it would not seem fair for them to miss a chance at the novel. I believe you said I had the British and foreign rights. I dont think Jonathan Cape is the best publishing house in England but they're not the worst.

I had a long letter from Scott a few days ago saying he'd started his book, was seeing no one not drinking and working hard. He said he'd gotten $15,000 for some movie rights and this, with other things, would probably

---

[1]Ecclesiastes 1:18: "For in much wisdom is much grief and he that increaseth knowledge increaseth sorrow." This epigraph was cut before publication.

see them through until Christmas. I felt very touched by his precarious financial situation and told him that if he was worried about money I would write you to send all my royalties direct to him at the Villa Paqita, Juan les Pins .A.M.

Am working on a couple of stories.

La Navire D'Argent published a 15,000 word story of mine[1] translated a couple of months ago and various frenchmen got very excited and made extravagant statements about it so now they all want them and I have a fine french market (in francs) Am supposed to be the re-incarnation of Prosper Merimee[2] whom I've never read but always supposed was pretty bad. The good thing about being a popular French writer like Mr. Merimee and myself, rather than an imported great American name is that, I believe, the great names have to pay the translator which seems to me, if the law of supply and demand still operates, commercially unsound.

I was awfully sorry to be disappointed in Capt. Thomason's book.[3] There were too many bayonets in it somehow. If you are writing a book that isnt romantic and has that as one of its greatest assets it is a shame to get awfully romantic about bayonets. The bayonet is a fine and romantic thing but the very fact of its being attached to a rifle which is such a fine and practical thing automatically restricts its use in the hands of any practical man also presumably armed with grenades to purely ornamental killing—with which I am not in sympathy. Most of it is fine and the writing often is splendid. There was just that little journalistic something that was disappointing. When you tell so much of the truth you cant afford to have anything not true because it spoils the taste. A little Arthur Guy Empey[4] is awfully poisonous. It makes you realize though what an awfully good book Through The Wheat[5] was. I hear there is a good new war book called Toward The Flame.[6] Have you read it? After I read War and Peace I decided there wasnt any need to write a war book and I'm still sticking to that.

This is a long drooling letter but if it arrives at the same time as the Sun A.R. (the pig that you bought in a poke) you'll probably be so busy reading the pig that whatever this letter says will not be very important—nor is it.

> Yours very truly
> Ernest Hemingway.

[1]"The Undefeated," published as "L'invincible" (March 1926).
[2]Prosper Merimee (1803–1870), a French novelist, was the author of *Carmen* (1852).
[3]John W. Thomason, *Fix Bayonets* (New York: Scribners, 1926).
[4]Author of *Tales from a Dugout* (1918) and *First Call* (1918).
[5]World War I novel by Thomas Boyd (New York: Scribners, 1923).
[6]World War I novel by Hervey Allen (New York: Doran, 1926).

*CC, 4 pp.*[1]

May 18, 1926

Dear Mr. Hemingway:

"The Sun Also Rises" seems to me a most extraordinary performance. No one could conceive of a book with more life in it. All the scenes, and particularly those when they cross the Pyrenees and come into Spain, and when they fish in that cold river, and when the bulls are sent in with the steers, and when they are fought in the arena, are of such a quality as to be like actual experience. You have struck our pet phrase, "pity and irony," to death so I can't use it;[2] but the humor in the book and the satire—especially expressed by Gorton, and by the narrator,—are marvelous; and not in the least of a literary sort. But in connection with this there is one hard point—a hard one to raise too, because the passage in question comes in so aptly and so rightly. I mean the speech about Henry James.[3] I swear I do not see how that can be printed. It could not by any conception be printed while he was alive, if only for the fear of a lawsuit; and in a way it seems almost worse to print it after he is dead. I am not raising this you must believe, because we are his publishers. The matter referred to is peculiarly a personal one. It is not like something that a man could be criticized for,—some part of his conduct in life and which might therefore be considered open for comment. I want to put this before you at the very beginning. There are also one or two other things that I shall bring up in connection with the proof, but there is no need to speak of them here.

The book as a work of art seems to me astonishing, and the more so because it involves such an extraordinary range of experience and emotion, all brought together in the most skillful manner—the subtle ways of which are beautifully concealed—to form a complete design. I could not express my admiration too strongly.

As ever yours,

. . . . .

*To: Charles Scribner*  
*From: Maxwell Perkins*

*ALS, 4 pp.*[4]

May 27th 1926

Dear Charley:—.

You wanted to know the decision on Hemingway: We took it,—with misgiving. In the course of the debate I argued that the question was a crucial one

---

[1]52 words have been omitted from this letter.

[2]In *SAR*, Bill Gorton uses this phrase in a nonsense song ridiculing literary critics.

[3]In chapter 12 of *SAR*, Gorton alludes to the claim that James was supposedly rendered impotent by a horseback- or bicycle-riding accident.

[4]380 words have been omitted from this letter.

in respect to younger writers;—that we suffered by being called "ultra-conservative" (even if unjustly + with malice) + that this would become our reputation for the present when our declination of this book should, as it would, get about. That view of the matter influenced our decision largely. Wheelock[1] was called in, with a curious result: I thought he had been so much out of the world on that balcony of his, + in his generally hermit like life, as to be out of touch with modern tendencies in writing + therefore over sensitive; but to my amazement he thought there was no question whatever but that we should publish. There was of course a great one. I simply thought in the end that the balance was slightly in favor of acceptance, for all the worry + general misery involved.—But you wont see Hemingway: he's in Spain, Bull fighting I suspect.

. . . . .
. . . . .
. . . . .


*To: F. Scott Fitzgerald[2]*                             *AL, 3 pp., JFK*
*From: Maxwell Perkins*


May 29th 1926

Dear Scott:—

When you think of Hemingways' book you recall Scenes as if they were memories,—glorious ones of Spain, + fishing in a cold river, + bull fights, all full of life + color; + you recall people as hard + actual as real ones. That is the way you remember the book,—not as you do Thackeray where the style + all, the literary quality, is always a part of the recollection. Here the ms. wriggles with vitality. The art is marvelously concealed, + yet the whole is composed to the last word.—Yet the book is not an unmixed pleasure because it is almost unpublishable. It is about such people as I suppose you know in Paris. Hemingway must have known them,—that is, their like. They belong to "a lost generation." Several including the girl are what are now called "disintegrated personalities," I suppose. They are the war generation + have had too long + too fierce a dose of reality. They conceal nothing, + neither does Hemingway. The principle characters are naturally fine people + their situation is tragic. The true principles are a girl + a man who belong together; but they are alway + inivitably parted by the fact—+ what an ironic fact—that he (who tells the tale) has been so wounded that he can not sexually play the part of a man!—You may know all this so I wont go into it. You can guess that it presents a problem;—but the book is never erotic, +, in a true sense, it is always clean + healthy. There is one passage—a part of one of the best + most humorous conversations in the book—that simply must

---

[1]John Hall Wheelock, poet and associate editor at Scribners.
[2]Fitzgerald presumably gave EH the first three pages of this letter; the rest of the letter has not been located.

come out:—its about Henry James supposed incapacity in the matter of sex. During his life no one could have dreamed of printing it, + to do it now would really be worse. And there are many words seldom if ever used before in print;—possibly some can come out without damage, or with less than their presense will cause. Altogether it is a very strange + remarkable book, with many aspects. The beauty + cruelty of the world are curiously blent in it. One would naturally fall back on "irony + pity" to describe it, but there's a chap in the book, + he's a good one, who laughs that fine old phrase out of usage. What we publishers are to do for blurbs I don't know!

*TLS with holograph additions, 2 pp.*[1]

Dear Mr. Perkins =

· · · · ·

· · · · ·

· · · · ·

· · · · ·

I believe that, in the proofs, I will start the book at what is now page 16 in the Mss. There is nothing in those first sixteen pages that does not come out, or is explained, or re-stated in the rest of the book—or is unnecessary to state. I think it will move much faster from the start that way. Scott agrees with me. He suggested various things in it to cut out—in those first chapters—which I have never liked—but I think it is better to just lop that off and he agrees. He will probably write you what he thinks about it—the book in general. He said he was very excited by it.[2]

As for the Henry James thing—I haven't the second part of the Ms. here—it is over at Scott's—so I can't recall the wording. But I believe that it is a reference to some accident that is generally known to have happened to Henry James in his youth. To me Henry James is as historical a name as Byron, Keats, or any other great writer about whose life, personal and literary, books have been written. I do not believe that the reference is sneering, or if it is, it is not the writer who is sneering as the writer does not appear in this book. Henry James is dead and left no descendants to be hurt, nor any wife, and therefore I feel that he is as dead as he will ever be. I wish I had the ms. here to see exactly what it said. If Henry James never had an accident of that sort I should think it would be libelous to say he had no matter how long he were dead. But if he did I do not see how it can affect him—now he is dead. As I recall Gorton and Barnes are talking humourously around the subject of Barnes' mutilation and to them Henry James is not a man to be

---

[1]185 words have been omitted from this letter.

[2]For Fitzgerald's critique of *SAR,* see *F. Scott Fitzgerald: A Life in Letters,* ed. Matthew J. Bruccoli with the assistance of Judith Baughman (New York: Scribners, 1994), pp. 142–145.

insulted or protected from insult but simply an historical example. I remember there was something about an airplane and a bicycle—but that had nothing to do with James and was simply a non-sequitor. Scott said he saw nothing off-color about it.

Until the proofs come I do not want to think about the book as I am trying to write some stories and I want to see the proofs, when they come, from as new and removed a viewpoint as possible.

Up till now I have heard nothing about a story called—An Alpine Idyll—that I mailed to you sometime the first week in May. Did you ever receive it? I have another copy which I will send if you did not. In Madrid I wrote three stories ranging from 1400 to 3,000 words. I haven't had them re-typed and sent on as I was waiting word about The Alpine Idyll.[1]

What is the news about Torrents? Have any copies been mailed to me as yet?

Could you send me a check for $200. in a registered letter to the Guaranty Trust Co. address? It was very pleasant to get your letter and learn that you liked the book.

Yours very sincerely<br>Ernest Hemingway

Villa Paquita
Juan les Pins
    (A.M)
June 5, 1926

CC, 3 pp.

July 20, 1926

Dear Hemingway:

The complete galley proof goes out today, C/o The Guaranty Trust Company. I have hardly made a mark on it,- though I can see the point about cutting at the start. What is there said is later said, and in the course of narrative; but it is well said here if not according to the method of the book, and a reader to whom your way of writing will be new, and in many cases strange, would be helped by this beginning. But you write like yourself only, and I shall not attempt criticism. I couldn't with confidence. But there are two points to consider that bear on this publication: the danger of trouble from referring to real people in a way to reflect upon them, and the danger of suppression.

As for the first, it is slight, and rests upon passages:

(1.) I know who Roger Prescott is quite well.[2] Would not others recognize him? You might say, so much the better; but you cannot be sure about these birds, and why injure him? You will if certain people who guess point out his identity. Why not call him Prentiss. You don't want to harm him.

---

[1]The story was declined by *Scribner's Magazine*.
[2]Glenway Wescott; see EH's 21 August 1926 letter.

(2) An Englishman will actually sue for libel on the slightest provocation. This we know to our cost. The reference to Hillaire Belloc though apparently the most absolutely harmless of the lot, is really the most dangerous, so far as material results are concerned. The English have a reticence and a sense of the right to it, a right to privacy, unknown in the U.S.A. I think we'll have to disguise the name of Belloc in some way.[1]

(3) I don't know what Hergesheimer might do about being announced as a "garter snapper",- probably not much. We can quote what a man has written but not what he is reported to have said, or even is known for sure to have said, without his permission. Besides, he and Mencken are friends. I don't think we have a right to impair their relationship.[2]

(4) As for the Henry James, you know how we feel about it. I know too, how you feel about it,- that he is as much a historic character as Balzac is. But in truth, this town and Boston are full of people who knew him and who cannot regard him as you do. There are four right in this office who were his friends,- two his close friends.

Then, as to the fact, I have inquired into it and it is at most, extremely doubtful. Van Wyck Brooks who questioned everyone who knew James, does not believe it, nor Willard Huntington Wright, nor anyone here. There are a variety of rumors, and many obvious lies, but no certainty.[3]

As for the other aspect I question:-

The book is of course a healthy book with marked satirical implications upon novels which are not.— Sentimentalized, subjective novels, marked by sloppy, hazy thought. That is one of the first things it is. But as I said, people are afraid of words. We don't want to divert attention from its intrinsic qualities to details of purely extrinsic importance. It would be a pretty thing if the very significance of so original a book should be disregarded because of the howls of a lot of cheap, prurient, moronic yappers. You probably don't appreciate this disgusting possibility because you've been too long abroad, and out of that atmosphere. Those who breathe its stagnant vapors now attack a book, not only on grounds of eroticism which could not hold here, but upon that of "decency", which means words.

In view of this, I suggest that a particular adjunct of the Bulls, referred to a number of times by Mike, be not spelled out, but covered by a blank[4]; and I rather inconsistently suggest that in the passage about Irony and Pity, you do not so plainly indicate the second line, but leave it as if Barnes did not hear it well, for Gorton was humming.—[5] By this you would lose little and

---

[1]Anecdote cut from the opening about Braddocks (English novelist Ford Madox Ford) mistaking diabolist Aleister Crowley for Belloc. EH recycled this anecdote in "Ford Madox Ford and the Devil's Disciple" (*A Moveable Feast* [New York: Scribners, 1964]).

[2]American author Joseph Hergesheimer (1880–1954); the name was changed to "Hoffenheimer" (Chapter 6).

[3]"Henry James" was changed to "Henry" in the published version.

[4]See EH's letter of 24 July 1926 for revision.

[5]The implied word is *shitty*. No revision was made (Chapter 6).

would tend to avoid the raising of an utterly false issue which might give your book an entirely false reputation and identify it with that very type of book which it should counteract.

But in general I recommend doing nothing that would <u>really</u> <u>harm</u> the text in this matter of words, but large reducing so far as you rightly can the profanity, etc.

I hope Pamplona has been as wonderful this time as in your manuscript. I'm afraid I've misled you about The Younger Son.[1] I see it gets to be theatrical. I was so impressed by the killing of that terrible Raven (like that of Rasputin) and then by the news of Trafalgar, that I thought the book must be a marvel. Maybe it is later. I've been too busy to find out.

Yours as ever,

TLS, 2 pp.[2]

Hotel Valencia—Valencia—Spain<br>July 24, 1926.

Dear Mr. Perkins:

. . . . .

I imagine we are in accord about the use of certain <u>words</u> and I never use a word without first considering if it is replaceable. But in the proof I will go over it all very carefully. I have thought of one place where Mike when drunk and wanting to insult the bull fighter keeps saying—tell him bulls have no balls. That can be changed—and I believe with no appreciable loss to—bulls have no horns. But in the matter of the use of the <u>Bitch</u> by Brett—I have never once used this word ornamentally nor except when it was absolutely necessary and I believe the few places where it is used must stand. The whole problem is, it seems, that one should never use words which shock altogether out of their own value or connotation—such a word as for instance <u>fart</u> would stand out on a page, unless the whole matter were entirely rabelaisian, in such a manner that it would be entirely exaggerated and false and overdone in emphasis. Granted that it is a very old and classic English word for a breaking of wind. But you cannot use it. Altho I can think of a case where it might be used, under sufficiently tragic circumstances, as to be entirely acceptable. In a certain incident in the war of conversation among marching troops under shell fire.

I think that words—and I will cut anything I can—that are used in conversation in The Sun etc. are justified by the tragedy of the story. But of course I haven't seen it for some time and not at all in type.

The reason I haven't sent any more stories to the magazine is because Scott was so sure that it would buy anything that was publishable that my

[1]Edward John Trelawny, *The Adventures of a Younger Son* (1831).
[2]147 words have been omitted from this letter.

hopes got very high and after I'd tried both a long and a short story—and I suppose the stories aren't pleasant—and both were not publishable and it made me feel very discouraged; as I had counted on that as a certain source of income, and I suppose I have been foolish not to copy out more stories and send them. But I will when we get back to Paris the 10th of August. As yet no proofs have arrived.

. . . . .
. . . . .
. . . . .
. . . . .
. . . . .

Yours always,
Ernest Hemingway.

*TLS, 2 pp.*[1]

69 Rue Froidevaux,
Paris, France.
August 21, 1926.

Dear Mr. Perkins:

The proofs came ten days ago while we were at the Cap D'Antibes on our way home from Spain and I have been over them very carefully with the points you outlined in mind.

1st—I have commenced with Cohn—I believe the book loses by eliminating this first part but it would have been pointless to include it with the Belloc eliminated—and I think that would be altogether pointless with Belloc's name out.

2nd—Roger Prescott is now Roger Prentiss. I believe I went to school with a Roger Prentiss but at least he was not Glenway.

3rd—Hergesheimer now changed to something else.

4th—Henry James now called either Henry or Whatsisname—whichever seems best to you.

5th—I do not believe that the blanks left in the Irony and pity song can be objectionable—anybody knowing what words to put in might as well put them in. In case they are offensive the word "pretty" can be inserted.

6th—The bulls now without appendages.

I've tried to reduce profanity but I reduced so much profanity when writing the book that I'm afraid not much could come out. Perhaps we will have to consider it simply as a profane book and hope that the next book will be less profane or perhaps more sacred.

. . . . .

In this same mail I am sending you a story—The Killers—which has

[1]284 words have been omitted from this letter.

been typed by the well known, admired author himself on a six year old Corona. . . .

. . . . .

. . . . .

With best regards,
Ernest Hemingway.

TLS, 2 pp.
Paris, France

August 26.

Dear Mr. Perkins—

I am sending the proofs tomorrow on the Mauretania so you should have them in a week now.

You did not send a proof of the quotations in the front or of the dedication and I have forgotten exactly what they were. For the quotations I want the quotation from Gertrude Stein which I believe was "You are all a lost generation" there may have been more to it—it's to go as it was on the Mss. and the quotation from Ecclesiastes.

The dedication is to be—

THIS BOOK IS FOR HADLEY AND FOR JOHN HADLEY NICANOR.

I may have changed a few more things and made more cuts before mailing the proofs but you will have seen all that by now. I believe that the book is really better starting as it does now directly with Cohn and omitting any preliminary warming up. After all if I'm trying to write books without any extra words I might as well stick to it. Now that it is finally out of my hands and there is no chance of doing anything to make it any better I feel rather cheerful now about The Sun. Hope you feel the same way.

A letter from Scott today said he was working very hard with the front door barred and all the blinds down and expected to sail for N.Y. on December 10th from Genoa.

If the Irony and pity ditty bothers there are a couple of things you could do—reduce the size of the dashes and omit periods after them. Or just run it all in together. No dashes and no periods. Do whatever you like with it. I don't care what happens to that as long as the words are not changed and nothing inserted.

The other things I believe are all fixed up. We've eliminated Belloc, changed Hergesheimer's name, made Henry James Henry, made Roger Prescott into Roger Prentiss and unfitted the bulls for a reproductive function.

Now I'll get this off so there won't be any further holding up. When do you expect that The Sun will be out? And how did Torrents go? You might send me a check for 200 dollars if you would. It is grand to have The Sun etc. finally off and to be able to start on something else without things to do on the book coming in and smashing up the production of anything else. I'd like to forget it now for a long time. It is a great mistake to put real people in a book and one I'll never make, I hope, again.

    With best regards,

        Yours very truly,

                Ernest Hemingway


*TL, 1 p., JFK*

*[September 1926]*

Dear Mr. Perkins:

I am awfully pleased about The Killers[1] and will send you some more. Everything you say about the arrangement of the title page etc. of The Sun seems to be very good. Unless you have already done it, in which case it doesn't matter, there is no necessity of changing the Roger Prentiss to Robert as I verified the name of the kid I was at school with and found it was Prentiss as a first name.

I was just joking about profanity in the next book. I have a grand novel to write when I get some tranquility in the head again. There will be no real people in it as there unfortunately were in The Sun etc. That is a thing that I'll never do again. You see last year after Pamplona Don Stewart[2] went to Vichy and took a five weeks cure for his liver and kidneys and I unfortunately cleansed mine out in writing The Sun Also Rises. But this is all only for you and me to know. In addition to Mr. Prescott you may have recognized Harold Stearns[3] in the gentleman who was always going off by himself like a cat and I'm afraid Ford may be in it and a number of other people and I am to assist in some major capacity at the marriage of Brett and Mike next month, the divorce having finally been obtained. That is I imagine I will assist if the book has not already appeared. All of which is very depressing.

*[The rest of the letter is missing and it may not have been completed.]*


*CC, 4 pp.*[4]


Oct. 30, 1926

Dear Hemingway:

    "The Sun Also Rises" has been out a week. The first real reviews appear

---

    [1]This story was published in the March 1927 issue of *Scribner's Magazine* (pp. 227–233); it was the first EH short story to appear in an American magazine.

    [2]American humorist Donald Ogden Stewart (1894–1980) was the model for Bill Gorton in *SAR*.

    [3]Harold Stearns (1891–1943), the model for Harvey Stone in *SAR*, was an alcoholic American journalist in Paris.

    [4]32 words have been omitted from this letter.

tomorrow. Those in the Times and Herald Tribune are perhaps the most important, and both are admirable,- particularly the Herald Tribune. It is not that it speaks more highly of the book than the Times, but it shows better understanding, and it is a signed review, which gives it more authority.- The author of it is Conrad Aiken. If I cannot send both of these now because the advertising department may not be able to spare them, I will send them Monday. I do now enclose some advertisements, the largest an announcement advertisement which was for the newspapers, and also for the Publisher's Weekly.

Now there is one point I raise with certain hesitation, but it keeps coming back into my mind. I too, came to the conclusion that you did right in taking out the first chapter and part of the second. They are not written in the method of the book. Almost all that is in them comes out in the story. Artistically I think they therefore constituted a defect and in some other ways the book gains by their withdrawal.- For instance, Brett appears with much more effect when she has not been talked about in advance.

But a good deal of that material must have been written with an idea that your objective method did require—at least in this first novel in which it has been used and so is new, and to many also strange—a sort of preparation; and it occurred to me that possibly from the material of those three galleys, you might gain this effect without impairing the method of the book itself, by making up a foreword or prologue, or whatever it might be called. This could tell some of the things about Brett which were in the first galleys and did not altogether come out in the narrative. They are things that I think perhaps make one understand her better in the end.

I am not at all decided as to whether this suggestion is good. I suppose I really would not have made it if I had not greatly liked that early writing. I thought we might in this way be able to retain some part of it, remodelled, without actually making it a part of the story, by putting it in a prologue, which would come before the half title preceding the first page of the book. Perhaps I ought not to bother you about this, for you are thinking now of other things, and this may be merely disconcerting. But you can discard it instantly. My idea was that if you thought well of it and did it, we could not only use it in later printings, but could even use it in all books unbound at the time that you sent it over. Anyhow, I am enclosing the galleys so that if you want to consider the matter, you will have the material.

. . . . .

I wish you could send over some stories now,—possibly "Fifty Grand" curtailed. I think that gentleman will find he has tackled something considerable though, when he begins his cutting.

Yours,

TLS *with holograph inserts, 4 pp.*[1]

*[c. 16 November 1926]*          *Paris, France*

Dear Mr. Perkins:

Thanks so much for sending the reviews and advertisements. The portrait, Bloomshield's drawing, looks much as I had imagined Jake Barnes; it looks very much like a writer who had been saddened by the loss or atrophy of certain non replaceable parts. It is a pity it couldn't have been Barnes instead of Hemingway. Still it is fine to have at last succeeded in looking like a writer. The ads and the blurb seem excellent.

I wish that I could do as you suggest about inserting some of the matter about Brett. It doubtless would be of value to anyone reading the stuff for the first time and there is some very good dope on Brett. On the other hand any sort of a foreword or preface would seem to me to break up the unity of the book and altho it does not show there is a certain rhythm in all that book that if it were broken would be very much missed. It was a complete unit with all that first stuff including the Belloc episode—I could cut it where I did and have it stay a unit—but the hard luck we had with Fifty Grand shows the difficulty of cutting that sort of stuff and further tinkering wouldn't help, I'm afraid.

I am terribly sorry because I would like very much to do it for you but I think we'll find maybe, in the end, that what I lose by not compromising now we may all cash in on later. I know that you would not ask me to put that back in unless you really liked it and I know it would be good in many ways but I think in the end perhaps we would both lose by it. You see I would like, if you wanted, to write books for Scribner's to publish, for many years and would like them to be good books—better all the time—sometimes they might not be so good—but as well as I could write and perhaps with luck learning to write better all the time—and learning how things work and what the whole thing is about—and not getting bitter—So if this one doesn't sell maybe sometime one will—I'm very sure one will if they really are good—and if I learn to make them a lot better—but I'll never be able to do that and will just get caught in the machine if I start worrying about that—or considering it the selling. Altho God knows I need the money at this present time and I would so like to see the book really go because you have been so very decent to me.

The other thing is that Brett Ashley is a real person and as long as there were no changes in the way other real people James, Belloc, Hergesheimer etc. were handled I did not mind what happened to <u>my</u> people—but since they the others were protected I might as well leave out that stuff so long as it is not actually necessary. That was the only stuff in the book that was not imaginary—the Brett biography.

I see that Mr. Bill Benet is very disappointed to find me lifting a character

<hr />

[1]34 words have been omitted from this letter.

from Michael Arland and that is rather funny as I have never read a word of Arland but went around, after the war, with Lady Duff Twisden, Nancy Cunard, Mary Beerbohm who took Arland or Arlen up as a deserving Armenian youth and let him in on a few things and then dropped him as soon as he became annoyingly Armenian and less deserving—but not before he had gotten a little way behind the scenes into various people's lives.[1]

So now it is pretty amusing to have known a girl and drawn her so close to life that it makes me feel very badly—except that I don't imagine she would ever read anything—and watch her go to hell completely—and assist at the depart—and then feeling pretty damned badly about it all learn that you had with boyish enthusiasm lifted a character from the un-read writings of some little Armenian sucker after London names. What do you suppose it is—that Benet imagines that nobody ever really had a title? Was it the title that offended him? Or do people only have titles in books written for servant girls? But as I haven't read Arland I don't know—and now I'm afraid to—because maybe it is like Arland. That would be awfully funny.

Maybe Arland would write a couple of chapters and it would sell millions. Perhaps Benet could get a hold of him for us.

Komroff[2] finally cut only a couple of hundred words out of Fifty Grand. Maybe you could run it some time between serials or if Mr. Phelps were sick and copy was short. You might offer Mr. Phelps from me that if he will condense and give me the space I'll pay him whatever it's worth a page where I overlap into him. or I'll split the price of the story with him. I'd like to have that story published sometimes before boxing is abolished. Or magazines abolished.[3]

Everything I publish over here is stolen by Samuel Roth[4] who has never had my permission to publish one word and and pirates everything that appears here as fast as it comes out and has never paid me a cent. I've seen the advertisements in the Nation and New Republic for his Two Worlds Monthly.

Joyce is all broken up about it. Roth has stolen his Ulysses without permission, never paid Joyce a cent, is publishing Ulysses in monthly installments and expurgating it. I saw Joyce today and he has just received a copy of an interview Roth gave to some N.Y. paper in which he declares that he is publishing Ulysses with Joyce's consent, that he has a financial arrangement with Joyce greatly to Joyce's advantage which he cannot at present divulge and that Joyce has made large sums selling the book under cover in America. Joyce is in absolute despair. The work of thirteen years of his life being stolen from him by a man by a man who not content with that trys to blacken

[1] Michael Arlen (1895–1956), author of *The Green Hat* (1926).
[2] Manuel Komroff was asked to edit the story because EH was unable to cut it.
[3] William Lyon Phelps was a columnist for *Scribner's Magazine*. For more information on the publication of "Fifty Grand," see Scott Donaldson's "The Wooing of Ernest Hemingway," *American Literature* 53 (January 1982): 691–710.
[4] Samuel Roth was a New York publisher of pirated works.

Joyce's character—and not content with stealing a man's life work and lieing about it then garbles it.

Kenneth Simpson who is in the district attorney's office has promised to nail Roth as soon as he gets back to N.Y. Joyce meantime is trying to get an injunction against Roth.

It is a horrible and discouraging business and does not make one love the Jews any better. I feel badly about his stealing my stories—but that is a small matter compared to his theft of Joyce's entire book—but it does seem as though reputable publications like The Nation should refuse to accept his, Roth's, advertising. Isn't there some national organization that can blacklist the advertising of crooks?

. . . . .

. . . . .

I still have a check for 200 dollars that I haven't cashed because the franc has been too high—but it looks as though it were going to stay there. I hope the Sun will sell so that I may get some more from you when I need it—it seems as though it should—it's pretty interesting and there seems to be a difference of opinion about it—I've always heard that was good. The Times review I had to read to the end before I found whether they really liked it or not. Aiken seemed to like it. Archie MacLeish[1] tells me he's a good critic— Aiken I mean. Maybe that will encourage some of the other boys to like it. It's funny to write a book that seems as tragic as that and have them take it for a jazz superficial story. If you went any deeper inside they couldn't read it because they would be crying all the time. Life's all very funny today and the typewriter seems to have run away with itsself

Yours

Ernest Hemingway

*TLS with holograph additions, 2 pp.*
*Paris, France*

November 19, 1926

Dear Mr. Perkins:

I don't know whether the magazine would care for any humorous stuff. Anyway here is a piece and if they should not want it will you use your judgement about turning it over to Edmund Wilson care of The New Republic—who has written saying they will pay me $50 for a page of 1200 words on more or less anything—or perhaps to Reynolds who wrote Scott they would like something more of mine——and who might be able to get me some money for it.[2]

---

[1] Archibald MacLeish (1892–1982) was an American poet.

[2] "My Own Life," a parody of Frank Harris's "My Life"; *The New Yorker* 2 (12 February 1927): 23–24.

Thank you for the Transcript review. They did very nobly by us all. It was refreshing to see someone have some doubts that I took the Gertrude Stein thing very seriously—I meant to play off against that splendid bombast (Gertrude's assumption of prophetic roles) (Nobody knows about the generation that follows them and certainly has no right to Judge.)—the quotation from Eccles.—one generation passeth and another generation cometh but the earth abideth forever—The sun also Ariseth. What I would like you to do in any further printings is to lop off the Vanity of vanities, saith the preacher, vanity of vanities; all is vanity—What profit hath a man of all his labour which he taketh under the sun?—delete all that. And start the quotation with and use only the 4th, 5th 6th and 7th verses of Ecclesiastes. That is starting with One generation passeth away——and finishing with unto the place from whence the rivers come thither they return again.

That makes it much clearer. The point of the book to me was that the earth abideth forever—having a great deal of fondness and admiration for the earth and not a hell of a lot for my generation and caring little about Vanities. I only hesitated at the start to cut the writing of a better writer—but it seems necessary. I didn't mean the book to be a hollow or bitter satire but a damn tragedy with the earth abiding for ever as the hero.

Also have discovered that most people don't think in words—as they do in everybody's writing now—and so in Sun A. R. the critics miss their interior monologues and aren't happy—or disappointed. I cut out 40,000 words of the stuff that would have made them happy out of the first Mss—it would have made them happy but it would have rung as false 10 years from now as Bromfield.[1]

The Sun Also rises could have been and should have been a better book—but first Don Stewart was taking a cure for his liver in Vichy while I wrote the first draft of S.A.R. instead—and secondly I figure it is better to write about what you can write about and try and make it come off than have epoch making canvasses etc.—and you figure what age the novelists had that wrote the really great novels. There can be the tour de force by a kid like The Red Badge of Courage—but in general they were pretty well along and they knew a few things—and in the time they were learning and going through it they learned how to write by writing.

Well I'd better stop before I start getting like a critic myself which would be pretty bad. I hope you like this funny one anyway.

With Best regards<br>Ernest Hemingway

---

[1] Louis Bromfield (1896–1956), an American novelist whose work EH held in contempt.

*TLS, 3 pp., JFK*[1]

New York Dec. 1, 1926

Dear Hemingway:

. . . . .

. . . Your letter with the correction also came, and we made the correction;- and we made also the correction in the quotation from Ecclesiastes. I see that I also misunderstood the relations of these two quotations;- but I did not misunderstand the underlying emotion of the book about the earth and its relation to people. That for me was the strongest quality in the book although it was an underlying quality. It has not been remarked upon by most reviewers, but I often doubt if the emotion itself is not one which is felt by a very few people of the book reading class. I believe it is felt by simpler people.

. . . . .

Yours,
Maxwell E. Perkins

*TLS, 3 pp.*

December 6, 1926

[*In Perkins's hand*] March No. out Feby

Dear Mr. Perkins:

Thanks so much for the reviews and the information about the Sun's prospects. As for movie rights please get the best you can i.e. the most money—I do not go to the movies and would not care what changes they made. That is their gain or loss—I don't write movies. Although if they would film Pamplona they could make a wonderful picture. All that racing of the bulls through the streets and the people running ahead and into the ring, amateurs being tossed, the bulls charging into the crowd etc. really happens every morning between the 7th and 12th of July and they could get some wonderful stuff. We made a movie from inside the ring one year with a German portable camera—the sort that takes full size movies; you have only to load it and press down a button to keep it shooting—no cranking—and had the rush of people coming into the ring, coming faster and faster and then finally falling all over themselves and piling up and the bulls jamming over them and right into the camera. It was a wonderful thing but so short that it wasn't of any commercial value. Have another one of Don Stewart being tossed in the amateur fight and one of me bull fighting. When I come over to the states will bring them and we can run them off sometime.

About the stories—I have ten stories now—Two long ones The Undefeated—a bull fight story of between 12 and 15,000 words; and Fifty Grand.

[1]128 words have been omitted from this letter.

52

Eight others will average around three thousand words or so. I don't know whether that is enough for a book. In any event do you think it would be wise to have another book out so soon as Spring—rather than wait until early fall? In Our Time came out last November—Torrents in the early summer—The Sun in Oct. Don't you think we might give them a rest? Or isn't that how it's done?

I will keep the bull fight book going and might do the first part and get it out of the way up to date. It will have illustrations—drawings and photographs—and I think should have some colored reproductions. It is a long one to write because it is not to be just a history and text book or apologia for bull fighting—but instead, if possible, bull fighting its-self. As it's a thing that nobody knows about in English I'd like to take it first from altogether outside—how I happened to be interested in it, how it seemed before I saw it—how it was when I didn't understand it—my own experience with it, how it reacts on other the gradual finding out about it and try and build it up from the outside and then go all the way inside with chapters on everything. It might be interesting to people because nobody knows anything about it—and it really is terribly interesting—being a matter of life and death—and anything that a young peasant or bootblack can make 80,000 dollars a year in before he is twenty three does something to people. I think a really true book if it were fairly well written about the one thing that has, with the exception of the ritual of the church, come down to us intact from the old days would have a certain permanent value. But it has to be solid and true and have all the dope and be interesting—and it won't be ready for a long time. But you can figure on it for the future if you like.

I think the next thing to figure on is a book of stories—and I think it's very important that it should be awfully good and not hurried. Because if The Sun should have some success there will be a lot of people with the knife out very eager to see me slipping—and the best way to handle that is not to slip. Then I'd like to write another novel when things get straightened out and my head gets tranquil. In the meantime I might as well write stories for a while. I had a note from Scott that he was leaving for Genoa—so I imagine you may see him before you get this letter.

My own typewriter is broken and this borrowed one has so many wretched individual traits that my mind is half occupied all the time I'm writing with the malignancy of the machine and I haven't been able to re-write the other story I was going to send you or do anything new. I'll enclose the proofs of the little canary story with this and perhaps you will turn them over to Mr. Bridges with my compliments.[1]

Yours always,<br>
Ernest Hemingway

---

[1]"A Canary for One," *Scribner's Magazine* 81 (April 1927): 358–360. Robert Bridges was editor of *Scribner's Magazine*.

*TLS, 2 pp.*
*Paris, France*

December 7, 1926

Dear Mr. Perkins;

Today your letter of Nov. 26 came. I don't think the book could have been better made nor finer looking.

One thing I would like—four copies only were sent me—and I would like a few more as I had to buy it here at 70 francs a copy to send over to Curtis Brown for his negotiations with Heinemann etc. I have set a trap for Roth by letting a local N.J. printer get out a few hundred copies of a thing of mine called Today Is Friday—which Roth will be very liable to lift for one of his publications. This I have had copyrighted and have just received the certificate of copyright registration from Washington. We may be able to bag him with that.[1]

About the drawing—it really makes no difference. At the time I hated to have my family think that I really looked like that. They feel, I understand, very humiliated because of "the way I write." A copy of The Literary Digest Book Review Magazine from my father has underlined in blue and red pencil the following—The Penn Publishing Company, of Philadelphia, which reports a constantly increasing sale for the books of Temple Bailey, wrote in part—"Our feeling is that there is a strong reaction against the sex novel, and even the highbrow realistic novel————and that (later on) the clean, romantic, or stirring adventure tale will always command the wider public." But the drawing may have pleased them. And it seems to reproduce very well.

What you say about The Green Hat is quite true. My contact with Arlen was through Scott's talking about him and his stuff when we once drove Scott's car from Lyons to Paris.[2] I remember telling Scott who the people were that had taken Arlen up—and even getting quite irritated about Arlen—Don Stewart talked about him too. I took it for granted that the Green Hat must be a cheap book when I heard that the heroine killed herself—because the one very essential fact about all those people that Arlen knew was that none of them had the guts to kill themselves. So I guess it was really protesting about that sort of twaddle that I made Brett so damned accurate that practically nobody seemed to believe in her. Maybe they do now though. Anyway it was very funny.

There really is, to me anyway, very great glamour in life—and places and all sorts of things and I would like sometime to get it into stuff. People aren't all as bad as Ring Lardner[3] finds them—or as hollowed out and

---

[1]*Today Is Friday* (Englewood, N.J.: As Stable, 1926); nothing resulted from EH's attempt to trap Roth.

[2]For EH's account of this trip, see "Scott Fitzgerald" in *MF.*

[3]Ring Lardner (1885–1933), an American sportswriter and short story writer, was one of MP's authors.

exhausted emotionally as some of The Sun generation. I've known some very wonderful people who even though they were going directly toward the grave (which is what makes any story a tragedy if carried out until the end) managed to put up a very fine performance enroute. Impotence is a pretty dull subject compared with war or love or the old lucha por la vida. I do hope though that The Sun will sell a tremendous lot because while the subject is dull the book isn't. Then maybe sometime, and with that impetus to go on, we'll have a novel where the subject won't be dull and try and keep the good qualities of this one. Only, of course, you don't have subjects—Louis Bromfield has subjects—but just write them and if God is good to you they come out well. But it would always be much better to write than to talk about writing.

My son looks forward very much to the Christmas book and told his mother very excitedly—Max Perkins va me donner un joli cadeau! When she asked him what it was he said it was a very beautiful big book not written by papa.

Yours always<br>Ernest Hemingway

*ALS, Chicago Daily News (Paris office) stationery, 6 pp.*[1]

PARIS December 21 1926

Dear Mr. Perkins:

Thanks for the figures on The Sun. I do hope it will go on again after the New Year and think it may as there seems to be much divergence of opinion etc. which must mean discussion. John Bishop showed me a letter from Edmund Wilson last night in which Wilson was very enthusiastic saying he thought it best novel by any one of my generation—but that plenty of other didn't and what did he, Bishop, think. Maybe Wilson will write something about it. I'm awfully glad he liked it.

I think it is a splendid idea of Bridges about running the three stories together—they are all short—none of them long enough to make much of a show alone—but all 3 compliment one another and would make a fine group.[2] And perhaps cheer up Dos,[3] Allen Tate and the other boys who fear I'm on the toboggan.

I take it for granted then he's buying In Another Country—and if he wants to send it I could use the check.

Thank you ever so much for the Christmas book for Bumby. And a very merry holiday time

Ernest Hemingway.

[1]63 words have been omitted from this letter.
[2]Bridges's plan was to publish "The Killers" with "In Another Country" and "A Canary for One" in a single issue. The latter two stories appeared in the April 1927 issue (pp. 355–360).
[3]American novelist John Dos Passos (1896–1970).

Dos Passos' sent me a carbon of his review. I think it was fine about his not liking the book and wanting it to be better but a poor criticism that Pamplona in the book wasnt as good as Pamplona in real life—because I think it was maybe pretty exciting to people who'd never been there—and that was who it was written for It would be easy to write about it for Dos and make it very exciting—because he's been there. But written for him it wouldnt mean anything to the quite abstract reader that one tries to write for—

. . . . .

. . . . .

Cape took The Sun with a 50 pound advance—10—15—20—royalties and Spring publication.[1]

I have been writing some more stories I have given my wife all The Sun royalties both British and American—and I hope they will be considerable.[2] I dont know when the royalty checks come out. When one does I wish you could consider the advance on Torrents as $500 and that paid on The Sun as $1000 and let the check go on when the earnings commence after the $1000 is paid off.

I dont imagine that Torrents earned $500 but you can deduct the difference from my next books.

. . . . .

I imagine, now that they seem to be rowing about it that The Sun may go very well. The chief criticism seems to be that people are so unattractive—which seems very funny as criticism when you consider the attractiveness of the people in, say, Ulysses, The Old Testament, Judge Fielding and other people some of the critics like. I wonder where these thoroughly attractive people hang out and how they behave when they're drunk and what do <u>they</u> think about nights. Oh hell. There's at least one highly moral hotel keeper in the book. That's my contention and I'll stick to it. And an exemplary Englishman named Harris.

And why not make a Jew a bounder in literature as well as in life? Do Jews always have to be so splendid in writing?

I think maybe next book we can save money on the clippings.

Critics. this is still Mr. Tate—have the a habit of hanging attributes on you themselves—and then when they find you're not that way accusing you of sailing under false colours—Mr Tate feels so badly that I'm not as hardboiled as he had publicly announced. As a matter of fact I have not been at all hard boiled since July 8 1918—on the night of which I discovered that that also was Vanity.

---

[1] Jonathan Cape published the novel in London as *Fiesta* in 1927.
[2] EH had assigned the royalties from *SAR* to his first wife, Hadley, as part of a divorce settlement.

# HEMINGWAY/PERKINS CHRONOLOGY
## 1927–1929

◆

| | |
|---|---|
| March 1927 | *Scribner's Magazine* publishes "The Killers," Hemingway's first story in an American magazine. |
| April 1927 | *Scribner's Magazine* publishes "In Another Country" and "A Canary for One." |
| 14 April 1927 | Hemingway's divorce from Hadley Richardson Hemingway becomes final. |
| 10 May 1927 | Hemingway marries Pauline Pfeiffer. |
| 14 October 1927 | Scribners publishes *Men Without Women,* Hemingway's second story collection. |
| 22 November 1927 | Hemingway tells Fitzgerald he has 50,000 words done on a new novel tentatively titled "A New Slain Knight." |
| March 1928 | Hemingway abandons novel in progress to begin writing what would become *A Farewell to Arms.* |
| April 1928 | The Hemingways take up residence in Key West, Florida. |
| 20–22 August 1928 | Hemingway completes the first draft of *A Farewell to Arms.* |
| c. 8–12 November 1928 | Hemingway comes to New York; he may have discussed possibility of serializing *A Farewell to Arms* in *Scribner's Magazine.* |
| c. 27 November–5 December 1928 | Hemingway comes to New York; he meets Ring Lardner for the only time, probably introduced by Perkins. |
| 6 December 1928 | Hemingway's father commits suicide. |
| c. 25 January–9 February 1929 | Perkins comes to Key West to fish and to get the typescript of *A Farewell to Arms.* |
| May 1929 | First installment of the novel appears in *Scribner's Magazine.* |

| | |
|---|---|
| June 1929 | In Paris, Morley Callaghan and Hemingway box; Fitzgerald serves as timekeeper. |
| 21 June 1929 | June issue of *Scribner's Magazine* is banned in Boston because of *A Farewell to Arms*. |
| 27 September 1929 | Scribners publishes *A Farewell to Arms*. |
| 18 October 1929 | Scribners publishes Thomas Wolfe's first novel, *Look Homeward, Angel*. |

—R.W.T.

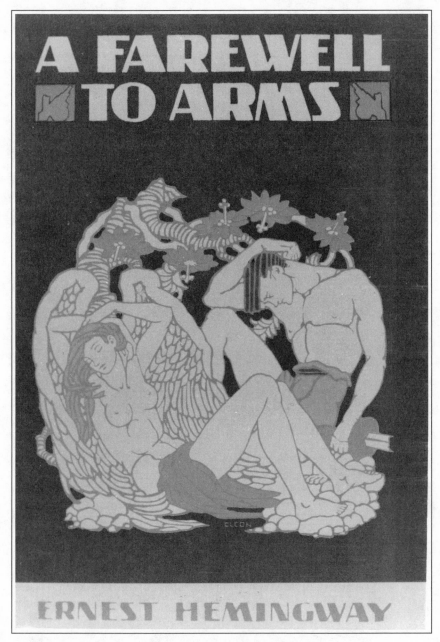

Front of dust jacket by CLEON.

*CC, 3 pp.*

April 13, 1927

Dear Hemingway:

It so often happened that when I wrote you, a letter crossed mine which gave me the information I asked for, that I have lately rather delayed, awaiting news from you. I thought it best now, though, to write to say that although we are making up a dummy on "Men Without Women", using "The Killers" for text material, we could now with great advantage use the manuscript itself. I hope you will therefore send it as soon as you can. It is short according to your figuring, and we do not above all things want to make it look padded. This we shall not do in any case, beyond putting in half titles between stories, which is proper. But Scott thinks that you must have much more material than forty-five or fifty thousand words. He spoke of various things that I had never heard of. If you have other stories that would go into this book without any regret on your part, send them too.- But if you are not satisfied that they are good ones, let the book remain short, and we shall do very well that way. Anyhow I suspect there are many more words according to our figuring than you think.

I am forwarding today a letter to Mr. Scott Fitzgerald, which is evidently one from you. I wish there were one for me. You ought to come over and see Ellersley Mansion, Brandywine Hundred, with the big Delaware River right beyond it. You had better come soon too, because nobody could live in such a house and not be modified. Zelda will soon be a stately lady of the manor, and the drinking will be port by candle light, accompanied with walnuts.

As ever yours,

*CC, 4 pp.*

June 8, 1927

Dear Hemingway:

I thought the two stories that came with your letter of the 27th were most excellent. The book will have a great deal of variety, among its other qualities. It is a notable collection. I still hope for the other bull fight story by July first or thereabouts, and perhaps some others. "Italy"[1] we already had got, and I am trying to find the Little Review story.[2]

Here is an advertisement, the first in a new series. Something different from what we have used before. The book goes on. It has been suppressed in Boston, but not until about a dozen other books had been. Boston suppressions do not even have a publicity value any longer.

---

[1]"Italy—1927," *The New Republic* 50 (18 May 1927): 350–353; reprinted as "Che Ti Dice La Patria?" in *MWW*.

[2]"Banal Story," *The Little Review* 12 (Spring–Summer 1926): 22–23.

The Liveright incident is definitely closed apparently and so I should like to say that the terms they offered you are the terms we will give you any time. And if you want any more money in advance on "Men Without Women" as the summer goes on, you have only to let us know. And do always let us know when you are in that position. I always hesitate to propose advances myself, or to suggest a high figure, because unless it is necessary for some reason, it is better that an author should not be running behind the game. With Scott, for instance—and I am sure you know about it in general from him, so I can speak of it freely—we have never stated an advance. We have simply given him what he required when he wanted it; and this has worked very well excepting that he has sometimes got royalty reports which showed a considerable earning, and yet has received no money with them. The only trouble with Scott has been that being unusually strict about money matters, and accurate, he has often felt as if he were in debt to us, and has apologized for asking for money which he could just as easily have had without any obligation whatever, as an advance. This I have often told him because his conscience seemed to trouble him.- It was only the other day I got an apologetic telegram asking for money which we would have given him long ago without a quiver as an advance on a novel he is now finishing. I say all this so that you will understand that you also can call on us, either for large advances, or for money against your work when you require it.

I was very much pleased to get your letter, and appreciated to the full your attitude. I hope you have a wonderful summer.

As ever yours,

*TLS with holograph postscript, 2 pp.*[1]
*Paris, France*

June 24

Dear Mr. Perkins,

I am enclosing a copy of a letter which arrived with a check for 25,483.40 francs enclosed yesterday morning. Also enclosing a draft of the letter I am sending returning the check.[2]

---

[1] 57 words have been omitted from this letter.

[2] Ray Long, executive of the Hearst's magazines, attempted to obtain serial and movie rights to EH's unwritten novel. On 24 June, the same day that he wrote MP, EH declined the offer in a letter to Temple:

At any rate I am satisfied with the prices and with your whole handling of the matter and, if you like, I will send you some stories for Mr. Long when I have them, and I give you my word that I will not enter into any negociations with any one else for serializing the novel. When it is done if I decide to serialize it Mr. Long can have it if he wishes at the price stated in the offer, $12,000 with the $30,000 movie option.

I write this so that you will see that I am not trying to hold things up in order to get a better offer somewhere else on the strength of this one. There are only two

Mildred Temple is the new Hearst representative over here. She flew over last week with a copy of this letter except that the serial price was 10,000 and the movie rights 15,000 and it did not contain the clause about no cutting. They came up over the week end. I had said I didnt think I'd do it anyway but certainly not on the original terms.

I was pretty badly tempted as it is a splendid chance to sell stories but I really think that the pressure would be too strong and too subtle in regard to the novel. It is a hell of a job for me to write anyway and with the pressure of a possible 42,000 dollars if it turned out to be what they wanted—somehow it seemed like too much extraweight to take on at this time in my career.

This is the sort of thing I would like to have eventually—but I can't see it doing me any good now—and I have never seen an American writer survive it. Then eventually something else may smash me and I never get it. But that's covered by the expression—What the hell.

Only it seems bad luck to have it come now and lose it instead of having it it 15 years—or even ten years—when it could harm no one.

Of course I would not sign anything without consulting you about the serial thing. All my instinct is against it—granted that I were strong enough not to have it affect me it would be splendid—but has anybody ever survived that sort of thing?

So will you please advise me about the serializing business—practically—from the publishing standpoint—and also as my friend.

In considering it please throw the money end out. We both take it for granted that money would be a fine thing to have but for the next ten years it must be a side issue. I always took you at your word about the question of advances etc.—I have plenty of money now to last several months.

I really think that eventually I might have a book which might sell a great deal—or one which, on being completed, might serialize well. But now doesn't seem like the time to get into what seems to me to be the greased shutes.

Your letter was awfully nice about the Liveright thing. I only mentioned it so that you wouldn't hear any different versions or rumours.

As for the horse and eagle offal I don't know what to do. Could we leave a dash? S—— might be all right.[1]

Walpole's review was in the June 4 Nation. Cape has gotten the Sun out in the cheapest form possible is advertsing it as an amusing story of the sort of thing young Americans are doing in the Latin quarter today and is trying hard to sell it as a hammock book. On that basis it is getting and will get panned. I feel disgusted with Cape and always have been. They cut the In

---

difficulties in the way of signing the contract. The first that I would not wish to serialize against Scribner's wishes. The second that, after consideration, I do not want to take an advance which might even unconsciously affect the writing of a novel because of the necessity of submitting it for serialization.

[1]In "A Pursuit Race"; *MWW* printed the word as "s——."

Our Time, changed many words, anglicized it to make walked along the ties read walked along the <u>sleepers</u> etc. etc.[1]

This must make the boat so I'll close. There is no need to cable about the serialization thing—a letter would be better. Please tell me all you think. I don't even know whether it is supposed to be good or bad for the sale of a book.

. . . . .

Yours always
Ernest Hemingway.

. . . . .

*TLS, 3 pp.*

Hotel Barron—Hendaye Plage
(Basse Pyrenees)
Frankreich
September 15.

Dear Mr. Perkins

That was a grand picture and caption and I hope that very clever youngster from Washington, Paris and "roundabout" has every success with the new volumne. I bought a two week old World at the Gare in Hendaye and was made happy to learn who had the Harper Prize for 1927–8 and at the same time saw in the Chicago Tribune that Louis Bromfield was the American Fielding. So that made a big literary day.

What about all these prizes? I am now writing a novel myself so am very interested. As far as I know Harpers have been announcing The Grandmother's[2] for over a year so it seems to have fallen out very happily that it should be given a prize by the House its-self immediately on publication.

Couldn't we all chip in and get up say The New World Symphony Prize for 1927–8–9 and give it to Scott's new novel as an incentive that he finish it?[3] I'm sure mine would go faster and further if it were only assured of the Herman R. Scribner Memorial Prize for 1929 and in the meantime I could borrow money on the prize.

With the various litero-menstrual clubs (Book of the Month) The Something or other Guild and these prizes the whole things seems to be getting pretty filthy. Any time a sum over one thousand dollars is found under the pillow in the literary, ball playing, popular evangelistic or other world crookedness seems to result.

Before I had your wire about O'Brien[4] I had a very nice letter from him

---

[1]In "Big Two-Hearted River"; Cape published *IOT* in 1926.

[2]A 1927 novel by Glenway Wescott, which received the Harper Prize.

[3]Fitzgerald was working on what became *Tender Is the Night* (New York: Scribners, 1934).

[4]Edward O'Brien, editor of annual selections of the best short stories of the previous year.

saying he would never have asked for the 50G. if he had had any idea how things were and would appreciate very much having the Killers. I didn't think you'd mind letting him have it as it was short, only one out of 14 others, was published in the magazine, and was in no sense the piece de resistance whatever that may be of the book. I figured that as long as we have a product that but for the grace of God and yourself and the way things happen to be we couldn't get published at all—or that if published any number of gents would be glad to jump on—and may yet: having such a product I think it is no loss to take whatever opportunities present to make it seems classic and unsuppressable such as O'Brien, Scribner's magazine, The Atlantic etc. Because there must be at home other people besides my own family who do not care for the stuff and would be glad to suppress it—and these people have been in power once and at home we have a dangerous habit of making laws which later they say they can do nothing about—and these people may be in power again and we may have such laws.

You asked about the novel[1] and as it seems that the more they are spoken of the slower they progress—except in the case of the gents who dictate them—I don't know anything to say except that 99/9/10 remains to be written but that I am going on the six hour a day regime in Paris next week with nobody having the address and that as Glenway says in the World "frankly I desire immortality" but am afraid that usually you have to die to prove you have it and would prefer to commence by trying to write a good novel. Would suggest to Glenway that if he desires immortality hard enough he might bump himself off while he's still going good because there is a certain type of young man which or whom if he dies young enough is always a source of interest to certain people.

This may seem a very wise letter butthat is because of a dangerous facility in writing English which gives such a sense of security that it leads to positiveness after the humility of, having talked a language all summer in which there is a great deal of outspoken repartee and in which I know only one word for —— as we say in Men Without Women.

Yours always,

Ernest Hemingway.

Have in this same mail several letters (two) from girls who think The Sun Also Rises is a wonderful book, so vivid and interesting with descriptions of real places and mustn't I have had a vivid and interesting life myself and would I send a short account of it and a picture. One of them hopes to be a writer herself and her name is Ernestine and you can see what a bond that would be between us. There have been a number of these splendid letters written to lead up to such a sort of literary friendship that people would have with, say, Barrie.[2] On the principle that the customer is always right I answer them—but

---

[1] "A New Slain Knight"; EH never completed this novel, suspending work in March of 1928.

[2] James M. Barrie (1860–1937), Scottish author of Peter Pan (1904).

in order not to lead the customer astray try and answer them as I hope John Greenleaf Whittier would. If you have any pictures of white bearded new England gentlemen about the office that would be suitable for mailing you might have them autographed and held in readiness.

*CC, 4 pp.*

Oct. 14, 1927

Dear Hemingway:

The book is out and I am sending six copies. I am sending also the Times review, and a copy of the ad. we are using on the day of publication, that with your picture, and two follow-up ads. I am not sending the Tribune review because I notice the Tribune has sent it. It was an enraging review, first because it appeared a week too soon—and because of women without men, there being only editresses on the Tribune, whose promises are worthless—and then because it was by Virginia Woolf who spent a large part of her time in talking about the function of criticism instead of functioning as a critic. I am also enclosing an amusing note from Ezra Pound, clipped from the Tribune. I won't bother you with much more stuff, but I thought I would send these early indications to show that "Men without Women" was out and about.

Dashiel[1] told me that he had written of the Magazine's urgent desire for a story. In January, Scribner's is coming out in a new style, and a much better one.- Larger type, and less pictures. Pictures only when they are worthwhile as pictures,- at least in the estimation of the staff;- not any pictures just to be "illustrated". It is to be different also in other than physical ways, and although I know I ought not to add to your complications by saying it, we think it would be a grand thing if the novel you are writing, could be serialized there. I merely mention this for if serialization is to occur, the question of price should be a most important one, if not the most important. But I did want you to know that the Magazine would be delighted if it could serialize a novel by you. I suppose we could not have done "The Sun Also Rises". In fact, I do not think anybody could have serialized that with an eye to their heterogeneous public. But this novel might be different in those respects, and we might be able to make it possible in the other respect. I will say no more about it, but since all the other magazines have said something, I thought if we did not, you might possibly not realize the strength of our interest.

We went down to the Fitzgeralds for a week end. Ellerslie Mansion, which is solid and high and yellow, has more quality of its own than almost any house I was ever in. It is very old (for America) and the trees around it are big. It has columns at the front and back, and second-story verandas, and the lawn runs right down to the Delaware River.- But Scott is in bad shape,

---

[1]Alfred Dashiell was then associate editor of *Scribner's Magazine;* MP consistently misspelled his name.

although you had better not say anything about it to him. He is terribly nervous, even to an alarming degree. I wish he would take a month of hard exercise, and nothing else. He is perfectly O.K. physically, yet you feel as if he might have a breakdown nervously.- But Zelda is in great shape in every way.

Ever yours,

*CC, 4 pp.*[1]

Oct. 31, 1927

Dear Hemingway:

I hope you won't mind our sending the enclosed cheque without waiting till the regular royalty time which is far off. "Men Without" has earned $400 odd beyond this $1000, after deducting the $750 advanced. It's a hard feature of book writing that an author has to wait from six months to a year to realize a penny. "Men Without" is being wonderfully received and it ought to sell; and we should like to give you some advantage from this now. We shall gladly send more at any moment.- That's a fact.

Scott (as I implied by cable) is much better. He was here ten days ago and had a bad nervous spell, but the first in some days. He had to walk, he said, and wanted me to go for a drink. I said, "Well, I'll go if it's just one drink." He said, "You talk to me as if I were a Ring Lardner." So we did go and had a grand talk, and he was most keen about "Men Without",- not only about particular stories, but about the book as a whole, so generally uniform and solid in quality.- He'll have written you though.

He was much improved that day and then I saw John Biggs from Wilmington, who had been worried about him. He said Scott was now quite different, in really good shape. I put him on to a denicotinized cigarette called Sano. They're horrible and did me no good, but Scott has managed to stick to them. I think tobacco was hurting him more than drink,- which he had lately gone easy on anyway.

. . . . .
. . . . .

Ever yours,

*ALS, 3 pp., JFK*

Nov 30th 1927

Dear Hemingway:—

With some trepidation, I send you last weeks ad. The physiology of our bull has caused you some anxiety, but now what?[1] Note the curious incan-

---

[1]152 words have been omitted from this letter.

[2]The ad for *MWW* in the *New York Times Book Review* (27 November 1927) featured an illustration of a bull with a highlighted penis.

descence of his most bullish feature, + imagine my mixed emotions when I noted it + supposed a couple of hundred thousand of others would too.— But as the enclosed memo relates, only ten thousand bulls got loose in this heated condition, + those in the provinces. Heaven protect simple minded cattle there.—And it seems to be a fact that the divinity that so strangely shaped <u>this</u> end was Chance!

The Sale to date is 11,230 Copies. I enclose, while about it, a third 'Ed.' wrap. Scott, here, is now almost wholly recovered. Conrad Aiken, who has a remarkable talent, writes me: "Thank you for the Hemingway. It's a damned good book. The Undefeated is a Knock out. And Fifty Grand + the Killers not far Behind it. Hemingway makes me absolutely Sweat with Envy."

Have you happened to see the Padraic Colums in Paris. I like them much + I think you would too.

Ever Yours

Maxwell E. Perkins

*ALS, 6 pp.*[1]

*La Rochelle, France*

<u>March 17</u>

Dear Mr. Perkins—

Guy Hickock[2] showed me a cable today from Scribners asking about my good health and I hope you werent worried I was tired of recounting accidents so was not going to mention it. However it was the sky light in the toilet—a friend had pulled the cord that raised it instead of pulling the chain of the toilet—and cracked the glass so that when I tried to hook up the cord (going into the bathroom at 2 a m. and seeing it dangling) the whole thing fell. We stopped the hemmorage with 30 thicknesses of toilet paper (a magnificent absorbent which I've now used twice for that purpose in pretty much emergencies) and a tourniquet of kitchen towel and a stick of kindling wood. The first two tourniquets wouldnt stop it due to being too short— (face towels) and I was rather worried as we had no telephone. The chance of getting a doctor at 2 a.m. and there were two little arteries cut. But the third held it very well and we went out to Neuilly to Am. Hospital where they fixed it up, tying the arteries, putting in three stitches underneath and six to close it. No after effects but a damned nusiance.

. . . . .

. . . . .

. . . . .

I asked a (Mrs.) Emily Holmes Coleman to send you her novel about an insane asylum. (She was in one for a while as a patient and, I think, can

---

[1]366 words have been omitted from this letter.

[2]Foreign correspondent for the *Brooklyn Daily Eagle*.

write) I have never read it, but she was going to send it to Boni and Liveright (who published a book on psychology by her husband) and I prefferred if it should chance to be good that you see it.

I would like to have finished the novel—but (1) I have been laid up and out a good deal.

(2) It took me 5 years to write all the stories in In Our Time.

(3) It took 5 years to write the ones in Men Without Women.

(4) I wrote Sun Also Rises in 6 weeks but then did not look at it for 3 months—and then rewrote it for another three months. How much time I wasted in drinking around before I wrote it and how badly I busted up my life in one way or another I cant fit exactly in time.

(5) I work all the time. But I dont think I can make even an irregular schedule and keep up the quality. I know very well I could turn books out when they should come out And you have been very damned decent about not even asking me to or putting any pressure on me but we only want good ones—Both of us. You see my whole life and head and everything had a hell of a time for a while and you come back slowly (and must never let anyone know even that you were away or let the pack know you were wounded) But I would like to write a really damned good novel—and if the one I have 22 chaps and 45,000 words of done doesnt go after I get to America I will drop it and put it away and go on with the other one I am writing since two weeks that I thought was only a story but that goes on and goes wonderfully.[1]
The first one was supposed to be a sort of Modern Tom Jones. (Never mention that because I do not write comparison but only to name the sort of book) But there is a very very good chance that I dont know enough to write that yet and whatever success I have had has been through writing what I know about—

I know very well that Scott for his own good should have had his novel out a year or two years ago I dont want you to think that I am falling into that thing or alibi-ing to myself. But this next book has to be good. The thing for me to do is write but it may be better not to publish until I get the right one.

I should have gone to America two years ago when I planned. I was through with Europe and needed to go to America before I could write the book that happened there. But I didnt go—but now have, suddenly, a great kick out of the war and all the things and places and it has been going very well.

My wife says that she will see that I'm bled just as often as I cant write—judging by the way it's been going this last week. Hope to be able to work on the boat. If I find I've any readers in America will change my name.

. . . . .

. . . . .

. . . . .

[1]EH interrupted his novel about a boy and his father (working titles "Jimmy Breen" and "A New Slain Knight") to start writing A Farewell to Arms. He did not resume work on "Jimmy Breen."

. . . . .

I am glad you are publishing Morley. I was never off of him but only a poor correspondent—[1]

Yours always,
Ernest <u>Hemingway</u>

. . . . .

. . . . .

*CC, 3 pp.*[2]

April 10, 1928

Dear Hemingway:

. . . . .

Scott I believe, is to go abroad with Zelda on the 21st of April. I saw him last Friday. We had lunch at the Plaza with the Seldes, and afterward Scott said we must have a talk, and selected the Plaza roof for it. So we sat in the sunshine and overlooked the Park. He has got entirely over his nervous attacks, but he was very depressed,- perhaps partly because of a party the night before with Ring Lardner. It was evident that he would have to make some kind of a change, and although he had not decided when I left him, I thought that it would mean Europe. I had hoped he would stay here now for a long time, but after seeing him the way he was, I am glad that he won't. He seemed to have no resilience at all, which is most unusual in Scott. He has made no progress with his novel for a long time, always having to stop to write stories.

As for when you will have something done, I could not make out definitely at all from your letter. But we will just wait patiently and be mighty quick to jump when anything does come,- both here and in the Magazine.

I shall be sending you a royalty report in a day or two, and money whenever you want it.

Ever yours,

*TLS with holograph inserts and postscript, 3 pp.*

April 21—1928
Key West Fla.

Dear Mr. Perkins,

I'm terribly sorry to hear about Scott. Could you tell me the name of his ship and I will send him a cable. Perhaps it would be better to wire it the name of hid boat or where he is in a night letter as this place seems to be a long way

---

[1]Canadian novelist Morley Callaghan (1903–1990), who had worked with EH on the *Toronto Star.*

[2]135 words have been omitted from this letter.

from New York by mail. I wish he would finish his novel or throw it away and write a new one. I think he has just gotten stuck and does not believe in it any more himself from having foole with it so long and yet dreads giving it up. So he writes stories and uses any excuse to keep from having to bite on the nail and finish it. But I believe that everybody has had to give them up (novels) at some time and start others. I wish I could talk to him. He believes that this novel is so important because people came out and said such fine things about him after the Gatsby and then he had a rotten book of stories[1] (I mean there were cheap stories in it) and he feels that he must have a GREAT novel to live up to the critics. All that is such (    ) because the thing for Scott to do is WRITE novels and the good will come out with the bad and in the end the whole thing will be fine. But critics like Seldes[2] etc., are poison for him. He is scared and builds up all sorts of defences like the need for making money with stories etc. all to avoid facing the thing through. He could have written three novels in this length of time—and what if two of them were bad if one of them was a Gatsby. Let him throw away the bad ones. He is prolific as a Gueinea pig (mis-spelled) and instead he has been bamboozled by the critics (who have ruined every writer that reads them) into thinking he lays eggs like the Ostrich or the elephant.

What about the Books—I havnt seen Men Without advertized for a long time.

Glad you saw Waldo Pierce.[3] He wires he is coming down here. I don't know when but hope it will be soon. Dos Passos is on his way too. I don't know for how long.

Have been going very well. Worked every day and have 10,000 to 15,000 words done on the new book. It won't be awfully long and has been going finely. I wish I could have it for Fall because that seems like the only decent time to bring out a book but suppose, with the time necessary to leave it alone before re-writing, that is impossible. I forget when I got the mss. for the Sun to you but think it was sometime pretty early in the Spring. Please tell me if I am wrong. Would like to finish this down here—if possible—put it away for a couple or three months and then re-write it. The re-writing doesn't take more than six weeks or two months once it is done. But it is pretty important for me to let it cool off well before re-writing. I would like to stay right here until it is done as I have been going so very well here and it is such a fine healthy life and the fishing keeps my head from worrying in the afternoons when I don't work. But imagine we will have to go someplace for the baby to be born around the end of June. Ought to leave a month before. Still if I keep on going there will be a lot done by then.

---

[1]*All the Sad Young Men* (New York: Scribners, 1926) included "Winter Dreams," "The Rich Boy," and " 'The Sensible Thing.' "

[2]Gilbert Seldes had given *The Great Gatsby* a warmly admiring review in *The Dial*.

[3]Peirce was a painter from Maine; he had met EH in Paris in 1927, and the two became lifelong friends.

It is hot here but there is always a cool breeze and it isn't hot in the shade and you can sleep at night.

After I get the novel done—if it is too late for this fall—I could do quite a lot of stories and that would keep the stuff going until the next fall and then the novel would come out and we would have stories enough for a book of them to follow it.

Have been ctahcing tarpon, barracuda, jack, red snappers, etc. Caught the biggest tarpon they've had down here so far this season. Sixty three pounds. The really big ones are just stating to come in. These up to 125–140 lbs Also a barracuda on a fly rod. Great quantities of sharks, whip rays and other vermin. We sell the fish we get in the market (the edible ones) and get enough to buy gas and bait. Have been living on fish too. Tonight is a big night (Saturday) although not so cheerful because another cigar factory has closed down. This is a splendid place. Population formerly 26,000—now around ten thousand There was a pencilled insription derogotory to our fair city in the toilet at the station and somebody had written under it—'if you don't like this town get out and stay out.' Somebody else had written under that 'Everybody has.'

Would appreciate your asking them to send and charge to me 3 Sun Alsos and 3 Men Without Womens. (As soon as possible) Nobody believes me when I say I'm a writer. They think I represent Big Northern Bootleggers or Dope Peddlers—especially with this scar. The havent even heard of Scott. Several of the boys I know have just been moved by first reading of Kipling A man introducing Robert Stevens's works would coin money if there was any money to [coin]—[but] there isnt— Yrs always

Hemingway

Hope I get nothing incriminating as they open my mail.

*CC, 4 pp.*[1]

April 27, 1928

Dear Hemingway:

. . . . .

I am glad the writing is going so well. I must say the idea of your doing a sort of modern Tom Jones though, does excite me. I hope you will some time. If there is anything that ought to be written today, it is that very thing. We can certainly expect to publish at the very beginning of the year anyhow, unless serialization intervenes;- and even then we could publish a year from the present time. I wish it might be sooner, but I think you are dead right in proceeding the way you do. Can't you make Waldo try his hand at something with an eye to publication while he is with you,- although I know that if I were in a land where there was sun, I should do nothing but lie still in it, except perhaps try my hand at the sharks and snappers. Here there is a cold rain falling all the time, or at

[1]131 words have been omitted from this letter.

best a cold east wind blowing. It is the rottenest spring there ever was. I am going to take next week off, and simply stay at home.

I did not wire you Scott's boat because I did not think you could even reach him with a radio by the time your letter came. His address is the same old one, C/o Guaranty Trust Company, Paris. He came in the day before he sailed;- I had somewhat the same idea as you about the novel, but he told me that now he thought everything would be right, that there was nothing that he needed to finish it except time. I had got to think that he was attempting the impossible in this novel in which a son kills his mother, and that he might have come to feel the impossibility, and not be willing to acknowledge it.[1] If I could have got any response implying that this was right, I would have advised him to let it go hang and begin another. Anyhow, he did seem himself that day he called. I felt much better about him. It is true that Zelda, while very good for him in some ways, is incredibly extravagant. They ought to get a housekeeper. They could pay her a good salary and she could save them a lot of money. Scott could easily be in a position of independence today. He could have all the time he wanted for writing anything. He said that they had lived abroad so long that they could not get American values into their heads, and I know—John Biggs down there told me—that they run their house most carelessly, and that their servants robbed them.

. . . . .

Ever yours,

*ALS, 3 pp.*[2]

Piggott—ARKANSAS
<u>May 31</u>

[Dear] Mr. Perkins—

There was no Lady Ashley in Burkes or Debrett's Peerage when I sent you the Sun Mss. and none in either of those stud books when I corrected the proof. A young Ashley married a girl out of musical comedy the summer after the book came out. She might as well try and sue Robinson Crusoe.

You've probably seen Waldo. We had a grand time—I worked every morning too and did 200 pages—200 words or so to a page—in Key West. Am now at the above address—a christ offal place. Hope to get up to Michigan soon. Am delayed by impending child birth probably to take place at Kansas City or some such great obstetrical center.

Last winter (IE) the winter before last—I tried to argue Thornton Wilder out of Boni and Boni (He was commissioned to argue me into " " " [*Boni and Boni*]) but am afraid he would now have more arguments. I thought Bridge of S L.R. was a fine book of short stories—2 splendid ones—The Esteban

---

[1]Fitzgerald's projected matricide novel evolved into *Tender Is the Night*.
[2]50 words have been omitted from this letter.

and I think the other was about a little girl who worked for the Mother Superior. He can write very very well. Also a nice boy.

I think I will have to get a large advance on my next book to insure to assure it being advertized in Florid and Gigantic Manner in order that Scribners must sell a large number of copies to get the advance back. Glenway Wescott, Thornton Wilder and Julian Green have all gotten rich in a year in which I have made less than I made as a newspaper correspondent—And I'm the only one with wives and children to support. Something's going to have to be done. I dont want the present royalties until they are due. But I would like to make a chunk of money at one time so I could invest it. This bull market in beautiful letters isnt going to last forever and I do not want to always be one who is supposed to have made large sums and hasnt and doesn't. If I have as many accidents right along as I've had this last year they will be having to give a benefit for me in a couple of years. It did seem as though they laid off advertising Men Without Women when it was still going well just as much as they jumped out with enormous ads for Thorntons book the minute it started going. Of course I know nothing about it but after the first of the year—when Men Without was still selling well—it seemed as though they were satified with the sale and pretty well laid off.

Anyway am working steadily on the present novel and it seems to go well—and finally—I hope—toward an end. When I get it done I think I will go back to the one I dropped after 60,000 and finish it—It seems now as though it had never been difficult to work but I suppose that time will come again.

. . . . .

Yours always,
Ernest Hemingway
Address Piggott ARKansas for a while. <u>They will forward.</u>

*CC, 4 pp.*

August 8, 1928

Dear Hemingway:

I hope this letter will find you in a cooler land than that from which you last wrote and that everything may now be better with you. I can easily imagine what a time you have had in Kansas City. I think a period of anxiety is the most awful thing. It hits you every way, mentally, morally and physically - or rather, I should say it hits <u>me</u>. I hope everything is all right with your wife and the boy. Patrick is a fine name.

Your question about how much the Magazine would pay I put to the Magazine and it aroused a great deal of interest, seeming to imply that they could look forward to a chance at the serial. It did not, however, extract a definite reply because they feel that the price would depend on a good many things including length. The quality of course they would take for granted, the only question then being that there might be something in the character of the story which would make it "unavailable". But the expectation would be to pay as much as we ever can pay, but this does not compare well with the twenty-five to forty thousand dollar payments sometimes made by the popular magazines. The best way to put it for you would be to say that we would presumably pay a top price, for us, and that our prices for long serials by Galsworthy and Mrs. Wharton have been about ten thousand dollars. This is the most I can say, and is certainly in[definite]. We want your serial and should strain hard to get it, but for the present I think it ought to be looked at as in the neighborhood of a ten thousand dollar proposition. That anyway will give you something to judge by.

What was suggested was that I should ask you to submit a synopsis; but that is a hard thing for the author to do, and often harmful to his work. I would say, let it go until you come to New York or until you are ready to send us the final draft, or a preliminary one. It is not improbable that this novel will be unavailable for the popular magazines for some reason. It might be thought to be above their public. In that case we will do our best to pay a price that is worth while. And otherwise you could not make the sacrifice.

I was mighty glad to get from Scott a letter beginning with the following paragraph:

> "The novel goes fine. I think it's quite wonderful and I think those who've seen it (for I've read it around a little) have been quite excited. I was encouraged the other day when James Joyce came to dinner, when he said, 'Yes, I expect to finish my novel in three or four years more at the latest', and he works eleven hours a day to my intermittent eight. Mine will be done <u>sure</u> in September."

He has urged upon us an author named Andre Chamson and I am making a proposal for his novel, "Les Hommes de la route". The book, although very fine, is of the quiet sort which is difficult to sell in this day. But I think we might put it over if we publish it well enough.[1]

May you have good fishing.

Ever yours,<br>M.E.P.

<br>

ALS, Sheridan Inn stationery, 6 pp.<br>Sheridan, Wyoming

[20 August 1928]

Dear Mr. Perkins—

Thanks for the letter with the check.

I've not received Strange Fugitive yet and would <u>like</u> to see it.[2] From the advertizements in the Magazine I got the impression you were booming him

---

[1] Published as *The Road* (1929), trans. Van Wyck Brooks.
[2] Novel by Morley Callaghan (New York: Scribners, 1928).

as a newer and better Hemingway of some sort—grooming him in case the present Hem should be slipping. I read the two stories that were in the magazine in the station at K.C. worried to see whether the new H. was better than the old—then read there was to be a prize fight story next month bought it—read it and haven't worried since. I feel like a boxer when his opponent hits him flush on the jaw with a right hand and he says "Is that all you got" and knows the other guy cant hurt him.

The first draft of the book is finished—we've had a fine time ever since—bummed all over—caught our limit of trout nearly every day—saw Struthers Burt one evening—Have driven 760 miles in America this Summer—We come to N.Y. the middle of Oct—first November—Hope to see Scott then—Dont tell anyone but we wont be going back this fall—will stay in Key West—to rewrite the book—That was where I went best writing it and it should be a grand life—will get Waldo down—Couldnt you come down in the winter?—If we could work up some good excuse?

I havent thought about serialization much—need the money but am afraid the magazine wont take a chance under Dr. Bridges—I am sure he would not have run The Sun—He wanted me to cut 50 Grand—Owen Wister[1]—who seems a fine man—told me he was once going over some letters of Roosevelt's for his sister and all the good ones were one's B. had refused for the magazine.

So I dont know how much hope to give myself—But now my earnings are down to $90 a month again must look forward to something as life is expensive.

The fate of my stuff has been to always be turned down as too something or other and then after publication everybody say that of course they could have published it and it would have been fine—I think you'll like the book—The Mss. is in the safe in the bank of Piggott—

I did not mean to be catty about Morley—I have read much much better stories by him than those in the magazine—I think he will be a very fine writer and I'm awfully glad you have him—I want to see his book—

Writing whether you want it or not is competitive—Most of the time you compete against time and dead men—sometimes you get something from a living (contemporary competitor) that is so good it jars you. As the story of Esteban in Thornton's last book. But as you read them dead or living you unconsciously compete—I would give 6 mos. of life to have written it.

You know the ones you have no chance against and the others that, with luck, you can beat living and dead. Only never tell this to anyone because they might call it the megalomania or simply swollen head.

(shoot)

We hunt next week on the Crow reservations then back to Piggott via K.C. I'm going to Chicago for a few days then we'll come the N.Y. May drive.

---

[1]Owen Wister (1860–1938), author of *The Virginian* (1902), became a strong admirer of EH's work.

Pauline is well and strong again and we are both in very good shape. This part of the country is very like Spain—I can see how happy the Spaniards must have been when they found it—The only draw back is Dude Ranches—I could write a piece Dude Ranches vs. The West—They are frightful places Like either the Social Register or War time Y.M C A.—but the cabins and tents where the Tin can Tourists and sagebrushers stop are grand. Yours always
Hemingway.

*ALS, 6 pp., JFK*

Sept 17th 1928

Dear Hemingway:—

I'm writing by pen partly because of my stenographer's vacation, but more that I may speak personally, rather than officially, on the Serial question.—This is the truth: there is nothing that Scribner's wants as much as a Serial by you + they will do everything they can to get it, + if they do, will make more of it than they ever made of anything. That's absolutely straight, + from me to you. Against this, stands only the one danger that the story may have in it some element that would unfit it for magazine use,—as there was in The Sun Also.[1] Other wise there is absolutely no ghost of a question. If there is any such element it would presumably unfit the Story for any magazine, but what of it! The book sale should be large, to Speak moderately. The Size of the advance would be what would Suit You, + it would be paid as you pleased, beginning any time from now on. I could not over-state the degree to which this house is interested in this book, or in You;—+ if they were not it would be time to re-organize as a Dry Good House.

What the magazine meant to imply about Callaghan was, of course, that since the last writer they had put foreward was You, their predictions were obviously infallible (?) But it's the hardest thing to find Editors who do not run to comparisons,—not only in advertising but even in selecting; + the comparisions are usually with the Most Notable recent success, however remote the resemblance. Of course its the worst way to advertise + a still worse way to select. You can convince people that this is so for the moment, but you can't break them of it for good.

I don't know what the devil Scott's up to. He should be here now. I hear bad reports of him, but probably untrue. His letters sound good. I wish to Heaven he'd turn up though. There's a rumor he's to stay two years in France. I'll let you know when I know + I hope I'll be glad to do it.—I guess things are OK. I'm in one of those despirate states that come toward the end of the Hay Fever Season!! Three more days of it. Then I'll be an optimist!

---

[1] There was a marked difference between what could be published in magazines and books at that time. The postal authorities had the power to cancel a periodical's second-class-mail privileges on the grounds of obscenity.

Molly Colum says you look like Balzac. Do you know Sid Howard who, in profile, resembles Fielding. I wonder if I could make Key West. Maybe I wouldn't love to do it. Waldo's picture of you looked well in Brentano's Book Chat with an article by Malcolm Cowley.[1] I'll send it on. I won't tell a soul your plans but I'm glad you will stay here

Ever yours<br>Maxwell Perkins

*CC, 2 pp.*

Sept. 21, 1928

Dear Hemingway:

I've been worrying over this serial matter. I've given you nothing to prove our interest but words, and in such matters "What are words? Air!" At least, that's all they might be thought to be. What I should like to do is to send you now, as an advance on serial rights, without the attachment of any thread, a cheque for five thousand dollars. Please let us. This would not bind you to accept our final offer for serialization, but would be an advance on whatever serialization brought;- and we should accept any risk but should have the right to serialize elsewhere with your approval, in the very remote contingency of not being able to do it ourselves. (This I have to put in I suppose, but it's the barest possibility). What we want to do is to give you palpable evidence of the Magazine's interest, which is unprecedented in my experience.

Ever yours,<br><u>M.E.P.</u>

*AL, 5 pp.*

Piggott<br>Sept. 28

Dear Mr. Perkins

I hope the hay fever is over There's nothing worse and I do hope it is finished now. Arriving at Piggott I found two letters from you and one from Guy Hickock who said sat ,"next to me Scott Fitzgerald very white and equally sober—" So you can add that to your reports though by now Scott may be back. I hope he is and that he is in good shape—Though I don't know why I should wish him in US. for his own good—He wrote The Gatsby in Europe—He drinks no more there and what he does drink is not poisonous. I'm awfully anxious to see him.

[1] Malcolm Cowley, "The Hemingway Legend," *Brentano's Book Chat* (September–October 1928): 25–29.

Coming back here I am anxious to start re-writing the book—But it is only a month since I finished it and it probably is best to let it lie until we get settled in Florida. I finished The Sun in Sept. and did not start re-writing it until December. This will not take as much re-writing as each day to start with (while I was working on it) I wrote over what I had done the day before. But I want to make sure that I leave it alone long enough so I can find the places where I get the kick when writing it and neglect to convey it to the reader.

Appreciate the offer of the check for $5000 and nothing would please me more. I want to get together about 15000 to buy bonds with when I get to N.Y. in the attempt to add $75.00 a month to our income—$100.00 if possible if I can raise 20,000. Money in the bank does me no good at all. It simply vanishes. That is why I haven't cashed the $3700 royalty check—but if I can save in chunks and invest we can live very well on the income. Pat was very expensive and living in U.S. with nurse cook etc plus travelling is expensive too. So I want to make an investment before I dribble my captal away. With the 3700 and some other I have picked up have about 5000 to invest now and want to get enough more to do some good.[1]

The only draw back to accepting the 5000 advance is that I quite gratuitously promised Ray Long would let him have the first look at my next book if I decided to serialize it. I did this to shut them up when they were worrying me with propositions while I was working. To be completely frank I would greatly prefer to serialize in The Magazine—I do not care for serializing in Cosmopolitan and the difference of a few thousand—2 or 3—would not make me switch from Scribners to the International Magazine Co. I think it would be a good thing for me to serialize because it is not a good plan to wait too long between appearances and as will not have a book out this fall—nor until next fall—due to working so long on this one—it is good to keep something going.

As I said the money would be very welcome. I would write Ray Long and tell him but am afraid he would think I was trying to bid him up which is the last thing I want. If you can see anyway out of this would be very happy. In the meantime I feel like a damned fool not to take the check—I worry about the whole business and am prevented from writing the stories I wanted to do now in between by worrying about these bloody money matters.

Yet I know, and that is what worries me—that so far I have made no money—nor been able to get any ahead—and I have attended enough benefits for people who did make money and did not hang on to it so that I have no idea but that it is an absolute necessity to get some ahead.

Also on the other hand it would be no fun if the book was adjudged unserializable to send the money back.

So that is the situation—if this letter is muddled perhaps it is because the

[1]EH's second wife, Pauline, enjoyed the generosity of her wealthy family. The Hemingways did not live on his earnings.

situation seems muddled—Perhaps you can clarify it. If the hay fever season is not over don't try!

Anyway the encouraging thing is that I believe maybe the book is pretty bloody good—and I've 40,000 words on another one to follow it—have never felt better or stronger or healthier in the head or body—nor had better confidence or morale—haven't been sick since I've been in America—knocking on wood—nor had an accident—more knocking. The last few days my good eye that I cut last winter has been bothering me and that and worrying about the money has slowed me up—but today it is all right—

This letter has dragged on long enough—Perhaps on re-reading your letter I would not be breaking my promise to Long by taking the check—Anyway you will know I dont think I would accept his offer no matter how much it was—There's also a good chance he wouldn't want it. No one may want it. I suppose that's really why I want the cash in hand! Anyway you will know where I stand and what I can and cant do. Your conscience is as $\left\{ \begin{matrix} \text{good} \\ \text{bad} \end{matrix} \right\}$ as mine.

So good luck anyway and I certainly appreciate the offer.

> Yours always
> *[signature clipped]*

*CC, 2 pp.*

October 2, 1928

Dear Hemingway:

Anyhow, I send you the cheque, and feel easier for doing it, because, as we regard you, and as things have worked out, it seems as though we had sent you very little money. If in some way Ray Long does get this serial, the sum can stand as an advance against the book;- and in view of our expectations, or of your position now as a writer, we are certainly justified in making it, even on a very conservative business estimate.- I hope it will work out the way I proposed though, we to take whatever risk there may be of availability for serialization. When the manuscript is ready you could rightly, to the minds of publishers, including the Mind of Ray Long (sounds like a book title) say: that as Scribner's was the first general magazine to publish your stories, and as that house was publishing your books, it seemed only fair that they should have a chance at this serial.- This argument, easily enlarged on, would and should appeal to a publisher or editor, though it might not and need not appeal to an author. (There would be no reason, of course, why you should recognize this claim to priority unless you wanted to). I know Ray Long would recognize it since as editor he has urged it, and he might freely acknowledge it and clear the whole question. But I'd favor forgetting the question now, wholly, until the manuscript is finished. I didn't like to raise it, I knew it would be disturbing, but I saw there was some sort of doubt in your mind over the Magazine and I had to try to make the thing plain. I suspected you thought the Magazine rather luke-warm because they didn't take the "Fifty Grand", and only urgent because of the enthusiasm of the house in general, and pressure therefrom. The truth is, Bridges and Dashiel have asked me a thousand times when that serial by Hemingway would be finished. I was mad enough that they didn't break their blooming rule and give the whole issue to "Fifty Grand" if necessary,- as they would have done had Mr. Scribner been here then.- But how many people know when to break a rule! They are fully awake now to your significance and would put forward a serial by you with a vigor and emphasis that no one could excel.- And I believe, personally, that you would do better to appear in Scribner's than the Cosmopolitan,- which is the last word I'll volunteer on a perplexing subject, best forgotten until the time comes to act.

Scott sailed on the 29th. Zelda is so able and intelligent, and isn't she also quite a strong person? that I'm surprised she doesn't face the situation better, and show some sense about spending money. Most of their trouble, which may kill Scott in the end, comes from extravagance. All of his friends would have been busted long ago if they'd spent money like Scott and Zelda. Well, I'll let you know how Scott seems the moment I can. Perhaps the news will be really good.

Ever yours,

TLS with holograph additions, 2 pp.<br/>Piggot, Arkansas

Oct 11, 1928

Dear Mr. Perkins-

Thanks very much for sending the check. I will hang on to it and we or rather you can decide what it is for later. I imagine when I see Ray Long or some of his under Rays I can fix it up with them as you suggest. We will see anyway. I don't see why they shouldn't.

Have a story about 3/4 done. Will be leaving here as soon as it is finished to see Chicago and Toronto en route to N.Y. What about Scott? I am awfully anxious to hear.

Is Morley Callaghan in Toronto? Would like to see him.

Nigger To Nigger is very very good.[1] I enjoyed it greatly. Thanks very much for sending it and also for the Aiken book.[2] His story about the fellow rapping on the wall very funny and the old whore lady quite sad. Haven't read any others yet.

Anyone that would say hay fever was imagination could probably prove that child birth was too. My father had it and I was always grateful to it

---

[1] Novel by Edward C. L. Adams (New York: Scribners, 1928).
[2] *Costumes by Eros* (New York: Scribners, 1928).

because it kept us increasingly further north when I was a kid—but I know how hellish it is. I get the same feeling from dust. But it goes away after a couple of days.

Instead of thinking Zelda a possible good influence (what a phrase) for Scott—I think 90% of all the trouble he has comes from her. Almost Every bloody fool thing I have ever seen or known him to do has been directly or indirectly Zelda inspired. I'm probably wrong in this. But I often wonder if he would not have been the best writer we've ever had or likely to have if he hadnt been married to some one that would make him waste <u>Every thing</u>. I know no one that has ever had more talent or wasted it more. I wish to god he'd write a good book and finish it and not poop himself away on those lousy Post stories. I dont blame <u>Lorimer</u>[1] I blame Zelda.

[*In left margin beside last paragraph*] I would not have Scott imagine I believed <u>this for the world</u>.

Yours always,<br>Ernest Hemingway

Will leave here in about three days I'll give you an address in Toronto.

*CC, 4 pp.*[2]

Oct. 24, 1928

Dear Hemingway:

I have just left old Waldo, and Pat Morgan who came up while we were at lunch and sat with us,- and talked about going back to Paris soon to paint. I hope Scott may turn up this very afternoon, as he promised to do, but it is getting late. He has a way of not coming on the day he says he will. He is often about a day late. Anyhow, he seemed pretty well when he arrived, though he had evidently had a very stormy voyage, and seemed to have quarrelled with the purser, but to have made friends with all the stewards. He had a brief case, as they call them, in which he said was the complete manuscript on the novel, but not the finished manuscript. He has to work over parts of it, and he would not definitely say when it would be perfected. On the whole I felt discouraged after seeing him, even though the thing I had feared most — that he was in bad shape physically — was not true. Ring Lardner says (speaking from some experience and with feeling), that he will get to a point where he will feel so rotten about loss of time and pressure of debts, etc., that he will cut it all out.- But he is losing so much valuable time!

I infer from the fact that you are now in Chicago, and are yet to go to Toronto, that you won't be here for some ten days or so. I am afraid Waldo will have left. Scott, of course, will be about, and I hope you will see Ring

---

[1]George Horace Lorimer (1867–1937), editor of *The Saturday Evening Post*.
[2]179 words have been omitted from this letter.

Lardner, for of all the people in the world that I know of, he is one I am sure you would like.[1]

I would ask you if you would send us that story two-thirds done, except that I begin to feel like a regular hog,- asking you for everything.

Ever yours,

. . . . .

. . . . .

*Wire, 1 p.*
*Trenton, New Jersey*

1928 DEC 6 PM 5 19

PLEASE WIRE $100 IMMEDIATELY WESTERNUNION NORTH PHILADELPHIA STATION MY FATHER DEAD MUST GET FIRST TRAIN CHICAGO:
=ERNEST HEMINGWAY

*Wire, 1 p.*
*Philadelphia, Pennsylvania*

1928 DEC 6 PM 8 32

DISREGARD WIRE GOT MONEY FROM SCOTT=
HEMINGWAY

*AL, Illinois Central Railroad stationery, 3 pp.*

*[16 December 1928]*

Cornith Miss
<u>Sunday</u>

Dear Mr. Perkins—

Hope to be back at Key West Tuesday Morning and at work on the book again. My Father shot himself—Dont know whether it was in N.Y. papers. I didnt see any of the papers. I was very fond of him and feel like hell about it Got to Oak Park in plenty of time to handle things—Funeral was Sat. aft.— Have every thing fixed up except they will have damned little money— went over all that too. Realize of course that thing for me to do is not worry but get to work—finish my book properly so I can help them out with the proceeds. What makes me feel the worst is my father is the one I cared about—

You dont have to write any letter of condolence to me—Thanks very

---

[1]EH met Lardner in December 1928, but they did not take to each other.

much for the wire—There was no immediate need for money—When I get the serial money I will try and fix them up—

For your own information (Not Scott) there are my Mother and two Kids Girl 16 Boy 12 still at home—$25,000 insurance—a $15,000 mortgage on the house—(House should bring 10 to 15 Thousand over the Mortgage but sale difficult) Various worthless land in Michigan, Florida etc. with taxes to pay on all of it. No other capital—all gone—My father carried 20–30 yr. Endoment insurance which was paid and lost in Florida. He had Angina Pectoris and Diabetes preventing him from getting any more insurance—

Sunk all his savings, my grandfather's estate etc in Florida.

Hadnt been able to sleep with pain etc—knocked him temporarily out of his head.

I have what I hope wont prove to be the grippe so excuse such a louzy letter—Thought you might be worrying so wanted to give you the dope—

Yours always,

*[Margin of page two clipped]*

*ALS, 4 pp., JFK*[1]

Sunday January 7th '29

Dear Hemingway:—

I hope I may find a letter from you tomorrow to say how things go with you.—Not that I want to interrupt your work or your fishing. If I don't hear I'll consider the news good. And don't worry if you're behind Schedule on the novel. That would be natural enough Heaven Knows. We'll fit our plans to your time. I hope the Sun shines bright + steady + that the Germs of the Flu give a wriggle + die with it. Herabouts they seem to flourish, though we've had fine weather. Fine Skating too up to today.

Scott + Edmund Wilson are coming in for lunch tomorrow. I shall try to head them to the Chatham but the odds are Scott will have us in a Speak Easy, + about two drinks ruins me for work. Scott was up last week too, in fine spirits. The only trouble with him is that in talk he's all over the place. You can never finish up anything you Start to talk about. Wilson is thorough in his talk. I'll be glad to see them together. Wilson promises to leave the ms of his Novel, + I hope he will. He's worked it over twice, + gives signs of doing it again, + I'm afraid he'll hurt it in the end.[2]

By the way: You read of Elinor Wylie's death. Did you see her Magnificent Sonnets in the New Republic. You ought to for they are most amazing,— beyond anything she ever did. Now I'll tell you in confidence, though you may now know it, + certainly it can't be kept a secret, that she was here for

[1] 120 words have been omitted from this letter.
[2] *I Thought of Daisy* (New York: Scribners, 1929).

only a brief visit, meaning to return to England for good + <u>that</u> on account of the <u>Subject</u> of these Sonnets she was to leave poor Bill Benet who worshipped her + had stood God knows what for her, + had sunk himself, almost, as a writer, for her sake, + had given up his children. This might seem pretty raw after all that had happened in a woman probably nearer fifty than forty. But just read the Sonnets!

. . . . .

Now do you require money in view of all that's happened. We want you to tell us if you do, + I'd meant to write you Sooner to say So.

Ever yours
<u>Maxwell Perkins</u>

*ALS, 3 pp.*
*Key West, Florida*

*[Mid-January 1929]*

Dear Max—

I'm sorry to have mistered you so long—Early got the habit of mistering anyone from whom I received money—on the theory of never make a friend of either a servant or an employer—But we have been friends for a long time and it is cockeyed splendid that you are coming down.

Anytime now is fine—Waldo cant come I'm afraid. He doesnt want to leave Bangor until the end of February—He's really just gotten there—

Got 1500 gold marks from Rowohlt my German publishers—They published The Sun in Nov and it has had very much comment and whoopee reviews—They are bringing out Men Without in February and want to publish In Our Time in the late Spring or Summer following with the new book as soon as they can get it translated next Fall. They are an industrious people and always overdo everything. They have come up from 500 to 1500 marks advance so the books must be doing something.

Laid off work yesterday and the day before, and went down toward Tortugas King fishing for the market—We did not hit them the first day nor yesterday until on our way in at 3 o'clock—Then struck them and they were absolutely wild—using two hand lines and a rod we caught over 2,000 pounds of them between 3 and 6—Filled up the cockpit of the boat—Early in the afternoon we had hapooned a big loggerhead turtle weighing about 400 pounds and later on needed his room for King fish and we could not lift him to get him overboard. The King fish sell for 16 cents a pound at the dock. They jump high up in the air—sometimes 6 feet clear of the water and turn and come down on the spoon—I trolled only about 30 or 40 feet behind the boat—used a heavy rod and they fought clear of the water most of the time—when we were in the middle of the school you could not let the spoon go clear of the boat before they grabbed it—It took about 300 fish to make 2000 pounds—gutted—We got in last night at ten oclock—They typed up through Chapter 34 while I was gone—Must get to work now and read the typing—Book will be finished by middle of next week. When will you be down? Best always

Ernest Hemingway.

*ALS, Havana Special stationery, 4 pp.,*[1] *JFK*

Feb 9, 1929

Dear Ernest:- I've just finished re-reading the book. It's a most beautiful book I think,—perhaps. Especially the last part, after they get into Switzerland. I got a different kind of pleasure out of it this time, knowing the Story, + so not being diverted either by the interest of some of the material, as I was the first time, or by anxiety to see what happened + how things ended. Its full of lovely things. The characters are marvelously + deeply disclosed, all their qualities, not the 'good' or 'bad' only, coming out. The interest of the material is itself immensely strong + many readers may miss the deeper + rare things at first on that account.—As for the proprieties, I'm in complete agreement with You personally, + have argued that way all my life. I guess You understand that. I said all this before + this letter is superfluous as well as realy illigible.—But when you put down such a book you've got to say Something. If I Knew anyone on the train I could have taken it out on them.

Now I'm going to take Your absynthe + drink a lonely health to you all in the wash room. It was a grand time for me.

Ever yours
Maxwell Perkins

. . . . .

*TS for wire, 1 p.*

Feb. 13, 1929

Mr. Ernest Hemingway
Key West, Florida

Wish to serialize. First installment being set with some blanks. May ask omission of two or three brief passages in later ones but only with your approval. Price proposed sixteen thousand. Regards to all. Writing.

Maxwell Perkins

[1]50 words have been omitted from this letter.

Feb 9,
1929

AAVANA SPECIAL.
NEW YORK–KEY WEST–HAVANA

PENNSYLVANIA RAILROAD
RICHMOND FREDERICKSBURG & POTOMAC R. R.
ATLANTIC COAST LINE RAILROAD
FLORIDA EAST COAST RAILWAY

Dear Ernest :— I've just
finished re-reading the book.
It's a most beautiful book
I think, — perhaps, especially
the last part, after they get
into Switzerland. I got a
different kind of pleasure
out of it this time, knowing
the story, so not being
hurried either by the interest

First page of letter written by Perkins on his return train trip
after visiting Key West to accept delivery of *A Farewell to Arms*.

*Wire, 1 p.*
*Key West, Florida*

1929 FEB 14 PM 3 56

AWFULLY PLEASED PRICE OK=
=ERNEST HEMNYWAY.

*To: Charles Scribner*                    *TLS with holograph postscript, 5 pp.*[1]

New York, February 14, 1929

Dear Mr. Scribner:

I'd meant to write you the moment I got back from Key West—after a splendid, refreshing week of sunshine and outdoors—but found an accumulation of little time-taking troubles.- And I thought it better to wait perhaps till Mr. Bridges and Dashiel had read, "A Farewell to Arms."

This title is a bitter phrase: war taints and damages the beautiful and the gallant, and degrades everyone;- and this book which is a <u>farewell</u> to it, as useless and hateful, would be only grim reading if it were not illuminated with the beauty of the world, and of the characters, even though damaged, of some people, and by love; and if it were not also lively with incident and often, in spots, amusing. Its quality is that of "The Sun", though its range is much larger and its implications consequently more numerous and widely scattered. Its story in outline is not objectionable but many words and some passages in it are: we can blank the words and the worst passages can be revised.- The reading of the book will still be a violent experience because of the force, directness, and poignance of the writing. We wired Hemingway yesterday naming a price of $16,000 and the first instalment is being set.

The story begins after a year or so of war, with some such phrase as, "That summer we were in the mountains." You get the idea of a place of charm and beauty hurt and saddened by war; of troops and guns passing up and down, and of a fatigued, raw-nerved group of men in the officer's mess,- one of whom, the narrator, an American boy, named Henry, is in charge of an ambulance section. A likable, dissolute surgeon named Rinaldi, persuades him to go to a hospital to see a "lady English". She is a tall, 'tawny' beauty. Henry who has frankly been all over the place with all low sorts of girls approaches her like one of them;- but this approach is somewhat resented and he feels the cheapness of it. He goes to the front with a little "St. Anthony" she gives him for luck around his neck.- There while eating cheese with his men in a dugout, he is wounded in the legs by a shell.- All this is fiercely vivid, sharp, and painful.- It almost happens to the reader.

A couple of days after he arrives at the hospital—certain disagreeable physiological aspects in the care of him having been frankly described—

---

[1] 30 words have been omitted from this letter.

Katherine Barker arrives. The moment they meet Henry discovers that he is in love.- He had not meant to fall in love, his idea had been quite different, but he finds that he has, and it is a wholly new experience in spite of all his amorous adventures. She is a gallant, winning girl, and she also has fallen in love. And though not his nurse, she manages, by taking on more than her share of undesired night work, to stay with him at night. And as he recuperates, they go to hotels once or twice together. He wants her to marry him, but if she does this she will be sent home on account of regulations, and will be separated from him, and she keeps saying that she already is his wife,- that a ceremony is a mere technicality. At the same time he is worried, and before he goes back to the front he knows that he has cause to be. He gets back in time to be a part of the great Caparetto retreat. This is a magnificent episode in the book. It is the account of the experience of several individuals,- Henry, and his companions, ambulance drivers. The episode as described differs from conventional descriptions of a retreat in much the same way as Stendhal's account of Waterloo differs from conventional accounts of battles.[1] Henry gets loose from the great column of retreat which is constantly blocked, loses his cars in mud on a side road, loses one man by desertion, and another by a bullet, an Italian one too, finds himself at one time among detachments of Germans, finally rejoins the column at night as it approaches a river. On the other side of the river is a group of officers with battle police. They are flashing lights into the column and calling out officers from it. Two police come and seize Henry. He finds that all officers separated from their men are instantly shot. This is happening on the spot. He is indignant because he has behaved manfully throughout and has been true in every sense, and yet he knows he will be shot. He will be thought to be a German in Italian uniform. He breaks away, dives into the river, and with the help of a timber escapes. He is through with the Italian army.- He knows that they will finish him off if they get him anyhow. He gets civilian clothes from a friend, makes his way to a lake near the Swiss border where he hears that Katherine is, and is with her in the hotel there when late on a stormy night his friend the bar man tells him a squad has come to arrest him. He and Katherine get into a row boat and row up the lake in the storm with the help of the wind (a fine episode) until in the morning they have crossed the Swiss line. The rest of the book is most beautiful. It records the life of Katherine and Henry in Switzerland throughout the fall and the winter. It has the pathos of a happy time that is tinged with sorrow because those having it feel that it must end soon, and tragically. That sense of the beauty of nature and of its permanence, in contrast to the brevity and fluidity of an individual's affairs, pervades it. It is beautiful and affecting reading.

Henry tries several times to persuade Katherine to marry him, but she will not do it now because she says she looks too "matronly". They will get married later in America, when this is over with.- The reader knows by the tone of the narrative that when it is over with, Henry will have nobody to marry.

---

[1] In *The Charterhouse of Parma* (1839).

The last twenty pages of the book tell of the birth of the child which results in her death,- and rather fully, although not naturalistically. The reason it is recounted is to show what a brave, gallant person Katherine is. It is most painful and moving reading because of her bravery in suffering.

Mr. Bridges thinks the book a very strong one and its motif—a revelation of the tragic degradation of war, of which this love affair is a part—a fine one. Dashiel is very enthusiastic and regrets that even a word must be changed. I do not think that given the theme and the author, the book is any more difficult than was inevitable. It is Hemingway's principle both in life and literature never to flinch from facts, and it is in that sense only, that the book is difficult. It is not at all erotic, although love is represented as having a very large physical element.

I had a splendid eight days in Key West, and formed a very high opinion of Hemingway's character. Nobody could be more altogether healthy and decent in every sense, and no household could be more natural and simple than his, with his wife and sister and two children. We spent almost all of every day on the water fishing. Hemingway was determined I should get a tarpon, although I had considerable doubts of my ability to land one after quite exhausting struggles even with barracudas. At the very last possible moment, on my last day, it was Hemingway, and not I, who hooked a tarpon. He instantly wanted me to take his rod and was so violently insistent that I did it, and after about fifty fine and quite exhausting minutes made more exciting by a sudden storm which kept the spray flying over us all the time, and, added to the strength of the tarpon, kept me staggering all over the boat, we landed him. In view of the rarity of tarpons, and the value set upon them by sportsmen, I think this was a remarkably generous thing of Hemingway to do.

. . . . .

Ever sincerely yours,
Maxwell E. Perkins

P.S. I was somewhat constrained in bringing out the difficult points in "A Farewell" by dictating this to Miss Wykoff,[1] but I thought your familiarity with Hemingway's way would sufficiently suppliment what I have said

MEP

*ALS, 4 pp.*
*Key West, Florida*

Feb 16—

[*In top right corner and margin of page one*] Thanks ever so much for the books. So far have received the Russian one—one story—The horse thieves[2]—only one Ive read is <u>splendid</u> in almost all the way I'll read the one you recommended tonight.

[1]Irma Wykoff, MP's secretary.
[2]Short story by Anton Chekov (1860–1904).

Dear Max—

Here are the pictures of your fish. It was wonderful to have you here We all enjoyed it very greatly I would have written before but caught my old bad throat clearing fish out of the ice house and was in bed with the throat pretty bad. Before it happened—the Sunday after you left—had a wonderful day in the Gulf stream—It was calm, almost oily—hooked a sailfish that ran out 250 yards of line on the Vom Hofe reel and light rod and had 40 minute fight—He was just over 8 feet long. Record here for this year—Completely pooped me with the light tackle—He seemed strong as a tarpon ½ hour later Charles hooked a Mako shark out in the Gulf and fought him 3 hrs and 20 minutes—The shark jumped like a tarpon—Straight up high clear of the water—He lost him—after finally bringing him to gaff (and having the heaviest tarpon rod break) when the hook straightened—all the other boats came around to see the fight—We were way out where the big tankers were passing—Mike gaffed him 3 or 4 times but he couldnt hold him. I never saw a fish jump more beautifully—We hoped of course he was a Marlin—he was bigger than the one at Casa Marina—but he was a shark of a sort nobody had ever seen around here—So we called him a <u>Mako</u>—the kind they have in New Zealand that jumps so wonderfully—

I'm awfully glad they are going to serialize and the Price is fine.

About omissions—They can only be discussed in the concrete examples—I told you I would not be unreasonable—dont mind the leaving out of a word if a blank is left if the omission is unavoidable and as for passages—almost every part of the book depends on almost every other part—You know that—So if a passage is dropped—there should be something to show it—That will not hurt the serial and will help the book. People might be curious to see the book and see what that passage contained. It's not a regular serial anyway.

My point is that the operation of emasculation is a tiny one—It is very simple and easy to perform on men—animals and books—It is not a Major operation but its effects are great—It is <u>never</u> performed <u>intentionally</u> on books—What we must both watch is that it should not be performed unintentionally—

I know, on the other hand, that you will not want to print in a magazine certain words and, you say, certain passages. In that event what I ask is that when omissions are made a blank or some sign of omission be made that isnt to be confused with the dots that writers employ when they wish to avoid biting on the nail and writing a hard part of a book to do.

Still the dots may be that sign—I'm not Unreasonable—I know we both have to be careful because we have the same interest <u>ie</u> (literature or whatever you call it) and I know that you yourself are shooting for the same thing that I am. And I tell you that emasculation is a small operation and we dont want to perform it without realizing it.

Anyway enough of talking—I am not satisfied with the last page and will change it—but the change will in no way affect the serializability—(what a word.)

I think you are very fine about the price—If I havent said more about it it is because while we are friends I am no blanket friend of the entire organization and have the feeling from experience, that the bull fighter is worth whatever he gets paid. However I think you are fine about the price. You are generous and I appreciate it. I may want some of the money quite soon Will write This letter in great haste. Best to you always, Ernest Hemingway.

[*In left margin of page four*] Now will look forward to when you come to Piggott for the shooting. Ideal [wing] shoo[t] the duck so thick you can shoot at one and hit another!

*CC, 3 pp.*[1]

February 19, 1929

Dear Ernest:

. . . . .

Bridges is sending you today the proofs of the first installment, and there is one passage where he thinks a cut should be made, where cutting will go hard. I believe he is telling you why he thinks it necessary,- circulation as collateral reading in schools, and consideration of subscribers, etc. You as an ex-newspaperman know about such things, and that there is a practical side to running periodicals.- On the other hand, there is this other side which I cannot wholly overlook:- there was a great deal of hostility to "The Sun". It was routed and driven off the field by the book's qualities, and the adherence which they won. The hostility was very largely that which any new thing in art must meet, simply because it is disturbing. It shows life in a different aspect, and people are more comfortable when they have got it all conventionalized and smoothed down, and everything unpleasant hidden. Hostility also partly came from those who actually did not understand the book because its method of expression was a new one. Sisley Huddleston expressed their view.[2] It was the same failure to be understood that a wholly new painter meets. People simply do not understand because they can only understand what they are accustomed to.

Now this serialization is not the real thing, as the book is. If we considered "A Farewell to Arms" only in respect to its intrinsic quality, and refused to regard the question from any practical point of view, we would all be dead against serialization. It is an incidental and outside thing, and the best reason for it, to my mind, was on account of the practical aspects of it in widening your public, and in making you understandable to a great many more people, and generally in helping you to gain complete recognition. It is in view of all this that I think—as I judge you do by yo.ur letter of

[1]169 words have been omitted from this letter.
[2]Sisley Huddleston, *Paris Salons, Cafés, Studios: Being Social, Artistic and Literary Memories* (Philadelphia: Lippincott, 1928), pp. 121–123.

today—that cuts can be philosophically made, for if we can keep people from being diverted from the qualities of the material itself, by words and passages which have on account of <u>conventions,</u> an astonishingly exaggerated importance to them, a great thing will have been done. Your mind is so completely free of these conventions—and it is fortunate it is—that you do not realize the strength with which they are held. If you knew a few of the genteel!

I am afraid this discourse is not very well put, but what I am trying to argue is that if we can bring out this serial without arousing too serious objection, you will have enormously consolidated your position, and will henceforth be further beyond objectionable criticism of a kind which is very bad because it prevents so many people from looking at the thing itself on its merits.

. . . . .

Ever yours,

*ALS, 4 pp.*[1]
*Key West, Florida*

<u>Feb 23—</u>

Dear Max—

Have gone over the galleys—and returned them to Mr. Bridges. The blanks are all right <u>so far</u>. I'll consent to the omission of the lead pencil encircled passage in galley 12—It is bad for the story to omit it but does not cripple it. I would never consent to its omission in a book.[2]

In the foreward at the start of galley (1) I eliminated the words <u>of the sordidness</u>—they add nothing, give people a word to attack with and weaken the statement. Remember more people review the blurb than ever do the book.

I'm not trying to give sordidness—I have avoided it as much as possible—

———

Do you still care for the title?

I think the books so far looks fine in type—That is very good type too. I had a fine time reading it for the first time in type.

Could you send me a list of how much money I received from Scribners in 1928—So that I may make out an income tax.

---

[1]51 words have been omitted from this letter.

[2]"Because we would not wear any clothes because it was so hot and the windows open and the swallows flying over the roofs of the houses and when it was dark afterward and you went to the window very small bats hunting over the houses and close down over the trees and we would drink the Capri and the door locked and it hot and only a sheet and the whole night and we would both love each other all night in the hot night in Milan. That was how it ought to be. I would eat quickly and go and see Catherine Barkley." (Chapter 6)

Also would you send me a check for 6,000 of the 11,000 due on the serial? I want to send some money to my family.

. . . . .

Best always—
Ernest Hemingway

. . . . .

*CC, 3 pp.*[1]

Feb. 27, 1929

Dear Ernest:

I am sending the six thousand now. I shall be sending you a small check in a day or so from your royalty report, too. The passage you spoke of will do very well for the book and it is necessary really.- But anyhow, I never would ask you to take out anything, not even a word, unless it seemed to me that it simply had to be done; and I should not be just playing safe. I should play the other way, in fact. You are wholly right in taking out "of the sordidness". The statement is much more effective without it. And your own statement about Italy and autobiography will be used in some way that would be sufficiently conspicuous.

As for the title, I think it is very good indeed, though it is one of those titles that is better after you have read the book than before. But even at first sight it is a fine title. Everyone here thinks so too.

. . . . .

Ever yours,

. . . . .

*ALS, 8 pp.*[2]
*Key West, Florida*

<u>March 11</u>

Dear Max—

Read the proofs of the 2nd installment when we got home last night from Marquiesas.

In galley 2 two omissions have been made—the first of 6 lines in the Mss.[3] The 2nd of 10 lines in the Mss.

The 2nd cut has been made so that the resultant dialogue does not make

---

[1] 90 words have been omitted from this letter.

[2] 38 words have been omitted from this letter.

[3] "Sometimes I think you and he are a little that way. You know."

"No you don't."

"Yes I do sometimes. A little that way like the number of the first regiment of the Bregata Ancuna."

"Oh go to hell." (*FTA*, p. 71)

94

sense—Two consecutive sentences are left as dialogue both spoken by the same person.[1]

In the first cut the removal of one sentence would have been sufficient.

I thought it was understood that there would be no Cutting without consulting me and having my approval. This was cut on the Mss. without being set in the proof.

Read it yourself and see what you think.

If any passages are to be eliminated they must be eliminated from the proof so I can see how it looks and clean it up on the proof—I'd rather return the money and call it all off than have arbitrary eliminations made without any mention of the fact they are being made. If that's to be done let some one else sign it—By E.H. and A.B.—That's just anger! Half the writing I do is elimination. If someone else is doing it let them sign it. Private to you—

I was too damned angry to write Mr. Bridges about it. There was no mention of anything being cut out and the first intimation I get is when the dialogue doesnt make sense on the page. I'll argue any point and if they insist on cutting consent and help the best I can putting the responsibility on the Magazine but I'll be damned if it's to be cut in the Mss. without a word to me. It's so awkward to fix—I suppose I must write Mr. Bridges—That takes 1/2 a day—The chapter (10) was a fine one and it's ruined—I could have fixed the cuts from the galleys so they would make sense—

Ernest Hemingway.

Thanks ever so much for the income tax data—I've just made it out—We caught 7 tarpon at Marquesas—I got one weighed 96 pounds—

We sail April 5—

Later—

Wrote a calm letter to Mr. Bridges—There was a cut in galley 10 too that I concede if you think it's necessary—but it doesnt seem so.[2] Would you read the installment and my letter to Mr. Bridges and see if it's all right? You

---

[1]"Truly? I tell you something about your good women. Your goddesses. There is only one difference between taking a girl who has always been good and a woman. With a girl it is painful. That's all I know." He slapped the bed with his glove. "And you never know if the girl will really like it."
"Don't get angry."
"I'm not angry. I just tell you baby for your own good. To save you trouble."
"That's the only difference?"
"Yes. But millions of fools like you don't know it." (*FTA*, pp. 71–72)

[2]In the serial galley proofs, the passage recounting Frederic and Catherine's reunion in Milan the lines " 'Yes, I am. Come on.' " and " 'I'm crazy about you. Come on please.' " were changed to " 'Yes, I am.' " and " 'I'm crazy about you.' " The following passage was deleted:
"You really do love me?"
"Don't keep saying that. Come on. Please. Please Catherine."
"All right but only for a minute."
"All right," I said. "Shut the door."
"You can't. You shouldn't."
"Come on. Don't talk. Please come on." (*FTA*, p. 99)

know I'm not just trying to be difficult. Am not sore now—But it was snooty to cut passages on Mss. rather than on proof. I think it's fixed up all right. There's a big Norther blowing—Dos Passos read the book and he was very enthusiastic—He's always been my most bitterly severe critic—Waldo liked it much too—Dos liking it is the best news I've had since you did because he's always been hard as can be and if you, Mike, Waldo and Dos all like it that is 4 different views—

I'm not trying to be difficult about the Magazine—I want to help however I can—

. . . . .

. . . . .

*CC, 3 pp.*[1]

March 15, 1929

Dear Ernest:

. . . . .

Truly, Ernest, the change made in the galleys (I have just consulted Mr. Bridges most tactfully, and I have seen your letter to him which was fine) was made for only the one reason of simplifying things and speeding them up;- although I will admit that the simplification could only have been effective at this end. There is, and was, and never will be, any idea of making any change without your approval;- and I doubt if there will be any change except a few blanks hereafter, anyhow.

I am just writing now to assure you on that point.

Yours always,

. . . . .

*ALS, 2 pp.*[2]
*Havana, Cuba*

. . . . .

<u>April 3</u>

Dear Max—

This just a note before we go—Have corrected and am mailing the 4th installment to the Magazine—We leave tomorrow morning—In the middle of packing now—We'll try to get Waldo to witness the contract and mail it to you—Pauline got the grippe and is laid up in bed—Sunny[3] worse than useless. Thanks ever so much for all the grand books—Hope we get off—It

---

[1]128 words have been omitted from this letter.
[2]16 words have been omitted from this letter.
[3]EH's sister Madelaine.

seems impossible—I've lost my hat and my coat too blue suit stolen so have nothing to wear—Waldo painted a portrait of me looking like Molly Colum's friend Balzac—Wish it was as easy to write like him—Not but what he's a hell of a sloppy writer but what an amount of juice!

Well as Aiken says Farewell farewell farewell!                    Ernest

Please dont under any circumstances give Scott our Paris home address—Last time he was in Paris he got us kicked out of one apt. and in trouble all the time (Insulted the landlord—pee-ed on the front porch—tried to break down the door at 3-4 and 5 a.m etc.) Will meet him in public places but have this apt where we're quiet and comfortable and found it with great difficulty and he would get us ousted by only one performance—Bank is only address to give—I am very fond of Scott but I'll beat him up before I'll let him come and get us ousted from this place—as a matter of fact I'm afraid I'd kill him—It's the best home I've ever had and he would lose it for us without one thought—It's nothing to do with friendship—That implies obligations on both sides—When I heard he was going to Paris it gave me the horrors.

*CC, 4 pp.*[1]

May 7, 1929

Dear Ernest:

. . . . .

I have had very enthusiastic letters from Owen Wister.[2] He is somewhat off in his idea of "The Sun Also", however, or so it seems to me. But he is right about "The Farewell". There is one point that he raises some question of about which he is writing you.- Whether the extreme painfulness of the last scenes in the hospital are not too much in that they so completely absorb the reader, so torture him almost, as to obscure other things. This had occurred to me at the beginning, and I thought I would re-examine the passages in the book proof and possibly raise the question.- Although you have always turned out to be so extraordinarily right as to make me hesitate on such points. After all, you are the one who has gone to the bottom of the matter. Still, it is worth considering, especially when one so enthusiastic as Wister thinks it worth considering.[3]

. . . . .

. . . . .

[1]200 words have been omitted from this letter.
[2]Wister's letter, dated 18 February 1929, included the following paragraph:
   Kipling, who was hostile to E.H. on account of The Sun also Rises' until I reasoned with him, sent a message: 'Tell him that since you vouch for him, I'll believe in him.' This I intend some day to deliver, but not until after I have seen the new book.
[3]See Alan Price, " 'I'm Not an Old Fogey and You're Not a Young Ass': Owen Wister and Ernest Hemingway," *Hemingway Review* 9 (Fall 1989): 82–90.

CC, *3 pp.*

May 24, 1929

Dear Ernest:

I'm about to send you the book proof. Don't delay the reading because of the fact that we have a good margin in time, but still don't feel hurried. The book is so remarkable that if you want to work further on any parts of it, you ought to do it. A book that can touch one more deeply on the third reading than on the first, ought not to be rushed through the final stages.- So take the time you need.

It has been read now here by those who will be most active in "pushing" it: their interest in it is not less than fanatical. I have thought and talked about it for some three months now, and beyond the few slight comments on the margin of the proof I have one or two more serious ideas on it which I dare give you because I know you will know easily whether to reject them, and won't mind doing it;- and if you do it I'll believe you're right: I see plainly that you go down to the very bottom at any cost to test the truth of everything. Only you can do that—not many writers, even, have the strength to—and that brings the right decision.

The first point relates to the combination of the two elements of the book,- Love and War. They combine, to my mind, perfectly up to the point where Catherine and Lieutenant Henry get to Switzerland;- thereafter, the war is almost forgotten by them and by the reader,- though not quite. And psychologically it should be all but forgotten;- it would be by people so profoundly in love, and so I do not think what I at first thought, that you might bring more news of it or remembrances of it into this part. Still, I can't shake off the feeling that War, which has deeply conditioned this love story—and does so still passively—should still do so actively and decisively. It would if Catherine's death might probably not have occurred except for it, and I should think it likely that the life she had led as nurse, and all the exposure, etc., might have been largely responsible. If it were, and if the doctor said so during that awful night, in just a casual sentence, the whole story would turn back upon War in the realization of Henry and the reader.

I say this with the realization that a man in this work may make a principle into an obsession, as professors do. Unity? Nothing is so detestable as the <u>neat</u> ending. But Catherine was in a physical condition which made her unable to come through the Caesarian even if the Caesarian were required only because of her type of physical form. If it is true that the War produced that condition, I don't think it would make the conclusion <u>artificial</u>, or too <u>neat</u> if it were said, or implied. Of course in a deeper sense the reader does feel that War permeated the entire thing.- I can argue either way but even that fact makes the question worth raising.[1]

I know, by the way, that Wister wrote you about these two elements of

---

[1]EH did not act on MP's suggestion.

War and Love, and that he saw the question differently,- as if the story was really only one of Love with War as the impressive and conditioning background; or almost only that. But I could not quite see it that way. The elements are so fully interfused up to the Switzerland section that I hardly think War should be regarded as secondary to that degree.

The other point regards the intense pain of the hospital episode. It's physical painfulness is such as by itself—apart from all the rest of the story—to completely absorb the reader, and this may not be right. You might lessen it by reducing the physical detail, perhaps. Wister felt this strongly I know, and I needn't go further into it.- Wheelock here did not feel this way about it. But the bad thing is that Catherine is made to suffer so, and to die, and if the physical aspects of the affair are too intensely presented, the reader suffers and shudders not because it is Catherine, but merely because of the horror of the thing itself,- while Henry, on the spot, poor devil, would suffer because it was Catherine. This is confused, but will suggest whatever need be thought of, I guess. The pain is after all mainly due simply to Catherine's situation, which perhaps seems to a male especially awful.- Besides, I know that I am super-sensitive to the physical. I only want the matter brought up for your consideration.

Otherwise, there's nothing much to say, except that if you could reduce somewhat the implications of physical aspects in the relationship I doubt that harm would be done. But here I may be influenced by the dangers of censorship. My whole intention is to put these things in mind.- I have most absolute confidence in your judgment and wouldn't want to influence it if I could.

I hope you're all well now. Write if you can.

Ever yours,

*CC, 4 pp.*[1]

May 31, 1929

Dear Ernest:

I feel terribly mean about having got Wister in so wrong with you, and I thought I had better write you the whole story of the affair. A day or two after I got back from Key West, I found a letter from Wister. It was in answer to one I had sent him without knowing I had done it.- A letter accompanying Frank's "Re-discovery"[2] which was sent to a number of prominent people, asking them if they were interested by the book to tell what they thought of it. How Wister got on this list I do not know at all, but he took great pains with his answer, although it was so unfavorable that it was useless to us.

I wrote and thanked him for it, and told him that I had just come back

[1]465 words have been omitted from this letter.
[2]Waldo Frank, *The Re-Discovery of America* (New York: Scribners, 1929).

from Key West and had brought your novel which was a very fine one, and that we were to serialize it; and he wrote instantly saying that this was "the best possible news". It was then I wrote you to ask if I could send him proof.

I had an interested motive in this. I knew how people shrink from the truth, not only in life, but even more in literature,- and particularly those people beyond middle age who are not accustomed to it in their literature, certainly not in the pages of a magazine. I wanted to make these people aware that Scribner's was giving them something very remarkably fine, and beyond the reach of objection on grounds of conventional taboos; and this could only be done through the influence of someone, whatever his merits, who could speak with authority to them.- Such people regard Mr. Phelps, for instance, as something like the last word. (I do not mean to couple Wister with Phelps, by a long shot. There is no real comparison except that both are greatly admired by a certain class and age of person.) As soon as Wister read the galleys he wrote back the letter I quoted to you, and I simply thanked him for this and made no suggestion of anything further, but he said that whenever it was wanted, he would express his opinion publicly, and sent us the statement, a letter for the magazine. In the course of this correspondence, in which I asked nothing at all, he asked me if I thought you would mind his making a suggestion about the last part of the book. I told him I thought not.

My idea was that you would probably disregard his or any other person's suggestions, but that one might have some validity which you would accept, and that no harm would be done anyhow. There are people who write, and even some quite good ones, to whom you do not dare make suggestions because of an uncertainty in themselves.- I never saw any sign of this in you. Anyway the only way I knew what suggestions Wister made—and I never even thought much about them—was by his briefly mentioning them in order to ask if I thought you would object to his stating them.

I understand quite well how you look at him, but it seems all the more striking to me in that light that he was taken off his feet by your writing. You speak of him as having made his career, but I have understood that he did not regard himself as having had a career, but as a failure as a writer. He knows he has compromised, whatever he may think of Kipling. His realization that you never do is one of the things he so much admires. Of course, having been a man who did temper himself to his times, and the conventions, he has naturally many prejudices. But who has not? About six in a generation, the world over.

You think that what such a man says has no value,- that his bad opinion would be more of a compliment than his good opinion. This is certainly true of men in his group in one sense. It is not true in a publishing sense. What made "The Bridge"[1] such a supreme success in sales? Everyone knows, both the publisher and author have said, that Phelps' statement about it had a

---

[1] *The Bridge of San Luis Rey.*

tremendous effect. Of course an author ought not to think of that side of the question, and you do not; but his publisher ought to think of it.[1]

　　· · · · ·
　　· · · · ·
　　· · · · ·
　　· · · · ·

Ever yours,

*ALS, 9 pp.*
*Paris, France*

June 7 1929

Dear Max:—

I got the proofs—Two days ago—They were held up at the customs because the notation "Proofs For Correction"—was made in such small type—without capitals—on the label that the Customs People did not notice it—I cleared them at the Customs and was on them all day yesterday and today—

I am sorry to have made you so much trouble having the corrections made on the original galleys copied.

I find many more suggested—some of them very good. Others bad. When it makes no difference I am glad always to make it conventional as to punctuation

About the words—I have made a notation at the side about the bed pan—Originally I had about 2,000 words of that aspect of hospital life—It really <u>dominates</u> it—I cut it all out with the exception of the one reference to the bed pan.

It is the same with other words.

You say they have not been in print before—one may not have—but the others are all in Shakespeare—

But more recently you will find them in a book called All Quiet on The Western Front[2] which Scott gave me and which has sold in the 100s of thousand copies in Germany and is around 50,000 copies in England with the word shit, fart etc. Never dragged in for coloring but only used a few times for the thousands of times they are omitted. Please read the statement on page 15 of that book.

The trouble is Max that before my book will be out there will be this All Quiet on The Western Front book and possibly at the same time the Second volume of the man who wrote Sergeant Grischa[3]—who knows his eggs also—and I hate to kill the value of mine by emasculating it when I looked up in The Quiet on W.F. book to find the words to show you I had a very

---

[1]The letter of late May 1929 in which EH deprecated Wister's advice was destroyed by MP at EH's request; see EH's 24 June 1929 and MP's 14 August 1929 letters.

[2]By Erich Maria Remarque (Boston: Little, Brown, 1929).

[3]Arnold Zweig, *Education Before Verdun* (1936).

hard time finding them. They dont stand out. But you should not go backwards. If a word can be used and is needed in the text it is a <u>weakening</u> to omit it. If it <u>cannot</u> be printed without the book being suppressed all right.

There has always been first rate writing and then American writing— (genteel writing)

No one that has read the Mss. has been shocked by <u>words</u> The words do not stand out unless you put a ring around them

There is no good my pleading the case in a letter. You know my view point on it. What would have happened if they had cut the Sun Also? It would have flopped as a book and I would have written no more for you.

The first place you say you think a word must go is in Galley 13—[1]

I can consider you leaving that a blank—but in galley 51 where the same word is used by Piani if that is cut out it is pretty ruinous—I don't consent and is done over my head.

In galley 57 a word is used that is used again at the top of galley 60.

If you think this word will cause the suppression of the book make it C—— S——R.[2]

You see I have kept out all the words that are the constant vocabulary— but have given the sense of them by using once twice or three times the real words. Using then only the most classic words.

You know what General Cambrone said at the battle of Waterloo instead of "The Old Guard Dies but Never Surrenders! He said <u>Merde</u> when they called on him to surrender.

In a purely conversational way in a latin language in an argument one man says to another "Cogar su madre!"

You see there is Nothing Wrong with any of the words I have used except the last—the one of Galley 57—which is used an an expression of Supreme insult and contempt—The others are common enough and I dare say will all be in print in U.S.A. before the year is out.

It's unsatisfactory to write this and I hope you don't think I am getting snooty about it. I wish we could talk and you could tell me just how far you <u>can</u> go and what the danger is. I do not want to make trouble—But want everything that can be had without trouble—I thought you said if I accepted certain blanks etc for the serialization the book would be published as it was. I see in the 2nd installment cuts made without my knowledge but am of course in their hands.

Anyway am working all the time on this proof and will get it back to you as soon as possible—By a boat the first of the week.

I hope you got the Signed sheets OK. I mailed them about a week ago Am enclosing the contract.

Yours always
Ernest <u>Hemingway</u>

---

[1]The word was "shit"; it was replaced by "——" (Chapter 9).
[2]The word "cocksucker" was replaced by "——" (Chapter 28).

## A FAREWELL TO ARMS 209

looked up. She looked perhaps a year younger. Aymo
put his hand on the elder girl's thigh and she pushed it
away. He laughed at her.

"Good man," he pointed at himself. "Good man,"
he pointed at me. "Don't you worry." The girl looked
at him fiercely. The pair of them were like two wild
birds.

"What does she ride with me for if she doesn't like
me?" Aymo asked. "They got right up in the car the
minute I motioned to them." He turned to the girl.
"Don't worry," he said. "No danger of ~~fucking~~," using
the vulgar word. "No place for ~~fucking~~." I could see she
understood the word and that was all. Her eyes looked
at him very scared. She pulled the shawl tight. "Car
all full," Aymo said. "No danger of ~~fucking~~. No place
for ~~fucking~~." Every time he said the word the girl stif-
fened a little. Then sitting stiffly and looking at him
she began to cry. I saw her lips working and then
tears came down her plump cheeks. Her sister, not
looking up, took her hand and they sat there together.
The older one, who had been so fierce, began to sob.

"I guess I scared her," Aymo said. "I didn't mean
to scare her."

Bartolomeo brought out his knapsack and cut off
two pieces of cheese. "Here," he said. "Stop crying."

The older girl shook her head and still cried, but the
younger girl took the cheese and commenced to eat.
After a while the younger girl gave her sister the second piece of cheese and they both ate. The older sister
still sobbed a little.

"She'll be all right after a while," Aymo said.

An idea came to him. "Virgin?" he asked the girl
next to him. She nodded her head vigorously. "Virgin too?" he pointed to the sister. Both the girls nod-

Hemingway filled in the blanks in this copy (Memorial Library, University of Buffalo).

P.S.

I found the place in galley 38 where F.H. is talking to the hospital matron—I don't know what to do—It is supposed to be the deliberate insult and routing of a person through the use of direct language that she expected by her sex and position never to be exposed to—The final forced conflict between someone from the front and some one of the genteel base. Is the word so impossible of printing?[1]

If it is the incident is killed. It was the one word I remember we omitted from The Sun. Maybe if it had been printed then wed know now if it was printable.

If you decide that it is unprintable how about

     b—ls

I think that's the only solution.

I suppose on galley 57

     C—S——RS and C—KS——R will do for the other too.

         galley 60

Certainly those letters cannot corrupt anyone who has not heard or does not know the word. There's no proof it isnt cocksure

*ALS, 2 pp.*
*Paris, France*

<u>June 7</u>

Dear Max:—

I've just finished a labored letter on the word business and yours of May 29th has just come.

Please dont feel badly about the Wister thing. Your cable explained it—It's nothing—But dont think I blame you either. I havent thought of it since the cable came.

And I do hope your troubles whatever they are clear up the way mine have. Pauline is fine—We wont be coming back until Spring—Pat is well again—I was damned near bug house from worrying about Pauline or I wouldnt have blown up so about what I mistook for Wister's interference. Please take care of yourself and Dont worry about anything. I feel frightfully to have made you more worry and trouble.

Please believe that I understand and appreciate both your and Wister's suggestions and was a fool to blow up. And for God's sake, not to Mention your author's, dont worry and do take Care of yourself because soon you'll have the cursed hay fever anyway and that's enough of a hell for any man without anything else.

---

[1] In Chapter 22, Fredric Henry originally asked Miss Van Campen, " 'did you ever know a man who tried to disable himself by kicking himself in the balls?' "; see EH's 11 July 1929 letter.

I hate to add any worry to you with my attitude on the publishable or unpublishable word business—But that is only official worry remember—You know what I want—All we can possibly get. It's a fight with me for the return to the full use of the language and what we accomplish in that direction may be of more value in the end than anything I write. I never use a word if I can avoid it—but if I must have it I know it—Then if you decide it is unpublishable really unpublishable I suppose I must leave it blank. But I want the blanks to indicate what the word is.

It's been fine outside all day but I've been with the proofs. Now there is a big storm coming up—Dark sky and everyone shutting windows. Couldn't you come to Spain in Aug. or Sept. No hay fever—We could go in the car and fish. Boats run from NY to Corūna. We'll be at Santiago de Campostella—There will be no hay fever on the boat—We'll meet you with the car at Coruna. Would it do any good for me to refuse to publish the book unless you came over to straighten it out? Ernest.

*TLS, 2 pp.*[1]
*Paris, France*

Sunday June 24

Dear Max—

. . . . .

. . . . .

. . . . .

Owen Wister was here and we saw him twice and enjoyed it greatly. He agreed there was no change to be made in the last chapter and has read this ending and likes it very much he says. His last words were last night—Don't touch a thing! He is nice and damned kind and generous and I was certainly the last of the wahoos to get angry and write as I did to you. I wish you would destroy the letter. No one knows about it except ourselves and that would wipe it out perhaps and make me feel not quite so lousy about having exploded in such a foul way. The strain of going over and over and living through a thing each time trying to make it better and for two months getting nowhere coupled with other things may have had something to do with me misuderstanding it so completely. But without alibis I wish you would destroy the letter.

. . . . .

. . . Scott is working hard he says. I have seen Morely Callaghan several times and boxed with him five times I think. He has not the apperance but is an <u>excellent</u> boxer. I have been working hard over the book but have made almost no changes. Write them out, try and better it and then come back to the way it is. Will be awfully glad to see the last of it.

[1]190 words have been omitted from this letter.

Some one cabled that the June number was banned in Boston.[1] Wister was here at dinner and I told him that and he seemed to think it meant nothing. I hope it causes you no annoyance. Yours always Ernest

. . . . .

*CC, 3 pp.*[2]

June 27, 1929

Dear Ernest:

There's little more to tell you. At the moment there seems to be nothing we can do about Mass.- such is their law. The press the incident aroused was good,- so far as it went. I enclose Harry Hansen's column in the World which is all on our side;- but I don't like it. Of course it's written to meet a situation, but I don't think he knows what you're about or how you write. As I remember, he was, about "The Sun Also," highly favorable but dumb. Of course he's read only two installments, and the second first, at that.- There's the trouble with a serial, and for an author the only advantages are the money and publicity;- and in this case I hate the publicity, greatly helpful as it may well turn out to be. It's brought a frivolous and prejudicial attention to one aspect of a book which is deeply significant and beautiful, and it may be hard to break through that.- But it's impossible to think the book won't end by doing so.

This incident affects the possibility of book suppression. There are things in the book that never were in another,- since the 18th Century anyway. There are points that enemies could make a good deal of. All right then! But I don't think we can print those three words, Ernest.[3] I can't find <u>anyone</u> who thinks so. That supreme insult alone might turn a judge right around against us, and to the post office, it and the others, I think, would warrant (technically) action. It would be a dirty shame to have you associated in a way with that Jessica boy[4] and his sort,- people who write with an eye to tickle a cheap public. It would be disgusting. There would follow such an utterance of intelligent indignation against it as in the end would change it.- But harm would have been done,- at least from my point of view.

Well, let me tell you, Ernest, Dashiel was grand. He wrote that statement following the A.P. dispatch,- and if it had one slightly soft spot, it was due to

---

[1]On 20 June 1929 Michael H. Crowley, Superintendent of Police, banned the June issue of *Scribner's Magazine* from Boston newsstands on the grounds that "some persons deemed part of the instalment salacious"; see Scott Donaldson, "Censorship and *A Farewell to Arms*," *Studies in American Fiction* 19 (Spring 1991): 85–93.

[2]15 words have been omitted from this letter.

[3]The three words referred to are "cocksucker," "fucking," and "balls."

[4]Reference to Maxwell Bodenheim's *Replenishing Jessica* (New York: Boni & Liveright, 1925), a novel about a promiscuous woman that was the subject of an obscenity trial in New York in 1928.

haste.[1] But he's absolutely sound about the book. And you must be wrong about changes in the second installment. There were none. What did you think was changed? You're not in their hands, and there's no such idea here.- And (it's only important because I don't want you to think me that sort) I <u>did</u> say at Key West that I thought certain <u>words</u> could not be printed in the book: I remarked too, it was hard to see how this fact could be adjusted to the jaundice episode. But whatever is done you will be consulted,- that's too obvious to mention. The book is <u>your</u> book.

Will this business disturb you? I had to tell you about it, and you would have heard it anyway. We had previously lost eight or ten subscribers or so, and had a few stupid and violent kicks;- and many people who truly admired the story said they were astonished to see such things in print,- but I heard, or heard of, no cheap comment. Molly Colum wrote a fine indignant letter to the Times about the Boston act. Apparently "The Western Front" was very badly cut here, and the publishers were as much to blame as anyone. Not only many words, but passages, incidents, went.- So there's a book designed only to show how nasty and damaging is war, and its point must be blunted for the very people who ought to want those very things shown and would say they do.- By the way, that book is supposed to bring out the one great good thing of war,- comradeship. You do it in ten minutes of dialogue with a poignance beyond what that whole book contains.- Not that I mean to run down a fine book.

. . . . .

Ever yours,

---

[1]Alfred Dashiell's statement was included in "Boston Police Bar Scribner's Magazine," *New York Times* (21 June 1929), p. 2:

The very fact that Scribner's Magazine is publishing 'A Farewell to Arms' by Ernest Hemingway is evidence of our belief in its validity and its integrity. Mr. Hemingway is one of the finest and most highly regarded of the modern writers.

The ban on the sale of the magazine in Boston is an evidence of the improper use of censorship which bases its objections upon certain passages without taking into account the effect and purpose of the story as a whole. 'A Farewell to Arms' is in its effect distinctly moral. It is the story of a fine and faithful love, born, it is true, of physical desire.

If good can come from evil, if the fine can grow from the gross, how is a writer effectually to depict the progress of this evolution if he cannot describe the conditions from which the good evolved? If white is to be contrasted with black, thereby emphasizing its whiteness, the picture cannot be all white.

A dispatch from Boston emphasized the fact that the story is 'anti-war argument.' Mr. Hemingway set out neither to write a moral tract nor a thesis of any sort. His book is no more anti-war propaganda than are the Kellogg treaties.

The story will continue to run in Scribner's Magazine. Only one-third of it has yet been published.

*CC, 3 pp.*[1]

July 12, 1929

Dear Ernest:

I have just wired you as follows: "Galleys received stop Will not send you page proof unless you send word but will supply cape stop Writing." I did this in order that you would have plenty of time to say you wanted to see page proof, because it had been understood that I should send it, and I only changed from that idea when I heard you had gone to Spain. This, I thought, might occasion great delay in transmission of proof.- Besides, everything seemed right and plain with the proof, and I have put it into Meyer's hands,[2] for he will take the greatest care of it. He is reading the book for the first time now, and thinks it magnificent. He will send a set of page proof to Cape, and even if you have already supplied him with galleys this will do no harm.

. . . . .

Everything goes well. We considered taking the Boston ban to court, but all advice was that this could accomplish nothing in the specific instance, and probably nothing in a general sense. Their law is such that intelligent people in Massachusetts oppose it, but have not yet been able to get it changed.- Irish Catholics rule the town. There was, and there is still, considerable anxiety for fear of the federal authorities being stirred up. They seem to take curious activity of late, and if the post office should object, we would be in Dutch.- The thing could be fought out, but it would take so much time as to be very serious.- But we do not have to cross any such bridge as that until we come to it. The question does, however, affect the book in this way:- it has been immensely admired, but also it has aroused fierce objection. This means that when the book appears it will be scrutinized from a prejudiced standpoint, and this taken with everything else, did make us conclude, what we had always felt anyhow, that the three words we have talked so much about, could not be printed, or plainly indicated. This is bad in connection with Miss Van Campen except that I do not see how anybody could fail to get the sense. Anyhow, we went over this thing with the strongest inclination to play the game to the limit with you, and we felt that if we got in trouble in just a matter of words like this, you would be in the least defensible position, because they could easily be defined as indecent and impure, etc., etc. They would from a technical point, and they would arouse prejudice. This point of prejudice I think is hard for you to understand, but there is no question about the fact of it. Anyhow, that is the way the thing worked out after I had talked with Mr. Scribner at great length about it. Everything else in the book goes, of course, as you have put it, exactly.

As for your new ending, I think it is very fine. It is better not to have gone beyond the end of the story in speaking about Rinaldi, etc.- I only regretted most that terribly poignant line about waking up in the morning and finding

---

[1]248 words have been omitted from this letter.
[2]Wallace Meyer, editor at Scribners, became EH's editor after MP's death in 1947.

everything the same as ever, and it never was again.[1] But you are right about it, and I do not find that people feel the way I did about the painfulness of the last scenes.- Mr. Scribner did not, for instance.

. . . . .

Ever yours,

*ALS, 9 pp.*[2]

[*At top of page one*] What about saying—kicked in the <u>scrotum</u> in connection with Miss Van Campen Remember the last time balls was changed to Horns—isnt that O.K?

Hotel Regina

Valencia—Spain

July 26

Dear Max:—

. . . . .

. . . . .

. . . . .

As I understand it from your last letter the book is being published as it appears in the last galleys I sent you except that "the three words we have talked so much about can not be printed nor clearly indicated."

---

[1] The original conclusion was first published in Carlos Baker, *Ernest Hemingway: Critiques of Four Major Novels* (New York: Scribners, 1962).

It seems she had one hemorrhage after another. They couldn't stop it.

I went into the room and stayed with Catherine until she died. She was unconscious all the time, and it did not take her very long to die.

There are a great many more details, starting with my first meeting with an undertaker, and all the business of burial in a foreign country and going on with the rest of my life—which has gone on and seems likely to go on for a long time.

I could tell how Rinaldi was cured of the syphilis and lived to find that the technic learned in wartime surgery is not of much practical use in peace. I could tell how the priest in our mess lived to be a priest in Italy under Fascism. I could tell how Ettore became a Fascist and the part he took in that organization. I could tell how Piani got to be a taxi-driver in New York and what sort of a singer Simmons became. Many things have happened. Everything blunts and the world keeps on. It never stops. It only stops for you. Some of it stops while you are still alive. The rest goes on and you go on with it.

I could tell you what I have done since March, nineteen hundred and eighteen, when I walked that night in the rain back to the hotel where Catherine and I had lived and went upstairs to our room and undressed and slept finally, because I was so tired—to wake in the morning with the sun shining in the window; then suddenly to realize what had happened. I could tell what has happened since then, but that is the end of the story.

[2] 314 words have been omitted from this letter.

I take it this means the word b—— spoken to Miss Van Campen will be left blank. The other two words must be the word s—— spoken by Piani where the drivers are talking before leaving Goritzia on the retreat and the word spoken by Piani when Aymo is shot by the Italian rear guard and the same word spoken by the Lieutenant Henry when arrested by the battle police after crossing the Tagliamento. I take it these words are to be blank.

I understand your position I.E. Scribner's position. The Boston thing was to be expected. I do not see how it could be expected not to be banned in Boston when the Sun also was.

. . . . .

. . . . .

I regret very much the Boston incident but feel it was to be expected. The book—if _any_ of it were allowed to remain—could not pass the Boston Standard of censorship.

. . . . .

I understand your viewpoint about the words you cannot print—If you cannot print them—and I never expected you could print the one word (C——S——) then you cannot and that lets me out.

About the page proof—I do not want to delay the book in anyway. If the only deletions are the ones you have mentioned i.e. marked yourself with pencil on the galley returned and about which we had correspondence—if you prefer and if it will cause delay there is no need to send me the page proof. If there are any other changes I'd better see the proof.

———

What are you doing about the statement I wrote in which it was stated that there were no living people nor any actual units or organizations mentioned in the book? If it could be put in inconspicuously enough it would avoid any aspirant characters writing you.

The dedication stands To G. A. PFEIFFER. There couldnt be a less graceful name nor a much better man. I would use the full name but it happens to be Gustavus Adolphus.

There was one other thing too—

What about the signed Limited edition. What does it sell for and what is the royalty to be? I do not know what is custumary and leave it to you. I should think that unless the paper, printing, binding etc.—are on a very elaborate scale that a large part of the justification of the price would be that it was limited in No. and Signed—Therefore unless there is a great deal more expense, if the limited edition is printed from the same plates it might have a greater royalty. I know that royalty is a very delicate matter and if I shouldnt be right in this please dont be offended.

I would like to stop writing to you as the official representative of the Great Organization and ask you personally what about the advance business. You know I do not want any money I do not earn and prefer to have it paid after it is earned. Now that I have all these bloody people to support and cant write more than a book every 2 years I have to make all I legitimately can. Especially I have to have money ahead in the bank to see them through at least a year at a time. The best way is to get a good advance. But I dont want to become unpopular or to get in wrong with you or Scribners.

Especially not with you. I'm afraid I said something in one of the letters about the word business that offended you. But if I did it was not intentional and I hope I didn't. I write the damned letters when I'm pooped from working over the proofs and if I'm ever rude forgive me.

Am feeling badly now from trying every day to write stories and not being able to write a damned bit and so as always—this seems like my last book—Wister is such a sweet old bird—What a skunk I was to write cursing him out to you—You did destroy the letter didnt you?

. . . . .
. . . . .

As for any bloody senseless statements I made in letters about how I try to write (See July issue of magazine)—Please dont let them fall into anybody elses hands.

As old Foch said about conversations—"It is unfair to quote a man in conversation. We all say foolish things. The only things I stand by are those I have written and read the proof on"

. . . . .

But do not you get in opposition to me now; ie—you = "me" and me = the author who does not understand the risks of using words. Because we both run risks it is only that where the writer risks hundreds the publisher risks thousands—But it all comes from the writer who doesn't write until he has at least risked that. We all lose in the end. That is the one thing we can be sure of. You'll be dead and I will be dead and that is all we can be completely sure of. This, of course, all seems nonsense but it is really true—And when you write your guts out (and your life out) and you do not write easily it is bad to see a few organized ignorant Irish co-religionists try to sabotage it aided by a few extra dollar seeking book organizations that have given a great blow to all good writing or anyway attempts at good writing. There is damned little good writing and the way things are going there will be less.

I'm sick of all of it. Of course I have nothing to complain of. You have been swell (what a lousy word to mean so much) consistently. But I am sick of writing; of the disaster of a family debacle; of the shit-i-ness of critics—(Harry Hansen IE <u>Naughty Ernest</u> in the World which Wister just sent me)[1] of damned near everything but Pauline and to get back to Key West and Wyoming—Paris has been—nasty enough.

This letter is enough and too much—But don't confuse me with this un-understanding user of obsolete Anglo-Saxon words you consider your advesary as an officer of Scribners but rather (if only in P.S.es) as your fellow

---

[1]Harry Hansen wrote the "First Reader" column for the *New York World Telegram.*

absinthe drinker, tarpon seeker and non discusser of advertising (tho proba-
bly` have discussed much worse in this letter)

          Anyway
          Yours always
          <u>Ernest</u>

*ALS, 4 pp.* [1]
*Valencia, Spain*

<u>July 31</u>

Dear Max:——

. . . . .

Harry Hansen has been consentedly against the stuff—fundamentally
inside himself—While feeling that he had to praise it too. Although With
him it's mostly dumbness—Not being a gent—he fears always that something may offend and that he must be the first to denounce. He's really
almost the dumbest of the critics—He says "it is amazing that so simple a
story can become so interesting!" Than to say that the talk with the priest
about "sex aberrations"! may be highly objectionable. When did that occur?
As always he is not worth noticing. He's always a fool but manages to get in
something damaging—like

      "Naughty Ernest!"

Yeah I suppose I felt like Naughty Ernest writing that book.

You cut off the "Naughty Ernest" so that I wouldnt get in a rage but Owen
Wister sent it to me. He's always fine though. He has me all mixed up now
with Henry James but he doesnt always know whether it is me that is Henry
James or whether it is he that is H.J. Sometimes one sometimes the other. If
you want my honest to God opinion:—Neither of us is Henry James! However we must keep that from Wister. He is damned nice though and if I could
act on all his advice at once I would not only make hundreds of thousands of

                                  (F. Scott)

dollars but also be greater thatTolstoi, Dostoeffski, Fitzgerald, Dickens,

          (Henry and William)

James and Tarkington.

Vive Dashiel! That was a statement to ring men's hearts. It could not have
been more moving if SS. Van Dine had been attacked! (Am feeling good this
morning so do not show these irreligious sentiments to anyone.) No; seriously it was fine.

I will pay for any subscriptions Mr. Bridges loses up to 100—not counting
any that are discontinued after the October number.

Really though—Im not sore any more because it's over—but they did cut
a big chunk of Rinaldi's conversation with F. Henry in the field hospital and

---

[1]181 words have been omitted from this letter.

a couple of other places. I don't mention this except that you ask me what did I think was changed. If I had the magazine here could show you but it is of no importance now.

Molly Colum is a fine woman. Wish I could have seen the letter

This is a lousy letter and I wish it could be a good one.

I'm dreadfully sorry your daughter was ill and I know how terribly tragic the damned exams can be. People suffer in the world pretty much altogether in the measure of responsibility they bring to it—and exams coming at the time of life when things are most tragic are a terrible business anyway—I know how you worried—But you mustnt worry or put yourself too much in the place of you children (It's enough to go through that once yourself) because we, being older and with more perspective, ought to put that perspective (which is all $\left\{ \begin{array}{l} \text{we learn} \\ \text{you} \end{array} \right\}$ at the service of any younger ones—which of course is exactly what you did when you told her you didnt give a damn about the exams. Asthma and hay fever are so damned bad though. I hope she's all right now. And I hope too you're not having too bad a time with the hay fever.

. . . . .

. . . . .

I think Harry Hansen's column did more harm than the Boston Suppression. But you have to remember that no one has yet the part of the book that will make it IE. the retreat etc. And God knows nobody is going to suppress a book that ends with that last chapter as some of the work of Naughty Ernest whose mind is often on sex.

Had Molly Colum read the whole book or only the Magazine part? I think it must be hard to read as a serial Cant read it myself. On the other hand Rupert Hughes, the Hearst people write me, cant wait for the next issue. Vive Rupert Hughes.[1]

I ought to try and write now. Pauline has gone out to wander in the town so I can have the room—but I dread to start. We will come over in the Spring—March maybe—to go to Key West—If there are any warrants out for me will not come through N.Y. Have written Scott but havent heard from him. Long letter from Waldo. In case you wander who G.A. Pfeiffer is—he is an Uncle of Paulines who came over to Paris when her family felt pretty badly hearing that she was, after 14 years in the convent, to marry a citizen who had been married before, hailed as a drunk and a man of bad associates by the critics, etc. Uncle Gus made no inquiries about me at all. Pauline brought him one evening to the dreadful dump where I was living, he only stayed about ten minutes because he did not want to disturb my work (sic) and cabled the family about 500 words to say that Pauline could marry no better and finer citizen and the family instead of worrying should be proud and happy. So I owe him a couple of books on that anyway. He sent copies of The Sun Also and

[1]Hughes (1872–1956) was a popular novelist.

Men Without to all members of the family to prove what a fine citizen I was and I believe has sent them all subscriptions to the Magazine which may account for some of the cancellations. Wonderful bull fight yesterday. We ought to swim now but I'm going to try and write. Best always

Ernest

*ALS [letter fragment], 2 pp.*

[August 1929]                                                                               *Santiago de Compostela, Spain*

Have an idea for the next book. Maybe it is punk—but started to write some things about fishing—hunting—about Bull fights and bull fighters—About eating and drinking—About different places—Mostly things and places. Not so much people—though I know some funny ones about people. Several about fishing—If there were enough of these and they were good enough they might make a book. Started to write because my Goddamned imagination wasn't functioning—still tired may be—and still I know a lot of things—Thought it's better to write than constipate trying to write Master-pieces—When I'm writing then I can write stories too.—But when cant write then cant write anything—Maybe if I got some ahead the Magazine might publish some—They are quiet and not awfully exciting—More like that Big Two Hearted River story—and not so long—Might be good for the maga-zines—Somewhere between Essays and Remeniscences—The two worst qualifecations I could find—What do you think?—

I dont want to have any correspondence with Dr. Bridges about them yet—Want to write a bunch first—Will divide them into three kinds—Quiet ones—Funny ones—Immoral ones—He can have the quiet ones. Will help the magazine as much as that piece by Doc Phelps about how awful we pornographers are. Who are the other pornographers? What was funniest was where he said what the beastly public interest in murder stories was and stories of Crime. I thought there were 10 commandments and adultry was only the 7th![1]

But am going to write—I think that's Scott's trouble with his novel. Among other things of course more complicated. But he thought he had to write a masterpiece to follow The Gatsby—as good as Seldes etc. said he was—And to consciously write such a thing that had to be great just constipated him—

Then too you have to use up your material—You never use Anything you save. I thought I'd used up everything in In Our Time—Should always write as though you were going to die at the end of the book—(This doesnt seem to go with what's before but it's a good idea too!) Never for gods sake use or turn over to the advt. dept. anything I say in a letter—

I think I could write some pretty good things—About Key West—Here—

[1]Phelps's "As I Like It" in the August 1929 *Scribner's Magazine* (pp. 119–128); Phelps does not mention EH in this column.

Paris—Constantinople—Try to have more than meets the eye and the old iceberg stuff—but no more stories than that Che Ti Dice La Patria thing. What do you think? You'll say fine whether you think so or not because that is what you have to do with these bloody authors—But I could write some pretty good ones I think—Did you ever read Far Away and Long Ago—by W. H. Hudson—Like that only not so good—That's a swell book—Swell is a dreadful word—When I hear somebody say it that thinks I would like to hear it—Jews usually—my stomach turns over—
There wont be anything like Sherwood Anderson in Vanity Fair—[1]

Yours always<br>Ernest—

I'll write when I want the advances—

CC, 3 pp.[2]

Aug. 14, 1929

Dear Ernest:

. . . . .

. . . . .

Another is about the advance. There is every reason you should have one, and a considerable one. The great trouble about an advance is that it is very discouraging to an author (take Scott for example), to see his book doing very well, and then to find on the next royalty report, that he gets nothing from it, or very little, because of a large advance.- But I need not have made this point with you, I guess. We would readily send you five thousand at any time, or more. It is a question of what you need.

The other point was about the synonym or near-synonym you suggested for the blank word in the passage with Miss Van Campen. I think it is all right. We have put it in. It is an unusual word, but being said to her, a nurse, I think it is right.

I did destroy the letter immediately as you said to, but I fully understood why you felt the way you did. Writers have been ruined by successful old boys who slapped them on the back and took them right into a circle of old boys, and pinned ribbons on them, etc. You instinctively felt there might be something of this afoot.

I shall write you soon. All goes well.

Ever yours,

---

[1]Beginning in 1926, Anderson had been publishing articles in *Vanity Fair* about places where he had lived.

[2]52 words have been omitted from this letter.

*AL, 3 pp.*
*Santiago de Compostela, Spain*

<u>Aug 28</u>

Dear Max—

Excuse the beautiful edging on the paper—It's Paulines. I got your two letters of Aug 14 yesterday—Im awfully glad you had such a good summer.

You can certainly get drunk on Port and it is bad afterwards too—Those famous 3 and 4 bottle men were living all the time in the open air—hunting, shooting, always on a horse—In That life as in skiing or fishing you can drink any amount—

Am cheerful again—have written 3 pieces—have some more in my head—going to go over them again and copy off in Paris. We leave here day after tomorrow—for Madrid—want to see Sidney Franklin of Brooklyn—They say he's good—Be back in Paris in Oct 1—Maybe before—Glad Meyer likes the book—I hope to God it's better than The Sun—The comparative that way doesnt bother me.

Did I ever write you about seeing Morley Callaghan in Paris—several times—he was working hard. You would not believe it to look at him but he is a <u>very</u> good boxer—I boxed with him 3 or 4 times—one time I had a date to box with him at 5 pm—lunched with Scott and John Bishop—At Prunier's—at Homard Thermidor—all sorts of stuff—drunk several bottles of white burgundy—Knew I would be asleep by 5—so went around with Scott to get Morley to box right away—I couldnt see him hardly—had a couple of whiskey's enroute—Scott was to keep time and we were to box 1 minute rounds with 2 minute rests on acct. of my condition—I knew I could go a minute at a time and went fast and used all my wind—then Morley commenced to pop me and cut my mouth, mushed up my face in general—I was pooped as could be and thought I had never known such a long round but couldn't ask about it or Morley would think I was quitting—Finally Scott called time—Said he was very sorry and ashamed and would I forgive him. He had let the round go three minutes and 45 second—so interested to see if I was going to hit the floor! We boxed 5 more rounds and I finally fought myself out of the alcohol and went all right—Can still feel with my tongue the big scar on my lower lip—He is fast, knows a lot and is a pleasure to box with—He cant hit hard—if he could he would have killed me—I slipped and went down once and lit on my arm and put my left shoulder out in that first round and it pulled a tendon so that it was pretty sore afterwards and did not get a chance to box again before we left. Morley had been boxing nearly every day in Toronto for a year. He is fat and looks in bad shape but is really darned good.[1]

[1]This bout escalated into a feud and became one of the most widely circulated anecdotes about EH; see Callaghan, *That Summer in Paris* (New York: Coward–McCann, 1963), pp. 212–219, 243–251; and Bruccoli, *Fitzgerald and Hemingway,* pp. 120–128, 142–153.

What reminded me of this was how you could get rid of alcohol by exercise—after 5 rounds—during which I took a bad beating in the first—I was going well—Judgement of distance good—in really good shape and out pointing (or holding my own) with someone who had been beating me all over the place to sweat it out of me.

*[Rest of letter missing]*

*Cable, 1 p.*

MADRID SEPT 7 1929 NFT CHAPTER FORTY SHOULD READ QUOTES WE HAD A FINE LIFE STOP WE LIVED STOP THROUGH THE MONTHS OF JANUARY ETC AS IT APPEARED IN MAGAZINE WITH NOTHING BETWEEN THOSE FIRST TWO SENTENCES STOP FIND TODAY PARAGRAPH SUPPOSEDLY CROSSED OUT IN GALLEYS IN ENGLISH PAGE PROOFS THIS WOULD RUIN BOOK[1] HEMINGWAY THOMAS COOKS MADRID.

*ALS, 5 pp., JFK[1]*
*Paris, France*

October 3

Dear Max:—

The books havent come. But I heard today they were on sale at Galignani's and went down there and bought two.

Your cable about the first reviews came (Thanks ever so much) and your letter about newspaper syndicating—I agree with you about the latter and would not want it unless (1) It would help in every way the book (2) It would bring in some respectable sum of money (over 1000 dollars) I believe it would hurt rather than help the book. Don't want it.

Anyhow I dont like it and wont sell to anybody to cut—

God knows it's cut enough.

About the Jacket—You must know best but it seems lousy to me—I'm no actress wanting the name in Big electric lights—But the name must have some value as a selling point and comparing it to the jackets of the Sun Also its a little over half as big type and about 1/3 as big as on Men Without Women—All I know about the effect of the jacket is that with the book in a pile on the counter with other books and me looking for it I could not find it and the clerk had to find it for me.

It looks as though the jacket designer had been so wrapped up in the beautiful artistic effort on the front that she had tried to eliminate if possible

[1]The book galleys for Chapter 40 have not been located.

the title and author's name so they wouldn't intrude on the conception of that nude figure with those so horrible legs and those belly muscles like Wladek Zbyszko's who is labelled <u>Cleon</u>[1] (a character in the book I presume or the spirit of no sex appeal) and the big shouldered lad with the prominent nipples who is holding the broken axle (signifying no doubt the defeat of The Horse Drawn Vehicle)

A little more restraint by the artist would have left more room for the title. It has the same number of letters as The sun also Rises—and there would have been room for the author to be referred to as the author of The Sun and Men Without—

You understand this is a layman's criticism—The old Sun jacket that I didn't care for when I saw it—looks like a masterpiece now compared to this one of Mr. and Mrs Cleon among the poinsettias or The tragedy of the Broken Axle. Really and truly if the book is banned anywhere I think it will be on account of that girl on the cover.

In the blurb—Cap<u>o</u>retto is spelled with an A and Catherine Barklay as we finally agreed to spell her in the book is Katharine (as in Katharsis)

What about the Signed ones?—How many of those do I get?

Could you send me the proofs I corrected and sent back? If it's impossible I will write and try and get the other set of them from Cape. Although I hate to write them for favors because I think I am <u>through</u> with them I hope to god for good. I'm disgusted with his yellow deletions. They cut sentences out without a word to me and only sent me page proofs and wrote me on the 18th when going to America the 21st of Sept. What I want to do is to get them cut and bound up so I can have one copy of it as it was before the blanks.

Thornton Wilder said for me to write you that if you got in any trouble about the book or if they attacked it he would be glad to write or wire anything to help.

What I'm afraid of now that I've actually seen it is that in a little while it will all be over and when a respectable number are sold then it will be laid off being pushed and not sell any more and the book will be just the same only no one will ever buy it—I wont have another one for two years anyway

I always figured that if I could write good books they would always sell a certain amount if they were good and some day I could live on what they all would bring in honestly—But Scott tells me that is all bunk—That a book only sells for a short time and that afterwards it never sells and that it doesnt pay the publishers even to bother with it. So I guess it's all just a damned racket like all the rest of it and the way I feel tonight is to hell with all of it— All I got out of this book is disappointment—I couldn't pay any attention when my father died—Couldnt let myself feel <u>anything</u> because I would get out of the book and lose it—Of course the thing as a serial supports them all

---

[1]CLEON was the signature of Cleonike Damianakes (1895–1979), who provided the dust jacket art for several important Scribners books, including *SAR*.

and the book is going to have to too—But I would rather write and then go over it and when I know it's right stick to it and publish it that way the way it was if it never sells a damned one—That's what I should have done—Instead of starting in on the polite Owen Wister Compromise—The fact I do it on acct. of my family is no excuse and I know it—I'm a Professional Writer now—Than which there isn't anything lower. I never thought I'd be it (and I'm damned if I'm going to do it any more)—But if I can get one copy of it and I can see I got it set up the way it was (rather you set it up and deserve all credit) in type it will take some of the curse off it.

Dont think I'm sore at you—I'm not. You've <u>always</u> been grand to me. I just hate the whole damned thing. And the jacket and blurb on Julian Greens book by Harpers made me want to vomit[1]—They said he was to be compared to Balzac, Flaubert, Doestoevsky, Emily Bronte and Conrad—The one who compared him to Flaubert was Grant Overton who writes whole propaganda books for publishers—As much critical integrity as a crab between your dirty toes—

A $10,000 prize given to 2 women and 2 Fairies—The last two under contract already—How many books did Cumming's Enormous Room sell?

It's all a racket—Sometimes I wish to God you weren't my friend and instead I was with some firm I hated so I could put the screws on and rachet them from the other side.

This is a pretty letter all right—Did McAlmon come to see you? He's been unjustly treated—His Village was good enough to publish—But much of his stuff is terrible—His best stuff was a couple of stories of homosexuality in Berlin Underworld and quite unpublishable. Also he's a damned gossip—I swore to kill him once for a damned lying story he spread about me—(How I'd beaten Hadley while Bumby was being born!) But sometimes he's very intelligent and wish he could be published if only to take him out of the martyr class—But dont know what stuff he has with him and it may be terrible.

Anyway I'll end this before it goes on any further—Its been raining all day—raining outside now—Havent had a drink for a week.

Yours always<br>Ernest[2]

CC, 5 pp.[3]

Oct. 15, 1929

Dear Ernest:

The first printing was 30,000, the second, 10,000, and the third, 10,000. The second was made at the time of publication, and the third about a week

---

[1] Julian Green received the $2,000 Harper Prize Novel award for *The Dark Journey* in 1929.
[2] This letter may not have been sent to MP.
[3] 175 words have been omitted from this letter.

119

ago. The orders are not recorded beyond Friday, but then they were almost exactly 30,000 on the royalty card. That is absolute sales. Everything seems right.

. . . . .

By what strange fate do you always happen on something bad at the start—about the only review I did not send you was Isabel Paterson, because it disgusted me. The trouble with her is plain enough to my mind: she missed her step on "The Sun Also". She found that everyone disagreed with her and she is stubborn and wanted to see herself justified. She is always that way.- Somebody did her a wrong once, and it has always rankled.

As to the jacket, it seems to be working out well. When the very first reviews came, we took all the notes off the flaps and back, and put on endorsements. We had the greatest trouble with the design on the front. The lady who made it is about the best person in the market and always wins the prizes for jackets, but she made two attempts before she produced the present design. We were very nervous about the jacket because we did not want to bring out the book as a War book, that is as a combat book. Still less did we wish to after the appearance of "All Quiet". We wanted no helmets or artillery, or any of that sort of thing. We did consider simply a type jacket, but in the face of competition it is a desperate matter to make one that stands out. I am merely giving you the line of thought that led to the present design. I thought it did make the book stand out, and did have an emotional quality that was appealing. I felt some anxiety about it on the grounds you gave, but I think we have safely passed that now, for good and all.- And the main thing about a jacket is that it should give a book <u>visibility</u>.

. . . . .

Thanks for telling me about the Bromfield[1] matter. I should have been worried somewhat, but not very much because I should be all but certain that you would take up anything like that with me first.- And although I hope you never will, and there isn't much we would not do to prevent you from it, I do not want anything personal ever to hold you back from it. That is, if you got to feel dissatisfied and thought we could not rectify the trouble, I wouldn't want you to be held back just because I was such a wonder as a Tarpon Fisherman: I hardly dare say this, but I told Scott the same thing once and refused to tie him up with options on his "next ten books". If you plan to send a story to Scribner's and could send one now, or soon, there's a reason why we would snatch at it with a special eagerness.

Always yours,

---

[1]On 5 October 1929 EH explained that Louis Bromfield had spread a false story about Hemingway's disaffection with Scribners: "So if you hear that damned lie dont let it worry you."

*ALS, 4 pp., JFK[1]*

Enroute Berlin
<u>Sunday Nov 10</u>

Dear Max:—

... Am going up to Berlin to see various citizens and German publishers—to arrange about serialization—The German publisher wants to take 37% of what that brings on acct of furnishing the translator. (First they wanted 80%) but I am being hard boiled abt it as I have too damn many dependents to split too much with people after the thing is once written and finished—The translator wd have to translate the book in any event for book publication and if it is serialized first 15% of the serialization or 20%—is plenty—Sunny—(my useless sister you met at Key West) now has developed stomach ulcers—(Broke her engagement first—I thot I had her married off). Hope she gets well—I may have to shoot them all to hold down the overhead.

Have been writing well on a story last 3 days so dont give a damn about anything—I saw Scott last week—looking very well and healthy.

If you were me—and Christ knows I need money—not money advanced or loaned but money earned—would you sell the book to movies for cash now or gamble on a play—Reynolds is getting Laurence Stallings—Scott tells me Stallings no good—Maxwell Anderson is the goods he says—Play may flop—then Movie only bring 20,000 and have to split 3 ways—minus commission to Reynolds and all his friends—Now I can sell for 10 grand—1 to Reynolds makes 9 for me—I <u>would</u> sell for 17 grand—That would net me 15,000. I think that wd. be better may be—Then write a play myself sometime. To hell with plays with other people—May be best tho—But I think I could write a good play myself sometime—what do you think about the play or movie business?[2]

Anyway there isnt any news good or bad—Except the 42,000 cockeyed copies—once its past 60—it will be fine—If it can come again after Christmas it will be grand—The Sun did—You all must be sick of it. If you are I dont blame you—I think we should sell an awful lot of this though because the whole fiction racket is going to go to hell may be in a couple of years—

Owen Wister sent me a fine autographed set of his complete works—Damned sweet of him to do—He wrote some fine—very fine—stories—

It's dark outside and train rocking—Not stuffy—wish you were here and we'd go up to the diner and drink—Must be nearly to Belgian frontier—Hope the Market didnt hit you—

Best to you always—
<u>Ernest</u>

[1]40 words have been omitted from this letter.
[2]Stallings's adaptation of *FTA* played for three weeks on Broadway in September 1930; EH reported that his advance from the play was only $750. He received $24,000 from the sale of the movie rights.

Remember O.W. and et al wanting me to tone down or cut out some of the last chapter? That's why they're reading the damned book.

It's no fun for me on acct. of the blanks—Now I can never say shit in a book—Precedent—When you make your own precedent once you make the wrong precedent you're just as badly stuck by it—

It takes away the interest in writing fiction.[1]

*CC, 5 pp.*[2]

November 12, 1929

Dear Ernest:

There has been so much turbulence lately that I have not had a chance really to write you, and now there is so much to say that I do not know whether I shall be able to get it all into one letter. The sale to date is just 45,000. We have printed 70,000 and we have paper on hand for 20,000 more. Ever since publication "A Farewell" has been the best seller in all the lists, except in one list for one week, when "All Quiet" got ahead of it. That was two weeks ago. Last week again it was at the head of all lists. The danger now is on account of the sudden and distinct depression in business that came with the Wall Street crash.- But that is more likely to affect the general line of books—that it surely will affect—than so outstanding a book as "A Farewell". I shall let you know how things continue anyhow, so don't worry.

. . . . .

It has been fine the way you have met these anti-Scribner rumors. One would think there was a regular campaign afoot—I enclose some chatter from the Daily Mirror. The probability is that these publishers simply want to get you, and they open up by saying they have heard you were dissatisfied.- But the offers they make do, of course, put us under an obligation. A publisher will pay an author so outstanding, more than he can ever get back, simply for the sake of having him lead his list. An author would make a mistake to accept an offer of that kind, which would not be made in his interest, but only in that of the publisher. At the same time, his own publisher ought not to expect him to accept less than could be soundly given by another publisher, and if you want $25,000 for instance, I believe we would pay it at any time on this book. When it came to the next one, we could also make a big advance if you wanted one. We are not in a position to ask you to refuse offers without being willing to equal them ourselves. In connection with this there is the question about the royalty. When we first published for Scott costs were not what they are now, nor were discounts. 20% after a certain figure left a reasonable margin to the publisher, on account of the big sale he

[1]This letter may not have been sent to MP.
[2]802 words have been omitted from this letter.

had previously made.[1] The situation is different now, and most publishers feel that 20% is too much,- that 15% is about all that a book will bear if it is to be heavily advertised. Before the advent of the clubs and other influences, it was possible to get a book going strongly and then let it go on its own impetus.- But now along comes the new Club book and Guild book, and a great deal must be done to counteract the tendency of public attention to turn to these new books. The truth is if you demanded 20% royalty, even from the start, we would probably give it to you and face a loss, if necessary, but it is better that the publisher should have an adequate margin so that he may strongly support a book. I will tell you what,- we have this contract now, and the royalty report based upon it will not be rendered until six months after publication;- but of course if you want payments in the meantime, you can have them in advance. But when that report is rendered we shall know what the result of the whole publication is, and I could then give you in a very simple form, the exact figures about the profits, and the advertising, and everything else, and if you thought we ought, we could then revise the terms of the contract retroactively. If you should come through New York, or if I should have the chance to go to Key West, I could easily show you the whole thing, and we could talk it out.

. . . . .
. . . . .
. . . . .
. . . . .
. . . . .
. . . . .

Ever your friend,

*AL, 6 pp., JFK*
*Paris, France*

Sunday November 17—

Dear Max:—

Just back from Berlin arranged for serializing Farewell in Germany—am enclosing first English review—You can probably use extracts from it—

On arriving here yest. found Pauline worried by news from Scott about the book—Scott seemed very worried. Some contingency which was to prevent a big sale that he had heard from you.

His idea was that if sales started to fall off you should start advertising the book as a love story—which it certainly is as well as a war story—If other war books should start to crowd it—Why not do that?

[1] In a 22 October 1929 letter to MP, EH had written, "Scott says he has a contract whereby above certain large amounts of sales the royalty percentage rises. He told me what it was but I forgot it. What about this? Do you want to make some increase over 50,000? over 75,000? and over 100,000? Will you let me know about this. The principal thing I want is for it to keep on going of course and am not avaricious. But have heard this is done so write to ask you."

I have not spoken about advertising and told Scott I would rather not but he said I was a fool not to—So here goes and then I'll drop it—I think the advertizing has been excellent!—

The first ad I would find fault with was the one in the World which started—First Choice of Book Buyers in the following cities—You are in competition with people who make such ambiguous statements that any ambiguity is discounted—

I think

        The Best Selling Book in ——The names of the cities) is

        The Top of the Best Seller Lists

at least 10 times as effective as a statement which means that but doesnt say it—

That's all about advertising—

About any reasons that may now keep it from having a big sale—

I know that there were about 3 perfectly valid reasons why I should not have been able to complete it—If I completed it and it gets the reviews it has had and sells as it did for 3 weeks—I'm afraid that no reasons are going to be valid why it should not have a big sale—There are no alibis in a battle—You win it or you lose it in spite of all circumstances that come up—Afterwards it is won or lost. This has reached the battle stage. It is no longer a skirmish, or a preliminary encounter or a trial of strength. It's something to be won or lost. And there are no explanations.

You know I have denied all reports of difficulties, I'm loyal to you in my head and my actions, I've not tried to embarrass you, but I tell you how this book goes is damned serious to me.

About the advertising—I have said nothing—I find it excellent—It is your business—not mine——

If, however, later you would say—"if you had any suggestions to make why did you not make it?" I'll suggest that if the sale does not keep up with what you are doing why not hammer on it as a love story—

        These things are from an advertising standpoint—not my opinion or my judgement of the book—

| (1) The action of | (1) Takes place in war | / | Theres more than |
| A Farewell to Arms | | | War in |
| (2) The background of— | (2)—Is War | / | A Farewell to Arms. |
| But it is | | / | It is |
| The Great Modern Love Story | | / | The Great Modern Love Story |

What Shit!

It makes me sick to write such stuff and I'm damned if I will—but what sold the Bridge of San Thornton Wilder was the calling it loud, plenty and often—A Metaphysical Novel—Sure and what it was was well hung together collection of short stories—

You sell the intelligent ones first—Then you have to hammer hammer hammer on some simple thing to sell the rest.

Like this—

There Are Other War Books (Or Books of War.)

But
A Farewell To Arms
By
ERNST HEMINgSTein
is

⟶ A GreAT MODeRN LOVe STORY

This not my opinion or judgement it is only a suggestion for advertizing—
You sell the intelligent ones first—Then you have to hammer, hammer, hammer on something to sell the rest—I once worked for Richard H. Loper[1]
whose best business was selling whiskey by mail order. While working under
Mr. Loper we did not come in contact with the intelligent at all.

I only suggest this if you do not continue the sale as you would like with
the present line—I see it's The Sensation of the Season—In the ads—But
there will be other sensations and that is a pretty impermanent qualifica-
tion—The thing to do is dub it something The Great or A Great and then
stick to it—Anyone whose opinion matters will have read it long before—
What sold the Bridge of St. Thronton Wilder was (1) It was as damn good
collection of short stories (2) They dubbed it A Metaphysical Novel and
stuck to it.

Now a final suggestion from Mr. Richard H. Loper's 2nd in Command:

I would run this entire review in an ad—It has more sales force (what
filthy words) than any damn thing I ever read—In spite of having written the
bloody book and having worked over it so much that I am completely unable
to read it when I read this review I wanted to go right out and buy one—
Dont use the head lines—Just start the review—

A Farewell To Arms—By Ernest Hemingway—350 p. $2.50,
Charles Scribner's Sons—N.Y.

By James Aswell[2]

Then the review.   Then at the bottom—In The Richmond-Times Dispatch
Put any comment you want across the Top and the Bottom—But I swear that
review in it's entirety would make a swell ad. You could slug at the bottom
names and comments of various more prominent citizens who agree with
Mr. Aswell—

I'm not trying to interfere—These are two suggestions—

When you get through with the Aswell review will you please send it
back. It's the only one I'm keeping.[3]

---

[1]Loper was an editor of *The Cooperative Commonwealth,* a monthly magazine of the
Cooperative Society of America for which EH worked from December 1920 to October
1921.

[2]James Aswell, "Critic Lauds 'A Farewell To Arms'"—The Biography Of A Virginal
Mind," *Richmond Times-Dispatch,* (6 October 1929), Sunday supplement, p. 3.

[3]This letter was not sent; EH rewrote it as his 19 November letter.

*ALS, 3 pp.*[1]
*Paris, France*

<u>November 19</u>

Dear Max:—

Came back from Berlin and found Scott worried about my book—I believe and hope quite needlessly. Something he had heard from you about some contingency that might prevent it having a really big sale.

Scott's idea was that if the sale should start to fall off—other books with war in them coming out—you should start hammering it as a love story—i.e. Farewell To Arms—A Gt. Modern Love Story. (sic) It most certainly is a love story and most of the reviews called it so. This seems a good idea altho I am not mixing in your handling of it—

What ads I have seen have seemed excellent—only two things I would suggest—Many publishers advertisements are so ambiguous that it would always seem to be better to avoid ambiguity by an exact statement if that is possible—

[The First Choice of Book Buyers in such and such cities]
seems not nearly as effective as

The Best Selling Book or AT The Head of Best Selling Lists—To me, at least, it avoids stating something while another publisher—if he avoided stating it would only be avoiding because it was not true.

That is an awkward enough sentence but I think you see what I mean. The other was—The Sensation of The Season—That makes it old stuff in a month when there is a new sensation But that is not worth mentioning as I know that was just to be used for a short time—But it's best to dub a thing something and then stick to it—

About any reasons that may keep it from having a big sale—

There were about 3 perfectly valid reasons why I should not have been able to Complete the book. If it was completed, gets the reviews it has had, and goes as it did for three weeks I am afraid that no reasons are going to be valid why it should not have a very big sale. There are no alibis in a battle— You win it or you lose it in spite of all circumstances that come up—Then, afterwards it is won or lost. That is all that counts. This has reached the battle stage. It is no longer a skirmish, or a preliminary encounter or a trial of strength. It is something to be won or lost and there are no good explanations.

The last letter I've had from you was October 15—The last cable was Nov. 9 giving the sale as 42,000—I wired Saturday, after I'd seen Scott, asking about the sale. Today is Tuesday—May hear this afternoon—P.S. Wire has just come giving 46,000 sale last Friday—So it wd seem to be going steadily. One reason I want to keep track is to know how to regard the theatrical and moving picture negotiations. I would rather be writing than

[1]302 words have been omitted from this letter.

doing any of this. But what happens is that I get in the middle of a story and something comes up.

. . . . .
. . . . .

Yours always—<br>
<u>Ernest</u>

. . . . .
. . . . .

ALS, Guaranty Trust Writing Room stationery, 10 pp.[1]<br>
Paris, France

<u>November 20</u>

Dear Max:—

. . . . .

I'm glad to know Bridges is going—unless it means the Poorhouse or some hard luck—

Altho I have to thank his complete ignorance of this world for the publication of A Farewell in the Magazine—you were worried about it—But Bridges—being as dumb in one direction as he was in the other about 50 Grand—put it in—So the dumb have their uses. Not that it wasnt publishable—But it took a courage to do it that he replaced with ignorance—Still that's the most prevalent form of courage at that.

About the translations—Thanks for keeping me informed—Give me the information on their propositions as they send them in—or ask them to write me care of the Guaranty—here—That's best. Translation has been signed for Germany and Sweden

Thank you for sending the checks to Hadley—

About the royalty—

You know I am not trying to Shylock—But the contract was the same as for The Sun—There was no provision made for a big sale—I did not even sign it until after I had the proofs—Then only so there would be something of record to protect you in case any thing happened to me—

The Sun was a first novel with a First printing of, I believe, 5,000—

In spite of the book club competiton etc. this book had the publicity of The Sun, Men Without etc to help it and the first printing was 30,000 instead of 5,000—

I knew that our basis being what it is—one of mutual trust—you would do whatever is usual and just when this came up—(if we would have discussed this contract a provision would have been put in for sales above certain figures)

I've not quoted or tried to bother you with royalty % offers from other

---

[1] 145 words have been omitted from this letter.

publishers—Have no intention of trying to bid up—It was only when Scott asked me what my arrangements were for a big sale that I mentioned it to you—not quoting an outside elevated percentage but one I knew to be in existance. In the ordinary course I would have waited for you to mention it—

(This paper is too small to write on—They are doing some fumigating to the house and am turned out)

You're suggestion that we wait and talk it over after the 6 mos. is excellent except for one thing—If Scribner's decide now that after certain figures the royalty advances in proportion then we both feel we are making a certain amount—while if we wait 6 months the royalty always being considered 15% then Scribner's when another arrangement is made feel they are giving up a certain sum they would otherwise have had—I'd rather feel we were both earning it as we went along.

You know we have no fights about money. The only fundamental disagreement was about the words—I _knew_ certain ones could be published because I saw them in proof and they were all right—They shocked no one—I _had_ to have them—It meant everything to the integrity of the book. I was prepared with the book written and published intact as I wrote it to accept no advance—I didnt ask for one. Every one to whom I had obligations could take their chances along with me—If the book was suppressed I knew the suppression would not last and that it would be as well and better for all concerned in the end. I wrote about how I felt and how serious the matter was to me—That is our business—yours and mine—and I have talked to no one outside about it. But when I was over-ruled and knew that it was finally a commercial proposition (as of course it is and rightly so to you because you have the responsibility of Scribner's interests) and it was cut so it would be able to sell—I've had no interest in it as a _book_ since. It's something to sell—Some man in Town and Country has written that I am the one who made Joyce's integrity saleable and palatable—All right—with the words in they would see whether I was writing to sell or not—But now that I've lost my integrity on it let it sell By God and fix up my mother and the rest of them.

About the book of stories—You must have told me about it and I not paid any attention—I let O'Brien have The Undefeated because of an obligation I had to him—(He dedicated the book to me and broke his rules to publish a story that had never been published in a magazine. Or rather _did_ we let him have it? As I recall we refused to let him have it because it was too much a part of the book and made him take The Killers instead—But I may be wrong—He may have published it the year before and wanted Fifty Grand—Anyway we turned him down on something that year and made him take The Killers—[2]

Anyhow the obligation is gone because I read he has a book in which I confide to him on a lonely mt. top that I was a pure young man until the

---

[1]"My Old Man" was printed in _The Best Short Stories of 1923,_ edited by Edward J. O'Brien; "The Undefeated" and "The Killers" were, respectively, in the 1926 and 1927 volumes.

machines in the war turned me against everything etc.[1] Mike Strater and I once spent an evening with him in a monastery above Rapallo. I remember that Mike and I both drank several pitchers of wine. Am capable when tight of telling him I was a pure young girl of course and used to write under the name of Precious Bane but I dont think he shd put such assertions in a serious book—I hope I was a pure young boy once—even if my mother swears I never was—but dont see what that proves—

. . . . .

Anyway I was damned glad to hear from you—I get so many cables about and hear so many reports of trouble between us that I think sometimes there must be something to it and that you must be sore at me about something. The most purely inventive gossips I know are Bromfield and McAlmon—With both of them in N.Y. any story may start. Never worry about anything you dont hear from me—I'll try to worry you enough personally.

. . . . .

Yours always

<u>Ernest</u>

I am fixing up a trust fund for my mother—Have 30,000 promised from an outside source (<u>This confidential</u>) It's <u>not</u> a publisher. Will need to call on you for 20,000 against royalties due at the time when the will is made put in that 20,000 some time after the first of the year—(If I get cash from stories in meantime of course will not call on you. Then the trust will start paying off in April and I will have that off my hands. I wish there was someway I didnt have to pay income tax on that 20,000. There is no money in having to borrow money to pay income tax on money you never see! If you think of any way let me know.

P.S.

On income tax I only get credit for 2 dependents because that is all I have under the one roof—In reality I have 9 dependents! So if you know or hear of any way I can make or receive such a payment and not be liable for tax it will be good—Perhaps it could be sent direct to lawyer making trust and I would simply not declare it and if queried explain it—In the meantime want to take no more money this year if possible as it is all gone (paid out) and I'll have to borrow to pay tax as it is!

Once this is fixed up am all set though—

*CC, 4 pp.*

Nov. 21, 1929

Dear Ernest:

I can say definitely now that the sale has passed 50,000,- and we are printing another edition of 10,000, making 81,000 in all. We would have printed

---

[1]*The Dance of the Machines* (New York: Macaulay, 1929), pp. 236–242.

20,000 excepting that the smaller printing enables us to get finished copies sooner, and we can make another small printing very easily. The book market, like every other market at the moment, has been badly hurt by the break in stocks, and your book is the only one that does not seem to have been slowed up by it. This too, is the dull time of year—of every year. After Thanksgiving, if things are normal, trade will wake up. Most of the supposedly big novels that were published this year have flopped, and I believe Edith Wharton's is destined to do so.- But so far everything has gone well with "A Farewell".

I wish you would consider this idea—

You are not the kind of writer who produces novels at regular intervals, and you said once that you could not expect to do a novel in less than two years. If you are worried about finances in these periods between books (although I believe that your next book of stories will sell even better than the last one, and perhaps much better) it will be a bad thing because you will be under pressure, or else you may have to ask for an advance,- and in some way that often seems to a writer like asking for a favor, although Heaven knows we would not so regard it, and could not. I thought that on these accounts you might prefer it if we made some sort of an arrangement to pay you a minimum sum each year, upon which you could absolutely count. It would be almost like a salary and it could be deducted from the royalties earned, not all at once, but over a period agreed upon. In this way you would be assured of a much steadier income.

I do not know whether such an idea would interest you, but if it would, we could undoubtedly work out all the details easily enough, and you could then make your own plans for helping the people who are dependent upon you, more smoothly. On the other hand, you might well be very soon in a position where finances would not worry you anyhow. But I thought the scheme was worth suggesting.

I hope everything is right with you. I do think I can manage to go to Key West sometime, and I certainly look forward to it.

Remembrances to Pauline.

Ever yours,

*ALS, 3 pp.*
*Paris, France*

November 30

Dear Max—

Have read, heard and received cables about a report that I was going to leave Scribners. You offered to publish what I was writing before any one else did It was only by luck that I was in Austria and so did not get your letter which was waiting in Paris and accepted the cabled offer of another firm to publish my first book. You published a book which was refused by this first publisher. You published The Sun Also intact with the exception of one word which you have now published in this last book. You have been constantly loyal and you have been wholly admirable. If we have fought over you cutting words out of this last book you at least left blanks wherever you Cut and it has been our own fight and no outsider is going to profit by it. I have absolutely no intention of leaving Scribners and I hope to live long enough so you may publish my Collected Works if my kidneys hold out and I have luck enough to write any works worth Collecting.

Have read an article in the Bookman by a citizen who calls me a swine and one thing and another, to which opinion he is of course perfectly entitled, but what I look forward to is spanking in the physical sense the editor of the Bookman, who is young enough to know better, for publishing a review of a book written by a reviewer who is also a fellow novelist and who admits having read only a third of the way through the book he is reviewing and then advocates its suppression.[1] Reviewers on a monthly at least should be paid for reading the whole book or not at all. However we must not ask for too much and I will certainly not spank the editor of The Bookman unless he seems in physical condition to support it. In any event the projected spanking is promised entirely in the nature of a moral correction and the physical side will be minimized as much as possible.

Speaking of this book, will you repeat again that it is fiction, that I lay no claim even to have been in Italy, that I would never attempt to judge or picture Italy or Italians as such, but that I have only taken advantage of the tradition by which writers from the earliest times have laid the scenes of their books in that country.

> Yours always
> Ernest Hemingway

*ALS, 6 pp.*
*Paris, France*

Sunday Dec 7

Dear Max—

Thanks very much for your letters of Nov 21 and 25th—and the proof of ad in N Y Times which is very handsome—The ad—Glad everything is going well.

Had a letter from A Knopf asking to see me so went in order to tell him and his wife there was absolutely no truth in report I was leaving you—nor was I dis satisfied in any way. He is returning to N Y in a week and I asked him to deny the report wherever he heard it—which they both promised to do.

Thanks for writing about the salary business—I appreciated it but would

[1] Robert Herrick, "What Is dirt?," *The Bookman* 70 (November 1929): 258–262.

only think of it as a last resort—You know the difficulty I have of working under Contract—

About In Our Time—I wish you would get it from Liveright—There is no reason why they should hang on to the one book—Remind them that they promised me absolutely that they would sell the book to you if you wanted it—I remember wanting to get it settled at the time. The bringing out of the original Three Mts Press edition again sounds like a good idea—We can discuss it—I think it should, if issued, have Mike Strater's portrait reproduced as frontispiece—Not the punk wood cut made from it but a good reproduction—reproduce the original cover also maybe—The original edition was only 150[1] The idea of the English opinion ad sounds fine—Have you all the English clippings? There was a good one in New Statesman of Nov. 30—and Times Book Supplement of Nov 27—Glad to have that ad for Mr. R. Herrick to read—just for fun.

### Dec 10

Started to write you Sunday—Now it's Tuesday—Scott came to dinner last night and while drunk told me he had heard from you that McAlmon had told you various stories about me. He also told me of particularly filthy story Morley Calloghan had told him about me. Morley had gotten it from McAlmon.

So I write to ask if McAlmon has any new stories—His stories that I am familiar with are (1) That Pauline is a lesbian (2) that I am a homosexual (3) that I used to beat Hadley and as a result of one these beatings Bumby was born prematurely.

Did he tell you these or did he have new ones? I'd appreciate not a general but a particular answer.

Morley, it seems, asked Scott on meeting him if he knew it were true that I was a homo-sexual. He had just gotten the news from McAlmon! He may therefore be counted on to have spread it fairly thoroughly. He seems also to be having a great deal of success with a story about how I sneered at his boxing ability, he challenged me and knocked me cold.

I sent McAlmon with a letter to you because I have tried to help materially everyone I know who is writing whether a friend or an enemy. Have tried especially to help people I did not like since my judgement might be warped in favor of my friends and hate to see people bitter about never having had a chance even though I may feel sure personally there is good and abundant cause for their failure. I do not try to get them published That's your business not mine. but to obtain them an extra-fair presentation to the publisher.

But this has gone a little too far. There should be a limit to what lies people are allowed to tell under jealousies.

I did not know until last night that Calloghan was definitely in that class. It is all pretty disgusting. Pauline says it is my own fault for having had anything to do with such swine. She is right enough. There will be a certain satisfaction in beating up Calloghan because of his boasting and because he is a

[1]The 1924 Paris *IOT* was not republished by Scribners.

good enough boxer. There is none in beating up McAlmon—I would have done it years ago if he wasnt so pitiful. But I will go through with it as I should have long ago because the only thing such people fear is physical correction—They have no moral feelings to hurt.

I have, as far as I know, only one one other—perhaps two other "enemies", that is people willfuly seeking to do you harm through malice. One in a very minor way would seem to be Isabel Patterson whom I've never even seen and the other is a Russian Jew with a name like Lipschitzky who calls himself Pierre Loving and lies about everyone. He is a disappointed writer.[1]

Scott is the soul of honor when sober and completely irresponsible when drunk. If it's all the same I would rather you wrote me when you hear stories about me—not Scott. Please do not reproach Scott with a breach of confidence as he is absolutely incapable of such a thing sober and drunk he is no more responsible than an insane man. He did not say you had written him any definite stories—but told me stories he had heard from Calloghan as a type of thing McAlmon had probably told you.

I had to sit, drinking Vichey, cold sober, and listen to an hour or more of that sort of thing last night. When McAlmon told one of those stories in the presence of Evan Shipman[2]—Evan called him a liar and hit him. When McAlmon called Scott a homosexual to me (It is one of his manias) I told him he was a liar and a damned fool. It was not until after he had left for N.Y. that I heard the story he was telling about Pauline. Frankly I think he is crazy. Calloghan has no such excuse. He is a cheap, small town gossip anxious to believe and retail any filth no matter how improbable.

This seems to be the end of the letter—Your wires about the sale being 57,000 and 59,000 came yesterday and today. Thanks ever so much for sending them. I am glad it is going so well.

Yours always—
Ernest Hemingway

*[Two lines crossed out by EH]*

This is nothing—I was starting to make a reflection about people waiting 6 ms. to tell you when drunk some filthy story about you which they apparently never challenged physically or in any way but realized that since last night I have reflected entirely too damned much—But Ill be damned glad be in Key West and see people like Charles, Mike Strater and yourself and have no filth and jealousy. What the hell are they jealous of?—I dont want the publicity and I dont get the money. All I want is to work and be let alone and I damned well will be.[3]

---

[1]Paterson wrote the "Turns With a Bookworm" column for the *New York Herald Tribune Books* supplement. Loving wrote fiction and criticism.

[2]Shipman was a minor poet and horse-racing fancier; he met EH in 1924, and the two remained lifelong friends.

[3]See Appendix One for EH's drafts of this letter.

*CC, 4 pp.*[1]

Dec. 10, 1929

Dear Ernest:

. . . . .

. . . . .

. . . . .

Now as to the revision of the contract: I took it up finally today and everything went well about it. Your position and point of view were fully understood and accepted. In fact, I suggested a royalty of 17½% after 25,000 copies, and of 20% after 45,000, and Mr. Scribner said, "No, 20% after 25,000. I think I told you once that if you asked for 20% from the very first copy, we would give it, whatever the effect of our own profit on the book might be;- because we think the value of publishing for you is a great one in itself.- So if these new terms do not seem to you satisfactory, you have only to tell us what terms will. That is a fact. I am sure that if you wanted anything else, I could take it up, and they would give it. But from this moment on, you can figure anyhow on 20% after a sale of 25,000,- and the sale must actually have reached 60,000. It is bearly short of that on the royalty card.

. . . . .

Always yours,

*ALS, 4 pp.*[2]
*Paris, France*

—December 15—

Dear Max:—

Your letter of Dec 8 came yesterday and 2 others written Nov. 30 and Dec 4 came today—Also day before yesterday the wire about letter coming revising contract and sale. The sale is certainly damned fine. There was no hurry about any revision and no need to do it if it did not seem the thing to you.

I must certainly apologize—I think I have already—for having written that time after Scott got me alarmed about the sale stopping. But came home from Berlin feeling fine and found Scott had been here with some alarm. I went over to see him and he showed me a something you had written about the book going well and the only thing to watch was the market slump—I thought there was nothing alarming in what you had written but he knows so much more about the financial side of writing than I do that I imagined, he did not show me the whole letter, but only the part referring to the book that there was some contingencies I did not know about. Also he seemed so

---

[1] 320 words have been omitted from this letter.
[2] 146 words have been omitted from this letter.

alarmed. Am damned fond of Scott and would do anything for him but he's been a little trying lately. He came over the other day, a little tight, and said "People ought to let you alone. They ought to let you work and not worry you." And then proceeded to tell me the Goddamnedest stories about myself that I've ever heard. He has my interests at heart and wants only to help me but really I have been out in the world making a living for a long time—ordinarily get on with people have been familiar with slander, jealousy etc. although do not believe it exists as much as people make out and would prefer to ignore things—if they're not true they always die out. But when things are brought to your attention they make you sore as hell. Scott is working hard and well and I know he will be fine when he finally gets his book done.

. . . . .

If you are to worry about how you will go down in literary history I will have to write you a series of letters telling you what I really think of you— Am no good at that but will do it to remove any such idea from your head—

But the Xian Science business <u>was</u> something to worry over I can see.[1] Though I dont think <u>they</u> will make any trouble for A Farewell—They arent smart—They are simply wonderfully organized—If they were more intelligent they wouldnt be Xstian Scientists maybe. Anyway I hope you have luck with the book—The next 2 times that you would in your plans devote a large space to A Farewell please use 1/2 the space and the other 1/2 for the Eddy Book—I would be damned pleased if you would—

When I wrote you, angry about McAlmon and Calloghan it was only personal anger. I can and will handle my personal business with them (only hope I wont have to do any time in jail for making it thorough) but I do not want you to think I am against them as writers—I want them to succeed and would do nothing to hurt them as writers—altho it is dangerous when you have an enemy to do anything but kill him—and that's too expensive a luxury—

Wister is damned nice but all wrong though. Still there is this great thing about him—he does, personally, seem to belong to the same generation as we do—I mean you, me, Mike Strater, Waldo—for instance—All people of quite different ages—He has written about 3 or 4 damned fine stories—A Gift Horse—Pilgrim on the Gila part of The Honorable The Strawberries— How writing those he could write such a thing as Philosophy Four I don't know. Have just read that for the first time and feel ashamed even to read it—We all write shit but something should prevent you from publishing it or

---

[1]The Christian Science matter and the preceding reference to MP's place in literary history appear to be responses to a lost MP letter; MP reported to Owen Wister in a 17 October 1929 letter that the firm was "having quite a hot time with the Christian Scientists" because Scribners had published Fraden Dakin's *Mrs. Eddy: The Biography of a Virginal Mind* (1929).

at least re-publishing it—But I am very fond of him—If he wants to think of me as a "projection" there's no harm in it so long as he doesnt try to influence—He could have been a very great writer and the combination of circumstances that prevent that are always tragic—

. . . . .

. . . . .

. . . The idea that a writer can write a book then become a business man,—then a writer again is all —— as we say. It's hard enough to write—and writing prose is a full time job and all the best of it is done in your subconscious and when that is full of business, reviews, opinions etc you don't get a damned thing—

Speaking of all such worries the only fear I've ever had about the book was some Italian action to stop it—That may be cuckoo—But how would it be to run in the front matter the statement I wrote that was published in magazine when the first number of A Farewell appeared?[1] That seems to cover all aspects—The only thing I dont like is that people might think I was trying to compare myself with Shakespeare by making the crack about the Two Gentlemen of Verona—This only to run if you think so—

Must stop—Am trying to write an article on bull fighting as an industry for "Fortune" Archy MacLeish asked me for it—Written in journalese full of statistics. It's a romance of business magazine—There's no romance in the article—They probably wont take it—Am keeping it as dull as possible[2]—Every aspect I touch on if I could go on and write about would make a long chapter in a book—They wanted something between 5,000 and 20,000 words and I told them it would cost $2600—So they want something over 2500 words for $1000.00 instead. Their magazine came out just at the time of the crash which was hard luck—But if ever a magazine sounded like useless balls this one does—Am doing it for Archy—how he got mixed up with them God knows—

. . . . .

Ernest

. . . . .

[*Around right, top, and left margin of page four*] The book has stirred up a hell of a business in England. V. Sackville West broadcasted about it for the official British Broadcasting and the head of the B.B.C. raised hell and she, Waldpole etc replied—It's had much better reviews in England than U.S. Damned funny—I want to get to Key West and away from it all—Have never been as damn sick of anything as mention of this book—People write swell letters about it and I am so sick of it that a fine letter only makes you embarrassed and uneasy and vaguely sick.

[1]Scribners included a disclaimer in only the second printing of *FTA* (printed September 1929): "None of the characters in this book is a living person, nor are the units or military organizations mentioned actual units or organizations. E. H."
[2]"Bullfighting, Sport and Industry," *Fortune* 1 (March 1930): 83–88, 139–146, 150.

*CC, 2 pp.*

December 26, 1929

Dear Ernest:

I am only answering part of your letter.—The MacAlmon part. If he is talking on the line you tell me about I guess he knew it wouldn't interest me. I haven't hit anybody since I was fourteen so I don't believe I would have done that, but I would somehow have shut off that line of talk. I will tell you actually how he talked.—The way the once brilliant newspaper reporter, no longer young, talks about one who has become a brilliant correspondent, implying that he is a darn sight the better of the two and that, in fact, the other one learned about writing from him. It was just a case of rather malicious envy. He also belittles Scott as a writer and a number of other persons and of course it meant less to me than nothing at all. Its origin was only too obvious and only made me feel sorry, particularly as I like the rascal. And he has something too, but he is terribly stubborn and he has this idea of his importance as a writer. I am only writing this in a great hurry but I will write you at length very soon.

With remembrances to Pauline,
Ever yours,

*CC, 5 pp.*[1]

Dec. 27, 1929

Dear Ernest:

. . . . .

The only reason I spoke to Scott at all about McAlmon was that you sent him over here and wrote me a letter all about him,- and all presumably to help him. It was only on that account that his talk as I told it to you in a letter yesterday, impressed me. People like that are always depreciating other people, and it was only because you had played the friend to him that it seemed worth any comment. And I am sorry I said a word about it, for it had no significance of any kind in reality. Of course, he is not what you would want a man to be, by a considerable sight, but everyone who knows him knows that, I suppose.

When Callaghan got back here, I was having lunch with him. Bunny Wilson had told me the story you speak of, and it had seemed very improbable, and I said, "How about this story of you and Hemingway having a boxing bout?" and then he told me in an altogether decent way about how you asked him what he wanted to do, and mentioned boxing among other things, and how he, who had done a lot of it since he knew you, had said he was for that.- Then he gave an account of how you boxed, and the way Scott kept time. There was nothing about anyone getting knocked out or anything of the kind, but he only did so with pride, but not bragging that he had been

---

[1]201 words have been omitted from this letter.

able to hold you off through this heart-breaking round. He told me how he did not think he could last through the round, and could not imagine why it held out so long until he caught a glimpse of Scott out of the corner of his eye, apparently not taking any interest in his watch at all, or in the bout. This story was disseminated, as she admits, by Caroline Bancroft, of the Denver Post. She has admitted this and has corrected it so far as is possible. Scott wrote Callaghan about it, and so I sent Scott Callaghan's letter about it, and the statement he sent the Tribune which was printed.

. . . . .
. . . . .

Ever yours,

. . . . .

# HEMINGWAY/PERKINS CHRONOLOGY
## 1930–1935

◆

| | |
|---|---|
| 16 January 1930 | Hemingway is in New York and meets with Perkins. |
| 15–30 March 1930 | Perkins visits Key West; fishing group stranded on Dry Tortugas by storm. |
| August 1930 | *Scribner's Magazine* publishes "Wine of Wyoming." |
| 24 October 1930 | Scribners republishes *In Our Time*. |
| 1–c.10 March 1931 | Perkins visits Key West for another fishing trip; group is stranded on Dry Tortugas by engine trouble. |
| c. 5 October 1931 | Hemingway is in New York; he gives Perkins the photographs for *Death in the Afternoon*. |
| c. mid-January 1932 | Hemingway goes to New York to discuss business with Scribners. |
| 23 September 1932 | Scribners publishes *Death in the Afternoon*. |
| 16–21 December 1932 | Perkins and Hemingway hunt ducks in Watson, Arkansas. |
| c. 7–20 January 1933 | Hemingway is in New York; Perkins introduces him to Thomas Wolfe. |
| March 1933 | *Scribner's Magazine* publishes "A Clean, Well-Lighted Place." |
| April 1933 | *Scribner's Magazine* publishes "Homage to Switzerland." |
| May 1933 | *Scribner's Magazine* publishes "Give Us a Prescription, Doctor." |
| 27 October 1933 | Scribners publishes *Winner Take Nothing*, Hemingway's third story collection. |
| 10 December 1933 | The Hemingways arrive in Nairobi and begin a safari on 20 December. |

c. 2 April 1934 — Hemingway is in New York.

12 April 1934 — Scribners publishes Fitzgerald's fourth novel, *Tender Is the Night*.

23 January 1935 — Perkins and his wife, Louise, come to Key West so that he can read *Green Hills of Africa* and discuss publication plans.

8 March 1935 — Scribners publishes Wolfe's second novel, *Of Time and the River;* the novel is dedicated to Perkins.

May 1935 — *Scribner's Magazine* begins serializing *Green Hills of Africa.*

24 September– c. 25 October 1935 — Hemingway attends the Joe Louis–Max Baer fight in New York; he is in and out of the city during this period.

25 October 1935 — Scribners publishes *Green Hills of Africa.*

—R.W.T.

597 Fifth Avenue.

*ASL, Compagnie Générale Transatlantique stationery, 1 p.*

Thanks for fine wire

<u>Jan 10</u>

Dear Max—

Just a note to tell you got your cable and your letter of Dec 27 about Calloghan etc.—Pauline mailed by mistake a letter I'd written Calloghan and then, on Scott's more or less insistance decided better not send—

It was sent care Scribners—in my handwriting in a brown envelope—Will you hold it for me—I've just cabled you to this effect

In haste    Thanks    Ernest

*ALS, 2 pp.*[1]

*Key West, Florida*

*[c. 11 April 1930]*

Dear Max:—

  . . . . .

  . . . . .

  . . . . .

I would like very much to have the letters—Will you please send them to me?[2] I got out the 1st number of his magazine for him when he got hemmorages and had to leave Paris—Did him many favors—Was bitched by him in true Irish fashion—He wrote the attack on The Torrents in the New Masses—The Cheapest Book I Ever Read—After I'd told him I couldnt let him serialize it in This Quarter—Anyway I would like to have the letters— If you cannot sell the 3 Stories and 10 Poems for £ 35 I will pay you the difference between what you paid and what you sell—I do not believe the letters are shameful but they are probably libelous Send them to me without reading them and if I read them think they wd amuse you will send them to you—Walsh got up a prize The This Quarter Award of $2000.00 to be given to the Contributor who printed the best stuff in his Mag. He promised the award to Joyce, to Pound, and to me I found later. He got swell things from all of us on strength of his promise! I have his letter promising it to me—I'd like to keep my letters to him—But there must be more than 6— damn it—and will publish them and his some time when we're all broke—

  . . . . .

Yours always—<br>Ernest—

[1]190 words have been omitted from this letter.

[2]On 8 April 1930, MP informed EH that the Scribners Rare Book Department had acquired his letters to Ernest Walsh from the English dealer Elkin Mathews; see *Selected Letters,* ed. Carlos Baker (New York: Scribners, 1981), pp. 144–145, 152–153, 165, 169–171, 186–190, 192. EH wrote about Walsh as "The Man Who Was Marked for Death" in *MF.*

Ask them to buy any other letters from me to Walsh that come up for sale—
I'll trade you something else for them or write you some letters—

. . . . .

*CC, 4 pp.*[1]

Aug. 1, 1930

Dear Ernest:

. . . . .

. . . . .

"In Our Time" is certainly your book, and not mine, so make it exactly as
you please,- I will admit that in most of the arguments between us, you have
turned out to be right, but sometime, in some way, the original "In Our
Time" pieces ought to be printed consecutively, so that they could be read in
that way. I agree that the big thing is that you should go on writing while it
goes well, and anyhow that the important book is the one that is not done.-
Still, we ought to get out "In Our Time" not later than October, so if it comes
in right, get it fixed the way you want.

. . . . .

. . . . .

I'll tell you, Ernest, I think Scott is in a bad way, on account of Zelda. She
has evidently been desperately sick, and I infer on the edge of insanity,- if not
beyond it. In very recent and brief letter, he says, "Zelda is still sick as Hell"
and he speaks of himself as "somewhat harrassed and anxious about life." I
wouldn't quote these phrases to anyone else but you, but you ought to know
about it. He does not like to admit—at least to me—that he is worried, and
when he does, there is no doubt of it. I sometimes even think of going over
there,- but I never could do anything with him anyhow,- and anyhow, what's
to be done? Of course he can't work in these circumstances. I shall certainly
give him your messages, anyway.

                    Remembrances to Pauline.
                    Always yours,

*ALS, 3 pp.*
*Cooke City, Montana*

August 12—

Dear Max:—

Have gone over the IO.T. also The Up In Michigan. I've rewritten it to try
and keep it from being libelous but to do so takes all its character away. It
clearly refers to two people in a given town, both of them still alive, still liv-

[1]330 words have been omitted from this letter.

ing there and easily identified—If I take the town away it loses veracity—But I <u>can</u> leave out enough of the first part to eliminate libel. However I <u>know</u> you will not publish it with the last part entire and if <u>any</u> of that is cut out there is no story.[1]

I do not feel much like getting into a libel action or being suppressed now for the skin of a dead horse. The Farewell was worth making a fight on and I was willing to make it and take whatever came but this is an old story, one of the first I ever wrote, and I've published it once as I wrote it and do not feel like stirring up trouble with it now when I'm working.

What I would suggest is that you get Edmund Wilson, if he is willing, to write an introduction to the In Our Time. He is, of all critics or people, the one who has understood best what I am working at and I know an introduction by him would be of much value to the book as you are getting it out now. As I understand it you are getting it out somewhat as a new book i.e. you want new material from me and it is not fair to do this without explanation since it is <u>not</u> new but my first and earliest book. I'll be damned if I will write a preface but Wilson, if he would, could write what it would need as an introduction. If he wouldnt care to it would be better to have none—Allen Tate might write one. He is a good critic but Wilson knows my stuff very well and writes so damned well and it would be a shame not to have him do it if he were willing.[2]

Please let me know what you think of this—

I know I am not going in for putting out books because there should be something from me on the Scribners list—The In Our Time is, I really believe, a hell of a good book The stories, when I read them now, are as good as ever. and worth any ones two dollars but I am not going to jazz it up with any things of another period and try to make it sell as a new book—If you could publish the Up In Michigan without any trouble O.K. But show it to anyone and ask them. I'd like to have it published so people could see Morley's source book but its not worth getting into trouble over when I am still able to write and am writing—What it needs The In Our Time is a good introduction—What you are doing is making it really available for the first time to the people who have read the other books—I am too busy, too disinterested, too proud or too stupid or whatever you want to call it to write one for it. If you can get Wilson to it would be excellent—He is a damned fine critic of prose and he writes well—I believe that is the way it should be pub-

---

[1]In a copy of *Three Stories and Ten Poems* (Paris: Contact Editions, 1923), now in the Cohn Hemingway Collection at the University of Delaware, EH changed "Liv Coates" *to* "Mary Coates," "D.J. Smith" *to* "F.E. Smith," and "Jim Gilmore" *to* "Jim Dutton." He also deleted the sentence "Her breasts felt plump and firm and the nipples were erect under his hands" and emended "She felt Jim right through the back of the chair and she couldn't stand it and then something clicked inside of her and the feeling was warmer and softer" *to* "She couldn't stand it. She knew she couldn't stand it." The characters were identifiable people in Horton's Bay, Michigan. The story was not included in the 1930 *IOT*.

[2]Wilson provided an introduction for the book.

lished—My 1st book, now made generally available with an introduction by Wilson.

Anyway I will return the book to you with a few corrections, the original Mr. and Mrs. Elliott,[1] and with or without a couple of short pieces of the same period depending on how these seem in the book between now and then—Not later than the 1st week in September.

However we had better figure out a formula to put in the front about no living persons which wd absolutely prevent libel as there are three people who might if they were in desperate enough straits and the book suffcently prominent try a libel action. The reason most of the book seems so true is because most of it is true and I had no skill then, nor have much now, at changing names and circumstances. Regret this very much.

Am going well on the new book—Have something over 40,000 words done—Have worked well 6 days of every week since got here. Have 6 more cases of beer good for 6 more chapters—If I put in an expense account in this bull fight book it would be something for the Accounting Dept to study.

The check's came and your letter with them—Thanks ever so much— Also for the telegram about G. and D. jacket—I hated like hell to bother you about that—You have enough to worry about without Grossett and Dunlop. I'm so sorry to hear bad news of Scott—Please let me know what you hear and let me know <u>anything</u> you think of that I can do. I'd go over if you think it would do any good—

Best to you always—Please if I speak rudely in letters never take it personally—I'm working damned hard and a letter about some bloody problem or other is only a damned Interuption and Curse. Dont let me get on your nerves—We'll have a good time in March at Tortugas!

Yours always<br>
<u>Ernest</u>

ALS, 2 pp.[2]<br>
Cooke City, Montana

Sept 3

Dear Max:—

. . . Pauline is typing now on the Mr. and Mrs. Elliott and I'll send the book to you tomorrow if possible. Dont see how I can coscientiously put anything else in—have tried all day yesterday and this morning—Will try again this aft—

---

[1] The story was bowdlerized in the Boni & Liveright *IOT.* The Scribners edition reprinted the original version from *The Little Review* 10 (Autumn–Winter 1924–25): 9–12.

[2] 24 words have been omitted from this letter.

Later—Have been working all day on it—The Smyrna chapter can go as an Introduction by The Author—To follow Wilson's introduction. It goes pretty well that way. The original Mr. and Mrs Elliot is enclosed—I hope you could get Bunny to write the introduction—

Now we must get this straight—The book has been out 5 years and I've had no trouble about it but, also, it has had only a limited circulation so anyone tempted to make trouble might not have seen it nor thought it worth while to do so.

It is not worth while for me to now run any danger of trouble, Censorship or libel—I'd as sooner let the book go out of print—Its done its work and when Im dead they can always revive it if they want—or it can come out in my collected works—

So if you bring it out now you bring it out at your own risk. If you change the Elliot you change it at your own risk—You had better put a iron clad protective notice in the front that there are no actual characters and that the names are not those of any living people—You work out the wording and be responsible for it—

I'm on page 174 of this book I'm writing and have had it knocked out of my head for two days working on this In Our Time again and I've no interest in publishing it now, will take no risks and give no guarantees against libels nor slanders. All I'll guaranty is that Mr. and Mrs Elliots name was not Elliot nor anything like it[1]—But half the other characters in the book have their real christian names although there are no other last names or real last names used and I have fixed up the name in A Very Short Story.[2] So you had best be thoroughly covered.

It is all skinning dead horses to me.

You have seen me worried about possibility of libel and slander in past and nothing has ever happened so it may be all nonsense again But the above is how I feel about it. I'd rather write this book than get out anything—It is you that want to get the book out—Last Spring I came to N.Y to work and not see any one and instead just ran around doing business with one jew and another—

I <u>have</u> to stick at one thing when I'm writing a book and keep that in my head and nothing else and when I get to worrying and thinking and trying to fix up the old book it gets into my subconsious and buggars up everything—The Example of Scott ought to be evidence enough that a man has to stay in a book in his head until its finished——. I dont want excuses for not finishing my present book—<u>I want to write it</u>

Anyway am through with it now and I send the book to you with corrections, the Elliott Mss. and an Introduction By The Author to come after Wilsons Introduction but not to be mentioned on jacket nor in advertising but simply

[1]Mr. Elliot was based on the American poet Chard Powers Smith—not on T. S. Eliot.
[2]EH changed the nurse's name from "Ag" to "Luz," as well as the setting from Milan to Padua, to avoid a possible suit from Agnes Von Kurowsky, the nurse he had expected to

The last page of Hemingway's 3 September 1930 letter, showing
the problems of transcribing his holograph correspondence.

to be included in the book. You can advertise it as "new material" if you like. I've other stories but I've tried them—They break up the book, destroy the unity and being of a different period stand out in a way they shouldnt—

Best to you always—

Yours in haste—

Ernest

The real reason I wanted to get the book from Liverights for you was so you would have it if you ever wanted to bring out my collected works—A certain number of people are bound to buy whatever book I bring out after the sale of A Farewell—If that sale is pee-ed away in this getting out of In Our Time then the bull fight book will have to start from scratch again—Young Thornton harmed the sale of his book <u>enormously</u> be getting out that collection of 1 act masterpieces But then neither the book nor the masterpieces were much account anyway. Correct me in this if I am wrong—But I believe <u>any</u> attempt to bring this out as a new book or as anything new from me in anyway will be altogether harmful That's why the Wilson introduction is necessary—to make it clear this is an old book and what sort of an old book! Most people are dont follow the production of litrachoor as we do any any new book out is a new book. But this is really a <u>damned good book</u> and if they dont buy it under false pretences they'll get their 2 dollars worth—May be 2 and a half.

[*In margins of page one*] <u>Later in the evening</u>

My God Max I seem to write you the lousiest letters—But if I rewrite this and make it as decent as I wish it would sound it will take all tomorrow and the last mail for a week goes at breakfast—

Pauline sends her best and says pay no attention to me. I'm all smashed up from an accident it would take too long to write about—Have 6 inch gash in my jaw—But never healthier or in better shape in my life—Killed 2 big bear May take time to get the book out—what the hell do I know. I just re-read it and it's a damned fine book—Especially The Battler—Cat In The Rain—Out of Season and the first couple of stories—Those three I couldnt write any better now.

*CC, 4 pp.*[1]

Oct. 14, 1930

Dear Ernest:

What you tell about the bear and the sheep and the mountain and the wind, certainly sounds magnificent. It is what a man ought to be doing too, instead of sitting in a chair all day and watching the ever declining stock market quotations.- But I feel that you would be safer in Key West.

. . . . .

. . . . .

I do not know exactly what to do about Ford Maddox Ford. I have always

---

[1]112 words have been omitted from this letter.

liked him since a casual meeting, and I liked those three novels that were concerned with the war, a good deal. But in the first place, I daresay he is a man with an eye to a big advance, and it is always difficult too, to take on an older writer who has been all about and has become exacting, and who having changed so often, will probably change again. The great interest in publishing is to take on an author at the start, or reasonably near it, and then to publish not this book and that, but the whole author. It is not only more interesting, but it is sounder because your investment is in his whole output, and not in individual books. You can afford to lose on certain ones because of the gains you make on others.

My objection to the introduction[1] disappeared anyhow when I showed it to Edmund Wilson. I simply had an uneasy feeling which it is difficult fully to explain, that it might upset him in this way:- it is not, conventionally speaking, an introduction, and his introduction will presumably be one conventionally speaking. So he writes this introduction and then there comes an introduction by the author which disregards all rules, so to speak, and in that way might be thought, I feared, to say, "to Hell with introductions". The reason it ought not to do that is that it is so moving and genuine in itself that it ought not to arouse any after-thoughts of that kind. I did not think it would in other people, but Bunny is very sensitive, and he had already got a little cold-footed about doing his own introduction for fear he would say something you would not like—which I told him was bunk—and so I was very sensitive to any conceivable danger. But it is all right, and I am sorry I worried you about it.

Now I am simply asking you: if the bull fight book cannot be published until the fall of 1931 on account of the pictures, do you think it would be well—as it certainly would be for the Magazine—to publish certain pieces of it in the Magazine. You might think this would be a good thing. The question is only whether the pieces would suffer by being taken out of the book, or would give a wrong idea of the book if printed in advance of it.

Always yours,

P.S. John Bishop confirms the reports that Zelda is well again and that things look better for Scott. He plans to be back in this country before Christmas

ALS, dictated by EH to Pauline Hemingway, 5 pp.<br>Billings, Montana

Dec. 1—

Dear Max

The Enclosed introduction you can show to Wilson if you want, at the same time letting him see this letter. I have only the one complaint—that he

---

[1]MP is referring to "On the Quai at Smyrna," retitled as "Introduction by the Author" in the 1930 Scribners edition of *IOT*.

should have said "we cease to believe in them as real people" be cause I believe that is exceeding his authority since it is not an editorial [ ] he has a perfect right to say whatever he wants, and you know that. I've not ask to see what he wrote, or have anything to do with it. There has never been a word written in criticism or explanation of Miss Gertrude Stein's, or Mr James Joyce's work which was not a reflection or a derivation of something explained by Miss Stein or Mr Joyce to some critic in conversation. All interpretation of what they have done, explanations and glorifications, have originated with the writers themselves. This does not detract from the value of their work per se but it is some thing which would make the practice of letters unbearable to me. I do not explain because of some noble virtue you see in myself nor [ ] the friendship of critics but only because to do so would make writing not worth doing and all together disgusting. Writing is made to be read; the writer should keep out of it. If he explains something into it which is not there, it will only lose in the End. Shaw is an example of the explaining montabank who will be ridiculous within his own lifetime.

I hope you will tell Wilson that he is the only critic for whose writing I have any respect, but that I believe he is some times as wrong as when he claimed that Pound derived from Elliot, and when he speaks seriosously of Dorothy Parker who is also a friend of mine, and of Edna Millay as poets. If he were always right he would have been snatched to heaven in a chariot of fire long ago, but in the meantime reading him whenever I have the oportunity he seems nearly always right. If I disagree with him about the "romantic" ending of "A Farewell to Arms" it does not mean that I think him an ass, but that possibly I've seen more people die than he has and that we differ in our attitude toward the pleasure of sexual intercourse.

Something—this for your own information—has been wrong with the main nerve in my arm and I have been having hell with it for four weeks.[1] The only thing that I've discovered about pain—the subject Wilson says I'm so interested in—is that I cannot stand it as I could in my Twenties. I was all right for three weeks and then it got to me. I dont know whether this discovery is worth the field work I've put into it—I would like to ask one favor though of Scribner's and that is if I should ever be bumped off in any of these various affairs, that you would not as a good business venture have either Morley Callaghan or W. R. Burnett[2] write my biography—This last is a joke. In case I do not make any jokes clear, lay it to the fact of an unfamiliarity with dictation.

I am not in the least angry at Wilson who has a right to put in any thing he wants, but it gives me a pain to think of the wires I had to send because you feared I might hurt Wilson's feelings by calling my introduction an introduction and the fact that you thought I would feel fine to hear some one in my own book make me out a faking romanticist. Well, this seems to be all.

---

[1]EH's right arm was broken when he wrecked the car in which he, John Dos Passos, and Floyd Allington were riding outside of Billings, Montana, on 1 November 1930.
[2]W. R. Burnett (1899–1982), author of *Little Caesar* (1929).

Yours always,
Ernest
Per P.H.

P.S. You know that the only reason I asked for an introduction was not for any self glorification, but simply that it might be more clear to people buying the book that this was a re-issue of an old book and not a new book. I told you why I wanted an introduction at the time and I hope you explained this to Wilson.

E.

Dear Max—

This is the voice as well as the pen of Pauline. Ernest is really in pretty bad shape, after pain all the time for a month, and not sleeping nights. He's had nothing to do but think, always lying in the same position, and he's pretty nervous and depressed from the pain and worry. The numbness in the elbow and the paralysis in the wrist still persist, but the doctor expects this to be cleared up when the splint is taken off and the position of the arm changed. Today Ernest sat up for the first time, and tomorrow he will get up again, and we may leave a week from today, the 8th, but of course we may not, too. Thank you for sending all the books and papers. They have been a great help. Poor Ernest, its very sad to see him lying here so long. I wish you'd write him when you can. The mail's about the only thing that breaks the monotony.

*Wire, 1 p.*
*Billings, Montana*

1930 DEC 8 PM 5 01

DEAR MAX IGNORE MY LETTER ABOUT INTRODUCTION SORRY I EVER NOTICED IT THINGS NOT SO GOOD HERE SO PLEASE CONTINUE NEWSPAPER SUBSCRIPTION=
ERNEST.

*CC, 3 pp.*

Feb. 11, 1931

Dear Ernest:

You can count on the five thousand when you want it.

I am hoping to come, but the annual stockholders meeting is not until the tenth of March, and as things are now, it seems as if I ought to go to that.- I am Secy, you know. Who would read the minutes? But for Heaven's sake don't change your plans. I would be happy enough even if we did not get to the Tortugas,- even if we did the way we did the year before, and had John along, and saw the others. Maybe I shall be able to change later, but it does not look so.- You had better tell me what your plans are, and I shall fit them in so as not to overlap your trip to the Tortugas if you go on the first.

I should think that sailfish of Pauline's might be a record. Ever since I became a champion I have been ordering king fish whenever I saw it on a bill of fare, but it was always the wrong kind of a king fish.- Not my kind.- Anyway it did not taste the way it did when John cooked it.

I do not know whether you like that sort of a book, but one called, "Wilson the Unknown" is a very brilliant piece of that sort of writing.[1] His theory is inadequately supported by evidence, but it is mighty interesting,- the way a super detective story might be.

Scott's father died, and that brought him home. I saw him for about fifteen minutes. He is very greatly changed. He looks older, but it is more that he has lost, at least temporarily, all of the elam that was so characteristic. But he may be all the better for it because you feel that at bottom he is a very real person now. Zelda is in mighty bad shape. Scott's going back this week or next, and apparently he is not seeing anybody. He is to let me know when he goes through New York. He has been making lots of money on his stories though, more than ever before; but it must have been a terribly hard thing to write them under the conditions.

Always yours,

ALS, 9 pp.[2]<br>Key West, Florida

Monday April 27—

Dear Max:—

. . . . .

. . . . .

About business—

The February royalty report shows

2192.59 due me (I dont know exactly when) and me owing you $6500 which I borrowed as an advance on this next book—If you are willing to let that stand as advance on the book—(It does not seem exhorbitant to me but that is a matter for you to decide) If it does please say so and I'll borrow from the bank and pay it back to you. Will you please deposit $1,000.00 of the Royalty due in my account City Bank Farmers Branch, 43 Exchange Place, N.Y.C. on receipt of this and I will only call on you for the balance when and as I need it.

About the Cerf and Grosset business.[3] Since the putting of a book in these

---

[1] Wells Wells [pseud.], *Wilson the Unknown* (New York: Scribners, 1931).

[2] 270 words have been omitted from this letter.

[3] Bennett Cerf was co-owner of the Modern Library; Grosset and Dunlap published inexpensive hardback reprints. Both firms reprinted *FTA* in 1932.

reprints amounts, as much as I can gather from looking at the royalty figures, to saying good bye to all further income from its sale for an outright cash payment, at least for some time possibly, sure there is no check up on their honesty, forever, I know nothing about that—They may be honest—I do not want to do this unless the payment is considerable. Nor can I afford to.

5000 G and D must be sold to bring in the same royalty as 1000 regular copies—Maybe 10,000—(Later—it amounts to about 7,000).

The Cerf business does not wipe out the ordinary sale as completely as the G and D does—Because it is a different format for one thing—Also I like the Modern Library and do not give a damn about G and D. Some are novels of distinction and some merely stink—In the whole lot there are only 6 truly 1st rate ones—

In any event if the regular sale of the book is to be wiped out after such a short time I do not think it should be done without having both Cerf and G and D. take editions. Of course G and D. have the favor of the business end since if the publishers make a concession to them on one book G and D. will reciprocate on another book. While Cerf takes only good books (or what are supposed to be) Some of them aren't. so is not in a position to be of as much use. For myself I dont want to have it go to G and D. without assurance that Cerf will also take an edition. Dont you think this is correct? G and D. want it because it is going to be in the moom pictures—If they want it let them pay first—of course they are taking a good big edition as it is

Write this so you will know my standpoint as I might be on the water or difficult to come at by letter when you were deciding this.

Also I'll find and sign the In Our Time contract and send it to you—

Can't think of any more business

When I was first in this racket, and steadily until it has been proved to me that it is not that way, I thought that if I could write good books which were true and would last they would all sell a certain amount each year say $363 apiece on an average and when I had 7 of them written say and was 50 with my life work done and inside them they would if they had turned out to be good and had lasted, bring me in, say 2541.00 a year which with what I had been able to save during any times they had made money would be fine But instead you find, or rather I've found so far, that a book of stories is sold out piecemeal for the original $40 it brings from the anthology and the 40¢ a year thereafter until it has lost its cohesion and its capital is all disbursed. That a novel exists only for a few months and that what you get from it is entirely dependant on how violently it is pushed during those months and principally how long the push is kept up. And the chances are that when you are fifty if you should have written 7 good books your income from them will probably be about $300 a year—if that—and that if you do not save the chunks of capital that come into your hands—they will be giving benefits for you—It may be that the economic salvation of the aged writer is the collected works racket about which I know nothing yet—Anyway I'm not worrying. But you see why I want the best terms possible in the disposal of my capital to Messers Grosset and Cerf—Because I am not in the writing business with one to sell each year. I am not crabbing about the above—I have made more money already than a writer deserves to make or that is good for him—But have been protected from this by not getting most of it—

As for the Communism that everybody is so spooked about—What the hell? If we are all broke it is all right—If we dont like it we can get out of the country—If we hate it enough we can fight it and die—But I'll tell you something; we wont have it. We are the most cowardly people in the world. Let business be a little bad and everyone is spooked about communism. Personally I dont like it as a regime to live under. But if you dont like it you can get out—The trouble in the world is over population—plagues and wars will handle that—If you have studied the history of communism you will note that no country has ever had a Commune without first being defeated in a war—You need that to break down "sales resistance"—We will have no communistic govt here until after a military defeat—Such a defeat would be the greatest thing that could ever happen to us—

But at the Dry Tortugas[1] Max you gave me such confidence in the inherent military genius of America that I feel we would never fear this defeat—So you neednt think about the fate of five daughters under Communism. First we must have the war, then the defeat—You can argue that a sufficient economic defeat might do instead. You would have a point—But I dont think it would be enough—

Now about the Story for August—

I would have sent you one before but have not published anything for sometime and it is best not to publish anyth [  ] after a long absence.

[*Rest of page four torn off and missing*]

[*On the back of page four*] This is some valueless pooping on financial aspects of the literary life and some sage observations on Communism which I tore out to go on with the letter when your Grosset and Dunlop letter came and then thought you might be amused by—

Have just received yours of April 25—

Note that 75,000 of Grosset and Dunlop will bring in to me the same as about 9000 sale of the regular edition—

I would not expect Cerf to match their offer of number of copies guaranteed—But believe would be much better off if they each took 50,000—Cerf to publish without an introduction—To hell with introductions. Though I read Bunnys over and it was fair enough. Or get Cerf to take 25,000 later if that is the best they will do—I dont think the number means much except as size of advance—Why cant they publish simultaneously?

Well I will do what you say to do—But have put down my viewpoint to guide you—or anyway to acquaint you it—

About the story for August—

---

[1]MP went to Key West to fish with EH from 1 to 13 March; they had waited out a storm on one of the Dry Tortugas islands.

The only two stories I have that are in shape to publish with out re-writing (which would hold up work on my book on which I am going well)—(There is a lot of going over on the Standard Oil Man one)[1]—are

A Natural History of the Dead—

*[Bottom of page six torn off and missing]*

You read this one upstairs and you know whether the magazine will publish it or not—Black Sun Press[2] in Paris have offered $1500 for it but I dont want to sign any limited editions—That is a lousy racket—Will probably save it for in the B.F. book anyway.

A Sea Change—This is a damned good story—Would be better in a book though—However since I promised one you can have it. But publishing it is against my judgement—

I could try to write one in Madrid—or on the boat—once wrote 3 there in 2 days in Madrid including The Killers, Today is Friday and I forget the other—Started a hell of a good one here and stopped it because I thought it was a mistake to write any thing but on this book until it is finished—How late could you have one and still publish it in August? Whats the matter with Callaghan and the rest of your jackals? Cant they crack a few old bones up for the August number? Or get Mr. Thomas Wolfe to kill for you. He's no jackal. He really kills by himself. I'll bet he'll write swell books for you.

Anytime I dont write a book for over a year you get a Faux-Hemingway complete with mis-spelled words, mustache, inability to punctuate, naive rythms and all the visible faults of the original carefully photo-stated. The only trouble with them is that they're lousy. You ought to have more confidence in me, Max, and spend that money some other way.

Am not pooping on Caldwell[3]—Just read him. He seems very honest. Glad you're publishing him.

. . . . .

. . . . .

. . . . .

. . . . .

. . . . .

The only part of this letter you have to answer or read even is that about the reprint business—and give me a late report on Cap. Cohn—[4]

Best luck to you—

Ernest—

. . . . .

Max if I ever sound rude in a letter please forgive it. I am naturally a rude

[1] "Death of the Standard Oil Man"—an unfinished story.

[2] Imprint founded in 1927 by Harry and Caresse Crosby.

[3] Erskine Caldwell (1903–1987); Scribners published his *American Earth* (1931) and *Tobacco Road* (1932).

[4] Louis Henry Cohn, a New York bookdealer, compiled *A Bibliography of the Works of Ernest Hemingway* (New York: Random House, 1931); Cohn retained his World War I army rank of captain in civilian life.

bastard and the only way know not to be is always to be formally polite. You stopped me doing that when you asked me to un-mister you. So please remember that when I am loud mouthed, bitter, rude, son of a bitching and mistrustful I am really very reasonable and have great confidence and absolute trust in you.

The thing is I get so damned tired of being careful in letters—Christ, here I am starting to loud mouth again—But—anyway goodbye and good luck—
Ernest/

*ALS, 4 pp.*
*Key West, Florida*

Jan 5—
Dear Max—

The reason you have not received the Mss is that the typist sprained his ankle—Playing basketball—Pauline got sick—or rather overdid and had to rest in bed—The nurse has been laid up practically ever since weve been here—I had ulcerated throat. But he has it all typed now and I have been over 1/2 of it and you should have it by 1st part of next week if nothing else comes up—

Write this while staying up all night with Patrick who ate as near as we can figure 1/2 grain of arsenic in form of an Ant Button. Been vomiting etc since 6—its around 11 pm now—Done every thing that can be done—Hope to Christ he comes out all right—Dr says he wont be safe for 60 hours

A great life Max—a great life—But you will get your Mss. Never have any doubts about that—If they should feed me ant buttons you could publish it as it is by having someone check up on spelling and letting MacLeish correct proof—Dos could go over Spanish—If any thing should happen to me by any bad luck get it out with only a few illustrations—No color plates—Give Pauline the money they would cost—Pauline could pick the illustrations and write very short captions—Am sending the glossary and 2 appendices with the Mss—others will follow—

There have been plumbers—roofers—screeners—electricians etc here to drive you bughouse—

Since I started this book have had compound fracture of index finger—bad general smash up in that bear hunt—14 stitches in face inside and out—hole in leg—Then that right arm—musculo spiral paralysis—3 fingers in right hand broken:—16 stitches in left wrist and hand—Eyes went haywire in Spain—With glasses can't do more than about 4 hours before they go bad—

Paulines 2nd Caeserian etc—etc—etc—

Scott on the other hand had his wife go nutty which is much worse—Plenty more worse—

During Sun Also plenty happened while during Farewell to Arrums—outside of Patrick being born only incident was my father shooting himself and me acquiring 4 new dependents and mortgages—Then some shit faced critic writes Mr. Hemingway retires to his comfortable library to write about despair—Is that what I write about? I wonder—

It is blowing like hell outside—From the North-east—First Kings have just come—Mackerel too Charles and I killed 14 big snipe on Sunday—There are a world of cranes this year—Charles and Lorine are fine—Bra too—Burge came drunk on Xmas eve to tell me how he had quit drinking—or did I write you that—

The quail book is Monumental but dull—Eschew the Monumental—Shun the Epic—All the guys who can paint great big pictures can paint great small ones——

So Long Max——
Ernest

Jan 6—9 A M

Stayed up with Pat until 430—He is much better—Should be all right—Just got your wire about Ann Watkins relaying Metro Goldwyn-Meyers receptivity. Please thank Miss Watkins and tell her I have had other offers But that I am very busy at present—Too busy to go to coast at present. Do not consider her wire places me under any obligation to deal through her if I ever went out to whore for M.G.M They have been making offers for a long time. But dont worry—Am not going—only want to keep the record straight—EH

*CC, 1 p.*

Jan. 25, 1932

Dear Ernest:

I read the book all yesterday—Sunday—and after it I felt <u>good.</u> I went to bed happy for it in spite of innumerable troubles (not so bad really, I guess). The book piles upon you wonderfully, and becomes to one reading it—who at first thinks bull fighting only a very small matter—immensely important.

I'll write you about the practical matters. It's silly just to write you that it's a grand book, but it did do me great good to read it. That about America, the corn, is utterly right.[1] And I think of corn as in New Jersey in the winter,- the most unlikely time and place for corn.

Always yours,

[1]The final chapter of *DIA* included a long passage on the peninsula topography of Northern Michigan, Italy, and Spain, with a Wolfeian soliloquy on American corn. This material was deleted by EH in the galley proofs (see his 2 June 1932 letter). Selections have been published by Susan F. Beegel in *Hemingway's Craft of Omission* (Ann Arbor, Mich.: UMI Research Press, 1987), p. 58:

> The simplest thing to test with is a cornfield. Corn in Europe, and in the Bible, means wheat. Corn in America is maize, but we know it as corn and as nothing else. There is no one of us who does not have many and racial reactions to a cornfield. Whether it is memory of the thin fields of New England; corn planted in a clearing in Pennsylvania; crows keeping just out of shotgun range while corn is being planted on a plowed hillside in Michigan; memories of fine stands of corn on new

*CC, 3 pp.*[1]

Feb. 5, 1932

Dear Ernest:

Dashiell's writing you about magazine articles. The question is difficult—
that of selecting—but one thing that influenced it was my desire not just to pick
out the <u>best parts.</u>- For instance, that about "death" has unity, but it's one of
the finest things in the book and I think should be saved. You might argue the
same way about the Peninsular piece—which is magnificent—but that does
make a perfect article even alone. It's a mean business, picking articles out of
a book like this. But from the commercial standpoint, as we call it, it will help
it. In looking it over again, and reading it here and there, it seems immensely
impressive, and it has a wonderful completeness too, although nobody could
map out its organization. It gives the impression of having grown rather than
of having been planned.- And that is the characteristic of a great book.[2]

. . . . .

Yours,

. . . . .

. . . . .

. . . . .

*ALS, 2 pp.*
*Key West, Florida*

Monday Feb 7—
<u>1932</u>

Dear Max:—

Enclosed is a letter which I wish you would read rather carefully and send
on to Dashiell. Am working hard and going damned well so please forgive
not having written this all to you separately.

---

land that has been taken from the forest; corn being hoed in the hot weather (the weeds
cut at the roots by the hoe, its blade worn shiny, and the earth being hoed to a fine dust
around the corn roots); the great tall cornfields of Illinois and Iowa; cutting and shocking corn in the fall; ripe ears of corn thrown into a wagon; shocked corn in a field at
night with the moon on it; hunting through a cornfield with rabbits hidden in the
shocks; the first snow in a cornfield in winter; not to mention corncob pipes, an uncle
who lost a finger in a corn-sheller, the corncob as a joke; cobs around the grist mill;
corn in a silo; corn whiskey in a charred-oak keg (strapped to a horse; a keg on each
side and the charcoal to be strained out before drinking); hundreds and hundreds of
other things about the one word cornfield not to mention the word corn, which you
could fill a book with, that are the subconscious and racial memory of the people who
settled America. It is in this process of use and association that words acquire values.
The unrevised galleys for this chapter are at the Princeton University Library; Hemingway's revised galleys are at the Kennedy Library.

[1]182 words have been omitted from this letter.

[2]*DIA* was not excerpted in *Scribner's Magazine.*

I know Dashiell has had a hard time making up the articles and appreciate his good offices—You know I am not sympathetic toward Dashiell but you know too I would not let that enter into a question of what is best to do about writing—But Max you know truly that while I'm often wrong in personal matters I've always been right about the handling of my own stuff—literarily speaking—and I feel awfully strongly about this—Read the parts (the two chapters—and see if I'm not right—Both need the ends <u>absolutely</u>—Removing the ends ruins them. You can trust me to cut better on the other (the 5 good killers—than anybody can cut for me. I havent just tried to pick out the best—but in each selection you had picked, I have tried to preserve the feel of the book which is the important thing and which Dashiell had eliminated to make an article—I think the end chapter is much better, not published until the book comes out—Don't you on thinking it over? Now the beginning chapter is another matter. It could be published somewhere the same month the book comes out—Say in The Atlantic—And be very good for the book.

As to the prices—You know they are not exaggerated—I mean it truly about if the Magazine is hard up—They can pay the balance when they wish—6 ms. or a year if you want—But I know they are worth much more than what I ask and I want you to have them—Am not chargeing on a basis of what I can get at all—You know that—But it is my capital and my two solid years work I'm selling—

Either the Magazine can pay the rest in a year—or they will be dead from all this publishing 2nd rate stuff and can pay out of what it saves them to not publish at a loss—Would like to keep it alive because of its great usefulness to writers—

Please believe I'm very reasonable in this but know what I'm talking about—

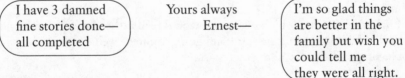

I have 3 damned
fine stories done—
all completed

Yours always
Ernest—

I'm so glad things
are better in the
family but wish you
could tell me
they were all right.

[*In right and left margin and top of page one*] Max:—One thing to remember is that when you buy cheaply the work of people who can sell their stuff for a big price it is because it is usually their 2nd run or odd lot stuff—I have given you the very best stuff I write, always, without offering it elsewhere. E. You know I turned down more for serialization of Farewell than it ever earned—(including movies)

I have not offered or sent a story to any other magazine since I sent you the Fifty Grand—You sold that for me—In the meantime and that includes this year, 1932, have had offers from every big and most small magazines and last price, 1932, offered for stories was $9,000 a story. Cosmopolitan offered 1000; for me to let them read the mss of this bull book with no obligation to me.

*TLS with holograph additions and postscript, 5 pp.*[1]

Key West, Fla.,<br>
April 4th, 1932

Dear Max,

Thank you for sending the proofs of the pictures in offset and the first nineteen galleys. The one of the two bulls looks very good; the others are not bad; fair enough. Really they are quite good—immeasureably better than half tones.

I have something over a hundred pictures necessary to make the book comprehensive; having brought this number down from two hundred to, at present, one hundred and twelve. What was it gave you the idea of suggesting sixteen illustrations for the book after I spent all summer and my own money getting the necessary illustrations and showed them to you in New York and we never discussing on any terms except the use of a great amount of illustrations? I will eliminate the colored frontispiece if you wish, in order to save expense, and have no reproduction of painting in colour although I ordered and paid for the paintings on your authorization, but paid myself and would not suggest you pay because I knew times were hard with you; but the book has to be properly illustrated. The reproductions in offset as you send them, printed flush with the page, will do this splendidly if enough of them are used; but sixteen is a ridiculous amount when I have written in the text that I have not described certain things in detail because photography has been brought to the point where it can represent some things better than a man can write of them, and when I spent the time that I spent ruining my eyes looking at negatives against an artificial light to get the pictures I needed after you had written and spoken about the scale you wanted to do the book on.

I spent a long time on that book, Max, over two years in the [actual] writing and rewriting and plenty of years in getting the material and to hell with getting it out now in a preoccupied with business worries manner and selling it down the river to the Book of the Month Club to get some one a sure seven thousand dollars to cover margins with. It may be that a hundred illustrations is a grotesque and impossible number, impossible to do in "these times," but Max, if you think about the trend in these times, other than their financial trend, you will know the value of pictures and that they will do more for the popularity of the book than any other thing. That is not what I want them for, but I know their value in that way. And I know the captions I can write.

If you read it over you will see that I wrote a pretty reasonable letter about the serialization. If you read it over five years from now you will see how much more reasonable it will seem. Since writing you about it I have not offered it anywhere nor done any negotiating for it. I turned down a thou-

---

[1]85 words have been omitted from this letter.

sand dollars to let Cosmopolitan read it with no option when I was in N.Y. plenty broke and I turned down seven thousand five hundred dollars when Lengel was down here for them to publish some extracts from it. This quite possibly has no value but at least should show you I am serious.

Listen, you have troubles, and they are real troubles, and Scott has bad troubles, and I have had some troubles and if Mr. Thomas Wolfe lives long enough, great writer though he should be, he will have plenty of troubles too but I get my work done in spite of all troubles and when it is done to hell with it being bitched by somebody elses troubles. The first and final thing you have to do in this world is last in it and not be smashed by it and your work the same way.

Now, how much do the offset illustrations cost and what is the limit you can make and stillsell the book at 3.50 with a profit to yourself? I should not put it that way because that gives you an opportunity to say that sixteen is all you can make thank you very much and I can take it or leave it. As you did on the serialization. But Max it is getting a little too serious for that and if there has to be a compromise between sixteen and one hundred that compromise is not sixteen nor is it thirty two. If I have to borrow the money to pay for making the illustrations or take it out of my capital and spend it for that I will do so as I've already paid for getting them. But first would like to know at what price will you have to sell the book to make money for you with sixty offset illustrations? That is the irreducible minimum. It will be no fun for me to publish it with that but I do not care to publish it at all with less. Nor do I want to make it too expensive for people to buy. But what is the difference in sale between a book at 2.50-one at 3.50-one at 4.00 one at 5.00

About the Deluxe edition—the only reason for a deluxe edition outside of snobbery and making money for the writer, publisher and rare book bastards is to have a limited edition for sale by subscription only which contains matter unpublisheable in a trade edition (which is bad for the trade edition since it marks it as emasculated) or which contains reproductions too expensive for the trade edition. If you want to reproduce enough more stuff to make a DeLuxe edition worthwhile it will be all right with me and you can get Captain Cohn to sign it—but just the two paintings by Roberto Domingo (the two gouache) and the Gris in colour in frontispiece won't be enough to make it worth 10 dollars in these times unless you get Dashiell to sign it too. I made the mistake of signing one once. Let Miss Gyzyka sign it. Or whoever has the handwriting in the Marlboro ads The only way I would sign it would be if you would put a statement in that my royalties from the DeLuxe edition are being paid direct to the Committee for the Defence of Political Prisoners

Scott told me what happened to Ring's book that was sold to a book club.

Will do the proofs when I get them all since it is not just correcting mechanically but necessity to see it altogether in type so I can tell what I want to do with it. Do you know a Spanish proof reader competent to go over the spelling of the spanish words? This should be done. Setting them without italics is quite correct.

Please send me the pictures I left with you; the photographs I mean. I need to see them all together to decide which ones I need.

Don't get too spooked about these times. Fortune at 10 dollars a year increased their circulation.

—Later—

I have been thinking over the book of the month business and this is how I stand—

If the book is offered to the book of the month through publishing necessity and against my natural wishes my advance is not to be deducted by Scribners from any payment made by Book of Month or other organization but is to remain as an advance against royalties on <u>this book only</u> to be deducted by Scribners from the money earned by the regular edition as sold by them. This to protect writer in times like these from publishers receiving seven thousands dollars from the book of month, recovering the 6500 advanced to the writer and then not being under the necessity to make as much of an effort to sell the book in times like these as the writer had to make to write it in the same times. The only reason for doing anything like this, as you say, is the depression. I do not mean it personally—only as a question of business policy in regard to Book of Month Club.

The second thing would be that if the book of the month club brought any pressure to bear for certain anglo saxon words or any portions of the text to be eliminated all these words, whenever eliminated, would be represented by blanks of the exact length of the word eliminated and all words or portions of the text eliminated would be restored in full in the regular trade edition to be published by the publishers and on which the advance of 6500 which I have received would apply.

Third thing would be that all review copies or presentation copies would be of the regular trade edition rather than the book of the month edition in case the book of the Month had eliminated any words from their text.[1]

How's that Max Or is it too business-like? You see I happen to believe in the book and it was you who said things were different in depressions and so on.

If the publishers need a sure 7,000 from that source all right—but I have to see that two things are not imperilled; the further sale, which helps you as much as it does me, and the integrity of the book which is the most imprtant thing to me. If anyone so acts as to put themselves out as a book of the month they cannot insist in ramming the good word shit or the sound old word xxxx down the throats of a lot clubwomen but when a book is offered for sale no one has to buy it that does not want to—and I will not have any pressure brought to bear to make me emasculate a book to make anyone seven thousand dollars, myself or anyone else. Understand this is all business not personal. I'm only trying to be as frank as in talking so you will know how I stand and so we won't get in a jam and if I write too strongly or sound

[1] *DIA* was not a Book-of-the-Month Club selection.

too snooty it is because I'm trying to make it frank and as honest and clear as possible. So don't let me insult you Max nor find any insults where none is intended but know I am fond of you and that we could not quarrel if we were together and if I'm rude I apologise sincerely.

If you want to publish two selections—the ones I outlined and Dashiell agreed to—in the magazine—Chapter Two—one was I believe—and the other the chapter on the bulls—saying they are from the book and giving them the place they should have in the magazine you can have them for nothing and use the money for illustrations for the book. Submitting proofs to me first of course. I won't sell them for less than they are worth but I will give them to you. That should show you whether I am friendly. But I am damned serious.

. . . . .

. . . . .

Yours always,<br>
Ernest/

I know you didnt say you would do Book of Month or anything else against my wishes—but only asked how I felt and I have written so frankly so you would know how I feel about everything I mention.

*CC, 3 pp.*[1]

April 7, 1932

Dear Ernest:

I've just read your letter and I'm answering off hand to get things going and save time. You may get another giving specific figures before you answer. But answer these questions soon:

(1) Would it be possible with respect to placing the inserts to have them backed up, i.e. one picture on the back of another? This I think we could do even on the present basis and not increase the price. But the pictures I thought of as so close to the text that they ought to come close to particular passages.

(2) Would you rather revert to halftones in order to have a large number of pictures?

If we did, I should think we could have 32 inserts and if backed up 64 pictures, and perhaps not greatly increase the price.- But increase in the number of inserts does add greatly to costs, even in respect to binding.- Then too, each additional picture would add a page of text. We—and that means I—may have looked at the pictures too much by themselves,- as pictures rather than illustrations.- So we wanted to give each the best kind of reproduction possible for its own sake. But look at the Thomas book[2] I sent you (a

[1]159 words have been omitted from this letter.
[2]George Clifford Thomas, Jr., and George C. Thomas III, *Game Fish of the Pacific* (Philadelphia: Lippincott, 1930).

good book, too) and see what you think of those pictures. That book we had to price at $5.00 even though he has a lower royalty than you, simply because a lower margin than that price yields was impossible.

In fact this question always ends with arithmetic, and the "hard times" makes that no different from what it always was. We don't try to increase the margin on account of that,- the tendency is the other way. The only influence of the bad times is on the retail price. We do want to keep the price at $3.50,- though we may have to give that up.[1] You know Steffens' book was a flat flop at its original price, but a great success when a Guild edition enabled Harcourt to bring it out anew and cheaper.

Another point: we always want to bring books out the way you want them, partly because you want them that way, and partly because you do have a sure instinct in these things. But you seem to think that Scribners are looking out for themselves as opposed to you. That is not so. I am separating myself from them and am speaking with absolute honesty. They are not like that and never have been. That is known, and the Author's League rates them first in their treatment of authors' interests. They would not think of doing as you said about the advance. They never have done it, and never would. And the Magazine would never publish anything and not pay for it— but they can't pay higher prices for things now than they could pay in good times. I know I've given you a wrong impression by glooming about the times to you. It was because of my own affairs. I always see things as too much one way or the other. I haven't had enough trouble, that's the trouble. But the slump only affects the question of retail price on the book and, on the Magazine, what we can't pay for we have to forget.

As for the Book Club, we don't like it any more than you do. And the limited likewise.- I wasn't urging a limited, but simply presenting an important possibility. At least that's what I should have been doing, and meant.

But write me quickly about the pictures and I'll write you more specifically before the week's over.

Yours,

. . . . .
. . . . .

*TS for wire, 1 p.*

April 8, 1932

Mr. Ernest Hemingway
Key West, Florida
Shall publish book only as you want it though price must depend on method stop Wrote yesterday
Max

---

[1] *DIA* was publsihed at $3.50.

*CC, 2 pp.*[1]

April 19, 1932

Dear Ernest:

I was mighty glad to get your telegram.[2] Now send the pictures and captions whenever you can.- But we are all right for making up the dummy which is the only immediate problem, and you will soon have all of the proof. There is that matter about what they have come to call the four-letter words.- I won't argue with you about it because you know all of the arguments, except that you may not realize that spelling them out does technically make us guilty under the obscenity clause, and so it does give any legal authority that wants it, the right to act irrespective of anything but the more technical fact; and also that those words do prohibit completely all library sale but a very very small one. Dos Passos has gone beyond anyone else apparently, and I was told he had actually spelled out the words, but he has not in "1919" and I daresay that leaving two of the four letters blank was found by Harcourt to be enough to avoid the technical point of guilt,- though that certainly does make the law what Shakespeare said it was, a fool. But we knew that anyhow.

I read the story in the Cosmop, and I thought it was a very fine story.[3] Are they to have any more? I do not know why you should not publish those that you have written. I hope you will write others about Key West. I hope this means that you have got to the point where you can write about it.

What I meant about Scott is rather complicated and sometime I'll write you from home about it.- But Zelda has written a novel which was here in manuscript but later was withdrawn by Zelda to revise. It was very much autobiographical,- about herself, and biographical about Scott. In fact, she even named her hero Amory Blaine.- I did not say anything to Scott when it came, and felt very much perplexed what to do—it looked as if there were a great deal that was good in it, but it seemed rather as though it somewhat dated back to the days of "The Beautiful and Damned"—when I got a letter from Scott about it. Zelda had sent him a copy, and of course it would not do at all the way it was, with Amory Blaine the hero. It would have been mighty rough on Scott.- But this was written apparently very recently, and I think when Zelda was ill with her breakdown,- though that did not show in it in any obvious way, except that it was so much about Amory Blaine. This all must be a secret. I think the novel will be quite a good one when she finishes it. The thing is that she is evidently passionately fond of Alabama, and that gets into the early part of the book. I did not read any of it consecutively but the early part because of what Scott said in his letter. I think he must still be at the Rennert Hotel, Baltimore, Md. because mail I sent him to Mont-

[1] 80 words have been omitted from this letter.
[2] On 15 April EH wired MP: "AWFULLY HAPPY ABOUT PICTURES YOUR IDEA ABOUT PLACING THEM AT END SEEMS VERY INTELLIGENT AND EXCELLENT SOLUTION."
[3] "After the Storm," *Cosmopolitan* 152 (May 1932): 38–41, 155.

gomery has come back. Zelda wrote me a note about the manuscript which was of a sort which seemed to show that she was not very badly off this time, but Scott is greatly worried about her.[1]

. . . . .

Yours,

*ALS, 4 pp.*
*Havana, Cuba*

June 2—<u>Friday</u>—

Dear Max:—

Sent the proofs—revised—cut and corrected today registered. Have had the pictures and captions for 2 days but spooked to send them through mail as customs might open and crack or soil or disarrange them—So <u>am</u> sending them tonight on The Cuba with the Captain—To deliver them to Pauline who will mail them registered from Key West. She comes over on Monday with Carol[2]—who will be here until she drives North with me—I could not get them under 70—without losing the very necessary effect. If that is an odd number to print can add two good ones and make 72—

Have cut a lot of text—With what is gone the book may be less fashionable (all this stating of creeds and principles which does not belong in literature at all by people who have failed in or lost belief in or abandoned writing the minute it got tough to save their bloody souls). But it will be permanent and solid and about what it is about—I will save what I cut and if it proves to be of permanent value you can publish it in my Notebooks—which will also contain this statement—

The William Lyon Phelps of Tomorrow are the William Harlan Hale's of Today—[3]

It's a good book Max and you know what Dos says—That the performance of the book should be judged by the author by the quality of the stuff he is able to cut—

I'm not ready to go into my long white beard yet And you shouldnt have to tell it if you have any wisdom—They'll find it out sooner or later—or if your a fool—

Will send the short appendix—Estimate of Franklin as a bull fighter and the one giving the dates of fights all over Spain Mexico and S. America—And that will be all—There will be a new Reglamento[4] soon. So why publish the old one—I'll give the new one and much other stuff I have if and when you get out another edition—That will save enough on the printed text to allow

---

[1]*Save Me the Waltz* was published by Scribners in October 1932, after Zelda Fitzgerald revised it. Sales were disappointing.

[2]EH's youngest sister.

[3]Hale (1910–1974) was a historian.

[4]Spanish government regulations for bullfights; it was not published in *DIA*.

Hemingway's lay-out for *Death in the Afternoon* illustrations,
page four of his 2 June 1932 letter.

for the extra pictures—Have said this in the glossary—Theres no sense to try to make it complete, exhaustive and comprehensive and then be bitched on the most necessary part for that—The pictures—

May not go to Africa until end of next June—If Mike agrees—Dont like to leave the country now (too much going on) and have too many damned good stories to write—Go from here to ranch the first of July—If we dont go to Africa will stay there through October—Africa wont get shot out with everybody too broke to travel—I want to get some more work done—Feel so good and healthy from this life I have as much juice writing as when I was a kid—only now I know how to do it—

Write me here to Hotel Ambos Mundos—Will you please—About 4 letter words—See your lawyers—If you are unwilling to print them entire at least leave 1st and last letters—You say that's legal—I'm the guy who has been the worst emasculated of any in publishing It's up to you to keep out of jail and from being suppressed I write the books—You publish them—But dont get spooked—

What about the Modern Library money? Any time they (Business office) get crabby tell them how much money I've made them outright being sold down the river in Grossett and Dunlop etc.

The Sun Also Movie money goes direct to Hadley—Not to be entered in my accounts at all—it's always been hers.

Cant you come down? It's cool here—Fine breeze always—Weve caught 27 Marlin—Will break a worlds record if we have luck.

What news of Scott?

If you ever publish any books by any wives of mine I'll bloody well shoot you—Family all in fine shape—Hope things are well with you—

Ernest

CC, 2 pp.[1]

June 11, 1932

Dear Ernest:

. . . . .

Your notebook would be fun to publish, but neither you nor I will have anything to do with that.- But still, I understand perfectly well why you cut everything you did. The passage about the peninsulas and the corn could easily be made into a magnificent article though. The book seems wonderfully fine and solid in looking at it all at once—the proofs and all the pictures and the captions. There won't be another book to compare with it this fall, in reality.

I did what you suggested about the <u>words.</u> I got our lawyer up here and talked to him. He would have infuriated you, and in fact I ended with quite an argument,- but then broke it off because I saw it was foolish. His advice was against the words, of course, and he suggested that "damn" could be

[1]20 words have been omitted from this letter.

used just as well as one of them, and that was where we got into trouble, for I began to try to show him how it couldn't. But further discussion was confined to the legal aspect of the matter which amounts to this:- the words are literally illegal, but much more latitude is now allowed than formerly, and the courts do not consider the words by themselves, but in their context and in their general intent and bearing on it all. But there is a serious danger, since this is the first time in a book of any consequence in which these words have been printed in full, that Mr. Sumner[1] or some of these Prohibitionistic people, would make a fight on the matter in order to stop any further progress that way. Lawyers are mighty careful what they say, but I really think he thought that if they did, we could probably win in court, but not until after sales had been held up and publication suspended, etc. His advice was strongly in favor of the omission of the two middle letters, at least.- Even that, he thought would show that an attempt to meet the law had been made, and would be in our favor. You will understand all about it, I guess. I have simply sent back the proof as it was because we can change those few instances in the page proof. So I shall send it to you as it stands, and we can look at it all in final form. There is no doubt that these words do seriously interfere with library sales. But that does not amount to very great numbers. It is a good sale though, and it gives a book a permanence and finality to which this book is entitled. This book is even a reference book.

One good thing for me, came out of this four-letter word question.- It led me to read all of Dos Passos' book, and I think it is much his best book, and grand reading. Do you suppose Harpers did not take it on account of the Morgan piece? It is all according to the records.[2]

Scott and Zelda seem to be settling down in Baltimore, and I hope they will stick to it, and be compelled to be quiet. And anyhow if Zelda can only begin to make money, and she might well do it, they ought to get into a good position where Scott can write.

I hope to thunder you do put off that African trip. I never liked the idea of it, anyhow.

Yours,

*Wire, 1 p.*
*Key West, Florida*

1932 JUN 27 PM 7 07
DO NOT GROUP ONE AND TWO STOP GROUP TWENTY TWO AND TWENTY THREE INSTEAD STOP OTHER GROUPINGS OK IF

[1]John S. Sumner, secretary of the New York State Society for the Suppression of Vice.
[2]*1919*, the second volume of Dos Passos's *U.S.A.* trilogy, was declined by Harper, presumably because of its biographical sketch of J. P. Morgan; the Morgan bank was a major investor in the publishing house.

GROUPINGS NECESSARY STOP WILL CORRECT ALL PROOFS IMMEDIATELY AND SEND FROM HERE BEFORE LEAVING DID IT SEEM VERY FUNNY TO SLUG EVERY GALLEY HEMINGWAYS DEATH OR WAS THAT WHAT YOU WANTED HAVE BEEN PLENTY SICK REGARDS=
        ERNEST.

*ALS, 4 pp.*[1]

*28 June 1932*

                    <u>Tuesday</u>—
                    Box 406
                    <u>Key West</u>

Dear Max—
. . . . .
Have done 233 pages of the page proof and all the captions. Will go right on through it and send it off to you with the list of fixed dates of fights in Spain—Central and South Am and Mexico. Would prefer not to call these appendices—Limitations of space and costs have aborted any attempt to make the book exhaustive so as it is appendices are only pretentious—So list them in the table of contents by their titles—<u>removing</u> the desegnations Appendix A B and C.

. . . . .
Will try and find contract and send it to you to protect you against worry in case of any such future contingancies. Know neither you nor I worry about the contract or would have sent it before—

But listen Max could you <u>bawl out</u> please or raise hell with the son of a bitch who slugged all those galley's Hemingways Death? You know I am superstitious and it is a hell of a damn dirty business to stare at that a thousand times even to haveing it (in this last filthy batch) written in with red and purple ink—If I would have passed out would have said your Goddamned lot put the curse on me—

About the combining of pictures—You dont want to open the illustrations with a double page—Also that seed bull and ox are too good to combine— That's why I sent you the wire—The two Villaltas combine much better—
                    22 and 23
Saw a publicity sheet sent out by Benjamin Hauser[2] presumabley re-hashing Scribner publicity—Mostly ballyhooing stuff I had cut out—What you will do is get everyone disappointed—I put all that stuff in so that anyone buying the book for no matter what reason would get their money

[1]80 words have been omitted from this letter.
[2]Publicist Benjamin Gayelord Hauser later became briefly famous for his diet and nutrition books.

worth—All that story, dialogue, etc is thrown in extra—The book is worth anybodys 3.50 who has 3.50 as a straight book on bull fighting—If you go to advertizing that it is so many damned other things all you will do is make people disappointed because it hasnt a cook book and a telephone directory as well.

If you try to sell it as a great classic Goddamned book on bull fighting rather than some fucking miscellany you may be able to sell a few—Let the critics claim it has something additional—But suppose all chance of that is gone now with that lovely Hauser stuff—If you want to try to find someone to speak well of it ask Dos Passos—

But thats Your business—not mine—

About the words—Youre the one who has gone into that—If you decide to cut out a letter or two to keep inside the law that is your business—I send the copy and you are supposed to know what will go to jail and what will not—F-ck the whole business—That looks all right—Its legal isnt it—

Max I feel damned sick still, but I could break the neck of the punk that slugged these galleys—

Oh yes—What about that Modern Library money? I'm flat broke—What is Mr. Dashiell's budget for stories now? Please answer these last two.

Also will you please have three sets of these <u>corrected</u> page proof galleys drawn as want one for Cape, one for Germany and one for my self—Best to you always—Ernest

If they feel disappointed and still want my "literary Credo" in a book on bull fighting they can run an insert saying "F-ck the whole goddamned lousy racket"—Hemingway—

If you want some pictures will get some taken but for Christ sake no more of these open mouth open collar wonders—Promise me that—

And <u>NIX</u> on that one of me lying with the sick steer—

Will send you painting by Luis Quintanilla who did the frescoes in the Casa del Pueblo that you can use—

[*In right margin of page one*] Not going to Africa this year—Wouldnt want to miss the literary teas

*CC, 3 pp.*[1]

July 7, 1932

Dear Ernest:

I never once saw that headline.- If I had I would have known what to do with it, because you cannot tell me anything about omens. I can see more omens than any man on the face of the earth, and once when things were bad and I was alone in the car and a black cat crossed the road, I actually shot around the corner.- When any of my family are in the car and that happens,

[1]40 words have been omitted from this letter.

I tell them not to be foolish. But the fact is, of course, they just followed the regular rule in the headline,- the author's name, and then the first important word of the title.- But I know you know that.

Everything has come back, and we are going through it all and I shall have another consultation about the words, and let you know. There was one other thing that bothered me a lot, and I hate to speak of it to you. I had had a hope that you might let Waldo Frank off a little easier in the end.[1] It is absolutely none of my business I know, but I cannot help remembering what Pope did to some of those fellows, so that the only thing they were remembered for was that. I hate to bother you about this, but I thought you might soften it by taking his name out. So that they thought of the book, and not of the man. I shall never be able to think of Waldo except as pictured on that eventful night.

I guess you must be all right, but it is a shame to have ended up such a grand period of health that way.

I hope to thunder you will send us stories. We shall do our absolutely best in the matter of price, but five hundred seems a great sight bigger now than it did only a year ago.

> Yours,

. . . . .

CC, 3 pp.[2]

July 22, 1932

Dear Ernest:

Everything seems now to be right with the book. And you will see when we send you the page proof, what we have done about the words, and it is not so bad. . . .

. . . Scott and I have got a grand tour of the Virginia battlefields planned, and although I do not see how I could take in more than two, it would be a great time if you were there. It all came from my going down to Baltimore and seeing Gettysburg, and really, Ernest, it was perfectly magnificent: you could understand every move in the whole battle if you had read about it. You could see the whole battlefield plain as day. There is a stone wall, as good as any in Connecticut, about two feet high, on Roundtop, built on the 3rd of July, by some Maine regiments. They knew all about stone walls.- It is as good as new today.

---

[1]EH was disgusted by Waldo Frank's work *Virgin Spain* (New York: Boni & Liveright, 1926). In Chapter 4 of *DIA*, EH retained his description of how Frank "lay naked in his bed in the night and God sent him things to write, how he 'was in touch ecstatically with the plunging and immobile all.' How he was, through the courtesy of God, '*everywhere* and *everywhen*.' " EH did cut the statement, ". . . it [America] is all free to Mr. Waldo Frank and his pals, all free except the ability to write English" in Chapter 20, which was part of a larger cut of two galleys; see MP's 25 January 1932 letter.

[2]304 words have been omitted from this letter.

Scott and Zelda are living about forty minutes out from Baltimore in a house on a big place that is filled with wonderful old trees. I wanted to walk around and look at the trees, but Scott thought we ought to settle down to gin-rickeys.- But you could see the trees from the piazza where we sat, and a little pond there, too. It was really a fine sort of melancholy place. Zelda is not nearly as pretty, and is quite a little different, but I thought she was better, and that there was more reality in her talk, and that she seemed well. She was very nice. She has a whole lot of drawings and paintings that she gets out of her subconscious, and they are very expressive.- Whether they really are any good or not, I do not know, but they are not negative, anyhow. Scott did not look so well, but he was in fine spirits, and talked a lot. He told me that if I went to Key West he would certainly go next time.- You know he was in Florida, and he began inquiring about the fishing. It seems he caught an amberjack, I think, that weighed about forty pounds. He asked me how big the fish we caught were, and maybe I stretched it a little, but I could see it worried Scott. He said he had had an awful fight with this amberjack. It was mighty good to see him anyhow. I wish you would come and go to Antietam with us. It is beautiful country all around.- The depression seems simply silly when you motor all over that country and see the crops and all the rich foliage, and the orchards coming along, and even the villages looking all neat and fresh. It makes you feel as if it were all a lunacy, this depression.

. . . . .

. . . . .

There is one more thing, but I wouldn't worry about it. A man named Sidney Barth came in here with thirty-six manuscript pages of your letters to that Ernest Morehead.[1] I may have the name wrong, but to the same couple that those earlier letters were written to. He wants to sell these letters (written in 1925 and 1926) for $1800. I don't think you would want to spend that much, and the times are too bad to do it, and I wouldn't suppose he could sell them at that price at present. I ran over the letters in typewriting, and except that they are personal letters, I see nothing about them that ought to trouble you.- The only thing was some comments on McAlmon, but they were really all right. They were not hard on him. You did say in effect, that you did not think he was as good as Mark Twain, but that might almost be conceded! I thought they were mighty good letters. If there is anything you want me to do about it, let me know. I am sure there is nothing in them that need trouble you.

Always yours,

---

[1]MP conflated the names Ernest Walsh and Ethel Moorhead, founders and editors of *This Quarter;* see EH's 11 April 1930 letter.

ALS, 2 pp.[1]
Cooke City, Montana

July 27

Dear Max—

Am sending the proofs that came yesterday air mail with this letter—Did them yest afternoon and last night. Hurrying to get this off in truck

Will you please erase the two cursings out of the compositors for still setting that Hemingways Death on those last galleys of the Dates of fights—I have the proof all packed and cant get to it—They are at the top of two of those last galleys—I wish to Christ you wouldnt have sent that slugged Hemingways Death again after all I'd written and wired—But want those erased as it does no good to slang the compositors—They arent responsible—

Hope you get these proofs and letter in pretty fast—Am sending them in to Gardner—64 miles to get them out today—

When do I get the page proofs? <u>What did you do to the words?</u> Why havent I seen frontspiece or jacket—You havent even asked what title goes on Frontispiece—

The Torero—By Juan Gris—

Will you tell Whitney Darrow[2] I got his very fine letter and will write him—He was very nice to write me.

Am feeling pretty good but dont seem to have a hell of a lot of pep—

The letters you refer to are to Ernest Walsh and Ethel Morehead—The bastards I helped get out their magazine when he was supposed to be dying of TB. Did die finally and she sold his letters. Tell the man who wants to sell them that I said for him to stick them up his ass—

. . . . .

Poor old Scott—He should have swapped Zelda when she was at her craziest but still saleable back 5 or 6 years ago before she was diagnosed as nutty—He is the great tragedy of talent in our bloody generation—

. . . . .

So long Max—Good luck—
Ernest

CC, 3 pp.[3]

Aug. 1, 1932

Dear Ernest:
. . . . .
. . . . .

[1] 57 words have been omitted from this letter.
[2] Darrow was sales manager for Scribners; EH disliked him.
[3] 167 words have been omitted from this letter.

If we could only fix Scott up for a clear six months, we might turn that tragedy into something else. But between us we have advanced him so much it is impossible to see how he could make anything out of a novel even if it were a great success.- And it is still more impossible for us to advance him substantially more. So I cannot think of any way out of it now. Maybe there will be a way later though, if conditions improve. And there isn't a bad chance really that Zelda might not turn out a writer of popular books. She has some mighty bad tricks of writing, but she is now getting over the worst of them. I think Scott could come through pretty well if he had a clear track given him.

Yours,

. . . . .

*ALS, 4 pp.*

August 9—1932
Cooke Montana

Dear Max:—

Enclosed the page proofs—Thanks for sending the foundry proof to Cape—I will give you an address to sent the German publisher a set—Same as Cape—Ernst Rowohlt—Berlin—

The others can wait—

The jacket looks fine—The blurbs also O.K.—hesitate to approve since they are complimentary—Seem restrained, to make no false promises, and know what the hell it is about—But you have done damned well—Didnt get frontispiece—Would like to see it—

Just read all the book—started at 6:45 finished at 4:50 It is really a hell of a good book. But Christ what an amount of work—

We have been down sage grouse shooting for five days—finest shooting ever in my life—Went down last Wednesday—Shot limit every day—Never shot better—Would have given anything for you to be there—Just got back today and found final proofs—Hit rock and broke bottom of Engine—oil pan or crank case—Coasted 4 miles back to Cooke

Book is to be dedicated—

To Pauline

Now what else—?

If you advertize like hell and realize there is a difference between Marcia Davenports Mozart etc (nice though they must be) you can sell plenty. If you got spooked or yellow out on trying to sell them naturally they will flop in these times—You will have to stick with it hard, as though it were selling big, through Christmas no matter how it goes. Like Sun also. Then it will go. It is really a swell book—

If you will give me 750 apiece will send three stories—excellent stories—so you can run them one after the other—Would like to do this to bitch Cosmopolitan—They have offered $1.00 a word up to 2500—$5000 above that for any stories—Homage To Switzerland—The Light of The World—The Mother of a Queen—You can have 3 for 2100—Paid to me <u>next year</u> January. This is about $9000 less than they are worth at offered price—But do not insist on that Just tell you—If you do not want stories from me at your regular rates O.K Do not want any shit from Dashiell—

Dont for Christ sake have that little shit Dashiell write back to me because would rather use them for bungwad than engage in polemics with that twirp who was cutting 2500 out of that fight story—Why did you trade Bridges for Bridges in [*two word illegible*]—If you arent the boss tell me who the son of a bitch is to write to—If you <u>arent</u> the boss they are goofy—And will go wherever you will be <u>boss</u>. Poor old Scott—but have seen an attack go bad before—(with better guys).

Yours always  Ernest—

On window display if you use
the Roberto Domingo Guache paintings <u>or oils</u> please have a card with his name below paintings as he deserves the publicity—Also on the Quintanilla portrait <u>use his name</u>

LUIS QUINTANILLA—-

And send me reproductions so I can send to him——

Remember I got you frontispiece—Jacket all illustrations—

If you can get photos of any window display with Roberto's or Quintanillas portraits please get them and send them to me—Please look after this even if it is irksome

---

EH

<u>Best to you</u>
Dos Passos will write a Blurb if you need one—he is 517 Commercial Street Provincetown—Mass He was pretty strong for book—

*CC, 4 pp.*[1]

Dec. 3, 1932

Dear Ernest:

. . . . .

. . . . .

You spoke, perhaps jokingly, about unfavorable comment, and that we might be asking waivers, etc. This is one of the times when I feel embarrassed to say anything, because to say anything is so totally superfluous. But I know so well how these things go. There is also the well known fact that there is in people a desire to pull down people who get up. But there are some few who cannot be pulled down because the foundation they stand on is too real to crumble. I know you must have been joking about it, and it is silly for me even to say this.

---

[1]355 words have been omitted from this letter.

We do not make much progress with the sale for although we get orders all the time, we get so many returns from outside the several big cities which are more or less cosmopolitan, and from libraries, that it keeps it about even. We have got the best weeks ahead of us still.- . . . .

. . . . .

. . . . .

Yours,

P.S. Let me know as soon as you can about about the book of stories. We ought to announce it in the spring list if it is to be published before August. If it is to be ready in time to be published before August, I believe it ought to be. If it is to be published later than June, or perhaps even in May, it should be a fall book. But I think it would help with "Death in the Afternoon" and everything if it could come out in the spring: Don't hurry it though,- of course you wouldn't.


*ALS, 4 pp.[1]*
*Piggot, Arkansas*


Dec 7 1932

Dear Max:—

Will you come out here and meet me at Memphis on December 15 to shoot ducks for a week from the houseboat Walter Adams—anchored in the Arkansas river at Watkins Ark. If you cant stay a week stay as long as you can. You dont need to bring anything but some warm clothes. I have everything else and have made the reservation and paid for you in advance. We could talk over everything and have the finest duck shooting in the world—I know how you enjoyed shooting the Goldwings and these ducks are so plentiful and come in to the decoys so often that you would have a swell time.

I know of course that business and your family affairs absolutely forbid it but I need to see you and you need to get away and we will have the sort of shooting our grandfathers and great grandfathers had. Please wire you are coming because it will be too late to get anyone else and I lose $100 if you dont come Tried to get Mike to come too but he wouldnt. Please come Max and if you dont have a better time than you ever had will push you back to N.Y. in a wheelbarrow—We will meet in Memphis on 15th get to Watson 16th—and start shooting that day—I will be waiting for a wire—From a business etc standpoint you really ought to—

You want to decide about book of stories—when—etc.

You need to hear about other new book I have under way—You ought to bring me that Contract—You need to convince me how hard you work to sell my volumes etc

(I promise not to mention a Goddamned one of these topics to you if you will come unless you bring them up for nothing else to talk about)

[1]146 words have been omitted from this letter.

178

. . . . .

Please wire—I have 2300 shells so you can miss 1845 ducks and still kill over your limit—

Thanks for yours of Dec 3—No I didnt make the statement about waivers seriously—Thanks for the Compten Mackenzie when it comes will read it and send it back—

Will you give this statement all the publicity you can? You know how I feel about publicity but would like to see you spread this statement around:

Mr Ernest Hemingway has asked his publishers to disclaim the romantic and false military and personal career imputed to him in a recent film publicity release. Mr. H., who is a writer of fiction, states that if he was in Italy during a small part of the late war it was only because a man was notoriously less liable to be killed there than in France. He drove, or attempted to drive, an ambulance and engaged in minor camp following activities and was never involved in heroic actions of any sort. Any sane person knows that writers do not knock out Middle Weight Champions; unless the writer's name happens to be Gene Tunney. While Mr. H. appreciates the publicity attempt to build him into a glamorous personality like Floyd Gibbons or Tom Mix's horse Tony he deprecates it and asks the motion picture people to leave his private life alone.

. . . . .

Best to you always—<br>Ernest/

. . . . .

. . . . .

Have been asked to lecture at Oxford (England) Do you want the name of the College?

*Form letter*[1]                                                          *TL, 1 p.*
*undated*

C
  O                                      Box 406, Keywest, Florida
    P
      Y

Dear Mr.—

Thank you for your letter. The fundamental reason that I used certain words no longer a part of the usual written language is that they are very much a part of the vocabulary of the people I was writing about and there was no way I could avoid using them and still give anything like a complete feeling of what I was trying to convey to the reader. If I wrote any approximation even of the speech of the bull ring, it would be unpublishable. I had

---

[1]EH provided this letter to be sent by Scribners to readers who complained about the language in *DIA;* it was not used.

to try to get the feeling by the use of two or three words, not using them directly, but indirectly as I used the Natural History of the Dead to make a point that you may have noticed.

I am trying, always, to convey to the reader a full and complete feeling of the thing I am dealing with; to make the person reading feel it has happened to them. In doing this I have to use many expedients, which, if they fail, seem needlessly shocking. Because it is very hard to do I must sometimes fail. But I might fail with one reader and succeed with another.

My use of words which have been eliminated from writing, but which persist in speech has nothing to do with the small boy chalking newly discovered words on fences. I use them for two reasons. 1st as outlined above. 2nd when there is no other word which means exactly the same thing and gives the same effect when spoken.

I always use them sparingly and never to give gratuitous shock—although sometimes to give calculated and what to me seems necessary shock.

Yours very truly,

(signed)       ERNEST HEMINGWAY

ALS, 4 pp.[1]

*[Early February 1933]*

Box 406<br>Key West<br><u>Monday</u>—     <u>Florida</u>

Dear Max:—

Pauline is typing the 3rd story for the series of 3—It is called The Gambler, The Nun and The Radio (at present) and runs to about 19 pages of this foolscap double spaced—Hope to send it off tomorrow. Somewhere between 8—9000 words. May be more. You havent any long short story contests on have you? This is worth 750 plus—but am always glad to give the lads their money's worth.

Thanks for sending the pictures. They arrived in good condition. <u>Beautifully</u> packed.

Glad about what you wrote of Tom Wolfe. He was awfully nice. He is like a great child and you must remember that. Genuises of that sort I guess are always children. Children, as you may have observed, Mr. Perkins, are a hell of a responsability. I liked him very, very much.

Have been working hard but it takes a while to get in training again.

How are you and all your troubles? Mine are bad. But realize now we were probably intended to have troubles and you can get used to anything if you dont worry about things happening to you before they happen.

Weather has been wonderful—like the best early morning feeling of

[1]72 words have been omitted from this letter.

Indian Summer. Bumby caught a 44 lb amber jack alone and un-aided. Have only been out twice.

Will you tell me, please,①about when to expect the royalty money on Death In Aft according to usual or present procedure.

②Whether I can draw on it before then.

③What present sale is.

I distrust that present system but understand it.

Also are you or will you be prepared to advance me $6,000 on the book of stories—This is figured as 15% on 20,000 sale at $2.00. The 20,000 is the minimum sale I have to have Mr. Darrow carry in his mind. Also the minimum that will hold poor old Papa's affectionate loyalty. The advance mentioned is less than sale on day of publication of this last $3.50 masterpiece.

Would it be any more palatable to you to advance 3000 or 4000 and the balance at say $200 a month?

If I take an advance on the new book will not need the Death In Aft royalties until they are due. But anyhow let me know when they are due.

Out of that check for the last story 200 went to a distingueshed writer to pay rent and eat (this will be repaid) 175.00 to Carol, 150.00 to another writer, unknown but damned good. Leaving 25.00 for Old Hem who needed all of it to start with.

Have $105.00 in bank as write this so please send the check for story promptly. Maybe would be better (it would be) if you would deposit it directly in my account City Bank Farmers Trust—22 William Street—

Because I tell you (personally) how broke I am dont think I am to be treated like all the poor little boys because my financial acumen (if necessary) is only equalled by my liberty of action (never necessary but present) and in reality I'm not asking any favor. You know that.

. . . . .

. . . . .

Am going well on a fine story. Have a fine plan for a novel. Will be working on the Gulf stream book from about 10th of April on—It may take 2 or 3 years more. Might get what I need this summer. Will see.

Best to you always, Max

Ernest/

I dont know, frankly, whether Scott will ever come out of this thing or not. He seems so damned perverse Does anyone think it is easy to get your work done properly? about wanting to fail—it's that damned, bloody romanticism. Why cant he grow up? That's a useless question. I wish to Christ I could see him sober.

Tom Wolfe will be fine—always within the limits of his intelligence—He has a great talent and a very delicate fine spirit—You've got to be a big part of his intelligence so for Christ sake dont lose his confidence

*CC, 3 pp.*[1]

February 10, 1933

Dear Ernest:

When a man calls for $3,000 or $4,000 even in boom times he is likely to get only $3,000, and he is likely to get only that in these times.- So we deposited only $3,000,- but we are bent upon doing exactly what you want. And we realize that you are trying to help us in suggesting the $200 a month.- So tell me when that ought to begin. The royalties on "Death in the Afternoon" are strictly due ten months after publication, which is July 23rd. We are altogether willing though to pay them now. I have got to take up with Charlie how we should charge this $3,000, whether as much as possible against the royalties, or whether as an advance on the stories.

I told Darrow what you said, and found him surprisingly willing to take your view as to what would have to be done with the stories. I hope you will get a fine title. Everything you say about your writing is splendid news, and I gather that what you will do will be to write the novel, and to write the Gulf Stream book over a long period.

. . . . .

Scott ended his last letter, of January 30th, with this sentence, "Will be getting in touch with you within the next few months on what I hope will be important business." I think that this means he thinks he will have his novel done. I wrote him that I had a hunch he would have published a novel within eighteen months, even allowing for serial. His letter sounded pretty good. But the best news I have is about Tom Wolfe. The day before you left I went to Baltimore. After you left Tom and me I said to him, "Why don't you come down to Baltimore and then we'll go to Washington too." He said he would, but I didn't expect him. But he did arrive there the next day and we had a good time out of it there and in Washington. On the way back he told me about a story he said he had written. He has a whole library of manuscripts, fragments of things. I said, "For Heaven's sake bring it in and let us publish it." Then there began all the regular series of procrastinations, but eventually he did turn up with about 60,000 words of his very best sort of thing, though far too much of the dithyrambic, too little of the dialogue and direct narrative.- But still the whole thing a unit. Some things had to go out of it obviously, too directly of the quality of autobiography, etc.; but even more obviously there were a lot of fragments I had already seen which fell right into it in place to complete the very motive of the manuscript. I called him up and said to him, "All you have to do now is to close your hand and you have your novel." We spent hours later talking about it, and of course Tom was all for breaking loose into all kinds of excursions away from the main thing, but I got him to promise that first he would put it together on the lines I suggested, with which he agreed.- If it needed enlargement thereafter (and

[1]178 words have been omitted from this letter.

182

it will need an awful lot of work in detail) he could do it, and see how it came. But he has promised first to deliver the manuscript. It does not seem possible now that he can avoid having a very fine book, in some ways better than "The Angel", much better structurally, for next fall.[1] I think it was a great piece of business having you and him meet. He did reproach him for some things, between ourselves. He said he thought it was pretty bad we had let him get within twenty dollars of starvation. I understood this, of course, from Tom perfectly well, but I did point out some of the other side of the matter;- but he said with a sly look he sometimes manages to take on, like the one his mother was described as having in the book,- he said, "Since we are talking business, how about the interest you earned on my $2,500 before it was spent?"

. . . . .

. . . . .

Ever yours,

*ALS, 2 pp.*[2]

Feb. 23/

Box 406

Key West

Florida/

Dear Max:

Enclosed is the story.[3] You'll have a good story in the Magazine for once or maybe several times. You can send the check here.

Do you want any more or is three the limit for a year? I had to wait on this to get the title right.

Am on Chapter 4 of the novel—going well. See my way all the way to the end. Dont know whether we ever talked about this one.[4]

When and if I get stuck will write another story or two and there will be the book of stories—

Thanks for making the deposit—My point about the advance was that I wanted 6000 <u>before the book came out</u>. Explained why. Didnt realize how few months intervened. Only suggested those monthly payments as a convenience for you in order not to draw too much out of your treasury at once. I detest any monthly payment status. Said 3 or 4 grand on same basis. What I ask for unqualifidly as to times is 6000—before book is out—15% on 20,000 @ 2.00—Look over the record and you will find I have always been

---

[1] Wolfe's second novel, *Of Time and the River,* was published in 1935.

[2] 120 words have been omitted from this letter.

[3] "Give Us a Prescription, Doctor," *Scribner's Magazine* (May 1933), pp. 272–278—retitled "The Gambler, the Nun, and The Radio" in *WTN*.

[4] *To Have and Have Not* (1936).

reasonable about advances and want to protect myself, my financial careeah (career) rather, and through me, you.

It is very good news about T. Wolfe—About Scott I dont know—The only things that would make a writer of him again would be (1) Zelda's death which might put a term to things in his mind. (2) For his stomach to give out completely so he couldnt drink. He's gone into that cheap irish love of defeat, betrayal of himself etc.

. . . . .
. . . . .
. . . . .
. . . . .

> Yours always,
> Ernest

. . . . .

*TLS with holograph inserts, 1 p.*[1]
*Key West, Florida*

Monday—March 13

Dear Max,

Am returning proofs of the third story to Dashiell today. Received them last night.

Thanks for your letter with royalty report and account of payments during the year and expenditures to the retail department. Also about the 3,000 to come. Our letters must have crossed as your suggestion was the same as mine.

There was no statement on Death In The Afternoon in the February royalty report. What about that? Also when would royalties due from that be payable?

When your banks are open could use check for this last story.

. . . . .

In case of getting into a jam in Cuba (know a few too many people there) I may ask you to give me a paper saying this will certify that Ernest Hemingway is at work on a book dealing with the migratory fish of the Gulf Stream, their habits and capture with special reference to the fishing in Cuban Waters from a sporting standpoint. The book on which Mr. Hemingway is working will be published by Charles Scribners Sons, 597 Fifth Avenue, New York City. Articles will be published on this subject by Scribners Magazine.

I wish you would have this made out To Whom It May Concern and typed on your most impressive stationery and signed, say, by Charley and send it down to me now. In a time of revolution it might keep me from getting shot and it would most certainly help me with the book.

---

[1] 58 words have been omitted from this letter.

184

I wish you could get something from the State Department stating the same thing. We used to get these, always, see enclosed which please return, from the Embassy in Paris before going someplace where we were liable to get into trouble and theye were often valuable as credentials (Can't find one. Must be in my trunk of papers over at Charles. Will send one when find. No hurry on that.)

Won't get you into any trouble and you needn't publish the book or articles either if you don't wish. But need some sort of strong credentials.

May want another set for going to Spain this summer the way things are.

Good luck. Hope everything is going for the best with you. All well here.

Best always—

Ernest

*TLS with holograph postscript, 2 pp.*[1]

March 31/ Key West/

Dear Max,

Thanks for your letter with royalty report. Since you explained to me in N.Y. that there was a slightly different system of crediting royalties due to your making no credit of those books sent out on consignment do you think it would be a good thing to give a statement of what books are out on consignment etc. I do not mean an official form statement perhaps but some sort of figure on them.

I notice your charge of $3000. against the Death In The Afternoon royalties. You wrote this sum would be one half of a six thousand dollar advance on a book of stories the other three thousand to be paid before publication; me to draw on it if and as I needed it otherwise to rest with you. Please let me know if there has been a change in this agreement.

About the corrections, billed for in excess, to the sum of $145.25 you may remember asking me to send you the mss. so that you could have it set up saying I could make any changes or corrections I wished in the proofs. It was you who were in a hurry for the mss. and suggested me sending it even though I contemplated changes. This is a matter of record.

Perhaps you remember agreeing that I was to spend up to 600 dollars getting the book properly illustrated. I spent a good deal more than that for photographs and illustrations and also provided painting for jacket of the book. I knew that things were comparatively good when you told me to get the illustrations etc. and bad when I had gotten them so I did not think of holding you to any such agreement. Also I figured I owed you something for the interest on the advance which I had held a little over a year before the delivery of the mss. I finished paying for the Domingo illustrations last month. You authorized me to order them. I ordered them, paid for them, accepted the fact when you told me times were too hard for such extensive

---

[1]22 words have been omitted from this letter.

illustration and did not feel badly about it. You might have gotten your money back for all deluxe items if we had agreed on a deluxe edition but it was a very bad time for De Luxe editions and later on a revised and de luxe edition will be a very good thing. Also a limited edition would have been bad business for you as a big part of your very good first sale came from the fact that the book was considered a first edition.

I do not consider you owe me anything, conditions being as they were, forwhat I spent on the book and I certainly do not consider that I owe you anything, conditions being as they were ie. you suggesting that I correct in proof rather than in mss. on corrections. If you look back over our business relation you will find that I did not make unreasonable or unjustified requests for advances; that after a considerable financial success with one book I stayed by you refusing very large cash and royalty offers and adverting guarantees from various publishers, that I never tried to get you to meet their terms nor promised you anything that I did not deliver.

All right. Now if you wish to bill me for corrections made at your request that I correct in galley rather than in Mss in order to speed up (your program; not mine) I will accept the charge. But do not expect me to do anything against my interests in the matter of speeding up in the future.

As a customer of your bookstore I spent $116.15 more than all the books you published by me except Death In The Afternoon during the last royalty period for books in book store. Getting no discount on any books I had not written myself. Whenever I buy anything I always try to buy through an individual hoping that individual will make something in case they are on any sort of commission basis. I have given away over half of what I've made this year to hard working people in bad shape from the depression and I am not particularly cockeyed tight about money so please do not think my protest is on that basis or that I do not know that times are bad.

I am not going to rush on a title. Perhaps it may not be such a good idea to get out a book of stories now anyway. Will be very pleased, in case you feel you are being badly treated, to send you back your advance three thousand dollars with interest. Or, if you want it, the 667.08 that statement says I owe you. Stories that are any good do not get sour and I am in no particular rush to publish.

Yours always,
Ernest

. . . . .

*TLS with holograph inserts, 3 pp.*

April 8
Key West

Dear Max,

I will get in touch with Franklin, find out what it is all about, and write you in detail. In the meantime, if I were you, would give the Belmonte woman say fifty dollars <u>for an option</u> to publish the translation the fifty to be part of advance on royalties in case you exercise the option to publish the book according to th usual terms. In case you decide not to publish it I will pay you the fifty dollars you lose.

I know the book. It is a very readable local color novel of Sevillian life and the bull fighting milieu (mis-spelled).[1] The holy week stuff and the bull stuff is interestingly and accurately treated. The book is romantic and sentimental, full of "local color" and is supposed to be based on the life of Francisco Peralto called Facultades. (He died a year ago of t.b.) While in no sense literature if well translated it would be a good spanish romance. Its bull stuff is much more authentic and better done than Blood and Sand, for instance, by Ibanez.

A translation with Franklin's name on it would be very valuable as a selling point. If he did not do the entire actual translating his supervising it would ensure accuracy and comprehension in the bull fight part and the innumerable local slang words which would baffle the average translator.

I would take an option on the book leaving it up to you to exercise it within 90 days of the time you receive the translation. Maybe sixty days would be plenty.

I have never heard of Senora Belmonte and want to find out from Sidney what his tie-up is. A very successful (in Spain) silent picture was made from the book.

With no negotiations finished for making a picture treatment of Death In The Afternoon it would be worth my while to have you have this book tied up with an option until I can find out what the picture angle is from Sidney. It would be worthwhile giving $100. option. Will guarantee you this in case you do not exercise it when you have the translation.

That is all I know about it, Max. Have given you as impartial report as though you had hired me as a reader.

The author is Alejandro Perez Lugin not Alexandra. At least it is supposed to be written by a man.

Now about the book of stories. It would be possible to call it After The Storm and other stories but if I can get a title which describes the whole book it is infinitely better. I have always had the greatest difficulty with titles and have always ended by getting good ones. Am at present in the middle of the period of greateet difficulty and would be a lousy quitting bastard to stop working on the title while there was a chance to get a great one. While I trust and have confidence in you you must know that while it is a book for your fall list to you, desireable to have because it will sell a certain amount of copies, and should be regarded as such; to me it is my life work, what I live for, what I care most about, and something which, if I hurry on (and I have not loafed on it) I cannot correct if I make a mistake.

---

[1]Alejandro Lugin's *Currito de la Crus,* published in English as *Shadows of the Sun* (New York: Scribners, 1934).

I'm not afraid to publish on account of fearing the critics will not find me a beautiful genius as some of your flock are. I only want to get out the very best book of stories it is possible to write. If I know it is as good as I can make it what anyone else says doesn't make any bloody difference.

At present I know that the book needs one more simple story of action to balance some of the difficult stories it contains. I thought I had it with the last story I wrote, one I just finished about the war, but that turned out to be a hell of a difficult one. Stories like Fifty Grand, My Old Man and that sort are no where near as good stories, in the end, as a story like Hills Like White Elephants, or Sea Change. But a book needs them because people understand them easily and it gives them the necessary confidence in the stories that are hard for them. A book of stories, that is a good one, is just as much a unit as a novel. You get the overtones by the juxtaposition of the stories or by what you put in between them. You cannot just have one good story and a lot of crap that you published in magazines as Scott's last book of stories was and make a book of it. Nor can you put everything you ever wrote together, as you did with Ring,[1] and not have the hate in them, the righteousness, and the cheating at the end of the bulk of them choke and throttle the fine ones.

Nor can you publish them all What makes a book of stories sell is <u>unpublished stories</u>.

I have thirteen stories now, all copied out and corrected. If anything should happen to me Pauline can send them to you and you can call it After The Storm and other stories paying her the other three grand before publication and making same contract as for Death In The Afternoon and inserting same disclaimer as in front of In Our Time. I will mark them in proper order. Went all over them yesterday. I write this not from any feelings of misaprehension but for <u>your</u> protection.

Now if things go as they should what is the latest date you should have mss. for eary fall publication? How late could you have it in case you got the title soon? How late could you have mss. in case of late fall publication?

Would you prefer to charge off that 3000 advance against the royalties due on Death In The Afternoon and pay me 3000 on receipt of the mss. and the other 3000 before publication? That would leave my conscience free.

I will be glad to pay you at the rate of 6% per annum on that $3000. until you get the manuscript. That will keep you from any loss as there is no other place you can get 6% as safely.

You are right that it would be a good thing for me to get a book of fiction out but when I know that I am liable to write a damned fine story or a piece in Cuba that would help make the book and that eventually I will get exactly the right title I hate to rush.

It was my fault because I got going on that novel. I thought it was a story,

---

[1]Ring Lardner's *Round Up* (New York: Scribners, 1929).

you see, and I used up six weeks that would have put this book in shape. It is a hell of a good novel and you will not be sorry that I worked on it but suddenly I realized that you have to do things one at a time and that it was really as bad for me to interrupt the job of getting out a book of stories as it was for Scott to have interrupted his bloody novel to write stories. So I put it away and then found myself with only two weeksbefore me. Wrote that Piave story,[1] no time to re-write it yet, and the story that I needed gone into the damned novel. For the long run it is a good thing since I have something well under way that I know, believe in and can go on with any time. But now have to perform the old miracle again to make a book of stories hang together—and I can do it if you can give me time. I hadn't realized how I was shortening your advance time because while I was in the novel I was so cockeyed happy to be going so well and so oblivious to what went on that I never noticed. I had thought you got the Men Without mss. in May or June because I remembered working on it then at Grau de Roi.

Lately when I am resting or wake up in the night I remember places, fine places and things that have happened, and I thought some of trying to get those in between the stories. If I could do that it would be very good. Anyway, however I do it, I want to get a good book. But always at your back you hear Sir Whitney Darrow hurrying near while before you lie deserts of lost publicity.[2]

I wish to hell you could come down. That is a shame about Charley. Couldn't you make it to get the mss? How are you anyway, Max? Don't let me worry you. I blow up but I want to serve your interests. My first obligation is to mine but that taken care of, like mercenary troops, will look after your interests better than the patriots.

You better charge off that 3000 against the royalties. Then you don't have to give me any money until I send the mss. That way I won't feel that I'm bitching you. When I send you the mss. you can send me the 3000 minus whatever I owe. I want to get the book out too. I want 6000 advance before publication. But I don't want to hold up your money nor gyp, bitch or delay you.

We go across Wed. the 12th. Can be reached at Ambos Mundos Hotel, Havana, Cuba.

Yours always

<u>Ernest</u>

Sorry to bother you with such a long letter!

---

[1]"A Way You'll Never Be."

[2]EH was alluding to lines from Andrew Marvell's "To His Coy Mistress": "But at my back I alwaies hear / Times winged Charriot hurrying near: / And yonder all before us lye / Desarts of vast Eternity."

*Wire, 1 pp.*
*Havana, Cuba*

1933 JUN 11 PM 7 02
TITLE IS WINNER TAKE NOTHING STOP WITH THIS QUOTATION
QUOTES UNLIKE ALL OTHER FORMS OF LUTTE OR COMBAT THE
CONDITIONS ARE THAT THE WINNER SHALL TAKE NOTHING
SEMICOLON NEITHER HIS EASE COMMA NOR HIS PLEASURE
COMMA NOR ANY NOTIONS OF GLORY SEMICOLON NOR
COMMA IF HE WIN FAR ENOUGH COMMA SHALL THERE BE ANY
REWARD WITHIN HIMSELF CLOSE QUOTE HOWS THAT TELL
YOUR FRIEND EASTMAN WILL BREAK HIS JAW REGARDS=[1]
ERNEST


*ALS, Hotel Ambos Mundos stationery, 4 pp.*[2]
*Havana, Cuba*


June 13/

Dear Max

. . . . .

. . . . .

. . . . .

Eastman has given me a new slant on my so-called friends in N.Y. If he
ever gets a solvent publisher to publish that libel between covers it will cost
the publisher plenty of money and Eastman will go to jail. Moe Speiser[3] will
see to that. I could use some of that dough.

If I ever see him anywhere or anytime, now or in the future, I will get my
own redress myself.

I am tempted never to publish another damned thing. The swine arent
worth writing for. I swear to Christ they're not. Every phase of the whole
racket is so disgusting that it makes you feel like vomiting. Every word I
wrote about the Spanish fighting bull was absolutely true and result of long
and careful and exhaustive observation. Then they pay Eastman, who knows
nothing about it, to say I write sentimental nonsense. He _really_ knows how
bulls are. They are like this—(he explains) I am like this—etc. (he explains) I
have seen 50 bulls do what that fool says—from his ignorance—no bull can
do—Its Too disgusting to write about—

And it is a commonplace that I lack confidence that I am a man—What
shit—And I'm supposed to go around with your good friends spreading that

[1]EH was reacting to Eastman's review of *DIA*, "Bull in the Afternoon," *The New Republic* 75 (7 June 1933): 94–97.
[2]200 words have been omitted from this letter.
[3]Maurice Speiser was EH's New York lawyer.

behind my back—And they imagine they will get away with it. Mr Crichton[1]—Mr. Eastman etc. Why dont you give them space to write it in the magazine? Whenever and wherever I meet any one of them their mouths will make a funny noise when they ever try to say it again after I get through working over them Mr. Crichton—the brave man who tells everybody things to their faces—We'll see—

They're a nice lot—The professional male beauties of other years—Max Eastman—a groper in sex (with the hands I mean) a traitor in politics and—hell I wont waste it on them.

It certainly is damned fine to have friends—They hear you are out of the country and they open up. Good. Bring on some more friends. I'll be a long way out of the country and they will all get very brave and say every thing they wish were true—Then I'll be back and we will see what will happen.

You see what they cant get over is 1 that I _am_ a man (2) that I can beat the shit out of any of them 3 that I can write. The last hurts them the worst. But they dont like any of it. But Papa will make them like it. Best to you—Ernest.

_ALS, 6 pp.,_[2] _Maryland and Princeton_[3]
_Havana, Cuba_

July 13/

Dear Max:

Here are the stories:
They go in this order—

|   |   |   |
|---|---|---|
| 1. | The Light of The World— | unpublished |
| 2 | A Clean, Well-Lighted Place | Scribners |
| 3 | After The Storm | Cosmopolitan—1932 |
| 4 | God Rest You Merry Gentlemen | 1933 House Bks Limited (Cohn limited) |
| 5 | The Sea Change— | This Quarter |
| 6 | A Way You'll Never Be | unpublished |
| 7 | The Mother of a Queen. | unpublished |
| 8 | A Day's Wait | unpublished |
| 9 | Homage To Switzerland | 1933 Scribners |
| 10 | One Reader Writes | unpublished |
| 11 | A Natural History of The Dead | (In book) |
| 12 | Wine of Wyoming | Scribners |
| 13 | The Gambler The Nun and The Radio | Scribners |

[1]Kyle Crichton was a Scribners editor who wrote leftist literary criticism as Robert Forsythe.

[2]131 words have been omitted from this letter.

[3]The first two pages of this letter are at the University of Maryland; the last four are in the Scribners Archive at Princeton.

[*In right margin*] Acknowledgements to [*torn*] Cohn [*torn*] s, This Quarter.

There is one more story I am re-writing and will send you from Key West—It is called—The Tomb of His Grandfather[1] and will be either next to last or last in the book. Although would like to reserve right to put it in another place in the batting order. It is about the same length as A Way You'll Never Be. Damned good story—Wrote it down here.

Plan to sail for Key West Monday Night—The 17th—May be a day or so later—

Havent written you because 1st was getting up at 5 and writing like a fool—then going out to fish—

2nd The huge fish finally came in—All this last ten days have been fighting huge ones—Landed one 12 feet 8 inches long—468 lb—hell of a fight—Have lost giant ones—Have caught 53—

Getting this Mss. now may be you can get me some proofs before we sail from here on August 7

Thanks for making the deposits when I wired and am so happy you took Evan's piece. He has some good stories—Thanks also for sending contract

Boat is leaking pretty badly—Marlin rammed it and the bill came clean through planking. Now has split plank a little—Have 8 bills broken off in the planking—

I wish to Christ you could have been here—Will write you about it. Too pooped now—

You might stress the fact that 6 of the stories in the book have never been published—One has been in a limited edition of 300 copies (verify number from Cohn) another only published abroad—(although copied freely here and a copy published by your esteemed selves)

(Could have sold A Way You'll Never Be and A Day's Wait for 1.00 a word—but want to have plenty of good unpublished stories to sell the book. Another thing—

Either I will mention in a foreword that A Natural History of The Dead was included because it was only available in a book published at 3.50 or you can say that I so requested in the front matter or the jacket—It was added to the original number of stories—Not put in to fill up.

Will you have it copied (typed) out of Death In The Afternoon—omitting the asides of Author and Old Lady—The Mss I enclose differs from the one in the book. Want to follow copy in the book.

. . . . .
. . . . .
. . . . .
. . . . .

Will probably want some more of that advance pretty shortly—

Will you wire when you get this Mss? If you get it later than Tuesday wire to Key West—I will get going over that other story as soon as get there—

As it stands without another story it is a damned good book—

[1]Published as "Fathers and Sons."

192

How do you like the title? Never lose confidence in old Papa—At the end of an hour the fish kills me—At the end of two hours I kill the fish.

Was sorry I got so sore about Eastman thing—But it was such a stinking lying piece of underhandedness—He wrote me a kissass letter—But he isnt out of the woods yet

When you send me proofs sent an extra set for me to send to Cape— Please—

. . . . .

Yours always.
Ernest/

*TLS with holograph inserts, 2 pp.*[1]

Key West
July 26

Dear Max,

Got back here July 20 and have been cleaning up getting ready to leave, waiting for proof or word from you and winding up affairs. Have everything pretty well cleared now and will start re-writing The Tomb of My Grandfather today.

. . . . .

Will be in Spain half of August and all of September. Maybe October. Will leave for Africa in November. This gives more time to work before start out again and time to get proofs all fixed up both with you and in England.

Poor old Gertrude Stein. Did you read the August Atlantic?[2] She's finally found a writer she can love and not be jealous of—the real american writer—Bromfield. It's damned wonderful how the story ends. She lost all sense of taste when she had the menopause. Was really an extraordinary business. Suddenly she couldn't tell a good picture from a bad one, a good writer from a bad one, it all went phtt.

Poor old Hem the fragile one. 99 days in the sun on the gulf stream. 54 swordfish. Seven in one day. A 468 pounder in 65 minutes, alone, no help except them holding me around the waist and pouring buckets of water on my head. Two hours and 20 minutes of straight hell with another. A 343 pounder that jumped 44 times, hooked in the bill. I killed him in an hour and forty five minutes. Poor fragile old Hem posing as a fisherman again. Weigh 187 lbs. Down from 211—

I'm going to write damned good memoirs when I write them because I'm jealous of no one, have a rat trap memory and the documents. Have plenty to write first though.

I imagine you are in more or less of a stew about certain words but tell me

[1] 128 words have been omitted from this letter.

[2] The *Atlantic Monthly* was serializing Stein's *The Autobiography of Alice B. Toklas;* the fourth and last installment, "Ernest Hemingway and the Post-War Decade," comments on his many injuries.

what you can and can't do and we will work it out. I'm not the little boy writing them on the wall to be smart. If I can make the effect without the word will always do so but sometimes can't. Also it is good for the language to restore its life that they bleed out of it. That is very important.

. . . . .

. . . . .

Yours always—
Ernest/

*Wire, 1 p.*

1933 JUL 31 PM 6 55

KEYWEST FLO
SEND PROOF AIR MAIL HOTEL AMBOS MUNDOS HAVANA CAN ARRIVE IN TIME IF MAILED THURSDAY IF AFFIX SUFFICIENT POSTAGE STOP CANT GET HERE IN TIME IF SENT WEDNESDAY PLEASE DEPOSIT SEVEN HUNDRED AND FIFTY CITY BANK FARMERS TRUST 22 WILLIAM ST WRITE DETAIL YOUR VIEWS ORDER STORIES LIGHT WORLD BETTER AND SHORTER STORY THAN MAISON TELLIER=[1]
    ERNEST.

*CC, 2 pp.*

August 2, 1933

Dear Ernest:

I am writing this letter now, in the morning, in the anticipation of being able to send you all the proof to Havana this afternoon. I have got most of it, and the rest is promised. I thought the war story a very fine story,- almost felt as if I were "that way" myself when I read it, and for sometime after it. It is a curious story, and most effective.[2]

I had been glancing at Gertrude Stein's articles, and that last one, of course, I read through. The truth might as well be known,- it ought to be—but in a way it is too bad she ever did that book for it seems to me that it blew her up. It showed her to be a petty character, I think, and a petty character cannot amount to much. She had this great reputation, and now she exploded it. What is more, I think there must have been contemptible malice in what she said about you. And mighty female malice too, which is the worst kind. The whole show seemed to me a poor affair. Now Cummings writes that book on

[1] "The Light of the World" features five whores; Guy DeMaupassant's story "La Maison Tellier" (1881) is set in a brothel.
[2] "A Way You'll Never Be."

Russia.[1] We had it here and I thought when he told me about it, it would be a wonderful book. But he wrote it in a way that hardly anyone would be willing to read it in. It requires more effort, and more of a kind of intuition, than you could expect of almost anybody who was not adept in reading. Why should he do it? Even in that form you can see that he has a wonderful eye and ear, and extraordinary humor. But humor is the very quality you cannot associate with writing in an utterly eccentric manner. The book was formless, of course, and always would have been that, but if it had been written, as it so easily could have been, so that anyone could have read it, it might have been a great book. There is nobody who seems more sane and honest than Cummings when you talk with him. There is some obscure reason why a man does things like that, and why Gertrude Stein also writes incomprehensibly. It is something about these times, I suppose. Or did some people always do it?

I hoped you had got over that trip to Africa. It always seemed to me a dangerous affair,- but my observation of your brittleness, or whatever she said, is that you are only brittle when you are under a skylight in a bathroom, or taking care of the baby, or driving a Ford on a high-road. So maybe you will pull through this too all right. Mike sent me a picture postcard showing some fish that he had caught weighing around eighty pounds. Is he going with you?

My point about the order of the stories is simply a practical one. The story you have put first is the one to which people will most object.- Utterly enrage all those who do get enraged in the most hateful way about those things. Its most conspicuous position would give it a tremendous emphasis, and would greatly damage the book in sales, and I think in other ways too, in reviews of such things. So I hoped you could put it elsewhere. I have underlined the words and phrases I think you ought to get around. There is one in "God Rest You" that you did not have in the version I read. I really think that one of the best of all the stories is "A Clean Well-Lighted Place" though it is of that kind, I suppose, which not many people would respond to as much as to others. I think "After the Storm" is probably the most popular sort of story.

I shall be writing you again soon. There are a lot of things I must tell you. But I must get this off.

Yours,

ALS, *Reina Del Pacifico stationery, 6 pp.*[2]

. . . . .

August 10—

Dear Max:—

The proofs never came—We arrived on Friday the 4th and I had your quite uneuthusiastic letter on Saturday (1st letter since I'd sent Mss.) saying

[1] *Eimi* (New York: Covici–Freide, 1933).
[2] 58 words have been omitted from this letter.

proofs sent same day—along with an envelop of front matter and table of contents (marked <u>returned for insufficient postage</u>) on Sunday—By Monday postoffice was closed and on Tuesday Did everything that could be done but could get nothing and I emphasized necessity of putting on sufficient postage in my wire as air-mail otherwise posted is <u>always</u> late—

. . . . .

Without the general strike would have received proofs in time even if the office hadn't mailed them properly—probably—I hope to Christ they get rid of that lousy tyrant

Saw everything that happened—No not everything—but what one person could see—keeping in the streets when supposed to be fatal and with my customary fragility or whatever G. Stein called it had no marks—Pauline and Jinny both fired on in the streets—food etc cut off for 3 days—

I suppose, from the tone in which you write (ie. <u>cautious defense of one or two stories</u>) that me having been attacked by your pal Eastman and poor old Stein you are all about ready to ask waivers—

But if you will go over the record you will find that I have cost the house of Scribner very little money—And I am in better shape and going better than I have ever been—It happens to be a time when I could appreciate a little loyalty (having just seen actions of Eastman, Stein and Co.) and if you feel you have been robbed by me taking a 6,000.00 advance (<u>Less</u> than the previous <u>non</u>fiction book had earned) (taking it in driblets so as not to embarrass your market comittments) (The state of the stock market being the accepted measure of a publishing enthusiasm for literature) will be very glad to return the

> 500
> 1000
> <u>750</u>

advance and call it all off—

But I tell you very sincerely that you would be very short sighted to do so—

<u>After</u> the stock market crash I turned down offers guarantying 25,000 advance etc. I have turned down plenty since—I paid for all the things in Death In The Afternoon that you promised to pay for—Your memory may be short or maybe you werent thinking about book but about something else and that's how I got impression I did. But didnt hear anything for 10 days after sent Mss. Then this letter—

And out of what has happened to me this year (details <u>not</u> <u>furnished on request</u>) you will make plenty when I write it—It wont be one of those Conrad Aiken stories So when your friends, who ardently hope for it, tell you that I am all washed up—I wouldnt take too much stock in it. Because I have a good 1/3 of a better novel done than any of the poor twirps you publish will ever come within a 100 leagues of doing—and am well and healthy and feeling fine—

And contrary to Gertrude I <u>last</u> where the others bastards break—

Thats why she said that—because being untrue she thought it would hurt me—

I will go over the order of the stories—When I asked you to write me in detail I had hoped you would—The book means something to me, you know too—Well—Good luck—Yours always

Ernest/

ALS, 3 pp., JFK[1]

[*Mid-August 1933*]

Dear Ernest: I meant Your present + future in my cable.[2] Never, since I read the first In Our Time have I had any question about You as a writer on real grounds. I have been terribly anxious on other grounds (not financial ones which I dont by nature think so much about) + I am somewhat now. A writer, + any artist, does reach a point after his first great sucess when he must meet opposition,—whether by the law of action + re-action, or from just plain cussedness in man, or what. But the real ones beat the opposition simply by having the reality or authenticity of their art. It can't be beat. You do give the opposition something obvious + easy to go against by ignoring the conventions + arouse a viscious hostility. But I know that while Bromfield etc. might + in the sort of writing they are willing to do, perhaps should, consider these things, the real writer should not. He should not be thinking about such things, of course, when he's writing. I really have been a buffer in this matter + I ought to be.—And I hate to speak to You about these things now because you're not the one to be worried about them. Then too You know everything I can tell You, I guess. I certainly think that I sound mighty silly in saying what I think of You as a writer. That has to go without saying. Suppose You heard someone tell Tolstoi he thought War + Peace was a great novel! By the way, I do think the last story You sent is a great story! As for the proofs, it is inexcusable + sickening. It seems they did not ask the P.O. about the packages till after they'd been mailed + I guess they carried too few stamps + will come back here. There's nothing to be said about it. Its done. Im enclosing the places marked that seem to me to be especially questionable.

The copy's safe.—I had it put away before the proof went.

Always Yours

Max

. . . . .

---

[1] 52 words have been omitted from this letter.
[2] "Not such blank fool to misjudge present or future" (15 August).

*ALS, 8 pp.*[1]

> Aug 31
> Hotel Biarritz
> Calle Victoria 2
> Madrid

Dear Max:

Thanks for your wireless and the two letters—Proofs came yesterday—

I'm sorry wrote a crabby letter—Not getting the proofs had my goat because I wasted time on them and would have had it on the boat—Also I'd done everything to get the copy to you in time and there was no way of missing them if they were posted properly—Then I would have sent them right on by the same boat and you would have had them from England a week ago—

Dont worry about me and opposition—Eastman trying to put his arm around me and stab me in the back got me very angry but it is only the first one of those that makes you feel bad—Had no reaction to the Stein thing at all. You know, of course, that I <u>forced</u> Ford to publish that long thing of hers and made him keep it in his magazine when he made very nasty scenes about throwing it out.[2] Was always completely loyal to G Stein until she practically threw me out of the house. She went quite gaga when she had change of life and it is unfair to judge her now. She lost all taste and judgement. She quarrelled with Picasso, with me, with André Masson and would have with Juan Gris if he hadnt died. Took up with a 4th rate lot of fairies. Now she has finally found a great writer Bromfield! That makes it all fine with me—she certainly invented some fine apochryphal incidents about me But what the hell I'm only sorry for her. It was a damned pitiful book.

(I got her to read The Enormous Room, for instance. Loaned it to her. I was crazy about it minute I read it! What I didnt like was Cumming's <u>drawings</u>—as published in Dial. She changed any fact to suit herself)

<u>About Proofs.</u>

I have changed the places you underlined and eliminated the three Anglo-Saxon phrases.

I do not do this happily. But I see your point very clearly and having taken money have no choice. Better to perform operation myself than have anyone else do it<u>—</u>If you want to leave off the K at the end of the word F—K in The Natural History of the Dead you can do so. It has been published once—So I dont care—I mean this seriously—I have never gone in much for fighting the conventions But for fighting the <u>Genteel</u> tradition which has been strangler of all English and U.S. literature.

Only a person who knows the conventions and has taste can do any good in this—as Erskine Caldwell cant—

[1]310 words have been omitted from this letter.
[2]The serialization of *The Making of Americans* in the *Transatlantic Review,* April 1924–January 1925.

. . . . .
. . . . .
. . . . .
. . . . .

. . . Am afraid will have to write my memoirs some time—But I swear to God Max that the small campaign I have made against the <u>genteel</u> tradition is quite different from Greenwich Village going against conventions—and that the fashions of speech are changing even in the bloody genteel circles of our native land.

However I have made the changes you request and see why you asked for them—

You can put The Light of The World 3rd opening with After The Storm—A Clean Well-Lighted Place 2nd—Then The Light if you think that better—

I do not want it any further down on account of it's chronological position in book—Also I thought it best to open with an unpublished story—However if you feel as strongly as you wrote about it put it in 3rd place—

It may make no difference anyway—

I might as well leave that last story as Fathers and Sons—

> The other titles I had were
> Long Time Ago Good.
> Tomb of a Grandfather
> Indian Summer.

---

If you prefer or Meyer, Hart and you all prefer any one of those titles please cable me—I have no one to consult with—Dos not here—Cant hold proofs until he comes—

Will you make a note in the jacket matter, somewhere inconspicuously, that A Natural History of The Dead is the only story previously published in a book (to hell with Cohns pamphlet) and it is reprinted at the authors request, because that book sold for $3.50 That there are 13 new stories. Put that first. One other published in limited edition of 250 copies. Now what else?

Oh yes What are these un-named worries about me?

I know that if I am fashionable (and should try to follow a fashion) I will be unfashionable (and would deserve it) That if I am popular I will be unpopular for a while. That if I make money my friends will hate me (Except those I support) That I will be attacked with more and more bitterness. I dont worry about any of those—You arent worrying about my private life are you? Dont.

All I want is for you to stick with me and not let attacks worry <u>you</u> and not let the business office get any goofy ideas about not pushing my books because someone has told them they aren't any good. They arent going to get any imitators of me that are going to make them the money that I will make them if they only have the loyalty to stick with me for a little while. I'm just getting to the age when a novelist really starts—And they all (critics) have tried to bury me after every book. Instead of being brittle am very durable (in spite of G. Stein) and only bones I've ever broken were broken by the full weight of a car turning over on my arm and by high explosive. Fished 97 days and caught 54 marlin swordfish without mis-hap—

If you send me the corrected proof when you get this (reading it carefully for spelling first) I will wire you o.k. on it—or wire any corrections. Then you can go right ahead and print. Will you please deposit balance of advance due in City Bank Farmers Trust—22 William Street—before date of publication?

Will you send duplicate <u>corrected</u> proof to Jonathan Cape Ltd?

Proof sent to Havana hasnt come yet—Dedication is

To A. MACLEISH

. . . . .

Yours always Ernest

. . . . .

[*In left margin of page one*] Max: This and the proof cannot catch any fast boat before the Majestic—sailing Sep 7—So you wont get it until 14th—but you check it yourself That means you cant get proof back to me before Oct 1 at earliest—When do you plan to publish? Would it be better not to wait for my OK.? Send me corrected proof anyway—I will check it and wire OK. and changes if any.

*CC, 3 pp.*[1]

September 22, 1933

Dear Ernest:

I got off the proofs to you yesterday. We ought to publish in October, and so we are going straight ahead. It seems to me that everything is all right. It was the first time I had seen the collection all as one, and I think it a most impressive one. All your stories in every book are better the fifth time you read them, which can be said of hardly anybody else, and I do not think you ever wrote a better story than "Fathers and Sons" (We have kept that title. We think it throws back into the past and future the way the story does more than any of the others, though "Tomb of a Grandfather" is a fine title). I did knock off that K. I ought to do the worrying, and I ought not to urge you any further toward concessions to the genteel than I can help.- And I admit too, that in the past I have probably gone too far that way because many things I feared have never happened. But we always have had very many vicious letters;- several self-righteous "gentlemen" probably in the Union Club, or the University, wrote that they were bringing "Death in the Afternoon" to the attention of William Sumner, for instance, and would never buy another Scribner book. I knew Sumner could not do anything about that book, and the other statement is like after the war when everyone said they would never trade again with Germany. But the Genteel have managed to murder several of the best writers there ever were;- though they were more fragile

---

[1]217 words have been omitted from this letter.

boys than you, and I suppose it was more on account of their conduct than their writings, too. We do want for every reason to stand back of everything you do and I am always afraid of being too timid about it because I come from people who were conventional in those regards, although never genteel. I was mighty amused by your account of the Englishmen. I know that they do use a lot of those words now under any circumstances. I read some piece somewhere the other day about how they had given up "bloody" and taken on substitutes. There is nothing but custom in the matter, and a strange thing about it is that what is objected to is the words, and not the reality at all. Those "un-named worries" are all on that score,- the fear of arousing unconquerable prejudices. But it is true that you have been righter than I have been so far, and I have always remembered that.

Scott called me up the other day, and the first thing he asked about was whether you had been bothered by Gertrude Stein.- I said I thought you were a little at first. He was very mad at her, and said she had done just that way before. He is supposed to come over here pretty soon. I want to hear what he thinks of the whole book. I must say it is the funniest thing she should have singled out Bromfield, who is obviously fake. It must be just that she likes him or something. Whitehead in Boston says that nothing she has about them in the book is true.

Everything about the Proof seemed to be clear and right. The dedication is to A. MacLeish. The order of the stories is plain. If you strike anything wrong, and can wire it, do that. If we do not hear anything we shall just go ahead and bind as few as possible, and if anything turns out wrong, we can print cancels.

. . . . .
. . . . .
. . . . .

Yours,

*ALS, 6 pp.*

November 17 1933
c/o Guaranty Trust Co. of N.Y.
4 Place de la Concorde
Paris
Cable address HEMINGWAY
GARRiTUS
PARIS

Dear Max:

Thanks for your two cables—of a week and two weeks ago and your letter of Nov. 6 enclosing some of the reviews. I cabled you yesterday because I had been seeing the N.Y. Times, Herald Tribune and Sat Review of Lit and they all were full of ads of a book of stories by Dotty Parker but nothing about this book. There was an ad in Sunday Times and I believe Daily Times the week the book came out. Then nothing. No follow up at all. Saw No mention of book in Sunday Herald Trib in number it was reviewed in. An ad in with your fall list in the week after. Believe there was an ad in Herald Trib the day it came out. The advertizing is your business—not mine. But if a publisher seems to give no importance to a book and make no Boom Ha Ha the public takes the cue from the publisher very quickly.

One of the reasons I always stuck by you was (in a commercial way) because you kept on pushing The Sun Also Rises through a terrificly slow start—And one of the things I did not care much about was the way after a wonderful start they dropped Death In The Afternoon absolutely cold. You know yourself.

This happens to be a book <u>you</u> have to do a little work to push—But in the end it doesnt do anyone any particular harm to publish literature once in a while—Especially as I have always paid my way.

You mention a review by Soskins in your letter but you didnt send it.

Also I have never had any August royalty reports—nor any accounting since I saw you in N.Y. (May have had a royalty report in the Spring) Will you please send them.

The bird,[1] when he labelled me as approaching middle-age was trying to get rid of me that way—Others having failed. So the advertizing department siezes on that to advertize the book by. If I write about <u>anybody</u>—automatically they label that character as me—when I write about somebody that can't possibly be me—as in After The Storm, that unfortunate convert to Economics religion Mr. Chamberlain,[2] says it is unusually imaginative or more imaginative than anything I've attempted. What shit.

When does Middle Age commience? That story—Wine of Wyoming is nothing but straight reporting of what heard and saw when was finishing A Farewell To Arms out in Sheridan and Big Horn—How old was I then? That was 1928 and I was just 30 years old while I was out there. Yet that bird says it is about middle aged people because <u>he himself</u> is middle-aged. I was 17 when first went to the war. (This for your own information) I write some stories absolutely as they happen ie. Wine of Wyoming—The letter one, A Day's Wait The Mother of a Queen, Gambler, Nun, Radio, and another word for word as it happened, to Bra, After The Storm,; (Chamberlain found that more imaginative than the others) others I invent completely Killers, Hills Like White Elephants, The Undefeated, Fifty Grand, Sea Change, A Simple Enquiry. <u>Nobody</u> can tell which ones I make up completely. The point is <u>I want</u> them all to sound as though they really

[1]Horace Gregory, "Ernest Hemingway Has Put On Maturity," *New York Herald Tribune Books* (29 October 1933), p. 5.
[2]John Chamberlain, daily reviewer for *The New York Times*.

happened. Then when I succeed those poor dumb pricks say they are all just skillful reporting.

I invented every word and every incident of A Farewell To Arms except possibly 3 or 4 incidents. All the best part is invented—95 per cent of The Sun Also was pure imagination. I took real people in that one and I controlled what they did—I made it all up—

A fool like Canby[1] thinks I'm a reporter. I'm a reporter <u>and an imaginative writer.</u> And I can still imagine plenty and there will be stories to write <u>As They Happened</u> as long as I live. Also I happen to be 35 years old and the last two stories I wrote in Havana were the best in the book[2]—And this 15,000 word one[3] is better than either of them. Several miles better.—So if you let all the people who want me over with kid you into believing Im through—or let the business office start to lay off me as a bad bet—You will be making a very considerable mistake because I havent started to write yet—(wont ever write you this again—)

I cant write better stories than some that I have written—What Mr. Fadiman[4] asks for—because you cant write any better stories than those—and nobody else can—But every once in a long while I can write one as good—And <u>all the time</u> I can write better stories than anybody else writing. But they want <u>better</u> ones and as good as <u>anyone ever</u> wrote.
God damn it. There cant be better ones. The one they pick out as "classic." Hills Like White Elephants not a damn critic thought <u>anything</u> of when it came out. I always knew how good it was but I'll be Goddamned if I like to have to say how good my stuff is in order to give the business office confidance enough to advertize it after they have read an unfavorable review and think I'm through.

So I wont Ever Again. Will do something else.

Will you please, for God's sake, because this is <u>very important</u> have a statement sent to me of all money paid me in 1933—in any forms—(And give the income tax people the same amount or total you send me when you report it to them.) Please send this on January First or whenever you know everything paid me in 1933—absolutely <u>as soon as possible.</u> (I will not ask for any more this year for anything) Please send this statement to the Guaranty Trust Co. of N.Y. 4 Place de la Concorde—Paris and Mark The Envelope in large letters—Please Forward By Air Mail. They will send it out to Tanganyika by Imperial Airways and I will be able to prepare my income tax report.

I wanted to have some idea before I left and wrote about it from Spain but have heard nothing.

This seems to be all.

<hr>

[1]Henry Seidel Canby, "Farewell to the Nineties," *Saturday Review of Literature* 10 (28 October 1933): 217.

[2]"Away You'll Never Be" and "Fathers and Sons."

[3]"One Trip Across" was published in *Cosmopolitan* (April 1934) before it was collected in *THHN*.

[4]Clifton Fadiman, "A Letter to Mr. Hemingway," *The New Yorker* 9 (28 October 1933): 74–75.

Does it seem of any significance to you that they all say there are 3 really good stories and nearly all pick 3 different ones? That Mr. Harry Hansen who doesnt understand these didnt understand A Farewell To Arms when it came out—Panned it—Now thinks it great novel etc. Oh hell—why go on. Why write as far as that goes? Because I have to.

If Cosmopolitan send this long story back to you—<u>Please hold it for my instructions.</u>

So long, Max. I hope you're fine and havent too many family worries. We sail on next Wed. This is Friday. Too many things to do.

Yours always,

<u>Ernest</u>

*CC, 3 pp.*[1]

January 12, 1933 [1934]

Dear Ernest:

The sale at the present moment amounts to thirteen thousand, six or seven hundred copies. We are now at that stage at which you came in last year,- many copies are on consignment of all the leading books, and we do not know what we may have sold out of the consignments. I hope we shall get to fifteen thousand by the time that is cleared up. It was not even a good depression year for publishers in general, but with the Longworth and Van Dine and Galsworthy and Sullivan[2] to help, we did a good deal better. We even sold about 3,000 of the first two volumes (which do not even touch the good part) of Churchill's Life of the Duke of Marlborough.- But we gave a big advance on that book long ago, and I don't believe we shall ever get it back. We hope to carry on "Winner Take Nothing" through the winter and spring. The salesmen have just gone out and should get some good orders.

. . . . .

Have you heard what I was bound for some reason not to tell you, that Scott has finished his novel? A mighty fine one too. We are running it in Scribner's. I have had some hard but funny sessions with him in the last several months. The book is truly very fine as a whole. It has a very tight plot. Some people would pretend to misunderstand the adjective in view of the authorship, but not you,- though it does somewhat apply in the wrong sense. It is based upon a psychiatrical situation. The hero, one Dr. Diver, had prepared to be a psychiatrist;- and Scott could never have written it unless he had come into contact with sanitariums, psychiatrists, etc., etc., on account of Zelda's illness. It is the sort of story you can imagine Henry James writing,

---

[1]220 words have been omitted from this letter.

[2]Alice Roosevelt Longworth, *Crowded Hours;* S.S. Van Dine, *The Dragon Murder Case;* John Galsworthy, *One More River;* and Mark Sullivan, *Over Here: 1914–1918* (Volume Five of *Our Times*).

but of course it is written like Fitzgerald, and not James. If you were in a place where I could get it to you safely, I would send you the whole thing in proof. It really ought not to be serialized, but authors must eat, and magazines must live. I shall send you a set of complete proofs anyhow, when I have them, whether they get to you or not.

I went down to Baltimore and tried to read the manuscript here in an extremely unfinished and chaotic form, with Scott handing me Tom Collinses every few minutes, and taking out sections of the manuscript to read aloud to me. But we did get it finished. It was the serialization that made him do it. He had to do it once that was agreed upon.

Then Tom Wolfe's book.- I have got here about seven or eight hundred thousand words of it, and I am not going to let it get away from here. Tom is supposed to come here every afternoon at 4:30 and we work for two hours, and on Saturday afternoons, and the book will be published this summer. When it is, I am going to take a vacation.

. . . . .
. . . . .
. . . . .
. . . . .

Yours,

. . . . .

*ALS, New Stanley Hotel stationery, 5 pp.*<br>*Nairobi, Kenya Colony*

Jan 17

Dear Max:

Thanks for your two letters enclosing royalty reports statistics for income tax etc.

I am afraid I do not understand your remark about "What business advice!" I gave Franklin. In order to aid you I went over his entire translation, 2 weeks of steady work, got him a jacket, explained every point to him that you asked me to, and showed him just why and how the contract you offered him was just. If you were unwilling or unable to push or advertize this last book as you have former books is no reason to act as though I were working against your interests with Franklin. If you knew the number of times I have explained to him that he could trust you absolutely you would not write in that tone.

Another thing you might remember is that there is a time in every mans life, if he is worth a damn, when he has to be unpopular. The only writers who survived the war were the ones who did not believe in it. <u>You have to believe in writing</u>. I am against and outside of this present damned YMCA economic hurrah business and you will find, when it is over, that I will be neither old fashioned, nor behind the times. I will be the same as always, only better, because I will have stuck to my job and will know a damned sight more. But when a publishing organization seems unable to keep up a pretense of believing in you——How is the public expected to respond.

Have seen 83 lions—I've shot 2 black maned ones—2 very big bull buffalo—excellent heads of Eland, Roan antelope, record Impalla, good Grant and Roberts Gazelle, Bushbuck and Water buck. Also a very big leopard and 2 cheetah.

Charles[1] has killed a fine lion and a marvellous buffalo—and has some fine heads.

He and Pauline are very well. I have had Tropical dysentery for last 2 weeks. Hunted every day but 2 with it But those 2 were <u>something.</u> OK now. Passed as much as a pint and 1/2 of blood a day. Flew in here about 400 miles yesterday over Ngororgoro Crater, Rift Escarpment to Arusha, then here, to get some injections Rejoining the Safari on the 21st at the Crater. It takes them 5 days to get there from where I got the plane—We hunt Rhino then greater and lesser Kudu and Sable. Have killed every thing, including Buffalo, with the Springfield 30-06 and the little Mannlicher. Ordered the Plane from Victoria Nyanza (Mumbashi think the station is)

Took the plane in to ease my ass and get the dysentery injections. That's a hell of a lousy disease. Your whole damn intestine tries to come out. Feels as though you were giving birth to a child. Will fly back out to meet the outfit. Dr. says am through the worst of it. Had really very light case.

This is the finest country I've ever been in. Believe we will settle out here. Wonderful people and splendid climate. Pauline is mad about it.

Come out of the bush on Feb 20—Go down to a little island off <u>Lamu</u> at the mouth of the <u>Tanu</u> river where have hired an empty Arab house to fish for swordfish—They report them 18 feet long (Probably bunk) Young Alfred Vanderbilt is going too and Philip Percival (who we've been hunting with) is going down to fish with us. He's the man who got Roosevelt his lions and is a wonderful bird. But would rather fish than do anything. Have had a wonderful time with him. Have heard some marvelous stories.

Well so long Max.
You would be crazy about this country.

Best luck,<br>Ernest/

CC, 4 pp.[2]

Feb. 7, 1934

Dear Ernest:

As you know, Cosmop took your story, and I finally got them to give me a set of proof, and read it in excitement.[3] It is one of your big stories,- takes

---

[1]Charles Thompson, EH's Key West friend, is Karl in *Green Hills of Africa*.
[2]142 words have been omitted from this letter.
[3]"One Trip Across."

two or three days to shake it off. There are four stories in "Winner Take Nothing" that are anyhow as fine in their own ways, but this is one of those spectacular stories which everybody will feel to the full effect. I am mighty glad you wrote it, and I'll bet there will be a lot of talk about it.

. . . . .

I believe that Scott will be completely reinstated, if not more, by his "Tender Is the Night". He has improved it immensely by his revision—it was chaotic almost when I read it—and he has made it into a really most extraordinary piece of work.- And I believe when he gets through with revising the first quarter for the book, he will have a genuine masterpiece in its kind. He is in a much better psychological state of mind too, having done it,- I was down there about ten days ago. Domestically things are still bad with him, but about himself he feels like a new man, I could see. He has all kinds of plans now for writing,- wants to begin another novel immediately. I shall soon have the last of the book proof in type and will send you a set.- But you may not want to read it because the book itself will be better than this proof.

You know mighty well that I know you did right by us, as well as by Franklin. He imposed rather hard terms—though not so bad really. But I was looking at the job as one of translation rather than of authorship, though his name was invaluable to it,- was in fact the biggest thing about it. But we never would have got the thing through at all if you had not been in it, I know that.

. . . . .

Always yours,

*TLS with holograph inserts and postscript, 3 pp.*
*Key West, Florida*

April 30, 1934

Dear Max:

When you get this will you deposit the 2000. you said I could borrow in my account in City Bank Farmers Branch, 22 William Street, N.Y.C. I would like it very much if you could make it 2500 instead of 2000. as I had to loan 400 dollars to a mutual friend on what he claimed was a matter of life and death (it sounded like it) and that has made me that much short on my boat financing. If you aren't in a position to let me take the 500 please wire when you get this and I will raise it somewhere else. But would much rather get it from you. Otherwise please wire deposit made (naming sum) and I will know it is ok to check against. Will you send me a note for this for me to sign bearing interest at 4 per cent. Then when I have a book ready on which I want an advance I will turn the note over to you for cancellation as part of the advance and pay you the interest from the date of loan until date of advance unless I should get the advance later than December 31 of this year.

In that case I will send you a check on Dec.31 for the interest from date of loan until the end of the year.

I rushed a book last year because I had taken an advance. It was no fault of yours. I felt the obligation to get it out although my best judgement told me it needed another story of the kind I know it needed to have people think they were getting their moneys worth. It is not enough to just give them their two dollars worth, anybodys two dollars worth, if they will read them over. You have to give them just ten times more than anybody else ever gives them for the same amt. of money. And I had kidded myself that you didn't.

But I am a careerist, as you can read in the papers, and my idea of a career is never to write a phony line, never fake, never cheat, never be sucked in by the y.m.c.a. movements of the moment, and to give them as much literature in a book as any son of a bitch has ever gotten into the same number of words. But that isn't enough. If you want to make a living out of it you have to, in addition every so often, without faking, cheating or deviating from the above to give them something they understand and that has a story—not a plot—just a story that they can follow instead of simply feel, the way most of the stories are. The story is there but I dont tell it to them in so many words. I knew it then, too. But because I had taken the damned advance I thought what the hell—that's good enough for them and more—they won't know it is—but what the hell.

But I am a professional and professionals learn by their mistakes instead of justifying them. So that won't happen again.

What has caught me right now about money is that I have had to loan to people in my same craft who were ill or in bad financial shape the sum of $1155.00 since March 26th of this year. This doesn't count money loaned to family etc. You cannot turn people down until you get to the place where you actually have no money to loan them and cannot borrow without imperilling your liberty of action. Have now reached that point so what happens to people in my craft does not concern me until I make some money again. And all I will do to make money is write and the ones that are saleable will be—and the others wont. I cant interfere with how they come out and my bloody dependents can all starve before I will write them anyway but the one and only way you can write them—Truly.

Now about Scott's book.[1] I finished it and it has all the brilliance and most of the defects he always has. In spite of marvellous places there is something wrong with it and, as a writer, this is what I believe is wrong. He starts with two people Gerald and Sara Murphy.[2] He has the accent of their voices, their home, their looks marvellously. But he knows nothing about them. Sara Murphy is a lovely and a marvellously strong woman. Gerald is a man of

---

[1] *Tender Is the Night.*

[2] The Murphys were celebrated Riviera hosts who befriended Fitzgerald and Hemingway; *Tender Is the Night* is dedicated to them.

great charm but very complicated emotionally and Scott depicts his charm very well at various times. He knows <u>nothing</u> about him emotionally.

But he takes these people who are formed by certain things, suffer from certain faults, which he knows nothing of because when he was with them he was busy making them into romantic figures instead of knowing what they were about (you do not learn about people by asking them questions), creating these romantic figures and then asking them concrete questions such as 'did you sleep with your wife before you married her?' in order to obtain "facts" to insert in the plasticine of his figures to try to make them seem true—it's awfully silly.

But anyway he takes a strong woman like Sara, a regular pioneer mother, and first arbitrarily makes her into a psychopathic case and then makes her into Zelda, then back into Sara, and finally into nothing. It's bloody hopeless.

Gerald is Gerald for a while, then made-up, the made-up part is good, then becomes Scott and has things happen to him that could never happen to Gerald. The beating up by the Carabiniere in Rome etc. So you are never convinced about him going to pieces.

He has taken a series of incidents, good incidents from his life and used them quite arbitrarily, made the story conform to the few wows he had saved up out of his life.

It isn't the way prose is written when the prose is any damned good—but then by Jesus he has so lousy much talent and he has suffered so without knowing why, has destroyed himself so and destroyed Zelda, though never as much as she has tried to destroy him, that out of this little children's, immature, misunderstood, whining for lost youth death-dance that they have been dragging into and out of insanity to the tune of, the guy all but makes a fine book, all but makes a splendid book.

But the hell of it is that you can't write Prose after you are thirty five unless you can think straight. And it is the flashes where he <u>does</u> think straight that carry this book in spite of all the worn christmas tree ornaments that are Scott's idea of literature.

The trouble is that he wouldn't learn his trade and he won't be honest. He is always the brilliant young gentleman writer, fallen gentleman writer, gent in the gutter, gent ruined, but never a man. If he is writing about a woman going crazy he has to take a woman who has gone crazy. He can't take one woman who would never go crazy and make her go. In life she wouldnt go crazy. Thats what makes it false. If he is writing about himself going to hell as a man and a writer he has to accept that and write about that. He can make it all up and imagine it all but he must imagine it truly. That is. If he wants it to be literature. You can make up every word, thought, and action. But you must make them up truly. Not fake them to suit your convenience or to fit some remembered actions. And you must know what things are about. He misunderstands everything. But he has this marvellous talent, this readability, and if he would write a good one now, making it all up, he could do it. But using actual stuff is the most difficult writing in the world to have good. Making it all up is the easiest and the best. But you have to know what things are about before you start and you have to have confidence. It is like navigating once you have dropped the shore out of sight astern. If you have confidence you are all right. But to have confidence you have to know your stuff.

Well this is a long letter.

Am going well but it is hard going. Have 20 good pages now on a story and 30 bad ones—discarded—Some are certainly easier to write than others. But am writing the kind that is hardest for me to do. Will do one of the easier ones next.

Get the boat May 9[1]—Then I can work in the morning and go out in the boat in the pm. Weather has been marvellous

Don't show any of this above to Scott or tell him I said anything I'll write him but have been too busy so far.

Best to you always,<br>Ernest

Please wire about money.

Am going to Havana tomorrow<br>to see May Day—<br>Back in a couple of days

CC, 3 pp.[2]

May 3, 1934

Dear Ernest:

. . . . .

I was extremely interested in what you said about Scott and about the novel. I knew that a great deal of this was true, and yet a great deal of the good writing he has done has come from that very fact of a sort of adolescent romanticism. I saw Scott last week in Baltimore and things are very far from right with him, and it is all based on this confusion in himself. There are certain fundamental things about which he has the strangest, most unreal ideas. It has always been so of him. But about one of these delusions I think I made an impression. Here he is, only about thirty-five or six years old, with immense ability in writing, and in a state of hopelessness. But it is useless to try to talk directly to him about it.- The only way one could make an impression would be by some oblique method, and that takes a cleverer person than I am.

. . . . .

Yours,

. . . . .

---

[1]EH used an advance from *Esquire* to purchase his fishing-cruiser, the *Pilar*.
[2]155 words have been omitted from this letter.

CC, 3 pp.[1]

May 23, 1934

Dear Ernest:

　. . . . .

　. . . . .

　. . . . .

If ever I get down there to Key West I would like to talk about Scott's book. Anyhow it was a mighty notable book, and is quite furiously discussed. I know of course, that there is that conflict in Scott's character, and a kind of basic illusion which causes a defect in the book and did not cause one in "The Great Gatsby" which was completely fitted to the illusion and the conflict. The other difficulty came very largely from the fact that Scott was too, too long in getting the book written, and he could not bear to exclude all of the superfluous material which he had gathered up in those years. He did exclude a good deal that was in the first manuscript, but he could not— though he prides himself in his relentlessness in this regard—bring himself to exclude a good deal more that should have been left out.

　. . . . .

Always yours,

CC, 5 pp.[2]

June 28, 1934

Dear Ernest:

　. . . . .

　. . . . .

I cannot come down now. I cannot leave as long as I can keep Tom going well, as he is doing now. We have over half the book finished, except for a little touching up on another reading. We have got a good system now. We work every evening from 8:30 (or as near as Tom can come to it) until 10:30 or 11:00, and Tom does actual writing at times, and does it well,- where pieces have to be joined up. We are organizing the book.- That is the best part of the work we are doing. It will be pretty well integrated in the end, and vastly more effectively arranged. The fact is, Tom could do the work but his impulse is all away from the hard detailed revision. He is mighty ingenious at times, when it comes to the organization of material. The scheme is pretty clear in his own head, but he shrinks from the sacrifices which are really cruel often. A couple of nights ago I told Tom that a whole lot of fine stuff he had in simply ought to come out because it resulted in blurring a very important effect. Literally, we sat here for an hour thereafter without saying a word, while Tom

[1] 168 words have been omitted from this letter.
[2] 321 words have been omitted from this letter.

glowered and pondered and fidgetted in his chair. Then he said, "Well, then will you take the responsibility?" And I said, "I have simply got to take the responsibility. And what's more," I said, "I will be blamed either way." But he did it, and in the end he knew he was right. We go over to "Chatham Walk" where you sit in the open, afterwards. Anyhow, we will have this book done by the end of July if we go on as we are going now.

. . . . .

. . . . .

Always yours,

*CC, 3 pp.*[1]

Oct. 6, 1934

Dear Ernest:

That about the novel is wonderful news.[2] I won't worry about how it compares with other people's novels. I'd felt morally certain you were doing a novel, but not quite, because when you were here you spoke of having written a great deal on a narrative and of thinking you might reduce it to a story. Sidney Franklin did not know what you were writing, but he did tell me you had written a lot. You do a novel, and we shall strain every muscle for it. Things look better now too,- if only they don't break them down in some new way. But let me know soon if The First Fifty-Seven[3] could be published in the fall or the spring, or when. If the novel were imminent I would do the novel first.

. . . . .

. . . . .

That word in Tom's subtitle is Hunger,- "A Legend of Man's Hunger". I do think with Tom pretentiousness may be right. That is the idea anyhow,- at least in my accepting the subtitle. And it is a darn sight less pretentious than it was when Tom started. We have got over half the book now in type, and if we can only keep Tom from writing in a lot more, we shall soon have it all in type, and out in January. Of course twice as much ought to be done to it as he will let us. And then my conscience bothers me about it often. A man ought to understand his own book better than anyone else can. But I just have to follow my judgment regardless. Somebody has to do it. There is no question but it needs about fifty percent cutting, and Tom won't give it one-tenth of one percent.

Don't get into too much danger down there.

Always yours,

[1]113 words have been omitted from this letter.
[2]On 3 October 1934 EH had written MP that he had "50,000 words done on this long thing."
[3]Projected title for a collected edition of EH's short stories.

*TLS, 2 pp.*[1]

Key West, Florida
November 16

Dear Max,

I finished the long bitch this morning, 492 mssspages, average, I suppose, something over a hundred and twenty words to the page.[2] Feel pretty good about it. Will write you about it later. Too pooped to write about it now. Also about the first fifty-five or the first fifty-six, or whatever we call it, Am writing in a hurry now before the train leaves to tell you that Luis Quintanilla who is one of the best friends I have in the world and, all friendship aside, absolutely the finest etcher alive is having a show opening November twentieth at the Pierre Matisse gallery in the Fuller building. I had arranged for the show before the October revolution in Spain. In that revolution Quintanila was arrested and is in jail in Madrid now charged with being a member of the revolutionary committee and the prosecuting attorney is trying to get him sixteen years of hard labor. I have written an introduction[3] to the catalogue and Dos has written another. I am putting up for the show and sent Luis the money to pull the etchings. Don't say anything about that. I was going to do it anyway before there was any jail tie up, and I had sent the money before he was arrested because of my belief in the etchings. When you see them you will know how marvelous they are. There have been no dry points come out of Spain as good since Goya and in some ways Quintanilla is a finer technitian even than Goya. Pierre Matisse is very excited about them and so is every body that has seen them.

Now what I want you to do is see what publicity the publicity department can get for the exhibition as a favor to me. You know that I have never bothered them to do any work for me. They can use my introduction and Dos' as first editions to hang something on if they want or they can make something of the row that I have picked in the introduction in order to help the show. If the etchings do not sell, although I am certain they will, I am going to give two autographed copies of any of my books to any purchaser of a print, but do not say anything about that yet as it may not be necessary and I do not want to do any circusing if we can put it over without that. The two introductions are damned good. Let the publicity department get the catalogue and they can get plenty to go ahead on out of them. In the second week if they havent sold will start with the book racket.

I would come up for the show and handle the publicity myself but am flat broke because I have not made any money during all the time I've been working on this long one. Am starting a story tomorrow. It has been fairly tough to keep going and run a God-damned scientific expedition on the

---

[1]110 words have been omitted from this letter.
[2]*GHA.*
[3]*Quintanilla* (New York: Pierre Matisse Gallery, 1934), p. 4

side,[1] but I have finished this thing without interrupting it, no matter what the temptation to make money writing on the side, and that is the only way you can write. There are quicker ways to make it than writing if you have to have it in a hurry, but me, I'm going to write now.

. . . . .

Glad you've got Tom Wolfe to the printers but I swear to God that last story in the magazine opened in the phoniest way and had the most Christ-awful grandiloquent title of anything I ever read.[2] You know why your geniuses stall so long and are afraid to publish may very well be because they have a big fear inside of them that it's phoney instead of being a World Masterpiece and are afraid somebody will find it out. It's better to write good ones one at a time and let the critics jump on what they don't like and have orgasms about what they do like and you know they're good yourself and write them and get them out and not give a good God-damn about what anybody says. But the only way you can do that is not to fake and most of the boys, if they don't fake, would be starved to death by Wednesday next. I suppose I'm getting to feel pretty good and may be a little snooty at having finished what started last April, so better sign off and not speak ill of my overassed and underbrained contemporaries, your World Geniuses. There's no feeling, Max, like knowing you can do the old stuff, even though it makes you fairly insufferable at the time to your publisher. On the other hand, I've never shot worse at birds in my life so I suppose what you make in Boston you lose in Chicago and after all I'm just a God-damned writer. . . .

Yours always
Ernest


*ALS, 4 pp.*[3]


Key West
Tuesday—Nov. 20—1934

Dear Max:

Thanks for the wire. I'm glad you liked the Esquire piece.[4] Wrote them another one Sunday and sent it off yesterday. Have been having a terrible lot of energy—Bad as disease—Have worked all day every day since we got back from Cuba—Maybe it's that worry to get your work done we always feel in the fall when the year dies—

I've just been looking at this I've finished to get an idea of the length I took pages at random and counted the words—page (6)—175—(31) 182 (92) 317 (93) 156 (111) 93 (135) 149 (156) 118 (211) 126 (233) 84 (262) 118 (303) 125 (311) 204 (382) 104 (411) 169 (450) 103 (468) 179—Those    16

[1] EH was compiling records of fish migration in the Gulf Stream.
[2] "Dark in the Forest, Strange as Time," *Scribner's Magazine* 96 (August 1934): 71–81.
[3] 62 words have been omitted from this letter.
[4] EH made an agreement with Arnold Gingrich of *Esquire* in 1933, committing himself to write monthly articles called "letters."

pages average out 150 words to the page—There are some very long ones in the first 150 pages—But I only took one really long one—The shortest ones are mostly conversation—There are 491 pages which would make it 73,650 words—

I've been over a little more than half of it 3 times re-writing and cutting so I dont imagine will cut more than 3 or 4 thousand words out of the last.

I started it as a short story about while we were hunting in Africa, wanting it to be a damned fine story to go at the end of the First Fifty Four and it kept going on and on—Until now it is as long as I tell you—But it has a beginning and an end—it the action covers almost a month—and after you have read it I think you will have been there—

It is more like the story at the end of In Our Time—Big Two Hearted river than anything else—in quality—It is as much landscape painting, making the country come alive, but a hell of a lot happens in this one and there is plenty of dialogue and action. There is plenty of excitement, I think—But you will know when you read it—I had never read anything that could make me see and feel Africa—It was not at all as I had imagined it or like any thing I'd ever read—When I started the story that was what I wanted to make—But just the straight story, the actual things that happened on that wonderful Goddamned kudu hunt—the relation between the people and the way it all worked up to a climax—seemed to me a very fine story. Anyway I have it done now—

Been starving me to do it for 8 months.

One thing I have learned this last year is how to make a story move—So that it seems short when it is really very long. I think this has that—Anyway we will see—

I've written it absolutely truly. <u>absolutely</u> with no faking or cheating of any kind but I think I have learned to make it smoother without sacrificing any honesty—This is as honest as the Big Two Hearted River and much more exciting—I make the excitement with the country—But there is so much more going on too—

Then we will have to figure how to handle it—I suppose 70,000 words is a little long for a story—It can be a book by its-self <u>Is!</u> but because I <u>know</u> how good it is I would like to throw it in free with something else to give them their supreme bloody moneys worth—I want to be <u>un</u>-pompous and give them what is really literature without being pretentious while your pompous guys blow themselves up like balloons and burst.

I notice you didnt say anything about it when I mentioned collecting the Esquire articles—What was the matter? Didnt you like them? I have 11 of them now—The 2 on big game in Africa are the only two that are weak. And they are O.K. But I didnt want to get into something there I was going to use—It would be possible to run this long one and follow it with the Esquire articles—calling it—say—The Highlands of Africa—

and Other Pieces

———

It is a swell thing, Max—I think the best Ive written—True narrative that is exciting and still is literature is very rare Because first it has to happen Then the person that it happens to has to be equipped to make it come true ie to realize it, so that it has all the dimensions You have to <u>make</u> the country—not describe it. It is as hard to do as paint a Cezanne—and I'm the only bastard right now who can do it. Because I've been working, learning how to do it all this time.

There's one way to handle it—another way would be to run it either as a story in or as the Introduction to The First Fifty-Four or whatever we call it—(For Christ sake keep that title <u>absolutely</u> to yourself or somebody will grab it for something else).

It is a hell of a good book by its-self—but I want to get out a book of <u>super value</u> for the money—That is the best way to sell a hell of a bloody lot of them—After whichever is published first—either the collected stories or the collected Essays—I want to follow with a novel that will knock them cold. But I am not in a hurry about it—And can always publish both books first— I'd even write another novel and let this one wait There is no hurry on anything that is any good. The hell of it is my mother and my fathers brother being alive[1] (That's a hell of a sentence to write isn't it? Let us wish my mother luck Hope she lives forever. Maybe that will take the curse off.)

Anyway So long, Max. Thanks for the books, the Lee the Gordon (Paulines read it I havent had time yet) the Henry James and The Duck book. Youre the only publisher that ever sends free books that are worth a damn. Thanks <u>very</u> much.

Can the retailers send me these and charge them—
The Random House—Proust—4 Vol 12.50
Dostoevsky—A life—Yomolinsky—Harcourt Brace—$3.75
Glory Hunter—(Gen Custer) Bobbs-Merrill—      $3.<u>75</u>
The Chianti Flask—Mrs Belloc-Lowndes[2]—(Publisher and Price unknown)
Taking of The Guy—Masefield[3]              "          "         "

Thank you very much—I hope you can come down this winter—Fishing, with the Pilar, is fine. We can run into Marquesas and be comfortable—or go to Tortugas or any place you say—Why dont you come down now and read this long story? It's worth reading. I'm going good.

Best luck always, Ernest

. . . . .

---

[1]EH did not write his projected novel about his family.

[2]Marie Adelaide Belloc Lowndes (1868–1947), British suspense writer; her works were among EH's favorites.

[3]John Masefield (1878–1967), British poet and novelist.

CC, 4 pp.[1]

November 28, 1934

Dear Ernest:

Maybe I might come down to Key West. I would like to do it mighty well. I'd like to spend an afternoon on the dock looking at those lazy turtles swimming around. The trouble is there is another author in Florida,- Marjorie Rawlings.[2] She is a fine author too, and a fine woman. But I never did feel comfortable alone with women (I suppose there is some complex involved in it) and the idea of visiting one with nobody else around (she is divorced) scares me to death. She is one of the best as a person, and a mighty good writer too, and she is just finishing a book. She has asked me to come down a lot of times, and if she ever knew I went to Key West and did not stop there, it would be mighty bad. You get that story finished anyway. Until then you will be busy.

. . . . .

I do not think I saw all the pieces in Esquire, though I must have read eight of them. The truth is I did like them, even including the one about Ring Lardner.[3] I had heard some of them criticized as that one was. But no one could have admired or been more fond of Ring than I was, and although knowing you, I may have read something into it, from you, I did like it. Ring was not, strictly speaking, a great writer. The truth is he never regarded himself seriously as a writer. He always thought of himself as a newspaperman anyhow. He had a sort of provincial scorn of literary people. If he had written much more, he would have been a great writer perhaps, but whatever it was that prevented him from writing more was the thing that prevented him from being a great writer. But he was a great man, and one of immense latent talent which got itself partly expressed. I guess Scott would think much the same way about it.

I think it is magnificent about the story. Couldn't you modify the title (which I am altogether for in general) to "In the Highlands of Africa". It would imply something that happened, or things that happened there. Without the "In" as a title alone, it might be what they call a "travel" book. You will suspect that in this suggestion, I am thinking of the trade and the wholesale department. I know they would bring the travel suggestion up against the title. But I have not told anyone about this book except Charlie and he has not told anyone. The title suggests a great deal to me, and all I want to do to it is to get in something that makes it seem as if it were a <u>story</u>.

I do not want to put anything so emphatically that it will embarrass you to overrule me if you must, but it is my strong conviction that this story ought to be published by itself. It detracts from a book to add anything else to the same volume. It does not make it more desirable, but less so. This comes

---

[1]192 words have been omitted from this letter.

[2]Rawlings (1896–1953) published her first book, *South Moon Under,* with Scribners in 1933; she is best known for *The Yearling* (New York: Scribners, 1938).

[3]"Defense of Dirty Words: A Cuban Letter," *Esquire* 2 (September 1934): 19, 158b, 158d had criticized Lardner's puritanism.

partly from the fact that publishers always are padding books, and everybody is on to it. They get a story of 25 or 30 thousand words and it is too short to interest the trade,- the price would have to be so low that the margin is too small. The public seems to object to small books, so then they proceed to pad it. Either they pad it by putting in a great many half titles and some illustrations, or much more often by asking the author for short pieces to add to it, or short stories. It is never so good as a complete unit. What is more, I do not think it is so good absolutely. "Spring Freshets" is really a long story, but it ought to be published by itself because it is a masterpiece, and ought not to be thought of with anything else, but only by itself.[1] If this book were only 40,000 words, I would say, publish it alone. Then, to revert to the purely practical: when the reviewers review the book with the short pieces added, their comments would be somewhat vitiated by being scattered to some extent over the other pieces. I hope you will publish it by itself.

The other possibility was to put it in the lead of "The First Fifty-Seven". That would make a very big book for one thing. But the chief objections I have to it are the same ones that apply to the addition of the Esquire pieces. The reviews then would be of all the stories. I see that you regard this as a story, not a novel, but that makes no difference.- It is a complete unit and considerably longer than would be necessary to make a full book. Besides, with this story you are writing you will have plenty to give "The First Fifty-Seven" the element of new material that is needed and fine things too. The reason I wrote about the last Esquire piece was mostly because of what it said about writing.[2] I thought that was magnificent, and as true as any utterance could be. Old Tom has been trying to change his book into kind of Marxian argument (having written most of it some years before he ever heard of Marx) and I had been trying to express to him that very thing, that what convictions you hold on economic subjects will be in whatever you write if they are really deep.- So you don't have to drag them in. I thought the whole piece was very interesting, but it was that writing part that particularly got me.

Always yours,

. . . . .

*ALS, 2 pp.*[3]

Piggott
December 28, 1934.

Dear Max:
Thanks for your letter, the check and the statement. Enclose check for interst for $66.12

---

[1] Novel by Ivan Turgenev, more commonly known as *The Torrents of Spring* (1871).
[2] "Old Newsman Writes: A Letter from Cuba," *Esquire* 2 (December 1934): 25–26.
[3] 92 words have been omitted from this letter.

It will be fine to see you and Mrs. Perkins at Key West. I hope to leave here Jan 1 and be there by Jan 5th but I will want at least a week (Better ten day) of uninterupted going over of my typed Mss. But if you come down before the 14th or 15th you can amuse yourselves until I'm through. I do not believe I could do revising and rewriting which is, with me, an un-alcoholic business requiring absolutely complete attention with Scott there but I would love to see him once that is over.

He was to come down with Gingrich and I spent a week getting ready for him. But his Mother was ill. I would like to see him very much but it would be better not when we are discussing, seriously, treatment of a book or when I am finishing a book. His judgement about a book—cutting re-writing etc. is deplorable. It is always to make it like the last considerable success. I will show you some time as a curiosity his suggestions to me on how to improve the type script of A Farewell To Arms which included writing in a flash where the hero reads about the victory of the U.S. Marines.[2] He got this idea quite legitimately from a story I told him about hearing about the U.S. Marines while I was in Italy and not believing it but it was un-necessary in the book since the book was a work of fiction designed to stand without last minute shots of sure fire journalism. He also made many other suggestions none of which I used. Some were funny, some were sad, all were well meant.

Thank you for the information about the N.RA code and the publishers stand. What is the name of the code that protects writers?

I dont believe I have any luck publishing in the Spring.

. . . . .
. . . . .

Best to you always,<br>Ernest

. . . . .

ALS, 5 pp., JFK

[c. 11 February 1935]

Dear Ernest:—

I explained that the "debt" to us was not to be reported as income to U. S. Govt.—So you don't have to put it in 1934 return.

Just got Your letter + am writing you this way unofficially because of akwardness in the price question. You named a price + I didn't + dont mean you to suffer. Never fear me as a man of business (alas!) Now I'm in the position of young U. S. Grant when he sold the horse for his father.—"Dad said to ask you $150—but if you won't give that etc."

When I went to Key West there were two things before the magazine—

---

[2]Fitzgerald's memo about *FTA* does not mention the Marines; see Bruccoli, *Fitzgerald and Hemingway*, pp. 111–115.

Villiers + Truslow Adams. They were indefinite but I had a faint anxiety that we were committed to so much that we would not have room for a serial + this was a matter that I had to talk about.—couldn't wire about. I did mention this to You, + bid for it, I should have asked to bring back your ms. Then, too, it would not be decent not to have Dashiell read the ms before we came to conclusions. He's supposed to run the Magazine. We probably would prefer to pay by instalments, but that isnt the real point: We run on so close a budget that if we exceed it in one number, or anyway in several, we cant offset it in later ones. We couldn't put "Green Hills" into 3 or 4 numbers. That's why I wanted to see if it could break up into seven, to spread the price. What was in my mind <u>then</u> was \$4,200,—600 a number, twice what we pay for anything else. You, when we last talked, mentioned \$5,000. Can't we stop here till we get the ms. I'll do rightly + I wont let you be put in a jam by any personal considerations. The whip is in <u>your</u> hand if we come to that.

Yours<br><u>Max</u>

How much does a really good shotgun cost?

It must have done me great good to get that rest. I thought I was well + I was, but the change freshened everything up + the world has looked better to me ever since

MP.

Wire, 1 p.<br>Key West, Florida

FEB 18 1935

LETTER JUST RECEIVED SORRY UNABLE UNDERSTAND YOUR ATTITUDE PRICE UNLESS YOU MEAN YOU WANT ME TO REFUSE IT TO RELEASE YOU FROM PURCHASING STOP WHAT DOES WE DO NOT INTEND THERE SHALL BE ANY HARD FEELINGS ABOUT PRICE MEAN STOP AND ON HOW SOUND AN ECONOMIC BASIS DID I OFFER IT TO YOU STOP THE MAGAZINE HAS NEVER BEEN ON A SOUND ECONOMIC BASIS AND NEITHER HAVE I BUT IVE NEVER COST A PUBLISHER ANYWHERE ANY MONEY EITHER EXCEPT LIVERIGHT BY LEAVING HIM STOP WHEN OFFERED YOU FIFTY GRAND YOU WANTED TO CUT IT AS TOO LONG LATER YOU GAVE FIVE THOUSAND DOLLARS FOR A LONG SHORT STORY CONTEST STOP I TURNED DOWN THREE TIMES WHAT YOU PAID ME TO PUBLISH FAREWELL IN THE MAGAZINE STOP CAN YOU WONDER WHY DONT UNDERSTAND THIS WHEN OUR CLEAR AGREEMENTWAS YOU WERE TO WIRE ME AS SOON AS YOU REACHED NEWYORK WHAT YOU COULD PAY

ERNEST

*Wire, 1 p.*
*Key West, Florida*

1935 FEB 19 PM 3 22

OK SENDING SOME PICTURES WILL TOSS YOU FOR THE FIVE HUN-
DRED IF YOU LIKE=
　　ERNEST.

*CC, 4 pp.*

Feb. 19, 1935

Dear Ernest:

When there is a misunderstanding it never does any good to attempt
explanations. It generally makes things worse. But the truth is my attitude has
always been perfectly simple and there has never been in it any intention that
it should be anything else. What I intended you to think was that we would
make you the highest price we possibly could in view of the situation of the
magazine, which I tried to explain, and that in order to do this, if the road was
clear for the serial, we would have to spread it over as many numbers as we
could without detriment to time of book publication, for the sake of spreading the payment. If I misled you, it was in not discussing the price more specifically when I was there at the time you mentioned five thousand. I had begun
by saying between four and five thousand, and that was all that was said because
I could not tell how many numbers we could run the serial in, and I thought
it possible, though unwise, that we might be able to catch an earlier number
to start with, and run it in eight, which would have made the five thousand easy.
When I got back that was impossible. Anyway, it would have been too many
numbers. Seven is a good many to stretch something over that ought, ideally,
to be in one number. Surely I could never have given you the idea that we did
not want the serial. I had never considered the possibility of serialization before
you brought it up because I knew our price would seem low to you, and I simply regarded the thing as beyond our reach. In each of my letters I pretty clearly
said that we would meet your price for we always have been completely for you
since the first day we had anything here of yours,- unless you accept the matter of "Fifty Grand" and the magazine of that day.

Dashiell was slower in reading the serial than I hoped he would be, but he
was not unreasonably long as compared to any other magazine as I know, for
I have dealings with them.- And the delay too, was inevitable on account of
the situation he happened to be in. I daresay the editor of "Esquire" runs a
one man show where he can say Yes or No on an instant, without any regard
to anyone else. But it cannot be that way in a house like this. The man who
manages the magazine ought to have his say, and I do not believe that the
Cosmop or anything but "Esquire" and perhaps not that, could have acted
any more quickly. If you had suggested serialization to me before I came to

Key West, I could have been prepared to deal with it entirely. As it was, all I could say was that I was positive of our wanting "The Green Hills" for a serial unless we were blocked by other things which was a slight danger, and if we could pay an adequate price.

We shall begin the serial in the May number which appears about April 20th. The last number, which will have the longest installment, as it should have (and I think installments break up very well) will appear October 20th, and we can publish it that moment, which is a good time.

*CC, 2 pp.*[1]

Feb. 27, 1935

Dear Ernest:

. . . . .

. . . . .

The real reason I am writing is this: Scott has got back from four weeks in North Carolina and writes me "I have been on the absolute wagon for a month, not even beer or wine, and feel fine." He told Ober that he was never going to touch another drop. I thought maybe you could find some time and some reason to do something that would help him in the crisis he will have to meet after a bit. It would be a miracle if he could stop wholly and for good, but perhaps he will pull it off. I thought you might have some excuse to write him in a way that would do good. I suppose he is not telling people he has stopped, but I mean just something that would buck him up. His letter sounds fine and happy, but I know there will be a let down and a struggle.

Always yours,

*CC, 3 pp.*

April 4, 1935

Dear Ernest:

I am having a sample page made up for "Green Hills of Africa", the book, which I shall soon send you. The thing that has troubled me is what I spoke of yesterday,- that the book has the quality of an imaginative work,- is something utterly different from a mere narrative of an expedition. (I am not trying to tell you this, of course, but have to say it the way you have to begin in geometry by saying that a straight line is the shortest, etc.) Just the same, it has also the value to hunters and people who care for adventure, of a record. It tells so much about animals and the way things are in Africa, and about shooting and hunting.- This value it has as a record is enhanced by photographs, but the other and greater value, is injured by photographs. I there-

---

[1]114 words have been omitted from this letter.

That's the truth.—I say all this mostly because I sometimes have thought that You thought I ought to advise You, or keep You advised. I do that for lots of people who write as a trade. With You it seems superfluous + absurd because those things that are important to that kind of writer + affect his fortunes, ought not to have anything to do with You,—+ so far You have not let them. I hope You never will, too.

. . . . .

I'll send you the page proof next week. I request that you consider what You say of Gertrude Stein. I'm not afraid of libel + I don't care a hang about her, but what she has said was plainly spiteful + jealous + not worth so much notice from you, + almost all readers will not know what she said anyway but will sympathize with a bitch because she gets called a bitch. I simply submit this for Your consideration.

You spoke of what the Russians said. Can You send any of this to me. I think we could get Russian comments printed. If You have them in Russian I could get them translated. By the way,—the way Green Hills rises so wonderfully into the final episode is felt by every one in our office that has read it.—

. . . . .

Always Yours
Max

The third and fourth pages of Perkin's 30 August letter
written from the Harvard Club.

*TLS with holograph inserts, 5 pp.*[1]

Key West Sept. 7

Dear Max;

I was glad to have your letter and would have answered sooner except for the hurricane which came the same night I received it. We got only the outside edge. It was due for midnight and I went to bed at ten to get a couple of hours sleep if possible having made everything as safe as possible with the boat. Went with the barometer on a chair by the bed and a flashlight to use when the lights should go. At midnight the barometer had fallen to 29.50 and the wind was coming very high and in gusts of great strength tearing down trees branches etc. Car drowned out and got down to boat afoot and stood by until 5.a.m. when the wind shifting into the west we knew the storm had crossed to the north and was going away. All the next day the winds were too high to get out and there was no communication with the keys telephone, cable and telegraph all down too rough for boats to live. The next day we got across and found things in a terrible shape. Imagine you have read about it in the papers but nothing could give an idea of the destruction. Between 700 and 1000 dead. Many, today, still unburied. The foliage absolutely stripped as though by fire for forty miles and the land looking like the abandoned bed of a river. Not a building of any sort standing. Over thirty miles of railway washed and blown away. We were the first in to the camp five of the veterans who were working on the Highway construction. Out of 187 only 8 survived. Saw more dead than I'd seen in one place since the lower Piave in June of 1918.

The veterans in those camps were practically murdered. The Florida East Coast had a train ready for nearly twenty four hours to take them off the Keys. The people in charge are said to have wired Washington for orders. Washington wired Miami Weather Bureau which is said to have replied there was no danger and it would be a useless expense. The train did not start until the storm started. It never got within thirty miles of the two lower camps. The people in charge of the veterans and the weather bureau can split the responsibility between them.

What I know and can swear to is this; that while the storm was at its height on Matecumbe and most of the people already dead the Miami bureau sent a warning of winds of gale strength on the keys from Key Largo to Key West and of Hurricane intennsity in Florida straights below Key West. They lost the storm completely and didn not use the most rudimentary good sense in figuring its progress.

. . . . .
. . . . .
. . . . .
. . . . .

[1]260 words have been omitted from this letter.

226

Max, you can't imagine it. two women, naked, tossed up into the trees by the water, swollen and stinking, their breasts as big as baloons flies between their legs. Then, by figuring, you locate where it is and recognize them as the two very nice girls who ran a sandwich place and fillingstation three miles from the ferry. We located sixty nine bodies where no one had been able to get in. Indian Key absolutely swept clean, not a blade of grass, and over the high center of it were scattered live conchs that came in with the sea, craw fish, and dead morays. The whole bottom of the sea blew over it. I would like to have had that little literary bastard that wanted his hurricane along to rub his nose in some of it. Harry Hopkins and Roosevelt who sent those poor bonus march guys down there to get rid of them got rid of them all right all right. Now they say they should all be buried in Arlington and no bodies to be burned or buried on the spot which meant trying to carry stuff that came apart blown so tight that they burst when you lifted them rotten, running, putrid, decomposed, absolutely impossible to embalm, carry them out six, eight miles to a boat., on the boat for ten to twenty more to put them into boxes and the whole thing stinking to make you vomit—enroute to arlington. Most of the protests against burning or burying came from the Miami undertakers that get 100 dollars apiece per veteran. Plain pine boxes called coffins at $50 apiece. They could have been quicklimed right in where they are found, indentification made from their pay disks and papers and crosses put up Later dig up the bones and ship them

Joe Lowe the original of the Rummy in that story of mine One Trip Across was drowned at the Ferry Slip

Had just finished a damned good long story and was on another when this started with the warning on saturday night. They had all day Sunday and all day monday to get those vets out and never did it. If they had taken half the precautions with them that we took with our boat not a one would have been lost.

Feel too lousy now to write. Out rained on, sleeping on th deck of the run boat, nothing to drink through all that business so ought to remember it, but damned if I want it for my novel. We made five trips with provisions for survivors to different places and nothing but dead men to eat the grub.[1]

. . . . .

Imagine a love affair would help Scott if he has anything left to love with and the woman isn't so awful that he has to kid himself too much.

About the Stein thing—I was just trying to be completely honest. I don't mention her name and what proves it is Gertrude? what would you like me to put in place of bitch? Fat bitch? Lousy bitch? Old Bitch? Lesbian Bitch? What is the modifying adjective that would improve it? I don't know what word to replace bitch with. Certainly not whore. If anyone was ever a bitch that woman was a bitch. I'll see if I can change it. (Have just found it and read it over and don't see what the fuss is about. Unless you think it gives the critics some-

[1]See EH's "Who Murdered the Vets?" *The New Masses* 16 (17 September 1935): 9–10.

thing to burp about. For Christ sake Max don't you see that they have to attack me to believe in themselves. You can't be popular all the time unless you make a career of it like Galsworthy etc. I will survive this unpopularity and with one more good book of stories (only these are going to be with plenty of action so they can understand them) and one good novel you are in a place where they will all have to come around and eat shit again. I don't give a damn whether I am popular or not. You know I never went in for it when I was. The only thing bothers me is that your business office will not have the faith in me that I have and will not see that I am working on a long plan instead of trying to be popular every day like Mr. Roosevelt. I need a certain amount of money too

All right. Let us take up the word bitch again.

Would you prefer fat female?

That is possible. I'll change it to fat female. or just female. That's better. That will make her angrier than bitch, will please you by not calling a lady a bitch, will make it seem that I care less about her lying about me, and will please everyone but me who cares only about honesty.

Well I've fixed it up now. It's all right. Have gotten more how I really feel about her and given it the small degree of importance that it deserves. It's all right now. Don't worry.

. . . I appreciate what you wrote about writing

Enclosed is the way the Stein part goes so you can get it reset now for the page proof. This fixes it up all right and puts the emphasis where it belongs. Also betters the end of the chapter I think and avoids the word bitch as applied to a Lady writer.[1]

---

[1]In the second *Scribner's Magazine* installment of *GHA* (97 [June 1935]: 339), the passage read:

"Mr. J. P. is really awfully brave, you know he really is. He's *so* lovely."

"Yes, and he doesn't have to read books written by some bitch he's tried to help get published saying how he's yellow."

"She's just malicious. She knew that would make you angry."

"It did all right. She's skillful when she's malicious, with all that talent gone to malice and nonsense and self praise. Well, she's cashing in now. Anybody can whenever he wants. How would you like a little cash, Baby?"

For the book text (pp. 65–66), Hemingway revised the passage to read:

"Yes, but I'm dignified with him. Don't you think he's wonderful."

"Yes, and he doesn't have to read books written by some female he's tried to help get published saying how he's yellow."

"She's just jealous and malicious. You never should have helped her. Some people never forgive that."

"It's a damned shame, though, with all that talent gone to malice and nonsense and self-praise. It's a god-damned shame, really. It's a shame you never knew her before she went to pot. You know a funny thing; she never could write dialogue. It was terrible. She learned how to do it from my stuff and used it in that book. She had never written like that before. She never could forgive learning that and she was afraid people would notice it, where she'd learned it, so she had to attack me. It's a funny racket, really. But I swear she was damned nice before she got ambitious. You would have liked her then, really."

When you get this letter can you deposit $500 in my account at City Bank Farmers Branch 22 William Street, That will bring the advance up to $4800 I believe.

Will get going on the rest of the proofs now but wanted you to have the revised part to you without delay. Will send this down now.

> Good luck, Max.
> Yours always,
> Ernest/

*TLS, 1 p.[1]*
*Key West, Florida*

December 17, 1935

Dear Max:

. . . . .

. . . . .

My book was ruined by three things; First that price—it was much too high for the length of the book.[2] I protested about this in advance but it did no good.

2nd—without even thinking about it I had offended the daily critics deadlily and they ganged up on it. The sidicated critics did the same. This was my fault.

3rd—You had a big advance sale. With any book by anybody it needed advertisment to move this and get the other sale started. Nothing was done to overcome the bad daily reviews by putting ads in those paper quoting from the good weekly reviews when it would have done some good. Ads at that time would have moved our advance sale. Instead the offensive was allowed to bog down completely and never gotten moving at all.

My stuff is not now judged by whether it is good or bad interesting or dull but whether it is or is not A In Our Time B The Sun Also Rises C A Farewell to Arms D Death In The Afternoon. You may have noticed how this last which was hailed as lousy when it came out is now referred to with the hush-hushe. It all gives me a pain in the ass.

Haven't seen Bunny's piece.[3] From the title it sounds as though he must have felt pretty bad to go all the way to Russia and find them liking my stuff. Perhaps he will be able to put a stop to that.

. . . . .

I feel sort of bitter about a lot of things but I always get over that. How did you like my Ethipian piece in Jan. Esquire?[4] Considering I write them a

[1] 100 words have been omitted from this letter.
[2] The book was priced at $2.75.
[3] Edmund Wilson, "Letter to the Russians about Hemingway," *The New Republic* 85 (11 December 1935): 135–136.
[4] "Wings Always Over Africa: An ornithological letter," *Esquire* 5 (January 1936): 35, 174–175.

month ahead they seem to come out pretty close to the headlines. I'll be a strategist yet. Am thinking of cutting out writing for Esquire. Been working very hard.

Best to you always,
Ernest/

*CC, 3 pp.*[1]

Dec. 20, 1935

Dear Ernest:

I read "Wings Always Over Africa" and although I have been reading you for a long time so that there ought not to be any element of surprise left, I read it with the greatest admiration. There isn't a living man who can write about things like that or can do that kind of writing (which really is only minor writing for you) who can be compared with you. It really is astonishing, and if we have great turbulent times, and revolution, so that the much more important writing cannot be done, there will be something that you can do in that way. This goes for the last, or most of the last five, or six, or seven, articles in Esquire, and the one in the Masses. They ought to be published in what we used to call "more permanent form". When it comes to doing it though, it is my belief that they should be carefully selected so that only the best go in. I ought to be almost shock proof, but I think that about the birds shuffling over you is a terrible passage, and the practical and philosophical comments in the article are hard as nails and carry truth with them. There are lots of elements to be considered because you are doing so many things, but if you should think it wise seriously to consider the proletarian boys, the Marxists; we could show them what could be done in the way of dealing with actual events and class conflicts which would make their stuff look silly. I have always thought that your journalistic sense made you a wise judge of when and what should be done. Something should be done in that direction at some time, and before too long, but we have the book of stories for the fall, and the spring is a short season, and I do not think there are enough of these articles as yet to make a book. They are not ephemeral though.

As to the points you make in your letter: I knew, and I never dreamed that you did not, that you were telling plain truths to the reviewers in "Green Hills". I could have warned you about that, but I did not think you wanted it, and I do not believe you would have heeded it for an instant. Nor do I think you should have. You have always spoken out, and insisted on your way, and I think you are right in doing it. It is all a question of how long a view you take. You told the truth about them and it won't act against you over a fairly long space of time, but only momentarily.

As for advertising, it is a matter that nobody can ever speak of positively

---

[1] 66 words have been omitted from this letter.

and it would be silly for anybody to say they might not have done wrong about it.- But this is the fact. Orders were given that irrespective of results altogether, and because we knew we were right about the real value of the book, "Green Hills" should have the same backing in advertising as Sullivan, Van Dine, and "Europa".[1] We spent much more on "Europa" because of its long time of publication and its extraordinary sale, but not more within the same period. We do not believe that you can answer unfavorable reviews by following them up two or three days later. You might if you knew when they were to appear, in the same issue. We have tried every turn and twist in advertising, and we do not believe that the daily papers have any value comparable to the Times and Tribune supplements. It is stupid that this is so, but we have been convinced of it. When a book goes in great style, the daily use of the advertisement does keep it in people's minds, and so we used it on "Europa". We did do a good deal of it in the dailies on "Green Hills" but not until after you spoke of it.

I am not saying all this to dispute you, but merely to tell you what our idea was.- But nobody, not one bookseller, ever doubted the price of "Green Hills". Booksellers always kick about prices, that they ought to be higher or lower, and often cause publishers to change the prices. It is the one thing they do talk about if they have any doubt. Not one unfavorable criticism was made of the price of "Green Hills". It looked its price thoroughly.

. . . . .

Yours,

*TLS with holograph postscript, 1 p.*[2]
*[c. 30 December 1935]*                                          *Key West, Florida*

Dear Max;

Thanks for the letter. I'm glad you liked the Wings Over piece. You can see what Bunny amounts to when he has never read my last six or seven Esquire pieces and still feels it o.k. to lump them all as rubbish. Well what the hell. It used to make me damned angry to be lied about but now there is more solid satisfaction in being lied about by shits than being praised by them. You don't worry about whether you are on the wrong track or not. Sooner or later we might get out a book of the sort you write about. But as you say next fall we have the stories. It looks now as though there would be enough for a book of new ones. Will keep that in mind. After all no need to collect if have a good full book of new ones on hand. Will let you know. If I don't have sickness or accident should be o.k. Have five chapters done on what s should be a short novel or a hell of a long story. About down here.

---

[1] Mark Sullivan's *Our Times: The Twenties*, S. S. Van Dine's *The Garden Murder Case*, and Robert Briffault's *Europa*.
[2] 69 words have been omitted from this letter.

About the critics, offending same, I never thought about them at all. Only put down what I told the Austrian in response to questions and what I was thinking then. You remember Winner Take Nothing came out while we were away and I got the first reviews in Arusha and read them in the plane flying to Nairobi. That was how I happened to think about critics at all when I came back hunting after that time being ill in Nairobi. I didn't set out to offend them but to tell the truth and if the truth offended them tant pis. It is all to the good in a few years. But hard on you as publishers of present book.

About the other stuff—as I say I was never around N.Y. when a book came out before and certainly never will be again. Wrote my reactions. You do right to back the book regardless of immediate sale as you have a valuable property to protect and sooner or later will have a book that will outsell any of them. There is no hurry though. With the critics hating my gut the way they do could bring out Hamlet new and they would see no good in it. But who are the most talented and best writing of the kids coming up? Cantwell, O'Hara, Malraux say.[1] They are the ones that like and respect my stuff—not the disappointed bastards who write the columns and hate your guts because they think you are in the big money, because they know you despise them, because you called them angleworms in a bottle. The novelists can see how your writing develops. The critics can't al l they can do is remember how wonderful Lady Brett was in the sun also rises.

Will you let me know what the book has sold? In the office first I heard an advance sale of 12,000. Then Darrow got out his figures and proved it to be just a few under 10,000. Don't let it go backwards since I left N.Y.

. . . . .

. . . . .

Yrs always—
Ernest—

. . . . .

---

[1] Robert Cantwell (*The Land of Plenty*), John O'Hara (*Appointment in Samarra*), and André Malraux (*Man's Fate*).

# HEMINGWAY/PERKINS CHRONOLOGY
## 1937–1940

◆

| | |
|---|---|
| 13 January 1937 | Hemingway is in New York; he signs contract to cover Spanish Civil War for the North American Newspaper Alliance (NANA). |
| c. 17–27 February 1937 | Hemingway is in New York to meet with John Dos Passos, Archibald MacLeish, and Lillian Hellman about the documentary film *The Spanish Earth;* he sails for Spain 27 February. |
| 21 March 1937 | Hemingway begins residence at the Hotel Florida in Madrid. |
| 18–26 May 1937 | Hemingway is back in New York. |
| 4 June 1937 | Hemingway is in New York to deliver speech, "Fascism Is a Lie," at Second International Writer's Convention. |
| c. 20 June 1937 | Hemingway is in New York. |
| 5-c. 8 July 1937 | Hemingway is in New York for premiere of *The Spanish Earth.* |
| 10–17 August 1937 | Hemingway is in New York en route to Spain; on 11 August he gets into a scuffle with writer Max Eastman in Perkins's office as a result of Eastman's article "Bull in the Afternoon." |
| 15 October 1937 | Scribners publishes Hemingway's third novel, *To Have and Have Not.* |
| 31 December 1937 | Thomas Wolfe leaves Scribners. |
| c. late January 1938 | Hemingway is in New York. |
| 31 March 1938 | Hemingway returns to Spain with journalist Martha Gelhorn. |
| 1 April 1938 | Scribners publishes Marjorie Kinnan Rawlings's novel *The Yearling.* |

233

| | |
|---|---|
| 22 June 1938 | Hemingway is in New York for the Joe Louis-Max Schmeling fight. |
| 29–30 August 1938 | Hemingway is in New York en route to France; he has breakfast with Perkins on 30 August. |
| 15 September 1938 | Thomas Wolfe dies in Baltimore, Maryland; Perkins is named executor of his estate. |
| 14 October 1938 | Scribners publishes *The Fifth Column and the First Forty-nine Stories.* |
| 3 November 1938 | Hemingway returns to Spain for fourth and final time during the Spanish Civil War. |
| 24 November–5 December 1938 | Hemingway is in New York. |
| c. 2–24 January 1939 | Hemingway is in New York to assist with the revisions of *The Fifth Column* for Broadway production; he meets with Perkins. |
| 10 April 1939 | Hemingway is in Cuba writing his fourth novel, *For Whom the Bell Tolls;* he begins living with Martha Gelhorn at La Finca Vigía. |
| 20 September 1939 | Hemingway and Martha Gelhorn are guests of Sun Valley Lodge, Idaho; they stay until mid-December. |
| 7 March 1940 | *The Fifth Column* opens on Broadway; the reviews are bad. |
| c. 25 July–early August 1940 | Hemingway is in New York revising *For Whom the Bell Tolls.* |
| 21 October 1940 | Scribners publishes *For Whom the Bell Tolls.* |
| 4 November 1940 | Hemingway's divorce from Pauline Pfeiffer Hemingway is final. |
| 21 November 1940 | Hemingway and Martha Gelhorn are married. |
| c. early December 1940 | Hemingway is in New York preparing for his Far East trip. |
| 21 December 1940 | F. Scott Fitzgerald dies in Hollywood, California. |
| 28 December 1940 | Hemingway buys La Finca Vigía. |

—R.W.T.

# FOR WHOM THE BELL TOLLS

# Ernest Hemingway

Front of the dust jacket for the last Hemingway novel edited by Perkins.

*TLS with holograph inserts, 1 p.*[1]

*[c. 15 February 1936]*          *Key West, Florida*

Dear Max;

   . . . . .

   . . . . .

   . . . . .

Feel awfully about Scott. I tried to write him (wrote him several times) to cheer him up but he seems to almost take a pride in his shamelessness of defeat. The Esquire pieces seem to me to be so miserable. There is another one comeing too.[2] I always knew he couldn't think—he never could—but he had a marvellous talent and the thing is to use it—not whin e in public. Good God people go through that emptiness many times in life and come out and do work. I always thought, from when I first met him, that if Scott had gone to that war that he always felt so bad about missing, he would have been shot for cowardice. But that has nothing to do with his writing, a writer can be a coward but at least he should be a writer. Hell I can't write about this and it is rotten to speak against Scott after all he had to go through. But I saw all the first part of it and it was so avoidable and self imposed and always from the one source—though the source spread into many channels and some of them you would never believe came from the same spring. Maybe the Church would help him. You can't tell. Work would help him; noncommercial, honest work—aparagraph at a time. But he judged a paragraph by how much money it made him and ditched his juice into that channel because he got an instant satisfaction. While if you don't make so much and somebody said it was no good he would be afraid. It was a terrible thing for him to love youth so much that he jumped straight from youth to senility without going through manhood. The minute he felt youth going he was frightened again and thought there was nothing between youth and age. But it is so damned easy to criticize our friends and I shouldn't write this. I wish we could help him.

   . . . . .

Best to you always Max—Earnest/

*CC, 4 pp.*[3]

Feb. 27, 1936

Dear Ernest:

I'll give you the hard and fast figure on the sale of "Green Hills" the moment we know it. As it is, on account of copies out on a returnable basis, we cannot

[1] 310 words have been omitted from this letter.

[2] "The Crack-Up," *Esquire* 5 (February 1936): 41, 164; "Pasting It Together," *Esquire* 5 (March 1936): 35, 182–183; and "Handle With Care," *Esquire* 5 (April 1936): 39, 202.

[3] 82 words have been omitted from this letter.

yet know it exactly. The reason it is not on that last royalty statement is that it was not published until October 25th, and therefore no report is due on it until April 25th. But I do not think that it will be less than 10,000 copies.- Nor do I think that the reason it did not sell more was the reason you think. It was mostly due to something that often happens in publishing: the public gets a superficial impression of what a book is, and the one they got of this book was that it was an account of a hunting expedition to Africa, covering a short space of time, and was therefore a distinctly minor piece of work. Anyone would have thought that who judged by the outside, superficially. That is what it would seem to be on its face. If all the reviews had emphatically argued otherwise, that impression would have been effaced, but the reviewers too are mostly superficial judges. The qualities of the book that made it fine were, as they should have been, not spectacular. Many of the reviewers took a superficial view, and all of the public except a few individuals of discrimination. I should have foreseen it. The public regards you as a novelist. "Death in the Afternoon" was so manifestly a work of years in accumulation and reflection that it stood by itself. But this the public took as an interlude.

. . . . .

. . . . .

I have just had an appeal for money from Scott, and I suppose I shall give it to him, but I wish I knew what could be done about him. The one thing that gives me some hope is that nobody would write those two articles in Esquire if they were really true. I doubt if a hopeless man will tell about it, or a man who thinks he is beaten for good. Those people I should think would not say anything at all, just as those who really intend suicide never tell anybody. So I thought that in some deep way, when he wrote those articles, Scott must have been thinking that things would be different with him. He may have lost that passion in writing which he once had, but he is such a wonderful craftsman that he could certainly make out well if he were able to control himself and be reconciled to life. He is only forty. It is absurd for him to give up.

Always yours,

*TLS with holograph inserts and postscript, 3 pp.*[1]

April 9
Key West

Dear Max;

. . . . .

Here's the story situation.

I have 5 now—One Trip Across runs about 12,000. It is a very good story (I re-read it) and would carry a big part of a book of stories. I also have the one you read in Esquire called The Tradesman's Return which is 4275 words.

[1]142 words have been omitted from this letter.

Another one, one of the best I've ever written called, tentatively The Capitol which is 4500—which am going to publish in the June Esquire.[1] I was going so well on this long one I've just finished that would not interrupt to write an article so sent them that story at considerable loss. But made pl enty by finishing the long one which finished day before yest. It is about 11,000 words and is a very exciting story of Africa which I think can publish in Cosmopolitan. About the length they call a short novel. Their Editor was down here last week and said he would pay me 7,500 for stories as long as the One Trip Across grading down to 3,000 for the really short ones. This last story is tentatively titled A Budding Friendship.[2] Also have another story of A frica called The Happy Ending which is between 7200 and 7500 words long and a major story.[3] Of these five the weakest is the Tradesman's Return and you know it is a long way from lousy. The others all have almost as much action as the One Trip A cross and run, I suppose, about sixty percent dialogue. That means we have on hand approximately 39,000 words of new short stories.

Now do you think it best to add these five stories to the 44 stories of In Our Time, Men Without Women, Winner Take Nothing (not counting the chapters between the I.O.T. stories as stories) and bring out the big book as The First Forty-Nine? Or add some more stories to these five and publish as a separate book?

What I was working on was to have some <u>damned</u> good to end the big book with. That was my first job and I have done that now. But we can always bring out that collection and I have almost enough for a new book now. But I don't want to have a new book without unity and these all have so much action that I need a couple of quiet ones. In Winner Take Nothing they were all quiet ones except the first one. There was damn little—for the so-called plain reader. In these new ones only one story is difficult; The Happy Ending and it doesn't seem difficult when reading it because there is so much dialogue. But they are all very good ones because I was shooting all the works figuring on ending with them—

The other problem is when to publish—if I am bringing out a book of stories I want it to be one that is going to knock them over he says, modestly! When is the latest you would have to have title and copy for fall publication? I have two other long stories one with about six thousand words done on it—another with not quite that much which I am going to finish in Cuba. It is always cool there in the mornings and have done some of my best stuff there. Have been working like hell lately and am beggining to get not stale but plenty tired.

Any time have a minute is taken up writing to recommend people for the Houghton Mifflin Fellowship. How many of these fellowships are there? If th ere is only one have written over 1000 dollars worth of letter writing

---

[1] Published as "The Horns of the Bull," *Esquire* 5 (June 1936): 31, 190–193; retitled "The Capital of the World" in *The Fifth Column and the First Forty-nine Stories* (1938).
[2] Retitled "The Short Happy Life of Francis Macomber."
[3] Retitled "The Snows of Kilimanjaro."

myself. As far as can recall never had any fellowship myself except drunken more or less good fellowship when starting writing but they say times are different now.

You will be delighted to know that I made quite a lot of money gambling which has kept me from hitting you for any since some time. Esquire is also getting prosperous. Sully and I are thinking of opening up a high class gambling joint next winter. I hope we can count on your patronage. You will also be delighted to know that I have stopped gambling now and will not be gambling any more until my winnings are gone. Then I want to make enough to go to Africa. Mr. Josie is laying off the operation of his highly successful joint because he is getting bartenders foot from standing up all d ay and all night and the day after the farewell ball of the Fireman's Convention he is going over to Cuba with me and we plan to put in two weeks of intensive recuperation from our orduous winter. Why don't you come down? You could fly down. I will let you read all these stories and we can discuss the book. Havana is a marvellous place especially when you have just made a little money and been going well. I've had a belle epoque of working lately—like the best I've ever had. You have the same juice only now you can handle a wider range and you have more knowledge under your belt. Have been working like a horse and the day finished went out in the aft at 3p.m. with Patrick and caught two big sailfish 7feet 8 and 7 feet 11.

Thank you also for the invitation to meet Miss Nancy Hale at your home which I received too late to make the trip up.[1] I would like to get a good idea from her sometime for a story to be called Sea Change and then get Dashiel to publish it. Please tell her how sorry I was I could not come.

The other angle about publishing is: if I sell A Budding Friendship to Cosmo they couldn't publish it before July or A ug. Then if they bought The Happy Ending that would carry into Sept. that would be o.k. But if I had another one that was saleable that would be Nov. or Dec. Well we can see and they might not want any of them but A Budding Frien dship (I hope to God I can beat that as a title) is a swell story as fool proof as One Trip Across or Fifty Grand.) and the guy was down here asking for them. But maybe he was just making conversation.

Gingrich wired me too that Scott seemed better. I wish he would pull out of that shamelessness of defeat. We're all going to die. Isn't it time enough to quit then? What is he doing? What is he going to do? He can't have adopted being through as a career can he? He and Maxie Baer have something in common.[2]

. . . . .

So Long Max—
Ernest

[1]Nancy Hale (1908–1988) was one of MP's authors.

[2]Heavyweight boxer Max Baer was accused of quitting in his fight with Joe Louis; EH reported the 24 September 1935 bout in "Million Dollar Fright: A New York Letter," *Esquire* 4 (December 1935): 35, 190b.

. . . . .

Dont tell Darrow I made any money I dont want my sales dropped below what he considers the danger mark. Green Hills came out in England April 3—Havent heard yet. They made a very nice looking book and I took out 7 bloodies, one son of a bitch and 4 or five shits (voluntarily to see what difference it would make) to please them and Owen Wister. A shame I couldnt have removed a cocksucker as a special gift to Jonathan Cape Ltd. See if it will sail as well or as badly with those reefs.

With Up In Michigan, to come in 2nd position in the book, that would make 6 stories and probably give the necessary diversification. Then even if I published the Happy Ending in early fall we could come out in the fall.

Am working on a title

CC, 3 pp.[1]

April 15, 1936

Dear Ernest:

. . . . .

I think you could take three and a half more months on the stories. If we had copy on August first we could publish comfortably in October which would be a perfectly good time to do it, as good as any. Later than October would be bad. Can you make that date? I hope you can. I do think the book would be better for several quiet stories, and we could also, as you say, put in "Up In Michigan". I think what you tell of would bring it to 54,000 words which would be enough, and if you could do the quiet stories there would be plenty.

There is also another possibility, and I am not suggesting it from the point of view of quantity. You could put into this book either in a separate group, or scattered through, "Wings Over Africa" and the hurricane piece (these two ought to be printed, and I do not know how they are ever likely to be unless in this way) and several of the very best of the Esquire pieces,- those you thought were most entitled to be in what we are accustomed to call "a more permanent form". Some of these pieces about fishing, etc., would go well with stories. I think it is worth considering. It might be better, with you, to bring out a book which is unusual, not just on the conventional formula.- And those two pieces would undoubtedly be wanted by many. Some sorts of people would prize them beyond the stories,- those who like journalism that transcends journalism. They would get a little of the radical vote too. What do you think about it? I see there may be some difficulties about the two long stories on account of Cosmop, but it ought to be possible to work it out if you can get them to them.

. . . . .

I think too that Scott is better, but not very much. I have been hearing

[1]213 words have been omitted from this letter.

241

from him more which is always a good sign, and not requests for money, either. I also heard a rumor that a movie company wanted to buy one of his stories, which might help him out. He has taken Zelda to a new sanitarium in North Carolina, and I have heard that she is not doing well at all.

I do not stand a chance of getting away for quite a while,- not until summer.

Always yours,

*TLS with holograph inserts, 1 p.*

Key West, April 19, 1936

Dear Max;

Thanks for your letter and for the London press cuttings. Glad it's off to a good start there. Cape wrote me and seemed very happy about it. Would appreciate seeing the other weekly reviews when they come in.

Dinamov, who edits International Literature, wrote me (letter yest.) the Sun Also was a big success in Russia. They are commencing to serialize A Farewell To Arms in the Russian edition of International Literature this spring and publish it in the fall. They want to publish Green Hills and anything else I will send them. They sent me an official explanatory review of Sun Al so which shows that it is the bourgeois world that is despaired of; not the communist world and that the author should make this clear and doesn't. But they compare the writing to Tolstoi. Maybe I'll make a writer yet. In the last number of the russian edition of International Literature they publish The Undefeated. Think I'll have to go over to the p amirs and shoot Ovis Poli on my royalties. They wrote me they hoped to have good fishing and shooting soon. I'll have to go over there and stay a while. Boy I'll bet that would break Comrade Cowley's heart.[1] Because n o matter how Comrade Cowley would follow the true dogma I don't think a great many people in any country, any language or under any regime would ever care to read his works because he cannot create anything, is purely imitative, and while he wants to be honest he is dull as cold tallow and as permanent.

Am also going good in Norway, Sweeden, Hungary, Czecho-Slovakia, France, Spain and the Bahama Islands. But would rather go well as I have been lately in Key West and it would not matter if the whole world thought you wer e lousy.

A m not very hot about mixing in articles and stories, Max. That just gives them the opportunity to dismiss it all, as Wilson did, as the trash I write for that Men's Clothing Trade magazine. If I publish a book of sportin g and political pieces let it be bought by those who would buy it and damn ed by everybody else. But don't think it would be a good idea to take a book of the best short stories I've done and get it damned as a hybred book and c ursed

---

[1] Malcolm Cowley (1898–1989) was at that time book-review editor of *The New Republic*.

by all that N. Y. outfit that foam at the mouthe at the mention of fishing or shooting or the idea that I ever have any fun or any right to have any fun. By being in N.Y. last fall and seeing how it worked I know that they don't read books; just look for a damning point or a praising point and that must be economic. They can't tell literature from shit and I have no more illusions on that score, nor any of fairness., nor any idea but what they want to put me out of business. Nor will I ever again notice them, mention them, pay any attention to them, n or read them. Nor will I kiss their asses, kiss their arses, make friends with them, nor truckle to them. Am going to work by myself, for myself and for the long future as I have always done. If we should have another boom such as England is haveing now you would see most of that literary fashionable communist crowd believeing as violently in the new mysticism of the boom as in the last thing they believed in. If it hadn't been for the well meaning buggering up of the New Deal we would now be going through the same boom England is. We'll probably pea away our chance at it and then have to fight the same war they are fattening on preparing for. Boy I only hope Scott is not too old to go to it. He always wanted to go to a war. But by now, doubtless, his ill health wouldn't allow it.

I had Pauline count the One Trip Across and it is 14,500 words. Sent this new one to Cosmo today. If they take it will have enough Jack so won't have to publish any of the others so it ought to be all right for October. Have a dose of Flu, all the servants in bed with it, and 800 cases in town, so if this doesn't make too good reading lay it to that.

Best always,   Ernest

ALS, Cat Cay Bahamas, BWI stationery, 4 pp.

July 11

Dear Max:

Gingrich was down here and I showed him the 30,000 words I had done on the Key West—Havana novel of which One Trip Across and The Tradesman's Return were a part—I had taken these for the book of stories and he seemed to think that was crazy—I hadnt even looked at the 30,000 since I left off to finish the book of stories—Anyway Ive decided to go on and finish that book now when we go out West—That will only take 2 stories from a book—and will have plenty of others by the time you want the stories, and it can come out after this book—

The book contrasts the two places—and shows the inter-relation—also contains what I know about the mechanics of revolution and what it does to the people engaged in it—There are two themes in it—The decline of the individual—The man Harry—who shows up first in One Trip Across—and then his re-emergence as Key West goes down around him—and the story of a shipment of dynamite and all of the consequences that happened from it—There is a hell of a lot more that I wont inflict on you—But with luck it is a good book—Gingrich was very steamed up about what he read and wanted me to promise not to bring out the stories until I'd finished this—I got the last stuff I needed for it on my last trip across—Also have the hurricane and the vets in it.

I owe you as I recall 1100 dollars advance on the book of stories—I have enough stories for a book but not if I take out One Trip Across and The Tradesman's Return—I can return you the 1100 if you want—or you can let that ride on the next book of stories—or let it ride on this new book—Tell me which you prefer? Have arranged with Gingrich to write only 6 pieces a year for Esquire instead of what I was doing so as not to interfere—Am to get same amount for six as formerly for 12—But do not have to have them in if let him know in advance and I refused an advance so I wouldnt <u>have</u> to turn them out if busy on any of this other—Did you read The Snows of Kilimanjaro[1] and The Short Happy Life of Francis Macomber?)[2] Would have written you this before but had to get it all straightened out—I stink so to the N.Y critics that if I bring out a book of stories no matter how good this fall they will all try to kill it—Well I will be able to give them both barrels next Spring and Fall with a book and a book of stories if you want to play it that way—Meantime the stuff I publish will not hurt my reputation any—All I want to do is get out west and settled down in a cabin writing—We caught a 514 and a 610 lb of tuna—So far have been bitched on marlin—Lost one over 700 and one over 1000—He straightened the hook straight as a pencil! Well what the hell I really have another trade beside marlin fishing and am very anxious to get back to work at it—We will stay out west until Oct or so. Then back to K.W. to work hard before the bloody sons of bitching winter visitors come.

I hope I've not let you down about the story book.

Please let me know to K.W. Leave here Thursday if catch some decent weather—It's been blowing a gale for 3 days—Will try to get this off on plane today—Dont think Im trying to stall on the story book as have

> Up In Michigan
> One Trip Across
> The Horns of the Capitol
> Tradesman's Return
> Short Happy Life of Francis Macomber
> The Snows of Kilimanjaro

besides whats new and unnamed—But if I can lift those 2 and finish this other then with only a couple more stories I have 2 books instead of one and one of them that thing the pricks all love—a novel—

> Best always—
> Ernest/

[1] Esquire 6 (August 1936): 27, 194–201.
[2] Cosmopolitan 101 (September 1936): 30–33, 166–172.

*CC, 4 pp.*[1]

July 21, 1936

Dear Ernest:

I read "The Snows of Kilimanjaro" last Thursday on a train, and with the greatest pleasure. It was the day it was advertised in the papers so magnificently,- looked like a full page given to you alone. It is a very fine story,- the end magnificent. The "Short Happy Life" is not out yet,- probably in the September number. Waxman told me about that story, and I am mighty anxious to read it.

About your change of plans, I wired that I was delighted, and the fact is I could not have got a letter that would have bucked me up more. It is a fine change, and the novel ought to be all by itself, and much better from our point of view, than a book of stories.- Much better to have a novel come before a book of stories. The only thing that has ever worried me is the long interval between your books of fiction—that is the way publishers look at things, being conscious of the trade— but I had actually been reflecting upon the postponement of the book of stories anyhow, this being a Presidential year, and the time of publication necessarily rather late. I hope we can bring it out very early in '37. But everything now is first-rate, and it looks to me as if things were shaping up better in many ways.

. . . . .
. . . . .

Always yours,

. . . . .

*TLS, 1 p.*[2]

July 23, 1936
Key West/

Dear Max:

. . . . .
. . . . .
. . . . .

I got a letter from Scott who was sore because I used his name in that Snows of Kilimanjaro story.[3] He has only been writing those awful things about himself since Feb. in Esquire but if I took issue with his analysis of his proclaimed break-up he gets sore. I told him that for five years I have not written a line about anybody I knew because I was so sorry for them all but that I felt time was getting short now and am going to cease being a gent and

[1] 131 words have been omitted from this letter.
[2] 325 words have been omitted from this letter.
[3] The *Esquire* text states that "poor Scott Fitzgerald" was "wrecked" by his "romantic awe" of the rich. "Snows" also quotes Fitzgerald's assertion in "The Rich Boy" that "The very rich are different from you and me," followed by the apocryphal rejoinder that "they have more money." See Bruccoli, *Fitzgerald and Hemingway*, pp. 190–194.

go back to being a novelist. Most of my friends were not of my own selection anyway. Can't wait to get out west and settled down to writing again. Have a big head of steam now.

. . . . .

. . . . .

. . . . .

Yours always,<br>
Ernest/

*CC, 4 pp.*[1]

Oct. 1, 1936

Dear Ernest:

You must have failed to get one letter I wrote you, because I told you in it that I thought "The Snows of Kilimanjaro" was a most extraordinary story. What's more, it showed a new vein in your talent, or at any rate showed it somewhat more clearly, though I can remember other stories that had it clearly. The last part of the story created a most curious and magical feeling which nobody will ever forget who has read it. I thought what a magnificent tale could be written of the defense of the Alcazar.[2] If you had been there, and got out of it safely, what a story! But I wish you would not go to Spain. Those Alcazar boys made me pretty nearly decide to vote for the Rebels though I think they will bring no good to Spain if they win.- And if you aim to go there among the bullets, I shall hope that they hurry up and take Madrid and perhaps stop the fighting for a time. Anyhow, I hope you will let nothing prevent the publication of a novel in the Spring. And it should be early too. I am awfully glad you wrote me about it. I had wondered how it was going. Let that big grizzly alone until you are finished.

. . . . .

I opened a telegram addressed to you to see whether it was important enough to forward, and it was from Scott. I don't know exactly what you could do for him, but the interview he gave the Post was frightful.[3] It gave me a chill to read it. It seemed as if Scott were bent upon destroying himself. He was trusting the reporter, and so was his nurse—when a man gets himself a trained nurse, it's time to despair of him—and both of them said things which the reporter must have known were not meant to go into print,- the nurse said them when Scott was out of the room. It gave you the impression of a completely licked and very drunk person, bereft of hope, acquiescing in his ruin. Scott had just written me that his mother had died, and that he was

---

[1] 50 words have been omitted from this letter.

[2] The siege of Alcázar during the early months of the Spanish Civil War (20 July–26 September 1936).

[3] Michel Mok, "The Other Side of Paradise, Scott Fitzgerald, 40, Engulfed in Despair," *New York Post* (25 September 1936), 1, 15.

to come into twenty thousand dollars. I had known that this was a probability, and I had thought that there was his chance. So I wrote him that he must take that opportunity to work two years on ten thousand a year, without anxiety or the necessity of potboiling. I told him this was the only way to answer what this reporter had done. I hope Scott will turn up here tomorrow. It may be that having hit bottom, and having the shock of this story, he might rebound with the help of the money. Fortunately, hardly anybody reads the New York Post.

. . . . .

Always yours,

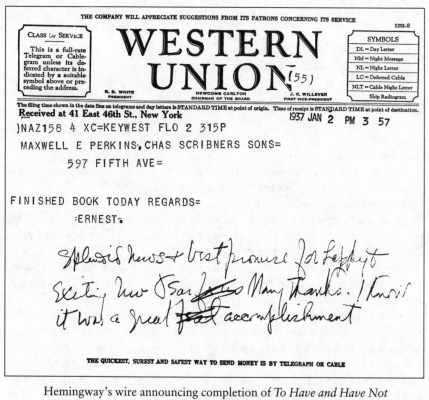

Hemingway's wire announcing completion of *To Have and Have Not* with Perkins's draft reply.

*CC, 2 pp.*[1]

Jan. 7, 1937

Dear Ernest:

I was ever so glad to hear that you had finished the novel. Have you found a title? Now that it is done, it can be talked about better.—It has seemed to me that it had one great superficial advantage in being about a region that I think nobody has ever written well about, and a very rich and colorful scene. I remember the first time I was down there asking you why you did not write about what you saw, and your telling me why in a way I understood. But you did get around to it when you had absorbed a sense of it and knew what part everything did play in the scheme of things. So I am not more anxious for anything than to see this novel come out.

. . . . .

Yours,

*ALS, 3 pp.*
*[Early February 1937]*                                   *Key West, Florida*

<u>Tuesday</u>.

Dear Max:

Here is the preface. I'm sorry I'm so late with it. Hope it will please Jerry. Please apologize for me for my delaying his publication.[2]

Am working like hell on a title. Have a long list.

Am going to go over the book entirely before and after I am in Spain. The version I complete before going to Spain (I am principally trying to better The Bradley part) will leave at the Guaranty Trust Co of N.Y., 4 Place de la Concorde, Paris with instructions to mail it to you in case I shouldnt be able to. But I hope to go over it again in time to get it to you to set up in June Is that date O.K? What is the latest date you can set it up?

I found I needed more time to leave it alone to get a proper perspective on it. But you know the length, you can set up a few chapters of the first part (where I am making no changes) for the dummy as soon as we have a title and Mr Darrow can get going with it. Moe Speiser read it and liked it very much but when I told him how much I wanted to try to strengthen a part of it (which incidentally he did <u>not</u> think needed strengthening) he agreed that there was no necessity to set it up at once. We have plenty of time. I plan to leave for Spain before the end of this month. Going by way of Paris and clearing up everything so I can work on the book on the boat. I will complete a publishable draft Leave it where it can be sent to you. And then try, again, to improve it when I come out.

[1] 66 words have been omitted from this letter.
[2] EH provided the preface for Jerome Bahr's collection of short stories, *All Good Americans* (New York: Scribners, 1937).

248

Will also leave one copy here with Pauline so there is no chance of losing it. When you get this will you please deposit $500.00 in my account City Bank Farmers Trust 22 Williams Street against the advance on the book. I think this brings the advance to $2000.00

Have been working on the book hard but need to be a little further away from it still to get that detached eye I need for re-writing. Am putting in more of the town too.

May be seeing you next week for a few minutes.

> Best luck always,
> Ernest.

See if you can get me that Blue Ribbon reprint money that I agreed to today with Darrow will you? I can use it.

<br>

> ALS, *The Anchorage stationery, 7 pp.*
> *Bimini, Bahamas*

[*c.* 10 *June* 1937]

Thursday

Dear Max:—

Coming down on the plane had what may be good idea for the book—To overcome the prejudice of mixing a novel with 3 stories why not have something entirely new That is an omnibus of unpublished material—

Title—(Temporarily)

——To Have and Have Not.

A novel, three stories, an article, a newspaper (or Some News Dispatches) despatch and a speech

By Ernest Hemingway.

Table of Contents—

Novel

Harry Morgan—(Temporary Title) Between 40–55,000

Stories

The Short Happy Life of Francis Macomber—11,000—

The Capitol of The World— 4,500—

The Snows of Kilimanjaro— 8,500.

Article

Who Murdered The Vets— 1500(?)

News—Dispatch or Dispatches.

MADRID APRIL 10TH— 1000.

or perhaps those reprinted in the New Republic—only better edited. Will re-read two of the mail stories too—The one about the blind man and the one about the chauffeurs.[1] Say 4,500—

> Could be much more.

<br>

[1] "A New Kind of War" (14 April 1937) and "The Chauffeurs of Madrid" (23 May 1937)—two of the dispatches on the Spanish Civil War that EH wrote for the North American Newspaper Alliance (NANA).

Speech—
Carnegie Hall—June 4—
(I read this over and it is O.K.)

1200—
_____
Book between 75,—85,000 words.

_____

This would be a new sort of book—A living omnibus—and would take away the disadvantage of combining a novel with a book of stories to disadvantage of both—You could sell it as a major book by me and it would give them their moneys worth. I will be in Spain when it comes out and it will have the advantage of leaving things sort of tidied up. Also you have a good timely book in case I should run into any bad luck.

It looks as though it were going to be quite a business now this summer and fall and I would like to have every thing in good order.

So Max will you get your operatives to work to obtain for me and send to me care of Miami Aero Corporation

36th Street Airport
Miami

( For—Capt. Ernest Hemingway )
    Yacht Pilar
        Bimini BWI

immediately if possible—
Copy of New Masses with—Who Murdered The Vets in it. (Sept 1935)
Copy of New Masses with Carniegie Hall Speech (Current Number)[1]
Copy of New Republic with exerpts from my Spanish Articles—(Sometime in May)[2]
Ask John N. Wheeler of N.A.N.A. for a complete file of my dispatches for me. Send—whatever you get as fast as you get it. Please. My time is very short and I am working hard. If you cannot get copy of the Vets photostat it from public library. I think this is a damned good idea. An exciting novel—3 good stories—and this other stuff that brings it all up to date—But is worth preserving—For Titles I thought of
                    The Various Arms
That is the novel, the story, the article, the newsdispatch and the speech.
                            or
                    Return To The Wars.

Can maybe do better.

Please wire me to Bimini when you get this letter if you agree with the omnibus idea.

If anything should happen to me. You can always get back the story book advance by an omnibus of all my short stories—If am OK, and expect to be, we have that in reserve and I will write you a real novel. I wish I had the time

_____

[1]"Fascism Is a Lie," *The New Masses* 23 (22 June 1937): 4. EH addressed the American Writers' Congress in New York on 4 June 1937.
[2]"Hemingway Reports Spain," *The New Republic* 90 (5 May 1937): 376–379.

to write it now—But after this fall will be better—I'll have the end of summer, fall and winter then in it—Have winter, Spring and early Summer now. Please wire when you get this—

Also will you send any pictures of me you have in the files I promised some to people in Spain and havent any—

So long Max—Good luck—everything fine here—Am working now editing the Harry Morgan. if you send the stuff promptly can have all mss to you on July 5th—Then when would I get proofs?

Best always,
Ernest/

*CC, 4 pp.*[1]

June 17, 1937

Dear Ernest:

I could not get the speech until today, but now I have sent it air mail. It was this speech that made me hesitate to speak completely in favor of your plan,- though I am altogether in favor of it in every other respect. I do think that bringing in a speech, just because it is one, does tend to make the book seem too miscellaneous perhaps. I would rather favor leaving it out. I just read it, and it is as good as when delivered, but it deals with current events partly in a current way, in speaking of Bilbao, etc.- though not in what it says about writing, which is everlastingly true—and the articles, especially the New Republic one, while dealing with current events, do it in a way which raises them above that level. They make you feel the way the thing all was, and have almost the quality of fiction. I sent off the Wheeler ones right away and have only read those of them that were in the Times. But they must represent the rest.- Certainly the New Republic material is worthy of the book, and so is "Who Murdered the Vets" which I always wanted to see get into a book. I think all that will add to the value of the book.- In reading over the speech, and especially the part about writing, I thought perhaps the book might have a preface. I have got now to like the title "To Have and To Have Not" very much.- Certainly it fits the Vets in a literal fashion, and in some sense it fits everything that will be in the book. I would be for sticking to it.[2]

. . . . .
. . . . .

Always yours,

[1] 214 words have been omitted from this letter.
[2] The plan for an omnibus volume was dropped; *THAHN* was published alone.

*CC, 4 pp.*[1]

Aug. 5, 1937

Dear Ernest:

. . . . .

. . . . .

Scott wrote me a very cheerful letter, and I have heard about him from people who were in Hollywood,- all much impressed with the change in him. And he is paying his debts. My pockets are full of money from the check that comes every week. If he will only begin to dramatize himself as the man who came back now, everything may turn out rightly.

I haven't any fear we won't get a good jacket with that title,- but I shall be disappointed if we cannot have on the jacket something that gives you the feeling of the gulf stream, because the title does not, of course, suggest that, and I think that the scene of the book is in itself a great asset. The Gulf appeals to everyone's imagination.

. . . . .

. . . . .

. . . . .

Yours,

\*　　　　\*　　　　\*

*On 11 August 1937 MP and Max Eastman were talking in MP's office when EH came in. EH's angry remarks about Eastman's statement "Come out from behind that fake hair on your chest, Ernest" in "Bull in the Afternoon" led to a scuffle. Both writers ended up on the floor. Eastman then informed the press that he had knocked down EH; and EH issued his own statement (see "Hemingway Slaps Eastman in Face," New York Times [14 August 1937]: 15). MP sent Fitzgerald a detailed report of the episode: "I think Eastman does think that he beat Ernest at least in a wrestling match but in reality Ernest could have killed him, and probably would have if he had not regained his temper" (see Dear Scott/Dear Max, ed. John Kuehl and Jackson R. Bryer [New York: Scribners, 1971], pp. 238–240).*

*Cable, 1 p.*
*Paris, France*

*[Early January 1938]*

WHATS SALE WILL HAVE ENOUGH STORIES FOR NEW BOOK WITH THOSE PLAN WRITE ALSO MUST REMEMBER PLAY[2] HIGHLY PUB-LISH-ABLE PROBABLY BEST THING EYVE EVER WRITTEN WOULD

---

[1] 241 words have been omitted from this letter.
[2] Published in *The Fifth Column and the First Forty-nine Stories* (New York: Scribners, 1938).

BE POSSIBLE COMBINE IT WITH PRESENT THREE UNPUBLISHED STORIES MAKE GOOD LENGTH BOOK COULD SETUP IMMEDIATELY PLAY ARRIVING NEWYORK TEN DAYS ANSWER GARRITUS ERNEST

*TLS, 1 p.*[1]

Key West/Feb 1—1938

Dear Max;

I was going to send you the enclosed wire and then I thought you might not take it as a joke.[2] It's a joke. The only papers I've seen since getting back were Herald Tribune Books that had accumulated here. I saw the Times both daily and Sunday while I was away. Mathews[3] and I had it sent to the Embassy from Brentanos in Paris. Aside from the big full page ad you sent me I didnt see much mention of the book or any sort of a campaign to push it when it had begun to sell. But as I say I was not in any position to see one if it had been made. Seems a mistake not to exploit any kind of a break-through—if there was any kind of a break-through.

Am sorry about the Tom Wolfe business. All I know is what I read in Time. I guess he is like Franco. He got to believeing his own communiques.[4]

I have a lot of funny things to tell you if I ever see you. Probably will have to come to N.Y. about the play. I did not want to leave Spain, Teruel was the best thing I've ever had I think, and all want to do now is get back. Would like to write some stories first. It is difficult to write though. Still too close.

Do you think you can get hold of your pal Max Eastman for me if I come to N.Y? I promise to fix him so he wont give any statements to the press for a while. And when I think how I promised you that day not to say anything about that business in order not to humiliate him. Read in the paper he was at a tea at your house. Wish he'd come to mine.

Will you tell me, quite frankly, whether you plan to try to sell anymore copies of the book?[5] I remember how you pushed the Sun Also after it got away to such a slow start and sold it for a long time after the first of the year. But that was a long time ago and the stock market was better and I guess it was a much more saleable book. Though the funny thing is; this is a good book. Could be sold too. But what the hell. If I sound bitter or gloomy throw it out. It's that it takes one kind of training and frame of mind to do what I've been doing and another to write prose. I'm making the shift, cutting out drinking during the day, nothing until five p.m. and nothing after dinner, and

---

[1]14 words have been omitted from this letter.
[2]Unlocated.
[3]Herbert Matthews, reporter for the *New York Times*.
[4]Wolfe moved from Scribners to Harpers at the end of 1937.
[5]*THAHN* was published 15 October 1937; it had sold some 36,000 copies by March 1938.

I'll write and it will be o.k. Meantime it is hell on the disposition and I also think the family and friends.

Please write me what the total advance I drew on the book was; with dates.

Good luck, always.

Ernest

. . . . .

*CC, 4 pp.*[1]

Feb. 3, 1938

Dear Ernest:

I am glad you wrote. I had been expecting you would turn up almost any day because I thought you would have to come about the play.- By the way: I don't know how matters stand in that regard, but if for any reason it would help for us to publish the play before it was produced, which has sometimes been done, we could do it, of course. But the general scheme is to publish immediately on production because the production is generally what makes the play sell, and it sells most while the run is going on. We sold about 10,000 of "Idiot's Delight" by Robert Sherwood that way,- even though he did not give us the copy until the play had run for quite a while.- But this play of yours would sell without a production, and it is possible that its publication might have some value in connection with arranging for production. I am only saying this because I know almost nothing except the little that Speiser told me, and it was that that made me think you would have to come up to New York right off.

I am getting up the figures you want, and I shall send them all tomorrow. I shall send a statement of everything.- There is that loan of a thousand dollars which can go on as a loan if you want, or be put as an advance against a new book. And there is some income tax point about which I have to get clear and explain. I shall also send you a list of the advertising we did on "To Have".- We spent $9,500 in newspaper and magazine advertising, and we sent out hundreds of thousands of lists and circulars and Bookbuyers. We sent out through our own store, and other stores, imprinted, 87,000 postcards announcing the book to individuals, to arrive on the day of publication. We kept the book at the top of every ad. through the season. Of course it would have sold more if it had not been for what they politely call the "recession". We cannot push it in any big way, but we shall carry it along in all our regular advertising through the Spring. I know plenty people who call this your best book, and I am sure that whether it was that or not—and comparisons always seem pointless to me, each book being something by itself alone—it did represent a breaking through into new territory, and an enlargement of technique. It showed a lot of things.

The Tom business is very curious and confused. The libel suit that Tom

[1]120 words have been omitted from this letter.

254

thinks we got him into was one feature. But another one came certainly from the fact that he had now got to a book in which he wanted to write about us.- When I saw him the other night, he said that he was writing a book that Scribners would be proud of!! I didn't say anything, but felt apprehensive. Another thing was that Tom may perhaps go through cycles like in manic-depressive, and for a long time he seemed almost insane,- like believing that we fomented a libel suit. In those stages he gets terribly desperate, and completely doubts his abilities. I had reassured him for so many years that it was no longer effective. I really think that when he put himself up to be bid for, he did it partly to restore his confidence,- and I think it has restored it. Another element was one that might be in an obscure way greatly in his favor: he had become dependent upon us to a degree that was never dreamed of with any other author that I ever heard of, so that we looked after all sorts of things for him, and he could not make a decision without referring it here.- I think that although he brought this about, he came to resent it, without perhaps being completely conscious of his resentment, and he determined to break himself loose and be his own man, and do his own work.- And if he only can do his own work, all of it, it will be his salvation, and it will be the only thing that could make him really top-notch. I believe that this had a lot to do with the whole thing.- I know he resented that silly dedication. Anyhow, I have to go over and testify for him in a lawsuit next week, and what's more, I think I put his lawyers in possession of material that will insure him of winning it. I ought to have been a lawyer,- maybe.

Scott was here twice last week, but I never saw him alone. He is sticking to his job well and has paid off a great deal of his debt, and has a better contract for another year which should clear him up.- And then if only we have another boom, he might get going. He has not been drinking at all, and he looked well. He hoped you were in town. He said you were the most dynamic personality at present,- in the world, I think it was, or anyhow in this country.

We did give a big tea, and invited all the authors, and almost all of them came. It was for Molly Colum. Thirteen years after beginning her book she finished and published it. (I am sending you a copy) One time a couple of years ago, Nancy Hale, whose book of stories we were publishing, was making what seemed to be unreasonable requirements about advertising and exploitation, and so I said sarcastically, "And wouldn't you like us to give you a tea?" and she took me right up, and I did it.- And Molly Colum came to it, and said, "Why don't you give me a tea, Maxwell?" And I said, "Well, we will when the book is out." Then I forgot about it until Molly didn't let me.- But we really have had good times at both those teas, except that there was such a mob of people.- And now, having given two of the women authors teas, I have got to keep it up with all of them, I suppose, and plan one for Marjorie Rawlings in late March or April. You will got an invitation, and I suppose Eastman will too, since he is on the list.- So what? I hope, nothing.

. . . . .

If we published a book of stories this Fall—that is, the omnibus book—we could do it quite early, even in August, and in that connection we could always carry it along as of equal importance with "To Have and Have Not". If we publish the play in the Fall too, I think it would do no harm either to the stories or to the play. A play is looked upon as a different thing altogether, generally speaking.

It must be mighty hard to settle down to a quiet and writing life after all that.

Always yours,


*TLS, 1 p.*[1]

[Mid-February 1938]                                        *Key West, Florida*


Dear Max;

Thank you for the good letter. I hope mine was not too unreasonable and violent. Also understand about the teas. I don't want a tea, pal, nor to make unreasonable demands about exploitation or advertising. (Only, please Max, don't invite me to anything that Eastman is invited to. If you have to invite Eastman .O.k. But there is no law that you have to invite me. Because I am, quite literally, not responsible for what I would do to him if I saw him. Just tell Mrs. Rawlings you can't invite me to her tea because you are asking Max Eastman. That's simple.

Have never had much of a break on publishing years. Farewell to Arms came out in Oct. 1929 the day the market broke. Had to wait eight years to hit the next break right on the nose.

You don't need to send the ads. I believe you, and I don't get any kick out of seeing my name in print. As you know I know very little about the business end of publishing. Certainly the Sun Also and Farewell to Arms were much easier books to sell than this. I know all the cards that were stacked against it. $9,500. sounds like a hell of a lot to have spent for advertising.

I never doubted the plan nor the strength of your original attack and if you had 9500 casualties before there was any break through (and I don't even know there <u>was</u> any breakthrough; although it did look as though it had started to go once) nobody has any business to tell anybody else to gamble with their reserves.

It may be necessary to publish the play first. I'll let you know. I am awfully sorry for Tom and I feel very badly for you about the business. You wrote very chic-ly about it. I think Tom acts like an enormous baby but then it must be very difficult to be a genius.

I would like to have seen old Scott. Jesus I never wanted to be dynamic. All I wanted to be was a writer. And by Jesus Christ I'm going to be a writer again. But Christ it is tough getting going now. But I know one thing that can make you write; being hungry. And if I have to go back to being hungry again

[1]224 words have been omitted from this letter.

to write why I'll go back. Am in such an unchristly gigantic jam of every bloody kind now that it's practically comic. Wont bother you with details. And max if I seem difficult or crabby or slightly screwball dont let me get on your nerves. Put up with me as much as you can because I am essentially reasonable. But have been in a tough racket for a while and you learn a lot; but you take quite a beating and I didn't want to come back this time at all and I'm not being too good at it. Oh well what the hell. . . .

Ernest

*TS for cable, 1 p.*

April 6, 1938

Mr. Ernest Hemingway
Guaranty Trust Company
Paris (France)
Greatly moved by play It is magnificent All good luck

Max

*CC, 3 pp.*

April 7, 1938

Dear Ernest:

I cabled you the moment I read the play. I think it extraordinarily fine. I was mightily impressed by it, and moved too. It means plenty,- and confirms what "To Have" showed, that you have marched forward into new fields, and large ones. I wish it were coming on right away.- But anyhow, I have sent it to the printer for an estimate. We ought to make something special of it, something like we did for the "Ethan Frome", a larger book than the usual play.

After reading that, and thinking about Spain and all, I almost hate bothering you about these things, but they are really important too, and we ought to try to get them right.

Now as to the stories, a publisher's impulse is to put anything new first. We could stick to a chronological arrangement with everything that was not new, and yet begin with the three or more new stories. But if you wanted to be strictly chronological, we could put them at the end, and of course we know that people really don't b begin a book of stories at the beginning and read straight through. They are almost as likely to begin with the last story. But leaving that question aside for the moment:- I would not like to see the book open with "Up in Michigan". It is certainly a grand story, but there are those old objections to it, and coming first would make it stand out conspicuously, since it is also in effect a new story.- But if we put the really new stories first, that could follow comfortably enough.

Another thing that could be done would be what I once urged upon you, and you were not much impressed with the idea at the time. But I felt so strongly about it that I thought I would bring it up again,- only don't let me over-persuade you. The original "In Our Time" published by the Three Mountain Press had in it those eighteen pieces, and they stood together with extraordinary effect. They presented our time. You remember when we took the later "In OurTime" over, I wanted to reset it and put these pieces together as a separate unit, consecutively. Why couldn't we do that now? I have the original book here and have just been looking it over. Don't you think they ought to stand that way as a unit? If we did do that, the original "In OurTime" would come first, one piece right after the other. Then could come "Up in Michigan" and then the other stories chronologically.[1] It would be the only book in which the original "In Our Time" stood as written and first published, excepting in the few copies of the limited edition,- one of which I have, thanks to you, and shall always keep.

We ought to send the stories to the printer by July first. If all this bothers you too much in the face of all the other things there are to bother you, let it go for a little, and we shall see how matters develop.- We do want this book to have as many strong features as we can, and I think the re-presentation of those "In Our Time" pieces in that way, would be one. People would see them anew that way.

I was mighty glad to get your letter, and I told Charlie and Meyer etc., what you said. And I am writing Scott who will be happy that you spoke of him. I think you have treated us swell. We all do. I owe you plenty. I only hope things will turn out well, or as well as they can in the circumstances. The play made me feel mean enough.

Always yours,

P.S. I wrote Pauline about the play, and to tell her I had heard from you. She came to our house the day after you sailed, for tea.

I have the dedication to the play right,- "To Marty and Herbert with love".[2] And by the way, I think that you will have a hard time beating the present title,—"The Fifth Column".

*CC, 4 pp.*[3]

May 13, 1938

Dear Ernest:

I always feel perfectly hopeless in writing to you. I read all the news about Spain that I can find—including your dispatches, but I really cannot make

---

[1]MP's plan was not acted on, but the vignettes from the Paris *iot* were placed between the stories as in the 1925 *IOT*.

[2]This dedication was not used. EH's separation from Pauline did not become final until the end of 1939. "Marty" was Martha Gellhorn, with whom EH was having an affair; she became his third wife in 1940.

[3]94 words have been omitted from this letter.

much of anything out of it. I can only hope it is going to end rightly in some way, but I wish it would end soon.

I wanted to tell you that I had sent you galleys of "The Fifth Column". I suppose they will wait for you in Paris, and I doubt if you will want to return them soon anyhow. But we ought, if we possibly can, to publish at the very moment of production. We made an announcement that we would, and then Maurice Speiser called up to say that the people who were to do the producing objected to this.- I told him I thought nothing but good could come of it, but that of course with a play the production was the main thing, and that he could count on us to cooperate, and not to do anything that we could not convince the producers was wise.

I got hold of Captain Cohn to get a copy of "Up in Michigan".- I had it photostated from his copy. At the same time, I went into the chronological order of the stories, about which he knows as much as anyone except you. He gave me all the information, and so in sending them over to be set up, I put them in accordance with the enclosed table of contents.- This puts the original "In Our Time" Fourth, as if it were a unit. I hope you will think it can be. I read it that way, of course, and it seemed then and does now, to be a unit. But anyhow, with all the stories in type we can do any arrangeming that is desirable.- I still have some doubt as to whether the new stories could not come first instead of last. I am not sending you the proof. I do not think you need read it unless you want to. I shall read it here, and have someone else read it too.

. . . . .

I saw John Bishop a couple of days ago for lunch. He looks pretty gray now, but he seemed in fine shape. I always liked him. I told him you had asked to be remembered, and that pleased him greatly. Scott figures he will take two more years in Hollywood to get clear of debt, but I really think he enjoys the work. People I see tell me he is mighty good at it.

In Detroit the authorities suppressed "To Have and Have Not". They were making a general raid on all kinds of literature, including magazines. A little bookseller there that we hardly know, named Hamer, immediately reacted with violence, got himself a lawyer, and is moving for an injunction against the authorities. We sent him all the material we could about the book, everything that would help him. We do not know much about him, nor anything about his lawyer, but the Civil Liberties Union is taking an interest in the case too and told me they would let me know whether he was well represented. It is the same old thing that used to happen in Boston, where they even once suppressed a book by Arthur Train![1]

. . . . .

Always yours,

---

[1] A lawyer who wrote very popular stories about a lawyer named Ephraim Tutt.

*CC, 4 pp.*[1]

July 1, 1938

Dear Ernest:

. . . . .

Now I am sending you the proof of the first forty-five galleys of "The First Forty-Eight". You do not have to read them, but I thought you ought to look at them so as to see the arrangement.- But the numbering is wrong, and the reason is that even before you got back, we had 30 galleys set up, but I thought it better not to say anything about that in order not to make your decision any more difficult. It would not have been very important if we had had to scrap them. But I began on the strictly chronological order. The shifting around of the numbers won't amount to anything at all, and will have to be done in the galleys when they are complete. And the new stories will all be at the end and will not be in the right order when they come. It is better not to give a printer directions after he has got started.- It gives him an alibi for not getting on fast. The only point is "Up In Michigan". I enclose a clipping from the Publisher's Weekly about the situation in Detroit which shows that so far everything is right enough.[2] But in reading over "Up In Michigan" I did begin to feel nervous about it. When I remembered it, it did not seem to me that there was any serious question. I did not remember the two phrases in it which would arouse the vindictiveness of a certain very numerous kind of person. I remembered it as in a sense a sad story. And it is. Except for these two phrases it is all right from any point of view. I think maybe you ought to read that story through. I certainly do not like to furnish those people with amunition with which to misrepresent your work. The story ought to be in because of its quality, and because it was your first story. We would not really be carrying out the idea of the book without it. Anyhow, we'll read a duplicate proof here, so that you need do no more reading than you want to.

Always yours,

*TLS with holograph postscript, 2 pp.*[3]

Key West/
July 12 1938

Dear Max;

I have delayed answering your letters because of two things. First the play. The producer failed to have the $25,000 up that was to be in escrow on July first and it has been a question of extending the option to permit him time to raise the money etc. This between ourselves as do not want talk to get out

---

[1]106 words have been omitted from this letter.
[2]"Case to Be Tried On Its Merits," *Publishers' Weekly* 133 (25 June 1938): 2434.
[3]110 words have been omitted from this letter.

about it which might embarrass him in his efforts to raise the necessary money to produce. Other producers have been after it, too, but everything is getting late. But whether it is produced or not we can figure on publishing in the fall. I have not returned the proofs as there seemed no hurry. Let me know if there is. The preface I would write, if you wanted a preface, would naturally be changed by whether the play was to be produced or not. Can write that in a day or two at the most at any time.

Now about the stories. The Up In Michigan seems to be just the same as it always was. Without that phrase the story is pointless. With it people who are looking for something to jump on have it right there.[1]

The book is supposed to be a definitive collection of all stories up to now. Without Up In Michigan it is not that. If the story is cut it loses all importance.

It is an important story in my work and one that has influenced many people, Callaghan etc. It is not dirty but is very sad. I did not write so well then, especially dialogue. Much of the dialogue is very wooden in that story. But there on the dock it suddenly got absolutely right and it is the point of the whole story and the beginning of all the naturalness I ever got.

(Have just re-read the story)
was writing from memory before.

Max I don't know what to say about it. If you cut it there's no sense in publishing it.

If you don't want to publish it -o.k. But if it is published I think it should go as it is.

Now here is another idea. Why not publish the play as the first story. Then the forty eight others.

Call it The Fifth Column and the first forty eight short stories of Ernest Hemingway.

You know all there is to strategy is to always be strong—and then always be strong at the right place.

How you get beat is by splitting up your strength.

In these two books we split badly. There is no last story that shows what I've learned since the first 48. And everybody will damn the play alone. Put them all together and no matter how they damn them nor what happens I won't feel bad because I know that there is the work that I have done, there you can see what I have learned, and all the vitality of dialogue and action is there in the play. and it comes after all that solid body of work.

It reads damned well you know.

In that event you could leave out the Up In Michigan. I would rather leave it out than cut it. But it does seem a shame not to publish it.

In this book Max we would like to give them so damned much for their money as well as have the whole business there.

Could write just a short introduction explaining Fifth Column was last thing written. It followed by the other new stories and the other stories in

[1]"Oh, it's so big and it hurts so."

chronological order. Would it make too big a book? I'd like to have a pretty big one for a change.

What do you think about all this?

. . . . .

. . . . .

I enclose that story I cabled to Ken the day we evacuated Amposta.
It would make a story for the book I think
An Old Man at a Bridge[1]
      What do you think?
                  Hope everything goes well with you.
                  Best Always Ernest/
The odds are 3—1 the play will <u>not</u> be produced this fall.


              *TLS with holograph insert, 2 pp.*
                       *Key West, Florida*


                  July 12—(later)

Dear Max:

Had the other letter written and sealed and then started going through the galleys on the stories.

I don't like the In Our Time there all by its-self with only numbers and not marked as chapters. They need the breaking apart that separate pages and the heading of chapters give. That would be the only possible way to have it published as one thing.

Then you have two of the chapters listed later as separate stories     No. 10 in the table of contents you sent me A VERY SHORT STORY is also Chapter 10 in In Our Time except that the girl's name in it as A VERY SHORT STORY has been changed from AG to Luz. It should stay as Luz in the book. Ag is libelous. Short for Agnes.

Story Number 12 in the table of contents THE REVOLUTIONIST is also Chapter Eleven in IN OUR TIME.

So you are short two stories of your 48 in that arrangement

I do not like the look of the In Our Time all run together that way at all. It should either be Chapters each one heading a page separately—or else be the way it was in the Liveright In Our Time and the one published by you in 1931.

Now Captain Cohns chronological order is all balls.

I wrote My Old Man before Out of Season. I wrote To-day Is Friday and The Killers on the same day in Madrid both of them a couple of years before Hills like White Elephants which was written three or four years after I wrote Fifty Grand. Lots of them I can't remember when I wrote them; but I know that as a chronological order it is all preposterous.

---

[1]"The Old Man at the Bridge," *Ken* 1 (19 May 1938): 36. It was included as the forty-ninth story in the collection.

What is the objection to simply running them in the order in which the three books were published? In Our Time, Men Without Women, and Winner Take Nothing, except put the three last stories first ie. The Short Happy Life of Francis Macomber first, then The Capitol of the World, then The Snows of Kilimanjaro, then, if you are useing it, Up In Michigan and the others just as they were published.

I cannot say just when any given story was written but I can check up on enough of them to know that the Cohn order is simply nonsense.

I was living with Hadley in the rue Notre Dame des Champs over the saw-mill when I wrote Fifty Grand. I was in Madrid in love with Pauline when I wrote the Killers and Today Is Friday. While a Banal story was written in Schruns at least a year before that. In the Chronological order it comes after A Canary For One which was written in Gerald Murphy's studio in Paris in Rue Foidevaux where was living after Hadley and I had busted up. Hills Like White Elephants was written in the rue Ferou in Paris over a year later than that. So I know that the Chronology is nonsense. But if you put me on the witness stand I could not tell exactly when each story was written. Nor do I give a good god-damn. So if they are not to be chronological let's have them in the order they were in the books which was always carefully worked out The other thing about In Our Time chapters is that to get the effect I wanted with them (and it was a strange effect, and they made it,) I had them set in italics. They need those italics.

I think Max it's best to just have them in the order in which they were published in the three books with the three new stories first, then Up In Michigan (if you decide to publish it) If you don't publish Up In Michigan it is only 47 stories. Change the title of Introduction By The Author to On The Quay At Smyrna

Now what about the Fifth Column starting the whole thing off? Or doesn't that make sense. It would be a fine big lot of reading matter.

Or The Fifth Column and the three new stories. Saveing the collection for later.

I don't like to publish it without Up In Michigan and with them all gunning for you now it gives them something to go on.

Those last three stories are very readable and it would be a good book that way if the other seems too long.

Frankly I don't think the play will be produced. Too much money trouble. Probability of Catholic ban on sale to movies; and movie money has a lot to do with play producing now.

I think published separately they will just jump on them one at a time. Ignore one and pan the other. Together it is too big for them, too damned impressive.

On the other hand might seem sign of weakness to put everything together. I could explain that by saying in introduction that some people had complained that last novel was a little short so had decided that there should be plenty of reading matter in this book.

You want to remember, Max, there was about the biggest gang-up in the reviews on that last novel, which was not a bad novel, that you would almost ever see. So I would like to have something so extra good and extra big this time that there wouldn't be any question of that.

I don't think it is persecution mania or egotism if I say that there are a lot of critics who really seem to hate me very much and would like to put me out of business. And don't think I mean it conceitedly when I say that a lot of it is jealousy; I do what they would like to do, and I do what they are afraid to do; and they hate you for it. Now there is politics too. So I think the best thing to do is to make a book with so much good reading, and so obviously good that you have them on quality and bulk anyway.

What do you think?

I could write a modest, straight, and I think interesting introduction about writing the stories and the play. There are some things which are rather impressive if just stated baldy about the play and there are some interesting things about the stories.

If you like I could write it now. Maybe better do that and knock off this letter. Getting pretty long anyway.

I know some of the critic thing too is my fault. I have been very snooty and they hate you for that too

Well anyway the hell with it.

Ernest/

TLS with holograph postscript, 4 pp.[1]

Key West<br>August 3

Dear Max:

I have the proof of the Fifth Column all corrected, the changes and inserts typed and it is ready to go to you. What has held me up is the damned uncertainty about production. Losey,[2] who was to have the money in escrow on July First did not have it up. So I let him have more time. It is quite definite that he will not have it now although several times he has thought he would have. The last play he produced was a flop and this has made it hard for him to get money for this one I am sure.

Meantime several other people have been after it and there is a definite possibility, almost surety, of haveing it produced if I will permit it to be "play doctored" by certain people.

It has been very upsetting. Through all this I have held firmly to the idea of publishing as that is the only thing I know anything about—and the other things all seem so bloody unreliable and I have no taste for them. One producer died

[1]226 words have been omitted from this letter.
[2]Broadway writer, director, and producer Joseph Losey (1909–1984).

when going out to cast the play—another is a failure on financial backing. I think we might as well go ahead and publish and not fool with others.

But you can see how it has been a delay and a nuisance.

How do you feel now about haveing the whole thing together? The Fifth Column and then the stories in one volumne? Or do you think it better to be separate? Or to delay the Fifth Column until later, Spring say? and let the various production possibiloties work themselves out? Or what?

I have had nothing but trouble and loss out of the damned thing since last December.

Perhaps publishing it now would help it to be produced later on. If they wanted to do a Sherwood or Howard doctored version later they could and I could wash my hands of it. I want to leave it, definitely now and go on to something else.

Anyway I send you now my final version of it.

. . . . .
. . . . .
. . . . .
. . . . .
. . . . .

About the Quintanilla book by Modern Age.[1] Their conduct has been shitty in the extreme all through this. I have written no commentary for the pictures. The commentary is by either Jay Allen or Elliot Paul. I have written an Introduction and nothing more. I am getting no money out of it at all and they are trying to put a fast one over by announceing a book by me. They have a right to announce that the Introduction to the book is by me and nothing more. I wish your legal department would see that they do not exceed this as they have been absolutely shitty throughout their whole negociations with me and I will not have them announceing any Hemingway book which is a harmful thing to both Scribners and myself. I anticipated that they would do some such skullduggery and so warned you long ago.

Am terribly sorry to hear Tom Wolfe is ill—and so dangerously ill. I hope he will be better by now.

Max what do you really think about the book. Should the play be in with the stories or not? Would it be any solution to publish them simultaneously and sell them boxed?

My feeling is that a collection of stories by me needs something later than the Snows of Kilimanjaro and The Short Happy Life story.

The little story of the Amposta bridge is not enough. O.K. but too short and slight.

Rather than write my best stuff into stories I have wanted to save it for a novel.

I have written two new stories of about 3000 and 4200 words but both of them are imperfect still. I have them typed in final form but I know that I can

[1] Luis Quintanilla, *All the Brave* (New York: Modern Age Books, 1939).

improve them on another re-writing. They are about Chicote's Bar—a famous place before the war—and deal with it in wartime They are good stories but I have written better ones and can make these better with time.[1]

So here is the problem. Do we have a stronger book and one that will sell more by including the Fifth Column with the other stories? I think it would give them God's amount of reading matter and reading it over today and going all over it I know it is o.k. to read no matter how it would play.

I have sort of lost my perspective on my stuff with the going back and forth to the war and all and I wish you could advise me soundly.

It seemed to me that the Have and Have Not book was reviewed so very unjustly in many quarters that it was necessary to give several times the value for the money this time so that we sort of swarm over them. But I may be wrong. Do you think the stories and the play together could do better than the two separate? It seems to me they might. That makes the play, which is exciting reading, even if I wrote it I know that, and some twenty five to thirty thousand words of new stuff they haven't read and all the back-log of the other stories.

Anyway I sent it to you now. I will send the galleys of the stories en-route or when I get to the ranch. There will a couple of names to change in Up In Michigan.
I think the order of reversing the stories in general time but using book order and finishing with Up In Michigan o.k. Or it can come at the beginning of the In Or Time stories where it was designed to go in the book. Might be better and less conspicuous that way.

Will you write me to the ranch when you get this. I am prepared to publish and turn down production or let it depend on the thing being published first.

. . . . .

. . . . .

Ernest.<br>
Send Tom Wolfe all my sympathy if you are in<br>
communication with him.

*AL and TLS, 3 pp.*<br>
*Cooke City, Montana*

Aug 17

Dear Max:

Have just finished the proofs. Return them herewith I read all the In Our Time chapters but they will need to be re-set in Italics—I cut out the two that appear as separate stories A Very Short Story—and The Revolutionist—
The order is Now
The Fifth Column—

---

[1]"The Denunciation" and "The Butterfly and the Tank" (*Esquire*, November and December 1938) were not used in *The First 49*.

The Short Happy Life of Francis MacCumber
   Old Man at the Bridge
The Snows of Kilimanjaro
The Capitol of The World
Followed by the stories in the order which
they appear in
Winner Take Nothing
Men Without Women
then Up In Michagan—
Then the stories in the order in which they
appear in In Our Time with the chapters
set in Italics between them exactly as in
the Liveright Edition.
The story called Introduction by the Author
which is now called On The Quai at Smyrna
Follows Up In Michigan
   and proceeds the story Indian Camp in The In Our Time group.

Although it does seem sort of goofy to work backwards all the way like that and it would probably be sounder since we are not following chronology completely either backwards or forward to simply state in the preface that the play and the first four stories were the last things written and so are put first and then follow with the other stories in the order of Up In Michigan In Our Time, Men Without Women, and Winner Take Nothing. I think that give the book a more logical reading arrangement.

But if you want it the other way go ahead.

I put the Old Man at the Bridge between the Francis Macomber and The Snows of Kilimanjaro quite arbitrarily because it is better for the readability. Will mention in the preface that it is the last story written and Up In Michigan the first.

The only proof that needs to be read now is the Old Man at the Bridge and the In Our Time italics.

I really think it is best to put the order In Our Time, Men Without Women and, Winner Take Nothing with the play first followed by the new stories.

The going backwards is maybe logical but it does not make so good a book because there is a line in all the Nick stories that is continuous and running it backwards is confusing.

We want to make the best book possible and if you are not following chronology either way I think that arrangement is the best.

I worked hard in each book to make it a unity and a balanced arrangement and makeing them go backwards doesn't go so good.

As a matter of fact, to make a book, it might be better to
Have Fifth Column
   Short Happy Life
   Capitol of the World
   Snows of Kilimanjaro

Old Man at the Bridge
Up In Michigan
On the Quai at Smyrna
followed by the Liveright In Our Time
Men Without Women
Winner Take Nothing.

That is the order that after reading them all overand thinking it all over I believe to be the soundest and would like to go on unless you have objections to it.

It places the last thing I wrote next to the first thing I wrote and then proceeds in order of publishing through the three books haveing given, in this new book, all the new stuff first but in a good order for reading it.

In makeing a book of short stories readable there is a hell of a lot to haveing them placed properly in relation to each other. will now go ahead on the preface. It's raining here and snowing higher up.

What delayed me on the proofs was cutting my lousy eye again. Was crippled from it for about a week. The other one went bad—sympathetically. Wish it would show more sympathy for the owner and less for the partner.

No time to write, Max. Must get busy on the preface.

I think it will make a fine book, really.

Thanks for makeing the deposit and for wiring me the money to Denver. I was delayed in Palm Beach two days in bed with the eye. That was what made me late. Then driving one-bleary-eyed across the country. 3200 miles.

Am glad Tom is better. Did what I changed make it all right about Scott?[1] Please tell Tom when you write him that I hope he'll be well soon.

Best always
Ernest/

*CC, 3 pp.*[2]

August 23, 1938

Dear Ernest:

. . . . .

. . . . .

. . . . .

As to the Scott passage, you amended it very neatly.- But I greatly wish his name could come out altogether. If people reading the story do not identify "Scott" as F. S. F., it might as well be some other name (one realizes he is a writer in the very next sentence) and if they do identify him, it seems to me it takes them out of the story for a moment. It takes their attention to the question of

[1]EH wanted to retain "Scott" without the surname in "The Snows of Kilimanjaro"; the reading in *The First 49* was "Julian."
[2]555 words have been omitted from this letter.

what this means about Scott. You did take out the things that could hurt and I showed the amended passage to two people who had never read the story and they thought Scott might still feel badly, being very sensitive, but that they hardly thought there was much reason for it now. If his name could come out without hurting, it would be good.- But I'll bring up the matter when you are here.

. . . . .

Old Tom seems to be making out pretty well, and he wrote me—though he should not have done it, and his hand looked feeble—a mighty nice letter. He certainly had a bad time though.

Yours always,

*CC, 3 pp.*[1]

Oct. 14, 1938

Dear Ernest:

. . . . .

You must have had a dreadful time trying to work over there in the midst of the war crisis,- though perhaps you discovered sooner than the rest of us, that nobody really meant to have a war. Or did they? I can't understand it. But everything seems now to be worse than ever so far as human decency is concerned.

You will have read, of course, of Tom's death which was an awful business too. I never want to go through such a day as I did at Baltimore when he was operated on, [with that terrific, emotional family,- like a day out of "Look Homeward, Angel".][2] But I am enclosing a copy of Tom's last letter, which he wrote just before his illness took its fatal turn. It is a remarkable and beautiful letter, I think.[3]

I hope you have been able to write, but I swear I do not see how you could have done much recently. Maybe you have, though. You wrote "The Fifth Column" in Madrid. You ought to be back here by Thanksgiving anyhow. . . .

Yours always,

---

[1]115 words have been omitted from this letter.
[2]Bracketed material is crossed out in the carbon copy.
[3]See *The Letters of Thomas Wolfe*, ed. Elizabeth Nowell (New York: Scribners, 1956), pp. 777–778.

*TLS with holograph postscript, 3 pp.*[1]

c/o Guaranty Trust Co. of N.Y.
4 Place de la Concorde
Paris
Oct 28/

Dear Max;

I should have written you a long time ago how sorry I was about old Tom. But I knew you would know and it never does any good to discuss casualties. You must have had a hell of a time with it all. That was a good letter he wrote. Everybody writes you fond letters when they think they are going to die. You ought to get quite a collection. Hope I'll write you a lot of them in the next fifty years.

Well we thought we had something pretty unbeatable in that book didn't we? But you can't beat those guys. They can gang up to play it down. You know Max I think I'll still be around and going pretty good when there is a whole new generation of critics. You see those guys all buried me and it is awkward and difficult for them to see you rising like Lazarus. I always thought Lazarus must have been awkward to have around myself. What was it they said "Lord he stinketh."

I don't give a shit about any of it except the aspect of interfering with my livelihood. When I got the book and saw all those stories I knew I was all right as a sort of lasting business if I kicked off tomorrow. Which, by the way,—oh well let us neither talk nor write balls.

Pauline wrote that on the day the book came out there wasn't a copy visible in the window. But I'm sure there must be a mistake. Is there any connection with the size of the reviews and the size of the ads? I can see how a large ad could <u>not</u> get a large review. But a small ad might be used as an indication of size of review. Must be quite a racket.

Think you might emphasise in the advertising that there is 185 pages of hitherto unpublished material. Give the length of the new stories. Mention that Up In Michigan is only obtainable in a book which now sells for $350. a copy. and emphasize the size and number of words in the book.

Those seem to me to be sound points.

There is enough new stuff in the book to make a book a good deal longer than Of Mice and Men say.

Mention that. I think you will have to push it to sell it with those kind of reviews. But I do think, truly, that you offer a very good bargain and that it can be sold if the strong points are emphasized.

I worked like a bastard right up until that Wednesday. Thought maybe it would be last chance ever to write and wrote well. Did two long stories. One was just unfinished when the war was called off. Finished it afterwards. Since, in the mess everything's in, the sort of let down and carnival of

---

[1]77 words have been omitted from this letter.

treachery and rotten-ness that's going on, coupled with being upset about the damn book (not hearing anything and then everything I hear being bad) it's been hard to work. But I have two Chapters done on the novel.[1] Look like will be back pretty soon now. Ask Pauline to show you the copy of one of the stories I sent her—Night Before Battle. It is ten thousand some words long.[2]

Will work again on the novel today. Writing is a hard business Max but nothing makes you feel better.

. . . . .

I haven't written the napoleonic story yet. But will.[3] Going to look in on Bercelona next week before comeing home. Max I am a little bit gloomy so I will terminate this.

Remember if anything ever happens to me I think just as much of you as Tom Wolfe even if I can't put it so well.

So long Max.<br>Ernest

. . . . .

ALS, 4 pp.[4]<br>Key West, Florida

Dec 24.

Dear Max:

Thank you for depositing the check and for the wire about the sale. Wouldnt have wired if I'd had your letter which came just after I sent the wire.

The book on Grant Lee and Sherman is very good and I enjoyed it greatly.[5] You cant agree with all of it but it is a first rate book within its limits and its prejudices. The limits are self imposed and the prejudices are understandable in an Englishman. The Shotgun book too is very good—really.[6] Walker Evans photographs are superb. But how did you ever publish that utterly tripy The Captains and The Kings Depart.[7]

I'll bet you havent read it. The man reveals himself as a fool, as an idiot in military affairs, as a snob, a sychophant, (his dispatches—no not dispatches—his ass kissing love notes to Douglas Haig) are as disgusting reading as you could find. As a monument to the British misconduct of war it

---

[1] EH did not continue work on this novel, and it has not been identified.
[2] *Esquire* 11 (February 1939): 27-29, 91-92, 95, 97.
[3] This story was not written.
[4] 122 words have been omitted from this letter.
[5] Col. Alfred H. Burne, *Lee, Grant and Sherman* (New York: Scribners, 1938).
[6] Lawrence B. Smith, *Shot-Gun Psychology* (New York: Scribners, 1938).
[7] *The Captains and the Kings Depart: The Journals and Letters of Reginald, Viscount Esher* (New York: Scribners, 1938).

should be compulsory reading You <u>read</u> the damned thing. I'll bet anything you havent.

I'd like to see a review of it by Gen. Fuller or Lidell Hart, even, if they could write what they really think and not have to be respectful to the pompous dead. What a disgusting man Esher is when you see his mind work. And how marvellously impressive and fine a person he was, probably, to meet.

. . . . .

. . . . .

. . . . .

. . . . .

. . . . .

. . . . .

          Ernest/

I thought Bunny Wilsons review was rather pitiful.[1] All the "revolutionaries" who are really cowards and who took no part in the defense of the Spanish Republic feel a very natural obligation to discredit those people who did take such a part. That's O.K. with me. The poor pricks

*ALS, 5 pp.*
*Key West, Florida*

Feb 7—1939

Dear Max:

Thank you again for the Peter Scott book. It tells all about wild fowling in all the places Ive always wanted to go and never will get to now I guess.[2]

About the lectures. Tell them I am not free to lecture at present. Might as well be polite—Must keep that in reserve in case ever get blind or anything so cant write.

Well, we've lost another war. Its bad enough to lose but to have Carney[3] lying and saying the International Brigades have been fighting in this last business is too lousy. The brigade people that Franco took prisoner were men without papers to prove their nationality who were held in camps near the frontier or in towns like Ripoll until the League of Nations commission could arrange for their repatriation. Theres only one thing to do with a war and that is win it. But in this one winning was made impossible by many circumstances outside of the control of the military.

When you get this will you please deposit a thousand dollars in my account City Bank Farmers Branch—22 William Street—N.Y.C? Need to pay income tax. Debit my Fifth Column royalties.

[1]Edmund Wilson, "Hemingway and the Wars," *The Nation* 147 (10 December 1938): 628, 630.
[2]Peter Scott, *Wild Chorus* (New York: Scribners, 1938).
[3]W. P. Carney, *New York Times* reporter.

Am going to Cuba next Monday, I think to work. I know to work. I think to go next Monday I mean. I ought to have enough new stories for a book in the fall or do you think that is too soon for another book of stories?

I have    The Denunciation     Esq

          The Butterfly and The Tank     Esq.

          Night Before Battle     Esq.

          Nobody Ever Dies     Cosmo—     <u>Read it in March No.</u>

          Landscape With Figures—Not sent out yet.[1]

And three very long ones I want to write now. One about Teruel—called Fatigue.[2] One about the old commercial fisherman who fought the swordfish all alone in his skiff for 4 days and four nights and the sharks finally eating it after he had it alongside and could not get it into the boat. That's a wonderful story of the Cuban coast.[3]

Im going out with old Carlos in his skiff so as to get it all right. Every thing he does and every thing he thinks in all that long fight with the boat out of sight of all the other boats all alone on the sea. Its a great story if I can get it right. One that would make the book.

Then I want to write that one of the storming of the Gudarrama pass by the Polish lancers. If I can do those three Ill make enough to support the family for the rest of the year and can then start on the novel again. I have to know how the war comes out to get that right anyway.[4]

Have heard nothing from the play Jews since I left. Maybe with the war gone bad they are hedging on the play. Christ how I wish Id written <u>that</u> as a novel. Well I couldnt. There wasnt time when we were waiting for Teruel. Am afraid I insulted them all the night I left any way got to feeling too good with you and Charley.

I have bad dreams every night about this retreat. Really awful ones in the greatest detail. It is strange because I never had any <u>ever</u> in Spain about anything that happened only the always recurring one about getting out of the trucks and haveing to attack without knowing where the objectives were and no one to explain the positions. Last night I was caught in this retreat again in the Goddamndest detail. I really must have a hell of an imagination. Thats why should <u>always</u> make up stories—<u>Not</u> try to remember what happened. Well so long Max. Give my best to Charley. Thank you both again for the book.

                      Yours always,
                      Ernest/

[1]This story was not published in EH's lifetime; it first appeared in *The Complete Short Stories of Ernest Hemingway: The Finca Vigía Edition* (New York: Scribners, 1987), pp. 590–596.

[2]This story was not written.

[3]This story idea became *The Old Man and the Sea* (New York: Scribners, 1952).

[4]This story was not written.

*TLS with holograph postscript, 2 pp.*[1]

Key West          March 25

Dear Max;

. . . . .

How has the book sold? What's the sale now?

I don't like to talk about this because it's bad luck but have been going awfully well writing. Got to Cuba intending to write these three stories. Instead wrote one about the war, Pauline thinks among best I've ever written, called Under The Ridge.[2] And then started on another I'd had no intention of writing for a long time and working steadily every day found I had fifteen thousand words done; that it was very exciting; and that it was a novel.[3] So I am going to write on on that until it is finished. I wish I could show it to you so far because I am very proud of it but that is bad luck too. So is talking about it. Anyway I have a wonderful place to work in Cuba with no telephone, nobody can possibly bother you, and I start work at 8.30 and work straight through until around two every day. I'm going to keep on doing that until this is finished. I turned down a lot of Hollywood money and other money and I may have to draw on you to keep going. If you want to see the collateral you can—but you don't need to so far. I promise you that. Have worked very slowly reading everyword over from the start every day. I hope it will be a good novel. Anyway it will be as good as I can write, being in good shape, putting all worries aside, and writeing as carefully and well as I can. It is 20 times better than that Night Before Battle which was flat where this is rounded and recalled where this is invented.

Am going to stay in one place now and work no matter what. After the way the French treated the Spanish Republic I feel no obligation to fight for the French and anyhow it is more important now for me to write and that is what am doing. To hell with comeing to N.Y. Have figured out that in any personal problems I am no good to anyone if I do not work. So am working where can work and not be interfered with. Bumby is here for his Easter vacation. Then I Am going back to Cuba. So it looks like we will have a book of stories and a novel. Have five new stories so far. The Denunciation. The Butterfly and The Tank. Night Before Battle. Nobody Ever Dies. Landscape With Figures. and this new one. Hell, that makes six.

Am down to 198 pounds. Have place where can play tennis and swim and am happy and healthy although always that hollow in the middle of yourself daily emptied out feeling you get when working well on a long book. Wish me luck Max. I find I know a lot more than when I used to write and think that is maybe what makes it easier in the end but it is still a very tough busi-

---

[1] 53 words have been omitted from this letter.
[2] *Cosmopolitan* 107 (October 1939): 34–35, 102–106.
[3] *For Whom the Bell Tolls.*

ness., But working the way I do now I feel as happy and as good as when I was going good on A Farewell to Arms

So long, Max. Give my best to Bill Webber, to Meyer and best to Charlie.

Ernest

I found Scotts Tender Is The Night in Cuba and read it over It's amazing how _excellent_ much of it is. If he had integrated it better it would have been a fine novel (as it is) Much of it is better than anything else he ever wrote. How I wish he would have kept on writing—Is it really all over or will he write again? If you write him give him my great affection (I always had a very stupid little boy feeling of superiority about Scott like a tough durable little boy sneering at a delicate but talented little boy) But) Reading that novel much of it was so good it was frightening——

*CC, 3 pp.*[1]

November 21, 1939

Dear Ernest:

I certainly did read your "Under the Ridge" and I do not know why I never told you of it because I was greatly moved by it.- There was horror in it of a kind I never remember before except in your own "The Killers". Those battle police, and the despair.- But Al Bessie[2] didn't like it ideologically! Now what in hell has a writer as good as he to do with ideology in a writer? I am only telling you this as a funny thing because he is your great admirer. Some of those other stories I haven't read though, or can't get by name. I remember "Night Before" mighty well of course, in every detail. Maybe as pure fiction it wasn't as good, but as a piece of writing it was remarkable. I remember also "Nobody Ever Dies" but I don't remember "The Butterfly and the Tank". I'll try to get it.

But it would be unwise in the circumstances, to publish a collection of stories until after this novel.- And if the novel is finished in January, it could comfortably come out in the Spring. It would be all right if it were a late Spring book because it could carry over safely into the Fall. It would not be hurt by the fact that the Spanish war seems to have been pushed far back into the past in the sense of a historical event. It will sell as a novel about people and the way things were, and such things as other people writing about the war wouldn't have any effect upon it. But I would give anything if I knew just a few of the elements in it to make a note from, and the title. Even if the title were changed later it would be O.K. And I would not need to know much to build up a note for the time being.

I would give anything if I could read half as fast as you can. It would be the greatest talent in the World for me. I have always been held back by slow

---

[1]253 words have been omitted from this letter.
[2]Alvah Bessie, a veteran of the Lincoln Brigade.

reading, and the better a thing is, the slower I tend to read it. I can force myself, but then I don't get anything but what the facts may be, and I forget them rapidly too.

I am sending you all the books,- "The Rivers"[1] with our compliments and a couple of others. Sanka especially on account of the illustrations.[2]

I had a letter from John Thomason in which he spoke very highly of Alvah Bessie's book,- "A fine piece of war writing" etc., and ending "I noted, however, very little that was new in the experiences of the infantry soldier— more planes, and more trouble—but the same old troubles as formerly. And of course the ideology. (Regulars don't have ideology—I hope I never have to bother with it)". He ends up, "Hunting season opens in Mexico now. I am getting some fine shooting." You like a lot of things he does, and ought some-time to get together with him.

I think Scott is fixed up O.K. now with Colliers. He has a fine subject, fine material, though I cannot tell you about it. He has not answered my last let-ter though, and I think he may be mad because he dropped a few hints that we might send him some money. But he owes us a lot, and I don't think he ever realizes that apart even from that large sum, we just wrote off six thou-sand when we serialized "Tender Is the Night". He never took that in, in those ginny days, I guess.- Anyhow, I think it will all come out right with him and Colliers.[3]

. . . . .
. . . . .

Always yours,
MEP

. . . . .


CC, 2 pp.[4]


Nov. 30, 1939

Dear Ernest:
Scott is in great despondency but he has a short book all planned, and partly done. I saw 6,000 words, and mighty good, new and stirring. It makes you aware of new transcontinental ways of life. This may not make sense, but the nature of the Gatsby like story is secret.

. . . . .
. . . . .

Always yours,

[1]Ward Allison Dorrance, *Where the Rivers Meet* (New York: Scribners, 1939).
[2]MP was apparently referring to *Manka, The Sky Gypsy*, written and illustrated by Denys Watkins-Pitchford (New York: Scribners, 1939).
[3]Fitzgerald was attempting to sell *Collier's* the serial rights for his Hollywood novel in progress, *The Love of The Last Tycoon;* but the deal fell through in late November.
[4]95 words have been omitted from this letter.

*TLS, 2 pp.*[1]

*[c. 14 January 1940]*

Hotel Ambos Mundos
Havana—Cuba

Dear Max;

Thanks very much for depositing the money. How is everything? I had a letter from Harry Bull of Town and Country that old Waldo was in town so I guess you have seen him.

Have a terrific hangover and can't write this morning (won't write rather as don't want to turn out any hung over pages   so write you instead. Make allowances for that in reading. Had been working steady and went on big drunk with some of the boys down here night before last.

Marty gets back in a couple of days now and then everything will be o.k. Am in the stretch on the book now. Of course I suppose people have to praise a book when the author lets them read it. They can't just say 'It's horsehit' probably even no matter what they th nk. But have let various people that I trust read this one and they think it's the best I ever wrote. Hope to God so. People like Esther Chambers, Joris Ivens, Chris LaFarge, Otto Bruce, Pauline hates me so much now she wouldn't read it and that is a damned shame because she has the best judgement of all. But what the hell. Maybe it isn't so good anymore too. As Dizzy Dean said of his arm. It aint so good as I used to be but hell what is?

But you haveing to pay out money on nothing but promises thought I would send you a chapter (it's just typed off from my hand-written mss. and isn't corrected. Copied it that way in case mss. was lost) to cheer you up. That is chapter 8.[2] I am now finishing chapter twenty two. You can let Charley read it to cheer him up too.

Have now worked on this book since the first of March and have not interrupted to make any outside money by writing anything at all. You know I could always write pretty good but I know so damned much more now that maybe I can write a hell of a book.

It is fine out here in the country. There are quit a lot of quail on the place and lots of doves. Patrick and Gregory were over for  he holidays and they had a fine time. I wish you could see this joint. Hope can renew the lease in June.

I don't care about going to war now. Would like to live a while and have fun after this book and write some stories. Also like the kids very much and we have good fun together. Also would like to have a daughter. I guess that sounds funny to a man with five of them but I would like to have one very much.

Don't let the ideology boys that have to claim we never killed anybody see

[1] 135 words have been omitted from this letter.
[2] Chapter 10 in the published text of *FWTBT*

that chapter. Poor Bessie. He is a wonde ful guy too. But it is as bad to have a ring in your brain that people lead you around by as to have a ring in your nose. Me I am faithful and loyal while under arms but when it is over I am a writer. Not a Catholic writer, nor a Party writer nor anything but a writer. Not even an American writer. Just a writer. (and today a writer with a hang-over) And in writing this I have learned how to give the effect of all the bad words without using them. I had to because Spanish is so truly obscene that you can't translate most of the stuff and have people believe it even. So have learne how to do that and there is not one obscene word in the book. If I have it right th t is something to have learned.

I'll let you know when need some more money. Maybe you better put in $250. when you get this. In the 22 William Street branch of City Bank Farmer's Trust.

Read Marty's piece in this week's Colliers.[1] It isn't so good militarily but boy she got out to that front when not a single correspondent had been there.

Oh yes. That was the other thing I had to write you about. She has a contract with that new outfit of Duell, Sloan and Pearce. It is a hell of a good book called A Stricken Field. I did not want her to show it to you because I think it is a bad idea for people in the same family or anything like that to be published by the same firm.

Anyway I have done all the business with Duell (who seems a fairly slippery young fellow) and he has sent me a contract full of what seem to be jokers. Would you send me a contract of the very worst that you ever make; that is including all the possible conditions that a publisher can impose on a writer so that I will have something to judge this contract by? If that is unethical I will have copy out all the seeming jokers and submit them to you. My tendency is to just tell them to go to hell as he agreed to send a contract in accordance to terms agreed upon by letter and then sent this thing full of jokers. They are all outside of my experience so I have to ask your advice. I remember you telling me that contracts were much stiffer now and it may be that this is o.k. So send me the stiffest one you have ever made so I can judge. I don't like Duell from his letters. It seems to me anyonw who would steal a writer from another firm might be expected to steal from the writer too. Or doesn't it work that way?

. . . . .

. . . . .

Please send the piece of Mss. back
Best always
Ernest/

---

[1] "Blood on the Snow," *Collier's* 105 (20 January 1940): 9–11.

*TS for wire, 1 p.*

Jan. 18, 1940

Mr. Ernest Hemingway
Hotel Ambos Mundos
Havana, Cuba
Extremely impressed stop Opening pages beautiful and chapter eight tremendous Will send contract but better if you copied out questionable clauses All confidential
      Max

*CC, 4 pp.*[1]

Jan. 19, 1940

Dear Ernest:

I cabled you the morning after I read what you sent of the ms. The impressions made by it are even stronger after the lapse of time. The scenes are more vivid and real than in the reading. That has always happened to me after reading your novels, and it is true of mighty few writers. That chapter eight is terrific, and as one gets further away from it the characters of those different men when they came out to be killed, and the ways they took it, seem as if one had seen it all, and had known them. It is truly wonderful,- the way the temper of the people changed as things went on, and they got drunk with killing, and with liquor too. The first chapter, or the first eight pages, had the old magic. Last night I had to talk about forthcoming books to the people in the bookstore, and I ended by saying what a simple thing it was to be a real writer, the easiest thing in the world, and I was going to give them an example to show it,- how anybody could do it, and then I read them, without saying who had written it, the first three pages through the point where Jordan gets his glasses adjusted, and sees the mill and the waterfall and all.- Having him do that makes the whole scene jump out at you as real as real. I said, "Why couldn't any of us do that? It's perfectly simple." But of course nobody can do it. Then I did tell them that they were the first pages of a novel by you, but I told them nothing else about it. You could see how even that little bit impressed them all. Well, of course I am mighty impatient to see more.

    . . . . .
    . . . . .
    . . . . .

      Always yours,

    . . . . .

[1]301 words have been omitted from this letter.

*CC, 3 pp.*[1]

February 14, 1940

Dear Ernest:

. . . . .

. . . . .

In the letter before this one which you may not remember since you described it as a hang-over letter, you spoke of not being "A Catholic writer, nor a party writer . . . not even an American writer. Just a writer." I don't see how anyone can think that this is not as it should be,- but an awful lot of these fellows do, even ones of true ability sometimes seem to. I don't think Bessie thinks so himself. I do not think his ideas would prevent his fiction from being that of a real writer. Another thing: I always understood your problem about the old four-letter words. One time—in-fact the last time I ever saw him—Owen Wister came in here to talk about this. And of course those words always worried him. I don't think he exactly objected himself so much, but he did think them completely unnecessary, and that they aroused prejudice. That time, he began telling me how magnificently Homer wrote of the Trojan war, and Tolstoi of war and peace. No four-letter words. He didn't seem to see though, that any circumlocutions, etc., would be inconsistent with the way you write. I tried to explain this, but I really never fully grasped how you do write, so I couldn't very well. But I pointed out as an instance that you almost never even used a simile. It is a different way of writing. I always knew it wasn't just a simple matter of not using words,- that it really did mean a deviation from your style or method or whatever, to avoid them. I knew it was a serious matter. I don't know exactly why I am saying all this, but many people never understood this, and it is hard to explain.

. . . . .

. . . . .

. . . . .

Always yours,

*TLS, 1 p.*[2]

[Mid-April 1940]                                          *Havana, Cuba*

Dear Max;

Harry Burton[3] should have gotten those 32 chapters last Saturday. I sent him 28 on Monday and he got them on Wed. Sent the other on Thursday

---

[1]543 words have been omitted from this letter.
[2]84 words have been omitted from this letter.
[3]Editor of *Cosmopolitan,* who was considering serializing *FWTBT. Scribner's Magazine* had stopped publishing in 1937.

and he should have had them on Saturday. Since it is now in the pay or not pay stage they become very cagy and the usual hurrah, hurrah, hurrah telegrams are suspended.

I wrote him to turn it over to you. You can show it to Cape. But for Chist sake Max not to Alvah Bessie and every other bastard that will want to see it. You read it. Charley. Bill Webber. Meyer if you want. But for Christ sake don't let any of those communists read it just because you like them and trust everybody you like.. Don't please argue with me on this. And please see <u>no one</u> outside of office reads it and that the Mss. doesn't leave office.

I was laid up five days. My heart was only hitting 52 at noon and Dr. said I was shot with over-work and should lay off for two months or so. Stayed in bed 2 days. Loafed three and went back to work last Wednesday. This is sat. Have been going good. Am on Chap. 35 (almost finishedthat chap) Yest. Ben Finney good tough guy F.F.V. Captain in Marines at 20 last war, first guy to ever run the Cresta from the top first try etc. Old friend. Came out here at 4.p.m. Started to read Mss. Read straight through without stopping until eleven o'clock and then I let him take it out to the yacht with him to finish. He thought it was the best and most exciting book I'd ever written. Twice while he was reading he called me in to see that he had an erection about the girl. Good sign because Finney pretty well fucked out. My desk swamped with cigarrette butts from Finney's reading.

He tried to make me admit I'd seen all that stuff. Hell no, I made it up, I told him. You're a goddamn liar, said Finney.[1]

That is what you want to do with writing. What I did once with Caporetto.

Christ I am tired though, Max. Me in the third person for a year and going on two months. Me that the third person can beat to death in a thousand words.

Will consult with you on all serilaization angles before doing anything.

Also no need to deposit that $500. Will size up how play goes and let you know. But it is an open and shut thing with Revenue Bureau. That's how they told it should be done. Can deposit thousand or fifteen hundred another month and be same.

Once I get this all cleared up am going to work with Author's League on tax situation to get a juster treatment for all writers. Went into that with Revenue Agent to get his advice. Ideal would be if we could get it on a crop basis the way farmers have. But would have to have some straight authors who are not gyppers and crooks meet with the department and talk things over. Then take various cases and carry them through and get rulings. I would be glad to do it when am in the clear again and not writing a novel. Trouble is that there are so many kind of writers. The law works to the advantage of the straight commercial writers.

. . . . .

. . . . .

[1]See Finney's autobiography, *Feet First* (New York: Crown, 1971), for his account of reading *FWTBT*.

Have worked two whole days with Bible, Shakespear etc. on title. (Worked plenty before. But this was on account your 22nd date.)

The Undiscovered Country is the nearest I can get with the necessary counter-point. But still it isn't right.

Have 24 others. None right. Still working. Will get it right.

Best always.
Ernest/

*TLS, 1 p.*
*Havana, Cuba*

Sunday.
April 21

Dear Max—

How about this for a title

For Whom The Bell Tolls
A Novel
By Ernest Hemingway

No man is an <u>Iland</u>, intire of itselfe; every man is a peece of the <u>Continent</u>, a part of the <u>maine</u>; if a <u>Clod</u> bee washed away by the <u>Sea</u>, <u>Europe</u> is lesse, as well as if a Promontorie were, as well as if a <u>Mannor</u> or of thy <u>friends</u> or of thine own were; any man's death diminishes me, because I am involved in <u>Mankinde</u>; And therefore never send to know for whom the <u>bell</u> tolls; It tolls for <u>thee</u>.

John Donne[1]

I think it has the magic that a title has to have. Maybe it isn't too easy to say. But maybe the book will make it easy. Anyway I have had thirty some titles and they were all possible but this is the first one that has made the bell toll for me.

Or do you suppose that people think only of tolls as long distance charges and of Bell as the Bell telephone system? If so it is out.

The Tolling of the Bell. No. That's not right. If there is no modern connotation of telephone to throw it off For Whom The Bell Tolls can be a good title I think

Anyway it is what I want to say. And so if it isn't right we will get it right. Meantime you have your provisional title for April 22.

Let me hear from you. Best to Charley. Going now to the Jai-Alai to try to make it 21 straight.

Best always
Ernest/

[1]John Donne, "Meditation XVII," *Devotions Upon Emergent Occasions* (1624).

*Wire, 3 pp.*
*Havana, Cuba*

1940 APR 22 AM 8 17

PROVISIONAL TITLE IS QUOTES FOR WHOM THE BELL TOLLS UNQUOTE FROM PASSAGE JOHN DONNE OXFOR BOOK OF ENGLISH PROSE BOTTOM PAGE ONE SEVENTY ONE STARTING QUOTES NO MAN AS AN ISLAND ETC STOP PLEASE REGISTER TITLE= IMMEDIATELY STOP SENT BURTON FOLLOWING WIRE WHAT PERKINS EYE HAVE TO KNOW TO DECIDE WHETHER SERIALIZATION MONTHLY MAGAZINE JUSTIFIES DELAYING PUBLICATION IS WHAT WILL YOU PAY HOW MANY INSTALLMENTS WHEN WOULD START AND WHEN FINISH STOP SCRIBNERS= MAKEING UP CATALOGUE MONDAY STOP BETWEEN FIFTEEN AND TWENTY THOUSAND MORE WORDS COMEING COMPLETING END MAY STOP BEST
ALWAYS ERNEST.

*TS for wire, 1 p.*

April 22, 1940

Ernest Hemingway
Hotel Ambos Mundos
Havana, Cuba
All knocked out by first five hundred twelve pages Think absolutely magnificent strange and new stop Would never show to outsider Title beautiful Congratulations
Max

*CC, 2 pp.*[1]

April 24, 1940

Dear Ernest:

I am just sending you a line to say that I have read all of the manuscript there is here, and am still in a kind of daze, half in that land, and half in this,- which has happened to me twice before in reading your manuscripts. I think this book has greater power, and larger dimensions, greater emotional force, than anything you have done, and I would not have supposed you could exceed what you had done before. It is a surprising book too. You know right off that you are in Spain, and the war, and then you expect something so different from what you get. You just naturally expect what you do conventionally get in a book that is in a war, what they call battle pieces, and all. Well, by God, that

[1]167 words have been omitted from this letter.

fight piece, where El Sordo dies, is a wonder. That surprises you, and you know for dead sure that that is the way it would be. The nearest thing I ever saw to that fight was perhaps one or two pieces in Tolstoi, one in a book that was called, I think, "TheThistle". You might not have seen it. But the way you write about war—nobody will ever forget the apparition of the cavalryman, his horse stepping along in the snow, and not seeing Robert until too late—all seems strange. And then you realize that that is because it is so utterly real. If the function of a writer is to reveal reality, no one ever so completely performed it. It was wonderful, too, to give this war—though of course that is not the point of the book—in the way you did, with these partisans, all extraordinarily solid people. A reader feels that it gives you people of Spain, as the war was to them, in a more real way than if it had been about the actual enlisted men. There isn't a person in it that anyone would ever forget, including old Goltz, the General. As for the girl, she is lovely, and as if one had known her.

Anyhow, reading it is an experience, that's all. Even now it has got so these things go through my head as if I had seen them. It is truly amazing. Well, I'll read it in proof, and I know I'll find greater depths in it the second time. It has them. All the memories that go through Jordan's head, which nobody can equal you in giving anyhow, are beautiful. It is an astonishing achievement. You are always in suspense because of the frame of the story.

As to the title, I don't believe you can possibly improve it, and I almost hope you won't try to,- and especially when you read that passage. Now the book has the spirit of that passage in it. I never read that before. But nobody who ever did would ever forget that either.

. . . . .

Yours,

. . . . .

*Wire, 1 p.*
*Havana, Cuba*

1940 JUL 1 3 47
PLEASE WIRE DEPOSIT THREE HUNDRED DOLLARS MY SPECIAL ACCOUNT FIRST NATIONAL BANK KEY WEST FLORIDA STOP ALSO AIRMAIL ME HAVANA COPY THAT CORN BUSINESS NOT USED IN DEATH IN AFTERNOON[1] STOP BRIDGE ALL BLOWN AM ENDING LAST CHAPTER=
ERNEST

[1]See MP's 25 January 1932 letter.

ALS, 1 p.[1]
*Havana, Cuba*

July 13—1940

Dear Max:

Hope to get up to N.Y. by the end of next week with the Mss. They are copying it all now except the last chapter where am still working on the end. The last chapter is the most exciting in the book. Its almost unbearably exciting during and after the bridge is blown. When I finished the part where—what the hell—will not tell you—You can read it—I was as limp and dead as though it had all happened to me—Anyhow it is a hell of a book—I knew I had to write a hell of a last chapter—But have it all now except the very end—The action and the emotion are all done—Been too shot about it all to write yest or today (The girl doesnt get killed) I hated to have that damned Jordan get what he got after living with the son of a bitch for 17 months. Felt worse than if it were me. Wrote 2600 words (all action) on last day. Almost like a genius. The hell of it is they all make sense so no chance of geniushood.

. . . . .
. . . . .

Best always,
Ernest/

. . . . .
. . . . .

*Perkins's typed note on the unwritten conclusion of* FWTBT *for the BOMC judges, CC, 1 p.*

Two short chapters, amounting to 1,500 words in all, will bring the book to a conclusion. In the first of these Karkov and Goltz meet after the failure of the attack, and in driving back from the front they talk together about it, and about Robert's message and his success in blowing up the bridge. In the second, Andrés and Gomez motorcycle back to the outpost and then Andrés makes his way over the ground he covered before, and eventually reaches the abandoned camp, sees the ruined bridge, and knows all that has happened there.

These chapters are written, but not yet to the complete satisfaction of the author. He wished to wait until after reading the proof up to this point before perfecting the end.

EDITOR

[1]120 words have been omitted from this letter.

*CC 3 pp.*[1]

August 13, 1940

Dear Ernest:

I read the book all through on Saturday and Sunday, and with amazement. I hadn't truly realized what a strange and cunningly contrived book it is. It stands all by itself, as a book should but almost never does. This comes partly from the very effective enlargement of scope that you made in the first two-thirds, or whatever it was, that I read a good many weeks ago. But it comes more, I think, just from reading it all at once. I have made a good many marks, but really they amount to very little indeed. Still, I'll draw up a memorandum and send it to you before the week is over. But what I do send you now is some additional typographical questions on points of style, uniformity, spelling, etc. Perhaps you yourself won't have to bother with this matter. We haven't had time here in the office to read through all the reader's set of proof, and all these possible corrections are on the galleys after page 106. They were made by Meyer, and he gave me this memorandum in handwriting, enclosed.[2]

. . . . .

. . . . .

Always yours,

MEP

P.S. Just got your telegram and have sent proofs to Duran, by air mail.

*CC, 4 pp.*

August 14, 1940

Dear Ernest:

( Hemingway wouldn't like this[3] )

Here are the very few things I have to say,- though some of them, being little more than typographical may duplicate on marks you have on the reader's set of proof, or those I sent you read by Meyer.

On galley 2, a little below the middle you say, "The man who will go with you (that was Anselmo)". I think that that parenthesis is entirely unnecessary,- that the reader would know this meant Anselmo. Still it would do no harm in there excepting that the reader is listening to Goltz's talk. He is under the illusion of being present in the person of Robert. This parenthesis tends to break the illusion somewhat. Anyhow I don't think it is needed at all.

On galley 5, I have marked two instances where it seems to me the verb should be changed to conform to the pronoun. I must say I am shaky on this

[1]30 words have been omitted from this letter.
[2]Unlocated.
[3]Written by MP.

"thee" and "thou" matter and the verbs that go with them, and besides I have taken it that you are perhaps somewhat modifying usage, as they call it in colleges, to suggest the way of Spanish speech. But there is no harm in pointing out these two instances.

On galley 17 in the paragraph considerably below the half-way point, beginning "not in joke" you put in a parenthesis to translate "la gente". I think this is wholly superfluous,- that that is one word everybody, however unfamiliar with any foreign language, would know. I think everyone could be expected to realize it meant "the people" and if so it is superfluous, and it too is in a direct quotation where one is hearing the person speak and tends to injure the effect and illusion.

On galley 18 I questioned whether the last paragraph might not be omitted. It is hard to take it out because it is very good. The reason to do it, if it should be done, is that so far in the story everything has been told as seen, and heard, and all, by Robert. This is the first place where you take the reader from him into someone else, apart from what he realized about the other person. I know it is good. The only point is whether it does not break the reader out of the story by the change from one person to another.[1]

The next time that happens is where Pablo talks to the horses. There it becomes perfectly right, and thereafter as you get to doing it, and very smoothly and rightly, it is always all right. It is just in this one instance where the change comes suddenly. In this book one gets to know all about Pilar, and I don't know that this is needed here because she is completely revealed as you go on.

On galley 19, where the gypsy is singing, about one-third down the galley, they have failed to italicize the third line in the verse, "But still I am a man". Probably this is already marked on the reader's set, though I do not remember its being.

On galley 29, about thirty lines down, you use the word "scretological".[2] It is all right, of course. The only point is that it comes as a surprise. Since you have been using the word "obscenity" it comes as a surprise and makes the reader think out of the book for a minute. It might be better to stick to the regular word.

On galley 42 it seems to me that the first two words of the second line might better be "them from" instead of "from them". This may have been queried on the reader's set.

On galley 50, the fourth paragraph from the bottom, about bigotry. It is certainly very shrewd psychology all the way through, but when I read this and came to that about being married, etc., I thought that Robert was married. But he was not. The reason one thinks this is that a young man, and not married, would not be likely to reflect upon that point of being married, etc., or so it seems to me. I think the reader when he reads that would get the

---

[1] The last paragraph of Chapter 4; EH did not revise this paragraph.
[2] MP's secretary misheard the word "scatological" in dictation.

impression that Robert was married. But he wasn't, and it is better that he should not be thought so, even for the moment.[1]

Galley 54 has a few typographical suggestions on it, and so does galley 59.

Somewhere a little previous to galley 71 Robert is sitting in the cave and thinking and remembering. It is extraordinarily good. And then right after that comes that about the smell of death which finally leads Pilar into a long and exceedingly effective and alive talk. I am not sure whether, despite the fact that there is nothing in all this which is not interesting to read, and deeply so, you might not find some way of shortening the thinking and the talk about the smell of death, etc. The point is only that the two long passages, though in a way very different, are of a sort that delay the story possibly longer than is advantageous.- I mention this with great trepidation, and wouldn't dare to suggest any specific point of cutting. I am doubtful if it can be done, and certainly it should only be done purely for the sake of the whole book, and not at all for the sake of the episodes themselves.[2]

On galley 73, in remembering about Gaylords and Karkov, you come to "a certain American journalist" who turns out to be named Mitchell, and about whom Karkov implies embezzlement. I haven't an idea who this man is, but you must consider the libel question. You will know whether it is safe. If the man is one whom many would recognize, unless the implication against him could be proved, and with the burden on us to do it, I think this passage is certainly libellous. But maybe the man is not recognizable, or if he is and is a bad egg, there may be reasons why he could not sue. But if he is recognizable and could, you might do something which would make him unrecognizable,- it is a point to consider anyhow.[3]

Galley 75 has some typographical suggestions on it.

Galley 94 is about El Sordo's fight, and nobody will ever forget it who reads it. It is all about El Sordo and his companions and the Spaniards who are attacking them. Nothing is known about it to Robert or his band, except that the fight is going on, and how it is bound to end. You say in it, (second paragraph galley 94) that "he had killed the young officer . . . the same one who had ridden up the pass that lead to Pablo's camp". Doesn't this take you out of it a little? El Sordo didn't know about what had happened at Pablo's

---

[1] EH cut the following passage from the galleys (Chapter 13, p. 164):

But what was the other thing that made as much for bigotry as continence? Sure. Being married to an unattractive wife and being faithful to her. Being married to such a woman and working at it was twice as strong a force for bigotry as continence. Twice as strong. Sure. But look at that old one from home with a beautiful wife who seemed, when you talked to her, twice as bigoted and witch-hunting as he was. Sure, he told himself. You'll have quite a time writing a true book. You better confine yourself to what happens.

Now, back to Maria.

[2] EH disregarded MP's advice.

[3] EH changed "American journalist who wrote for an American publication" to "British economist who had spent much time in Spain." He also deleted anecdotes about Mitchell being a fund-raiser for the Communists and close to Roosevelt.

camp. If it added to the effect to know that this was the same officer, it would be different. I don't think it does. The point is that everything is told as it seemed to El Sordo, and this takes you away from how it seemed to him. I thought it a point worth considering whether that ought not to be omitted.[1]

There is nothing later than this. The last chapters I did read very fast for they were the ones I had read last, and I thought too that I would read them over again when the last 1500 words came. But all the last chapters are magnificent, and I don't think there would be anything to be said about them beyond those little typographical matters, etc., that would be marked on the galleys read by Meyer.

Always yours,<br>MEP

P.S. I am sending you this entire set of galleys, but those I have referred to I have clipped together and put on top of the others.[2]

*CC, 2 pp.*[3]

August 26, 1940

Dear Ernest:

I'll tell you, I think that's mighty good news we got today about the Book-of-the-Month. I felt certain it would come out right from the start.- Everything seemed to go well with the book and that's always a sign that it will keep on going well. The fundamental reason, I suppose, for its going well is that the book has put everyone that had to do with it on their toes, because it was such a magnificent story. Anyhow, we can now go ahead with assurance of a very fine start and the best possible of prospects.

. . . . .
. . . . .
. . . . .

Yours always,

TLS *with holograph inserts, 4 pp.*[4]<br>*Havana, Cuba*

August <u>26th</u>

Dear Max;

I am air-mailing you today 123 galleys. I have gone over it all but I thought you might as well get going on these. I also enclose with this letter a style sheet

---

[1] EH deleted the line.
[2] MP's marked galleys are unlocated.
[3] 64 words have been omitted from this letter.
[4] 80 words have been omitted from this letter.

giveing the corrections that must be made throughout all the galleys. All of Meyers queries and suggestions are answered or embodied in this style sheet.

Your suggestions and Charlies I have taken up as I went along.

I send Charley a re-write of parts of galleys 21 (The Communist Business) and Galley 29—(the over-use of the word obscenity) to be set up and embodied in all galleys sent out.[1] He got these early last week.

I have cut the part about the man Mitchell drastically and removed all libel without, I think, removeing the flavour of Karkov's mind. It does no good to describe a man such as Karkov as witty and intelligent and then have no conversation to prove it.

I have made the thees and the thous as accurately used as possible without giveing the book an archaic-ness that would make it un-readable. When I use you instead of thee etc. I know what I am doing.

Throughout I removed the word unprintable as I thought it gave a literary connotation that was bad. I changed it to un-nameable or some other word.

I do not agree with you on the passage where something is written about Pilar at the end of galley 18. You thought it was o.k. when it was Pablo and the horses. I know it was necessary. It was simply that the first time it was done it would always be a shock to you. The second time o.k.

I got out that about bigotry etc. as you quite rightly suggested. It was confuseing on Jordan's status.

About the smell of death part. Unless this will impair the sale of the book seriously or cause its suppression I think it is necessary to leave it in. I have to make many effects that do not show at the time and it is like takeing either the bass viol or the oboe out of my orchestra because they each make an ugly noise when played alone.

If you or charley think that is a dangerous or unpublishable passage I could change it to read instead of wrap it around your head and try to breathe throgh it to——You raise this sack to your face and inhale deeply—and use this same phrase in the next sentence down.

Let me know about this. The passage is meant to be horrifying. It is not meant to be gratuitously obscene or unpublishable. But I have to somehow give that quality of Madrid and make the idea of the odour earthily and concretely and vulgarly believable—instead of seeming to be gypsy-cross-my-hand-with silver-nonsense. Real gypsies are a very strange people and the ones in this book are not book-gypsies anymore than my indians were ever book-indians.

On the Sordo fight galley 94 I agreed with your correction.

I fixed up the Onan so it would not bother Charley I hope. After all Robert Jordan is a man and the idea of holding some girl all night in your arms that you had intercourse with normally, on a night before an attack when he wanted to

---

[1]In galley 21 (Chapter 6, p. 66), EH changed Jordan's political affiliation—making him an anti-fascist instead of a Communist; in galley 29 (Chapter 9, pp. 92–93), EH substituted "besmirch," "un-nameable," and "befoul" in some places where "obscene" and "obscenity" were used in Agustín and Pilar's conversation.

get to sleep would bring up some sort of a problem. I tried to handle his rejection of one solution of the problem delicately. If it is repulsive to several people to whom you show it I can cut it out. But remember it is by the small things of that sort that the man becomes absolutely credible instead just a Hero.[1]

Be frank about this.

Now here is some more.

What would you think of ending the book as it ends now without the epilogue?

I have written it and re-written it and it is o.k. but it seems sort of like going back into the dressing room after the fight or following Catherine Barclay to the cemetery (as I originally did in Farewell to Arms) and explaining what happened to Rinaldi and all.

I have a strong tendency to do that always on account of wanting everything completely knit up and stowed away ship-shape.

I can write it like Tolstoi and make the book seem, larger, wiser and all the rest of it. But then I remember that was what I always skipped in Tolstoi.

What do you think? Is it o.k. as it is? (I have fixed the emotion some and made it better)

Please write me air-mail on this the day you get this. Ask everybody if they think it ends all right as it is.

I am leaveing here on Thursday to take the boat across and then drive and fly to Sun Valley. Should be there September 4th at latest. Will send you the re-maining 18 galleys before I leave.

Re-wrote on them all day yesterday.

You see the epilogue only shows that good generals suffer after an unsuccessful attack (which isn't new); that they get over it (that's a little newer) Golz haveing killed so much that day is forgiveing of Martybecause he has that kindliness you get sometimes. I can and do make Karkov see how it will all go. But that seems to me to date it. The part about Andres at the end is very good and very pitiful a and very fine.

But it really stops where Jordan is feeling his heart beating against the pine needle floor of the forest.

You see every damned word and action in this book depends on every other word and action. You see he's laying there on the pine needles at the start and that is where he is at the end. He has had his problem and all his life before him at the start and he has all his life in those days and, at the end there is only death there for him and he truly isn't afraid of it at all because he has a chance to finish his mission.

But would that all be clear?

Should I put on the epilogue?[2] Is it needed? Or would it just be grand manner writing and take you away from the emotion that the book ends on?

---

[1]In Chapter 31 (p. 342), EH replaced "There is no need to spill that on the pine needles now" with "There are no pine needles that need that now as I will need it tomorrow."

[2]The epilogue was not used and has not been located.

Ernest Hemingway     *Don't Lose This For Christ's Sake.* 1/26
                                                                    E 14.
                    Memorandum on corrections  of proof For Whom The Bell Tolls
These corrections may not have been made on this set of galleys due to lack of space .They
are uniform and each word and   usage should be checked throughout all the galleys .

       Throughout the book  use  Heinkel for planes --never Henkel .

       It is Golz --- never Goltz

       It is Estremadura -   never Extremadura .

        Rafael is the gypsy - never the Gypsy(except at the beginning of a sentence )

        Maria is referred to as guapa — not Guapa ( except at the beginning of
a sentence .)

        Maria is referred to as rabbit ® - not Rabbit   ( except at beginning of
a sentence .)

        It is viejo ( l.c.)  never Viejo ( except at beginning of a sentence .)

       It should be máquina  — never machina

       In Qué va  the accent aigu  should be used in every instance .

       ▓▓▓▓▓▓▓▓▓▓▓▓▓▓▓▓▓▓▓▓▓
        guerrillero   should be in italics  throughout the book .

        partizan   should be   italics and inl.c. through the book .

        It should be Agustín throught the book— never Augustín
                                                  Gredos
        In some places   the Sierra de Gredos  is referred to as the Gredos

(Robert Jordan always refers to them thus )   Sordo and Pablo would simply say Gredos
. Follow my corrected galleys  on this without querying  them .  I have checked all usage
carefully .


        Since I have cut chapter three into chapters three and four  the numeration
of all subsequent  chapters should be advanced by one . Check this carefully .


        Please check with some one who is familiar with Russian names as to
whether Kashkeen   should be spelled Kashkin . ( I  do not have my Russians here )
If it should be spelled Kashkin correct. the spelling to this through-out the book .

        I will wire you the name of a proper cavalry regiment to insert in the blank
left in galley 9I


        The dedication is to read :

        This book is for Martha Gellhorn .


        Check carefully my corrections  on the passage from  Donne . In the
galleys it was full of errors which I have corrected from the original .

Hemingway's "style sheet" for editing *For Whom the Bell Tolls*,
included with his 26 August 1940 letter.

Please write me when you get this.

There is also a paragraph on galley 127 that I would like your advice on. It is the long paragraph at the top of the galley. I could take out the last sentence which start's Comrade M arty's part is given only because etc.

Or I could take it out and the first part of the First sentence too and start it—Comrade Andre Marty's interference was probably only fortuitous as there was not one etc.

Let the rest of that go as it is and omit the last sentence.

Let me know about this.

I don't like to write like God. It is only because you never do it, though, that the critics think you can't do it.

The whole story of Marty and Karkov would take another entire volumne to tell. But that is no reason for starting something you do not finish. It was for this reason that I wrote that paragraph. It explains why there was no finish.[1]

Well I will send you the complete galleys by Wednesday.

These couple of corections (there are no question of any before galley 78 shuld not hold up your manfactureing up to there at once and if you write me by return air-mail I will get it Wednesday or Thursday and have plenty of time to fix all. Will probably work it out and fix it on my wn anyway first. But please write at once when you get this and remember it is ten cents for each 1/2 ounce.

Well so long Max. Best to Charley. Write me about the end. Maybe better wire about that when you get this letter. If that end is o.k. it would save a lot of time to know it and I would just work over and over that last Chapter until I send it.

Should have one proof on it just to make sure all my corrections are o.k. You can have that pulled and sent to me at Sun Valley—Idaho. by air-mail registered and mark it very prominently. <u>Please hold</u>. If there are no corrections I will simply wire to go ahead. If there are corrections will make them by air-mail same day. Send my corrected proof with the new proof so that I can check the additions faster.

. . . . .
. . . . .
. . . . .

> Best always,
> Ernest/

*Cable, 1 p.*
*Havana, Cuba*

400 P AUG 27 1940

:PLEASE ANSWER MY QUESTIONS ABOUT LAST CHAPTER ENDING BY WIRE TODAY I WILL PAY FOR IT BUT DO IT IN FULL STOP

[1]Chapter 42.

ACCORDING TO CHARLIES CABLED TIME SCHEDULE IT IS DEADLY
IMPORTANT THAT I KNOW PLEASED CLUB[1] THANKS=
:ERNEST.

*TS for wire, 1 p.*

AUGUST 28, 1940

ERNEST HEMINGWAY
HOTEL AMBOS MUNDOS
HAVANA, CUBA
   GALLEYS AND DIRECTIONS RECEIVED IN FINE SHAPE STOP
CAN WAIT TILL SEPTEMBER TWELFTH FOR LAST CHAPTER BUT
WOULD PREFER TENTH STOP DECISION ON ENDING HARD BUT
WE KNOW PRESENT ENDING IS IMMENSELY EFFECTIVE AND
COMPLETELY SATISFYING STOP ALL HERE FELT NOTHING MORE
COULD BE SAID ON READING GALLEYS BEFORE QUESTION WAS
RAISED STOP I THINK WE SHOULD DECIDE AGAINST EPILOGUE
   MAX

*CC, 4 pp.[2]*

Aug. 30, 1940

Dear Ernest:           ( Hemingway wouldn't like this[3] )
   . . . . .
   . . . . .
   . . . . .
   Of course much the hardest question of all was that about the ending. I did-
n't get your letter of the 26th in which you talked about it until the day after
you telephoned.- I thought it over all the time that afternoon and night, and
I had arrived at the conclusion myself that the only thing there was doubt about
was Andres. It really was only a question of that. The ending is tremendously
effective, and Weber and Wreden—who is mighty intelligent—and O'Connor,
all of them when they finished reading the galleys came and said that the book
was ended, they thought. The night of the day you telephoned, my daughter
Peg had just finished the book, and I asked her what she thought of the ending. She thought it was perfect.- Then I told her about the possibilities of bringing Andres back and of his feeling about what he found. Then she could see
there was a possibility. But at first she said she didn't see how it could go on further. I do see the value of Andres coming back because then the reader

[1]The Book-of-the-Month Club had chosen *FWTBT* as its October selection.
[2]304 words have been omitted from this letter.
[3]Written by MP.

would feel it as Andres felt it.- But it was only about that question that I was still hesitating. On the other hand we know that the ending really is an ending, a wonderful ending. Then you have amended it, or are doing so. I therefore thought that if we must decide, we ought to decide to have no epilogue.

. . . . .

. . . . .

Always yours,

*Wire, 1 p.*
*Sun Valley, Idaho*

1940 SEP 10 PM 4 05

JUST AIR MAILED LAST EIGHTEEN GALLEYS AND FRONT MATTER STOP DUE YOU TOMORROW NOON STOP CHECK CAREFULLY SPELLING ABURRIMIENTO THROUGHOUT BOOK AS WELL AS RECHECK ALL STYLESHEET SPELLINGS THIS LOOKS SLOPPILY DONE ON MY PAGE PROOFS STOP UNABLE DECIDE ON MAP AS EVERYONE READS IT UNDERSTANDS LOCATIONS PERFECTLY BUT ALL PICTURE THEM DIFFERENTLY AND MAP OF SEACOAST OF BOHEMIA[1] SOMETIMES CONFUSING STOP HAVE MADE MAP[2] IN CASE ITS NECESSARY BUT CANT LIKE IDEA YET STOP WILL HAVE TO SEE FINAL PROOF OF LAST THREE OR FOUR GALLEYS BUT WILL WIRE OKAY ON CORRECTIONS AS SOON AS RECEIVE PROOF REGARDS=
    ERNEST.

*Perkins's Article on Hemingway*[3]

*TS with holograph revisions, 4 pp.*

In spite of Ernest Hemingway's repugnance to publicity—his first and most emphatic request to his publishers was that nothing about his personal life should be given out—he is one of those about whom legends gather; and since he is disinclined to talk about himself it is hard to disentangle truth from rumor.

But one of the earliest stories significant of his character I do know to be fact. When still a boy, but large for his age and strong, his father, yielding to

---

[1]In *The Winter's Tale,* Shakespeare refers to the "seacoast of Bohemia," but Czechoslovakia is now a landlocked country; this putative error is frequently cited by editors in discussions about correcting texts.

[2]EH's map was not used and has not been located.

[3]Published as "Ernest Hemingway," *Book-of-the-Month Club News,* October 1940, p. 4. The bracketed material was not used in the printed article.

his urgency, gave him as a present the price of an advertised course in boxing. You paid the ex-fighter in advance and he turned you over to a pug. In the first lesson young Hemingway got rough treatment. His nose was broken. Few returned for a second lesson. But Hemingway did, and he finished the course. It never even occurred to him that this was a racket,- that you weren't supposed to come back ever.

That was in Chicago when he lived in Oak Park. Only a little later—he was certainly below sixteen—he left home, determined to take care of himself. In a surprisingly few years later he was taking care of a number of other people toward whom he thought he had loyalties. His first established job was that of reporter on the Kansas City Star,- though if his size had not beguiled a city editor into overestimating his age by several years, he would never have got it. Before this he had shown some inclination to write, for pieces by him had appeared in his school paper, but in Kansas City he really began to learn.

Then came the World War. Even when it ended Hemingway would have been barely old enough to enlist, but he was bound to see it, and finally got into the Ambulance Service on the Italian front, later to command a section, and then to transfer to the Infantry with a lieutenant's commission. He was wounded, and in the end received the highest decoration the Italians give.[1] It is commonly thought that the war scenes in "A Farewell to Arms" came directly from that experience. They didn't. The most famous ones of all, those in the account of the Caporetto Retreat were wholly his own creations. He wasn't there.

War is, we know, a revelation to one who can retain impressions. The book of Common Prayer says: "In the midst of life we are in death," but one could also say of war that in the midst of death we are in life. Many writers, like Tolstoi, have largely learned of life from war—for then life is quickened and intensified, and the qualities of men come sharply out. Hemingway saw it again after Versailles when, as correspondent for an American syndicate, he covered the Graeco Turkish war, and he said he learned far more of war from that, as an observer, than from the world war as a participant.

Then in Paris he turned wholly to writing, and lived for several years in poverty. This was in that post war renaissance which so deeply affected American literature. When about 1927, he came to America, it was by way of Cuba, for economy's sake. Then he crossed to Key West, liked it and stayed.

[It must require the intuition of an artist to learn quickly the geography of the ocean bottom and the ways of fish, but Hemingway learned in a year what often takes a decade or a lifetime. It was as though instinctively he projected himself into a fish,- knew how a tarpon or a kingfish felt and thought, and so what he would do. But the tarpon were rare. He was bent on my catching one and the afternoon before I was to leave, three of us with two rods went out into the harbour for the last chance. Hemingway was trolling to relieve me. A sud-

[1]MP accepted EH's legends about himself: there is no evidence that Hemingway ran away from home, and the account of his war record is largely apocryphal.

den storm struck down with driving rain and wind and whitened the waters, and just then he hooked a tarpon, and far astern it splendidly leapt out of the sea. It was his fish,- one doesn't lightly surrender a tarpon and it was fun enough to see the shining creature throw himself into the air over and over, and fight in the storm. But Hemingway was bound I should land a tarpon, and he thrust the rod on me and in some forty minutes we had him. But it should have been Hemingway's tarpon. That was just after "A Farewell to Arms" was finished.]

Hemingway became a great fisherman in those waters through which runs the deeply blue gulf stream: the fishing was needed as relief from the hardest work in the world, that in which everything is presented in final truth, where the essential quality of each thing told of is perceived and fixed. And that's why it was done,- that and the need of such a man for action. Obviously his first interest was in writing, and not <u>his</u> writing only.

Once when he came to New York and Tom Wolfe was in an agony to master the material of "Of Time and the River" I asked Ernest to talk to him. No writers could have been so far apart in style and method, yet Ernest was fully appreciative of Tom and he understood his torment in his work. I remember, at that luncheon which so encouraged Tom, Ernest told him some helpful things,- always, for instance, to break off work when you "are going good". Then you can rest easily and on the next day easily resume. For such as Tom, however critical he might be of some qualities in his work, Hemingway had a deep sympathy because of Wolfe's artistic honesty;- but not for the literary writers. When told of one who could not go on with his work until he found the right place to work in, he said, "There's only one place for a man to work. In his head."

Hemingway has too largely appeared as a man of force and action. He is that too and when he thought the people who were Spain were fighting for what was Spain, he gave all he could and was quite prepared to give his life. But his writings are surely enough to show what he is besides that, and what one soon learns who sees him is that he is always at his work; always aware. [Once when we were fishing where, off Key West, the shoals give that ocean the colors almost of a rainbow, I said, "Why don't you write about all this?" An old pelican was just then flapping by, and Hemingway said, "I might some day but not yet.- Take that pelican. I don't know yet what he is in the scheme of things here." He knew later + showed that life in "To Have and Have Not".

And in a later year a party of us were to go fishing, and at the last minute a stranger joined us who seemed pretty commonplace. Anyhow he did to the one woman present, and she rather ignored him,- though I only realized that in retrospect. But Hemingway was aware of it, and when at the end of the day we three were driving home, he remonstrated with her for neglecting the outsider.

"Why," she protested, "should I bother with him? He was just a Babbitt."

"Because," said Hemingway, "he was the least fortunate one in the party."

This talent of his to short-cut through the mazes of formal understanding is one of the secrets of his power.]

*CC, 2 pp.*[1]

Sept. 20, 1940

Dear Ernest:

Now that everything is done that can be done, and done magnificently on your part, I just want to say that I think that to have written this book in fifteen months' time was miraculous. This hardly need be said, but you seemed to think that you had taken a very long time to it. If you had taken five years to such a book nobody could have thought it was a long time,- apart from the fact that there isn't anybody alive who could have written such a book anyhow. It may be silly to say this, but you several times spoke of the time taken as if it worried you. Of course in a practical sense it might have worried you temporarily, but the fact of having done it in that space was a great feat.

. . . . .

Always yours,

*TLS with holograph insert, 1 p.*[2]

*29 October 1940*                                                   *Sun Valley, Idaho*

Dear Max;

. . . . .

Will you write me what has been done about Cape? Were page proofs sent him? Have you heard from him? He should have books sent him by clipper if he has not been sent page proofs.

I thought Bunny Wilson's review very dull.[3] He is interested only In the political and sectarian political aspect and writing means nothing to him anymore. Same for the Nation one.[4] He, Chamberlain[5] etc. all the non-fuck-men unite against the girl. Calling that unreal is the only thing they have left to attack. Well it isn't nreal and the thee and the thou way of speaking is the one thing they would know about if they were ever in a revolution.. Tu-toi-ing instead of saying vous or usted is the mark of comradeship in any language but nglish. But Bunny would have to ring in Maurice Hewlett. I care nothing about what any shits say now because they are just digging their own graves as critics by saying it. But John Chamberlain is a prick and Bunny is a man who has abandoned literature for politics and then tries to destroy it by mis-representation and lies as when he wrote that in Farwell to Arms the man rowed (impossibly) against the wind for thirty miles when what he did was to sail with the wind, useing an umbrella sometimes and sometimes his

---

[1]45 words have been omitted from this letter.
[2]167 words have been omitted from this letter.
[3]*The New Republic* 103 (28 October 1940): 591–592.
[4]Margaret Marshall, *The Nation* 151 (26 October 1940): 395–396.
[5]*The New York Herald Tribune Books*, 20 October 1940, pp. 1–2.

oars for a distance of a little under sixteen miles. But when they want to destroy you they lie and distort and fake. Well fuck them all say I and they are fucked by their own writings.

Think the Paramount deal o.k. I made it myse f and with Cooper we have quite a lot to say about how it will be done.[1] It was silly to hold out for 150,000 and maybe miss it when could sell for 100,000 plus ten cents a copy for each copy sold including the Book of Month. I wanted to sell before the counter-attack started.

How does the sale go actually?

I have to make some decisions about when to take the moneybetc. and how to take the picture money.

. . . . .

. . . . .

You know just because we had some good reviews you mustn't stop advertising the damned book now if we are really going to sell any. There are enough quotes in those bloody reviews to run a hell of an advertising campaign. And the more you sell the more you make as well as me.

. . . . .

. . . . .

> Your always
> Ernest
> Oct 29/

*CC, 3 pp.*[2]

October 31, 1940

Dear Ernest:

. . . . .

I think everything indicates that you made the right decision in regard to the sale of movie rights because the sale of the book goes on wonderfully well. I'll try to give you a statement now from which you can judge:

The Book of the Month Club first guaranteed and paid for 70,000 copies. The first printing for them was of 135,000 copies (we knowing that if they did not use all of that number we could use what they left ourselves); the second printing for them was 15,000 copies, and the third printing, which began yesterday, was 50,000 copies.- That is, we have printed in all for the Book of the Month Club on their wish and anticipation 200,000 copies. They might not sell all of these, and it might take a year for them to sell them all. But they do not expect to sell less than 200,000 copies.

As for ourselves alone, we started with an advance sale on the day of pub-

[1] *FWTBT* was made into a movie by Paramount starring Gary Cooper and Ingrid Bergman in 1943.

[2] 45 words have been omitted from this letter.

lication, of 40,000 copies. The total sale one week after publication was 61,000 copies,- that is, 21,000 in a week. And the total sale two weeks after publication (which I am anticipating safely because of orders for delivery on Monday) was 70,000 copies.

Our printings, apart from those of the Book of the Month Club have been first 75,000, second 35,000, and third which was begun yesterday, 50,000.- 160,000 in all. Our printings combined with Book of the Month Club printings total 360,000.

You must remember, of course—and the sales department urges me to caution you on this though I thought it hardly necessary—that a very great deal of this is in anticipation, but the book is going at the greatest rapidity, and we get orders from 80 to 120 store outlets (though many for from 1 to 5 copies up) a day. Just for fun I am mailing you the orders for your book of the last two days as they come up.- Throw them away when you have looked at them enough. These are just the day to day orders. The big orders come every several days from the jobbers, like Baker & Taylor or the American News. But every indication is most promising.

As for the advertising, I wanted to get it together and send it all to you, but the most impressive ad which quotes from about thirty reviewers,- a page in early November, was not among them. You have probably seen most of the others, but when that comes I'll send you all of them. But you needn't worry about the advertising.- And we are planning cooperation with the Paramount people in connection with it, and in publicity.

I was very disappointed in Bunny's review too, and somewhat surprised because I thought he had got himself oriented soundly and rightly as to the relation between politics, economics, literature and art. I hoped he had. I think he has a most interesting mind and he is doing a novel for us for which I have high expectations.- A peculiar kind of book that I don't think anyone else could do. It will have the social consciousness element in it very considerably, but I hope he will not let that keep him from writing rightly. Of course he is the kind of a critic who always criticizes in the popular sense of finding something the matter. He has always done that. But almost all reviews are now in. I haven't been sending you any reviews lately because I think you get them all from a clipping agency. But there is an article by Stephen Benet and his wife—I don't see how the two of them do it together—in this week's Tribune which in one part shows a great deal of discernment, and which is generally very good.[1] You will see it.

Ernest, I wish I could come out there, but since I got into all this trusteeing and executoring, I don't dare go away for any length of time.- It isn't that anything very important happens in those lines, but you always have to be signing your name to something.

I am hoping to hear from Scott.

Always yours,

---

[1] "The Byron of Our Day," *The New York Herald Tribune Books*, 3 November 1940, p.

*CC, 3 pp.*

Dec. 28, 1940

Dear Ernest:

I thought of telegraphing you about Scott but it didn't seem as if there were any use in it, and I shrank from doing it. Anyhow, he didn't suffer at all, that's one thing. It was a heart attack and his death was instantaneous,- though he had had some slight attack, as they realize now, a short time before. The Catholics would not allow a funeral from a Catholic church, or burial in a Catholic cemetery.- So I was glad Zelda did not come, for she has grown to be deeply religious, and would have been shocked by that.

One thing about it, Scott did leave something like forty thousand dollars, and there will be at least enough left I should suppose, to get Scottie through college and pay all his debts, and perhaps more than that. The will is very much confused and difficult. John Biggs and I are named as executors.- I am afraid this ends my last chance of getting to Cuba for awhile, for it will take some weeks to clear up confusions in the Will. It may be necessary for me to go to California. It will be in the end if I am executor. The point is that Harold Ober was first named, and then Scott changed him to me, and whether he did it legally is somewhat doubtful. But even apart from that, things must be done for Scottie. She ought at least to finish this year, and I think since she is so young, she should finish the next one, and means will be found for that, whatever happens. There is no use talking about Scott now.

The Murphys were on the train to and from Baltimore. I had met Gerald before. I think you told me what a person Sarah was. Anyhow, she is. It made you feel good to talk to such a one.

Well, our sale to a couple of days ago comes to 189,000 copies. I am enclosing herewith five of the bulletins sent out by Paramount to theatre people, etc. We think that this big Life feature will be next week.[1]

Yours always,

*CC, 2 pp.*[2]

Dec. 31, 1940

Dear Ernest:

. . . . .

. . . . .

I hope you didn't feel too badly about Scott. I am trying to think of some way that something could rightly be done to bring his writings forward.- But

---

[1]"The Hemingways in Sun Valley: The Novelist Takes a Wife" and "*Life* Documents His New Novel with War Shots," *Life* 10 (6 January 1941): 49–57.

[2]66 words have been been omitted from this letter.

the novel appears to have been very far from finished. In a way that is the worst thing about it all because this book might have vindicated Scott completely. It was going good. Well, I'll tell you all about it when you come up.

Yours always,

# HEMINGWAY/PERKINS CHRONOLOGY
# 1941–1961

◈

| | |
|---|---|
| 13 January 1941 | Hemingway goes with Martha Gelhorn Hemingway to New York to deliver her novel, *The Heart of Another*, to Scribners. |
| 11 February–6 May 1941 | The Hemingways tour the Far East as war correspondents. |
| 1 June 1941 | Hemingway is in New York; he probably sees Perkins. |
| March 1942 | Hemingway agrees to edit and write an introduction for an anthology of war stories, *Men at War*, to be published by Crown. |
| June 1942 | Hemingway begins patrolling for German submarines with his boat, the *Pilar;* his last patrol ends on 18 July 1943. |
| 22 October 1942 | *Men at War* is published. |
| c. April 1944 | Hemingway is in New York en route to England. |
| 17 May 1944 | Hemingway arrives in London as war correspondent for *Collier's;* he meets Mary Welsh Monks. |
| 28 July 1944 | Hemingway begins covering the 22nd Infantry Regiment. |
| c. 8 March 1945 | Hemingway is in New York for a week; he has a long lunch with Perkins during this visit. |
| 21 December 1945 | Hemingway's divorce from Martha Gelhorn Hemingway is final. |
| 14 March 1946 | Hemingway and Mary Welsh marry in Havana. |
| 1–c. 9 December 1946 | Hemingway is in New York and Long Island. |
| 17 June 1947 | Perkins dies in Connecticut. |

| | |
|---|---|
| 7 September 1950 | Scribners publishes Hemingway's fifth novel, *Across the River and Into the Trees*. |
| 8 September 1952 | Scribners publishes Hemingway's novelette, *The Old Man and the Sea;* Perkins and Charles Scribner, III, are the dedicatees. |
| 2 July 1961 | Hemingway commits suicide at his home in Ketchum, Idaho. |

—R.W.T.

Hemingway, Charles Scribner, and Perkins
in the Charles Scribner's Sons offices.

*CC, 3 pp.*[1]

April 4, 1941

Dear Ernest:

. . . . .

Everything goes along all right. The sale, which has slowed up, of course, in the face of a lot of big books like Marquand and Glasgow, has reached barely less than 491,000,[2] and the printings including one now under way, come to 565,000. . . .

We finally got a plan worked out about Scott's novel. It is the most tragic thing that it wasn't finished, for it broke into wholly new ground and showed Scott as advancing and broadening. But it is very much unfinished, both in that the last third of it anyhow was not written at all, and also internally. But it has to be published, and should be, and what we finally decided was that Bunny Wilson should edit it and comment on it, with an introduction, and with explanations at the end, and anything else that would help. Then we should publish it as "The Last Tycoon: An Unfinished Novel by Scott Fitzgerald" together with "The Great Gatsby" and selected stories. Wilson's introduction would also cover Scott's career as a writer and show his importance. It will be kind of an omnibus book of his best writings in fiction.- Bunny wanted to put in "Tender Is the Night". But even apart from the physical difficulty of such a large volume as that would make it, "Tender Is the Night" was too recently published. The Princeton Press too is planning to make up some kind of book of writings about Scott, and of some of his writings. I hate to think of the crack-up pieces going into it.- For one thing Scott was dramatizing his situation there. This novel shows that except for the physical side of it, he didn't crack up. He was just getting into a good state of mind. You ought sometime to talk to that Sheilah Graham[3] about it. I think she was mighty good for him, and a mighty good girl herself. I don't know that you ever saw her. We'll fix it up for Scottie to go through college if we can make her do it.[4] Scott wanted her to finish and she is only nineteen, with one more year to go.

. . . . .

. . . . .

. . . . .

. . . . .

Yours,

---

[1]747 words have been omitted from this letter.

[2]"Book of Mo 252,000 paid for; We 239,000" [*MP's note*].

[3]Sheilah Graham, a Hollywood columnist, was Fitzgerald's companion for the last three and a half years of his life.

[4]MP, Gerald Murphy, and Harold Ober, Fitzgerald's agent, put Scottie Fitzgerald through Vassar; she later repaid them.

*TLS with holograph postscript, 2 pp.*[1]

HongKong
April 29

Dear Max:

I was glad to get your ltters of April 4th and April 11th when flew in here from Rangoon last night. The lastleg of the trip from Kunming (Yunnanfu) to here was pretty bad and when we got over Hongkong the static was so bad the telefunken would not work and with a 200 foot ceiling we circled for nearly an hour before we could get down through. Have flown 18,000 some miles since I saw you last and have about 12,000 more to fly before see you a ain. Wish I was paid by the mile instead of by the word.[2]

I had a wire from Charley, two in fact, in answer to one I sent him from Chungking asking about the sale and another I sent saying I was not happy at haveing no word from any of you nor not too happy about the sale or lack of it.

Probably anyone who is not happy with a sale of half a million is headed for the booby hatch. On the other hand when I left you were announceing a printing of 500,000 and I had imagined that the sale had been pushed on. Regret that it was not.

Am damned tired just now and so do not want to be unjust but I sometimes onder if you, Charley and company ever worked as hard selling the damned book as I worked writing it what the sale would be—or rather what it would have been. Not that you didn't work. I know you did. And I know how I worked too when it was impossible

I hope it is not too late to keep on pushing it. It is bad luck to have gone away and then heard nothing, absolutely nothing when Hongkong is only eight days from Newyork by airmail; and then have heard finally the sort of news I id hear. And have to cable to hear that.

It doesn't make anybody feel good not to have a damned line from their publishers from late January until April 4th. Even if you thought I was comeing back in April that was no reason to let me go all of February and March with no word when air-mail only takes one day over a week. Especially when you look forward like hell to getting mail and make every arrangement to have it forwarded and each time you see a pilot with the letters there was never a damned thing.

I don't know how to put it in terms of horse so that Charley will get at its true meaning but I suppose it might correspond with how the quadraped would feel if you neither fed nor watered it on the day after you had given it a hell of a ride.

Hope Bunny Wilson will not knife Scott in that thing he is going to write. Since they both went to Princeton together and all that I suppose he won't.

---

[1]124 words have been omitted from this letter.
[2]EH was reporting on the war in China for *PM*, a New York newspaper.

It is damned hard on Scott to publish something unfinished any way you look at it but I suppose the worms won't mind. Writers are certainly dying like flies. It is a damned shame about old Sherwood.[1] He always liked living very much. I suppose finally no one will be left alive but the Sitwells.

. . . . .
. . . . .
. . . . .
. . . . .

Best always.
Ernest/

. . . . .


*TLS with holograph postscript, Finca Vigia stationery, 3 pp.*[2]
*Havana, Cuba*

—August 26—

Dear Max:
. . . . .
. . . . .

Charley sent me a royalty statement with amount to be deposited and he deducted from my royalties all his attorney's fees and expenses for that pathological case on the coast who sued Scribners, me and everybody else.[3]

As I understand it in the contract the author guarantees to the publisher that his work is free of plagiarism and libel. If there has v ry obviously been no libel and no plagiarism on the author's part and some insane person sues the publisher and the publisher (without a word to the author) then deducts all the publishers legal expenses from the authors royalties there is, from my standpoint, something very wrong.

Scribners, because they can deduct their expenses, makes a great deal more than I do out of that book even if our actual incomes from it were the same. Practically all of my profit goes into income tax. Books manufactured in great quantities are certainly much cheaper to produce. If advertising is greatly reduced or eliminated because the Book of the Month is doing the advertising and the publisher relies on the wonderful reviews his profits should increase correspondingly.

I had heard from Otto or Waldo, forget which, that you said Scribners and I were shareing the cost of that insane plagiarism action. I had told Speiser it was too ridiculous to defend even. In any case they could not serve

---

[1] Sherwood Anderson died on 8 March 1941.
[2] 26 words have been omitted from this letter.
[3] Playwright John Igual de Montijo had filed a plagiarism suit against EH, claiming parts of *FWTBT* had been taken from his film script, *Viva Madero;* the suit was thrown out of court eight months later.

me. It was Scribners, who have a branch office on the coast that the man was sueing.

Then Charley charges me with the whole thing and I suppose I am to be happy and think concessions are being made if Scribners assumes any part of it.

I went out to China and never heard anything from anyone about the book although I had made arrangements to have all letters forwarded by airmail so that I was never out of touch.

Then I asked you to deposit $500. the first of each month in Paulines account in the City Bank Farmers Trust.

She got the June money. There was no deposit made in July.

That kind of thing is hard on people and it isn't very businesslike.

I sent a check to her for the July money but it involved telegrams etc. and also involved me being delinquent in payments. This made me feel very badly.

It may be that I have no right to ask you to make such deposits and for the many other favours you do for me such as advanceing money for me to Evan, Otto etc. But in return I have always been glad to work any and all hours on such things as that proof business last year, I do almost impossible pieces of work to get proofs and copy in when I say I will and I am one author that you have had who has not gone out to work in Hollywood, or done the things that destroy the common property (my ability to write good books) which we both enjoy the fruit of. I have always turned down serialization (from which I only would benefit) if it would interfere with our mutual interests.

If you say what is the purpose of this letter it is just this: I have not gone nigger rich nor have I delusions of grandeur because a novel sold a certain amount of copies. I want to continue to publish with you as you well know. But I think you should look after the business end as carefully as I look after the writing end. If there was a way of writing me which I had carefully organized and kept open at considerable cable expense to give Mrs. Gellhorn our address at all times I think I should have heard. But we will drop that. That is just something I lost out on.

However if a regular sum was to paid to Pauline's bank it should be paid regularly.

If there is a plagiarism suit in which I have committed no plagiarism and Scribners and I have both enjoyed the fruits of my work Scribners should have proposed to me a just shareing of costs rather than deduct their whole legal costs from my royalties.

In writing me, too, I think Scribners should refer to the suit as a plagiarism suit rather than as a libel suit. Or was Charlie unfamilar with the suit? If he knew nothing about it that could explain his attitude toward it and his calling it a suit for libel.

Well that is how I feel about it.

Your grand-son sounds terrific. The infant hercules couldn't have d ne any better. I couldn't make out from Bunny Wilson's book whether my Wound was homo-sexuality or impotence or just plain mean-ness.[1] I still have a hell of a Bow though and that is what he can't forgive. Some day when I write my memoirs I will shoot him with it.

Best always,<br>Ernest/

Am trying to take some good pictures of Martha. The Hays ban on sweaters doesnt extend to writers does it?

CC, 4 pp.[2]

Aug. 29, 1941

Dear Ernest:

. . . . .

I must get it straight about Pauline. I am not making excuses, which I hate, but I did not understand that we were to make a deposit every month, and I can't find anything in your letters specifically to that effect. More than once you told me to make deposits on the first of two coming months. And other times you told me to make a deposit on the first of a coming month. If you want us to always make that deposit, it will always be done without error. I am not arguing that this is not my mistake at all. I just wish you would tell me for sure, and no further mistake will be made. I am now inferring from this letter that we should make a deposit for the first of September, and we did not make one for the first of August. If I was wrong about that, I am just mighty sorry. And so I am depositing a check for one thousand, and if that is not right, it can be easily set right. I am sorry about this, however it may be.

As to what I said to Waldo—I think it must have been—it was simply in discussion of the situation of an author, who is the victim of a racketeer, or as is more likely in this case, a lunatic.- But even then, his lawyers are racketeers. I said that the contract always made the author responsible in full, but that it didn't seem to me that it was fair that he should be when the suit was not at all his fault, when he was completely innocent of any offense, and I said that it might be thought then that since the publisher and author were equally victimized, they might share and share alike. This was merely what I was thinking at the time. I am only saying this so that you will understand it. If a publisher's contract could state that the author was only partially liable when he was sued without basis, or perhaps not at all, it would in my opinion be right. But the trouble is that a great many authors would always say they were sued without basis, as Tom himself did, although he unquestion-

---

[1] Edmund Wilson, "Ernest Hemingway: Bourdon Gauge of Morale," *Atlantic Monthly* 164 (July 1939): 36–46; rpt. in *The Wound and the Bow: Seven Studies in Literature* (Boston: Houghton Mifflin, 1941).
[2] 159 words have been omitted from this letter.

ably did write about a real person in a way which could be argued held her up to ridicule and contempt, in that libel case.[1] But I don't think the present wording of the contract is fair, and that is what I was saying to Waldo.

I know Charlie wrote you further about this anyhow. The trouble is though, that the darn suit isn't cleared up yet, though I should think all that was necessary was for a judge to read the book and the absurd scenario.

I just wanted to write you on those two points, and this further one,- that it isn't a matter of favors at all, these things you want attended to, and that I like to do them, and I hope you won't stop asking me.

Always yours,

. . . . .

*Wire, 4 pp.*
*Havana, Cuba*

1941 SEP 1 AM 7 41
AGREE RANDOM HOUSE RIDICULOUS QUOTES SIX BEST QUOTES EDITION IF FEE SPLIT FOUR HUNDRED ME AND ONE HUNDRED YOU[2] STOP ALSO DENY PERMISSION ANY REPRINTS OF ANY KIND EVER WITHOUT MY WRITTEN PERMISSION STOP SINCE SCRIBNERS STANDING ON CONTRACT AND DEDUCTING ALL THEIR LEGAL EXPENSES FROM MY ROYALTIES RATHER THAN GOING ON STRAIGHT ETHICAL BASIS AS FORMERLY AM PERFECTLY WILLING COMMIT HARIKARI RATHER THAN SUBMIT TO FURTHER GYPPING STOP AS TO LEGAL PROCEDURE SPEISERS LETTER TO ME CONDEMNS SCRIBNERS PROCEDURE IN CHARGING MY ROYALTIES WITHOUT DISCUSSION ON BOTH LEGAL AND ETHICAL GROUNDS BUT EVIDENTLY THOSE NO LONGER FIGURE STOP IF IT IS COWARDICE ABOUT ASSUMING ANY CORESPONSIBILITY IN DEFENDING OUR JOINT PROPERTY AGAINST A SUIT BY A LUNATIC AM GLAD TO HAVE THAT CLEAR NOW STOP PLEASE TELL CHARLIE THAT IT IS NOT GOOD POLICY TO CUT STEAKS OUT OF HIS RACE HORSES TO MAKE A DIME OR WHATEVER HORSE MEAT BRINGS A POUND STOP TELL CHARLIE IF HE NEEDS ANY MONEY WILL BE GLAD TO LOAN IT TO HIM RATHER THAN HAVE HIM STEAL IT FROM ME AND IN THE END WE WOULD BE BETTER FRIENDS AND HE WOULD HAVE MORE MONEY BEST REGARDS=
ERNEST.

[1]In 1936, Wolfe had been successfully sued by a person who could be recognized as a character in the story "No Door."
[2]Apparently a reference to proposed terms for including "The Snows of Kilimanjaro" in *Great Modern Short Stories* (New York: Modern Library, 1942).

*Wire, 1 p.*
*Havana, Cuba*

1941 SEP 1 AM 10 11
SORRY SENT LONG ANGRY NIGHT LETTER PLEASE DISREGARD
IT=
ERNEST.

*TLS with holograph inserts, 5 pp.*[1]
*Sun Valley, Idaho*

November 15, 1941

Dear Max,

First, about business. It is o.k. to let Robert Warren reprint "The Killers."[2]
I agree with you about the importance of having it in the school books, no
matter how hard it is on the poor students. Anyhow it is more interesting
than "A Dog of Flanders" and the stuff we had to read as short stories when
we were kids. I'll never forget how sick I was of "A Piece of String" and "The
Necklace" of de Maupassant. But I suppose they couldn't put his good ones
in the school books.

I read all of Scott's book[3] and I don't know whether I ought to tell you
what I truly think. There are very fine parts in it, but most of it has a deadness that is unbelievable from Scott. I think Bunnie Wilson did a very credible job in explaining, sorting, padding and arranging. But you know Scott
would never have finished it with that gigantic, preposterous outline of how
it was to be. I thought the part about Stahr was all very good. You can recognize Irving Thalberg, his charm and skill, and grasp of business, and the sentence of death over him. But the women were pretty preposterous. Scott had
gotten so far away from any knowledge of people that they are very strange.
He still had the technique and the romance of doing anything, but all the
dust was off the butterfly's wing for a long time even though the wing would
still move up until the butterfly was dead. The best book he ever wrote, I
think, is still "Tender Is The Night" with all of its mix-up of who was Scott
and Zelda and who was Sara and Gerald Murphy. I read it last year again and
it has all the realization of tragedy that Scott ever found. Wonderful atmosphere and magical descriptions and none of the impossible dramatic tricks
that he had outlined for the final book.

Scott died inside himself at around the age of thirty to thirty-five and his

---

[1]342 words have been omitted from this letter.
[2]*Understanding Fiction,* ed. Cleanth Brooks and Robert Penn Warren (New York:
Crofts, 1943).
[3]*The Last Tycoon An Unfinished Novel Together with The Great Gatsby and Selected
Stories* (New York: Scribners, 1941).

creative powers died somewhat later. This last book was written long after his creative power was dead, and he was just beginning to find out what things were about.

I read over the stories and I think Bunnie Wilson made a very poor selection. "The Rich Boy" if you read, it is really profoundly silly. "The Diamond As Big As The Ritz" is simply trash. When you read in "The Rich Boy" about his gradual decay and suddenly see that Scott has given twenty-eight as the age for this oldness setting in, it is hardly credible that he could write that way.

I am happy the book had such a fine review by J. Donald Adams in the Sunday Times with such a good picture of Scott. I think that should please Scotty very much and be very good for her because she never really knew how good Scott was. But J. Donald Adams is not really a very intelligent man, and to someone who knew Scott truly well and is in the same trade, the book has that deadness, the one quality about which nothing can be done in writing, as though it were a slab of bacon on which mold had grown. You can scrape off the mold, but if it has gone deep into the meat, there is nothing that can keep it from tasting like moldy bacon.

When you wrote Martha, you said that Hollywood had not hurt Scott. I guess perhaps it had not because he was long past being hurt before he went there. His heart died in him in France, and soon after he came back, and the rest of him just went on dying progressively after that. Reading the book was like seeing an old baseball pitcher with nothing left in his arm coming out and working with his intelligence for a few innings before he is knocked out of the box.

I know you're impressed by all the stuff about riding in aeroplanes on account of you not doing that and Scott had done it so recently that it impressed him too and he got something of the old magic into it. But in the things between men and women, the old magic was gone and Scott never really understood life well enough to write a novel that did not need the magic to make it come alive.

This sounds gloomy and critical, but I know you would want me to write what I really thought about it. You've had three guys. Scott, Tom Wolfe and me. Two of them are already dead, and no one can say what will happen to the third one. But I think it is best to criticize strongly so when you get the new ones that will come along afterwards, you can talk to them truly.

. . . . .

. . . . .

. . . . .

That's all I know about to write now. Please excuse the long letter, and if I sound deprecatory about Scott, remember I know how good he is and was only criticizing Wilson's selections and the posthumous work.

Best to you always,
Ernest/

*ALS, 2 pp.*[1]

San Antonio Texas
December 11, <u>1941</u>

Dear Max:

. . . . .

About the war Dont take Charley Sweeny[2] seriously when he baits you about the Civil War. When he is angry he always says such wild unjust things. Both he and John Thomason were both completely and fatally wrong about war with Japan when we argued it in Washington as events have proved Now the myth of our matchless navy has been exploded as badly as the myth of Gamelin the great General If we are to win this war rather than simply defend and cover up the incompetents who will lose it Knox should have been relieved as Sec of Navy within 24 hrs of the Pearl Harbour Debacle and those responsable at Oahu for that disaster shot. The above opinions are not for publication nor circulation.

Lastly, and to leave the war, I cannot tell you how badly I feel about Scribners failing to get a stenographer to take down Lewis's speech <u>after I had wired asking them to please do so</u>[3] From your own elementary best interests it would have been a useful thing to publish in pamphlet form. From my own interest it is all that I got out of the book that means anything to me (as a permanent record) and I will never get it to keep <u>nor ever even see it.</u>

Scribners not haveing it taken down as I requested as a favour was the most careless, shiftless and callous action I have ever met in civil life. I would like to present the firm with the Gold Medal so every time anyone should see it they would remember how I feel about it. I do not ever want to see it Ever.

Yes I know someone heard a rumour Macy would have a stenographer, or a report, or a promise of them. What I asked was for <u>Scribners</u> to have a stenographer take it down.

Yours always
Ernest/

*TLS, 3 pp., JFK*[4]

January 9, 1942

Dear Ernest:

I think this business of having to finance income tax payments is perfectly frightful, and I hate to think of you as struggling with it,- the last thing a writer should have to do. But you are dead right on what we report to the

---

[1]49 words have been omitted from this letter.

[2]A soldier of fortune EH met during the Greco-Turkish War in 1922; they became life-long friends.

[3]Sinclair Lewis made the presentation speech when *FWTBT* was awarded the Gold Medal of the Limited Edition Club on 26 November.

[4]215 words have been omitted from this letter

government as I wired you this morning. There is also one cent which I did not put in,- $137,357.01. The cash due you in accordance with the last statement was $804.17 and this we deposited yesterday in the Fifth Avenue branch of the Guaranty Trust Co. It would have been $1304.17 but for the check deposited to Pauline's account on January first.

The sales to January 8th since the last report are:

Regular sale, 5,428 copies which bring you $2,985.40

Book of the Month Club, 12,000 copies which bring you $1,815.00 The two together come to $4,800.40.

That is good news about the picture. I have often wondered where Bergman was. She was wonderful, and I had lost all track of her. Cooper's the right man for sure. There should be a fine picture edition.

As to Van Wyck,[1] it is something like you writing about Scott to me. He is my oldest friend, and so I am only saying to you that when I first heard about this book I was apprehensive. For one thing, Van Wyck never did really understand the contemporary writers. He had immersed himself in the past. You could see in "The Flowering of New England" that that was the golden age for him. He romanticized it,- and that is why, as I think, "New England Indian Summer" was much better. I remember hurting his feelings—for he is very sensitive—when he brushed Scott aside about the time of "The Great Gatsby" and I said, "The trouble with you is you are not interested in talent.- He was not interested in contemporary talent. I really understand it, but it is hard to explain about him. But it also comes about from his illness. That was terrible, as you know. And I think somehow instinctively, not consciously, it has made him protect himself from anything disturbing, violent, new. That is in it, I am sure.- He is amazingly detached, for instance, from the war. But he is not a frightened man. He would stand up all right. He is very shy and gentle, and wants everything to be pleasant and friendly. Age has something to do with it too. I do think it is too bad though. But now he'll stick to his histories.

. . . . .

I had a letter from Copeland[2] expressing great anxieties about the war, unless we waked up quickly. So I wrote him:

"In discussing this subject I have often quoted what you said in English 12 some decades ago, at the time of the San Francisco earthquake,- what a dreadful, tragic disaster it was and all, but quoting you: 'I think I perceive a certain feeling of satisfaction in that our earthquake was the greatest earthquake ever.'

"You knew that we take an even childish pleasure in having whatever we were concerned in the <u>biggest ever.</u> So when we get into a war we

[1]Literary scholar Van Wyck Brooks (1886–1963) was a childhood friend of MP; in 1941, Brooks published *On Literature Today* (New York: Dutton).

[2]Charles Townsend Copeland, professor of rhetoric, with whom Perkins had studied at Harvard.

aim to outdo everybody else in it. I think every American working man will feel that he is on the team, and will delight in making all other nations's production look diminutive along side ours.- And that this same characteristic will work throughout the army and the navy, and everything else. I think I perceive the development of a certain satisfaction in the prospect of the greatest debt ever,- and that is all right too for the time being."

Don't you think there is something in that, that we are that way? Remember Kipling's poem, "An American"?

Well Bumby would certainly make a fine looking soldier, and would be a fine officer. And he is your son. But I do think you are right,- that he would go ahead faster and more easily if he studied longer. Just the same—for all the trouble it gave you when you had to cram up on mathematics and such things,- it was probably much better that you did not go to college yourself.

. . . . .

Of course I realize that sooner or later you would be almost bound to cover some angle of this war.- But anyhow it is grand that you will be doing some writing for some months. I suppose that means stories, but I won't bother you about it. A collection should do very well indeed when you are ready.

> Yours,
> Max

CC, 3 pp.[1]

March 12, 1942

Dear Ernest:

. . . . .

And then there is another matter. A man named Wartels of Crown Publishers came in to see me. He said he had seen you in Cuba, and that you had been favorable to writing an introduction to an anthology of war stories.[2] I did not know who Crown Publishers were then, but I have inquired: they haven't a very high standing, but are perfectly reputable, and publish large collections and sell them at a low price relatively and merchandise them. Some writers would think their standing was not high enough perhaps for them to write introductions to their books. But to my mind this is absurd, for a book is a book whoever publishes it, and if they do a good anthology of war stories they will have done something. In fact I got so interested in the idea that I made several suggestions. For one thing, I told him about that magnificent episode from "War and Peace" where the boy Petya joins Denisov's band of partisans and then goes into the French camp with Dolokov, and then, the next morning in the attack gets himself killed.- But

[1] 55 words have been omitted from this letter.
[2] Published as *Men At War* (New York: Crown, 1942).

of course Tolstoi wrote wonderful war stories which really were stories. Still this piece can be taken-out intact.

Then Wartel told me they wanted two pieces out of your novels,- one El Sordo's fight, and the other the Caporetto retreat in "A Farewell". I didn't know how you would feel about having pieces taken out of the novels, or indeed about the whole matter. I wish you would let me know. If you want us to avoid it we will, but I myself would not be against it at all, if proper compensation were given. Anything that spreads a writer's public is to his advantage.

Always yours,

*TLS with holograph postscript, Finca Vigia stationery, 3 pp.*[1]
*Havana, Cuba*

May 30, 1942

Dear Max:

. . . . .

I have never been any good at writing those kind of advertisements that you sent in the letter, but I suppose if you have to do it, you have to do it, although by the time the back jacket of my book comes out the whole thing may be compulsory and that will solve the problem.[2] I have decided, or rather I decided several months before it started, or may be several years say, not to write any propaganda in this war at all. I am willing to go to it and will send my kids to it and will give what money I have to it but I want to write just what I believe all the way along through it and after it. It was the writers in the last war who wrote propaganda that finished themselves off that way. There is plenty of stuff that you believe absolutely that you can write which is useful enough without having to write propaganda. Do you remember poor old Owen Wister? Such a good man, and Mr. Britling sees It Through" and other things the last time? We have had Steinbeck's book so far and I would rather cut three fingers off my throwing hand than to have written it.[3] If we are fighting for what we believe in we might as well always keep on believing in what we have believed, and for me this is to write nothing that I do not think is the absolute truth. So stall along about me writing that stuff.

. . . . .

Now, about the war anthology man. I was very disappointed in his contents too. I have read over 370 galleys and have thrown out much of the worst stuff. I have also gotten him to include Frank Tinker's account of the Italian debacle at Guadalajara. Have got him to put in some good flying stuff. Have gotten him to include all the wonderful part about Waterloo from,

---

[1]418 words have been omitted from this letter.
[2]During the war patriotic statements by authors were printed on the dust jackets of their books.
[3]*Bombs Away: The Story of a Bomber Team* (New York: Viking, 1942).

"The Chartreuse de Parma" and got him to put in the account of the battle of Shiloh from that Lloyd Lewis book, "Sherman, Fighting Prophet", and I am insisting on him publishing an account of the first battle of Ypres by Frank Richards in, "Old Soldiers never Die", and an account of the fight on the Somme in 1916 by the same man. Have also had him throw out Ralph Bates' phoney story about the women machine gunners at Brunete as well as, "The Moment of Victory" by O'Henry, "The War Years" by James Hilton, "The Square EGg", by Saki, Arthur Guy Empey, the early life of your pal Winston by Richard Harding Davis (his, "The River War", would have been damned good to include), a terrible selection from, "Death of a Hero", by Richard Aldington, and a very phony, disorganized bit called, "West Canada Creek", from "Drums Along the Mohawk".

I hope the above hasn't confused you completely. Take your time and go over it and see if they were some of the weak things that you said he had included in his table of contents. If you have the table of contents, will you please check them.

Will you also, Max, please write me by return airmail what were the things you suggested to him which he did not include. Also, do you know what Charlie Sweeney suggested to him and he did not include? I think John Thomlinson must have suggested other things than just those pieces of his from, "Lone Star Preacher". They are very good, but, my God, that is not the story of our civil war. Please let me know about this as soon as possible as I do not want to have anything to do with the book unless it is as good a book as can be made. I still think it is a big mistake for us not to have taken the whole thing over and you have me edit it and write the introduction. Or had me edit and have John write the introduction. Wartels in his last letter said that he wanted to publish it as being edited with an introduction by Ernest Hemingway. I wrote him that I would not consider that as I had not edited it. But if I write an introduction to it I want it to be as good a book as can be gotten out and it is very much to the interests of everyone engaged in the present war that it be a really good book which can do some good. So, even though it is a bother for you, will you answer by return mail on the questions that I have asked you.

About my book of stories, I still have two long stories to complete. I am into both of them but was interrupted by this damned war anthology. I thought that it might do some active good if it was gotten out really well and so have been concentrating on it and my other work has suffered. Perhaps on account of that you should figure to publish in the spring rather than in the fall. Both stories are very long and very good. I had to stop on one while I waited to get some stuff that I needed for it to be really accurate. Then I got going on the other and I held it up when this war anthology came along. When they are finished I have enough stories for the book and the title will be either that of the best story or I will get as good a title as I can, as usual.[1] I

---

[1] EH did not publish another volume of stories.

don't want you to count on anything and not deliver exactly when I should. Usually you have needed to have the stuff by July in order to publish in the fall. Personally, I do not care anything about publishing this fall as will need whatever money the book brings in to keep my family and this house going next year wherever I am. I would rather turn the book over to you complete in the fall so you could bring it out whenever you wanted next year so that there would be enough money from it to handle the overhead wherever I am. I think there is going to be some sort of arrangement that if you are in the army your income tax can be deferred. Anyhow I need the book as a source of income for next year to handle necessary expenses and contingencies. Whenever the picture is released there will be some money, coming in from that edition too. Could you tell me what the sale has been since you gave me the $4,000 in February to pay on the income tax? Approximately what amount of cash is due to me now?

I am very sorry, Max, if you are disappointed in not having the manuscript by the end of June or early July as I had planned. It is that damned war anthology which has held me up. I take it you also know the difficulty of working in these times. I can really do it though but it involves putting yourself into a sort of temporary vacuum, and you do not feel very happy in that place. I have to do it though in order to be free to do what I want and I will do it and finish it.

Please write me right away about the war anthology and read this letter over carefully so you know what the points are I asked you about. If you see Charlie (Martha who hasgone up to see her mother, talked to him on the phone and he may be down here next week), ask him what the things were that he suggested so I can force Wartels to take them. Would it be too much to ask you to write John Thomlinson to ask him what he suggested to Wartels too. I would write him but I do not know him as well as you do. Tell him my excuse in bothering him is to try to make this book into a good weapon.

. . . . .
. . . . .

Best always,
Ernest
Ernest Hemingway

. . . . .

*CC, 3 pp.*[1]

June 8, 1942

Dear Ernest:

I hope my cable from Baltimore made some sense.- I know it won't help you much anyway. I couldn't answer your letter properly from there, but I

---

[1] 180 words have been omitted from this letter.

wanted you to understand that publication of your stories early in the year will be presumably as good as to do it now, and that my only disappointment is because I would like to see them out for the fun of it, and to read them, and all. Otherwise there isn't any harm whatever in the delay, and I rather inferred that they would have to be delayed. I think it is a miracle that anyone can do any sort of work now outside the Army and Navy, except the kind I do where there is a compulsion upon you. I understand exactly your position with regard to the advertisement, and that was why I just posted it to you without any particular comment. And it is easy to settle on that.

As to the anthology, I only saw the contents briefly, and I made hardly any comments then. I know that the Empey, Hilton and O. Henry should come out. The others you name I have not read. I am not sure whether he had in one very good story by Stephen Crane which tells of a sergeant taking out a squad on an autumn day down a country road, and how one of the men persuades the sergeant to let him climb a fence to get some fine apples, and then they go on and take up an outpost position in an abandoned farmhouse, and then comes the fighting, and it is a hell of a fight. I don't remember the name of that story so I am not sure he has got it. He should have it.

The other things I spoke about particularly were the obvious Incident at Owl Creek. And Winston Churchill's cavalry charge at Omdurman (of course there was no reason in the world for his putting in that biographical sketch by Dick Davis).

The rear guard action in the early part of "War and Peace" where Andrei joins Bagration and acts as an aide, is one of the finest "battle pieces" in the world, partly because it gives you a complete little battle that anyone can comprehend, and then partly because of the way that battery commander fought his guns, and then the way it all turned out to be so different from what Andrei thought it was going to be, his first battle.

Then there is the episode of the Russian partisan band's pursuit of the French in the rain, and their attack the next day: the boy Petya brings a message to the band from a German general and then when he finds there is going to be an attack on the French he persuades the leaders to let him stay and be in it, and then of course gets himself killed through recklessness.

Those two Tolstoi pieces have almost perfect unity, and Borodino, grand as it is, hasn't the same completeness, and is rather confusing, I should think—taken all by itself.

I did also suggest a story called "The Thistle" by Tolstoi, but I don't really think it should be in because it is perhaps about war on too small a scale.-No use talking about that.

I suggested "The Burial of the Guns" mostly because it does show what must be true,- the attachment men get to their weapons, and I should think especially to canon, and how they individually take on a personality of their own. And as compared to anything else of Page's it is told in a very straight-away manner. It does have some of the defects of the time, but for the most part, what you feel does come from a direct recording of the facts.- But don't you put it in if you do not like it. It is mostly that I know of no other story that does do that thing.

I'll write to both Charlie Sweeney and John Thomason.

I am enclosing a statement about the money situation that I think is perfectly clear.

As a matter of fact, I think perhaps we shall do better if we publish the stories early in the year before the market is crowded, possibly even in January.

Always yours,

. . . . .

*TLS, Finca Vigia stationery, 2 pp.*
*Havana, Cuba*

May 18

Dear Max:

Have just sent off a wire about the Grosset and Dunlop reprint business and the reprint of the Snows of Kilimanjaro. I thought latter had been sent off several days ago but when got in today found it hadn't.

My attitude toward that sixty-forty split as a minimum on Frances Macomber, Kilimanjaro and others is like this:

They were first published in 5thCol and First 49 stories which was pushed so vigorously that it was practically un-advertised and and a short time after it was out was not even being sold in the book-store. I.E. I couldn't buy a copy etc. You remember the whole histoire. This was <u>not</u> because a formidable sale had exhauseted the supply.

Later on I realized why this was: you had no necessity to sell any copies of the book at all to make a very large profit on the sale of re-print rights since at least two of the new long short stories would be in demand for collections and anthologies as long as they get out such collections of short stories.

You know how much you have made from your fifty percent of the reprint rights. I would say that it was considerable more than the royalties I received from the collection. Anyway I think it calls for a re-negotiation on the rights to certain stories; which rights are my only capital.

It is not as though I was a writer who you had to support and publish at a loss for years knowing you would finally get a fine selling book.

So far you lost money, on the advance anyway, of two books. Green Hills of Africa and Winner Take Nothing. I will bet you anything you want to bet they will both pay out. All the others made money. I owe you either ten or twelve thousand dollars, which, in the event of my death is secured by all comeing re-prints of last book already contracted for and with absolute security you get interest on the money as you should.

But it gripes me to the innermost part of where I actually feel and know what is right or wrong for you to publish a book as 5thCol and 1st 49 stories

322

was published and then take half of what some of those stories bring in for the rest of my life and whether I am alive or not.

ALSO I constantly get letters sent to me so late that it is necessary to answer by wire. All these wires are in regard to something on which we split 50-50 but the letter usually comes in a 3 cent stamp or with a six cent stamp and returned for insufficient postage which god to blessed jesus is what air-mail here costs per <u>half ounce</u>   not ounce   10 cents.

Then the arugement comes up that Scribners always gets 50 percent and therefore cant change and I say ok get it from everybody but not from me because there are special circumstances and you can say to the others as they come up "go on and write short stories for 20 years and bring us in so much and we will re-negociate with you."

Then there is the fact that other writers in other times didn't have all the money they made confiscated by taxes so that they could not build up an adequate reserve to last through the necessary time when you have to be fallow between books. It did not make so much difference what their re-print rights were because they made a capital on a book that sold 200,000 or 300,000 or as much as The Bell that they could live on and bring up their children on. But I had to pay $160,000 to the Government for writing For Whom The Bell Tolls. Scribners has capital, has a steady back-log of religious and educational books and has not one novel but many novels successful.

Due to the war and fact that spend 100 per cent time working at same I haven't written a line since that Introduction to Men At War a year ago August. As you could say it is not your fault; nor is it mine. It is the war. But if you make money in the war and I make not a nickel and yet, if I am alive after the war, you stand to make plenty of money from what I will write—and I will have something to write—then I think, with the arguments advanced before this there is a sound basis for me haveing a larger share in the re-print returns from my stories.[1]

As it is I have been living on the cash in savings account for past year and it is about gone.

Did you get my previous letter asking you to deposit 2,000. in my account in Guaranty Trust Co. of N.Y. Fifth Avenue Branch? I asked you to carry it as a loan and charge me interest and I would repay out of the money Cape said he was sending me in early May and which so far has not shown up. Asked you to wire when deposit made. That was some five days ago and haven't heard yet. Am leaving in the morning and am worried. If you didn't make the deposit will you please do so when you get this letter? If it hasn't been made am overdrawn now.

[1]In a postscript to his 28 May 1943 letter to EH, MP responded to these charges: "Ernest, there is one thing of which I only speak because we ought not by silence to seem to agree that we had followed a policy which really would make us out to be skunks as well as fools. Perhaps we are sometimes fools, but we are not skunks. We would be both if we took a book of yours, or of any other writer's, and said, 'We'll do nothing for this because we'll make plenty of money out of the permissions and reprints from it.'"

pauline's blood money keeps me broke between books. But that was what she really wanted it for so that it would be impossible for me to write. Once she had me ruined she could simply ask her family for any amount of money or income she needed. She is now behaveing abominably about the children; really wickedly. I think perhaps she is off her rocker as women often are at such times. But women who are that way continue to do their damage for years.

As it is we are both broke, Martha and I, and Martha will have to go to war again as a correspondent haveing used up the last of the money she made last summer on the Carribean, Surinam bout. It is a damned fine thing she likes it because Pauline has the cards stacked so she has to do it whether she likes it or not.

I am so sorry about your sister's boy. He sounds like such a good kid. It is fine John has such a good job. When you write him I wish you would tell him that young Saxon is with me now and is doing very well and that we will be on the water for the next two months.

Is Charley's book out yet?[1] Give him my very best and tell him if he does not hear from me it is because will be away for a while. Going on a scientific expedition.

I had a letter from Evan Shipman and will break this off now to write him.

Best to you always, Max
Ernest
Ernest Hemingway.

ALS, 6 pp.[2]

June 10 1943
At Sea

Dear Max:

. . . I wish you were on this trip Max so we could talk about things and you could explain them instead of me haveing to write a letter trying to put my affairs in order before going off for 2–3 months or more and then you getting angry and bitter at the letter.[3] I'm sorry the letter made you angry. I think you are the most honest, fair and squarest person I know and you know that. I also think the reprint split on certain of my stories (as I outlined) is an unfair one.

(Sorry it is so rough that writing is difficult but tomorrow morning is only

---

[1] Charles Sweeny, *Moment of Truth: A Realistic Examination of Our War Situation* (New York: Scribners, 1943).

[2] 170 words have been omitted from this letter.

[3] EH was using the *Pilar* as a Q-boat; from June 1942 to September 1943, he unsuccessfully searched for German submarines. These activities provided material for the final section of *Islands in the Stream* (1970).

chance to get this off and have a 12 hr day to put in and will be too tired to write tonight.

I know from hearing it from Charly that Publishers make no money. It is only authors who make money Oh the hell with it.

I can get bitter at enough things including getting 75% back on taxes in a year I made nothing instead of the year before when I had to pay 104,000 income tax without haveing to go back to reprint rights The hell with being bitter about anything. But you know I never called you or Scribners skunks so why say I did? If I spoke or wrote rudely or undiplomatically about the equity of reprint rights in new stories in 5th Col and 1st 49 after sale it enjoyed etc I'm sorry. If you want a more elaborate apology write it out and I'll sign it. Or I'll give you a power of attorney and you can sign it for me. Or I'll enclose a blank sheet for paper signed and you type in the apology.

As for items that require decisions—

Pocket Books—I am with you 100% and against Speiser on this "Samples" business.

He mislead me on the nature of the book which he said was all short stories In any event I believe Modern Library should be protected and agree with you fully on this.

Reading through your two letters see this is only item reqiuring a decision except for a paper Paramount sent me through Speiser asking permission from me and from Scribners for them to use my signature etc.

I am writing Speiser under no circumstance to give them this right which would seem to give them a chance to make me seem to endorse a picture I have not seen and which I would certainly not endorse unseen. I mistrust Speiser's handling of my affairs more each day. I hope to Christ this will not offend either you or Charley due to the fact he acted as your lawyer in that Montyo business. I have to have some one I can trust and can write frankly to and that person has always been you Max only now I cant write frankly about anything without fear of offending you.

. . . . .

Max please dont get sore at me. I need your sound advice, your judgement and your help—If Charley Scribner ever wants to pick a fight with me because I am insuffecently respectful or more bother than I am worth, or simply for any good reason at all that is okay—but dont you pick any fights because you are my most trusted friend as well as my God damned publisher and dont get yourself confused in your mind with too many institutions or I wont be able to speak ill of Harvard, Connecticut, the Confederate Army, Scribners, God or God knows what without being accused of imputive skunkhood and will only be able to curse women and still be your pal.

Which I still hope I am—

                          Ernest       Ernest Hemingway.

. . . . .

*CC, 4 pp.*[1]

June 21, 1943

Dear Ernest:

. . . . .

I could not, and would not have any right to get sore at you. And you have a right any time to cuss at Harvard, or the Army of Northern Virginia, or me, to any extent you want.- It is only that I wanted to have the record right. I don't mind your cussing out Scribners either. I didn't mind it when you did it. I just wanted you to know. As for women, you can even cuss them out to me without making me mad. You wouldn't even have to <u>smile,</u> when you did it.

I keep hearing that the picture is very wonderful, not only good for a movie, but really good. And I know that everything is set for the Grosset & Dunlap edition. The danger now is about paper, and that is getting serious. But I understand that they are perfectly safe for an edition of 100,000 copies,- and of course by next year they get a new lease on their allowance.

I do so well remember that night on the fishing snack, and the way the lights and the shadows looked in that cabin.- And I remember when we got back and you hailed John, and we could tell by his voice that he had been hitting the bottle, and you asked him about it, and he said, "I used my own judgment." And we found that he had, too. Once you wrote me about that little boy, I suppose he is now in the Army or the Navy, or something. All that now seems long ago.

I am sending you a copy of a book that is fascinating to read,- "The Shock of Recognition" which Bunny Wilson edited. He is the damnedest fellow. Once Scott told me he was a god-devoured man. But he talked to me not long ago as if he were a man-devouring god. He is getting the Jehovah complex. He always had it, but it is growing on him. But he truly is what we used to call "a man of letters".- And he says he made them make the book the way it is, physically I mean, and it is a beautiful little book.

. . . . .

Always yours,
MAXWELL E. PERKINS

*TL, Finca Vigía stationery, 2 pp.*[2]

*16 November 1943*                                              *Havana, Cuba*

Dear Max:

Thank you very much for your letters. Have tried to read the Christine Weston book[3] evenings on the water but it has a peculiarly un-readable qual-

---

[1]130 words have been omitted from this letter.
[2]160 words have been omitted from this letter.
[3]*Indigo* (New York: Scribners, 1943).

ity Her others were the same for me. She is so un-readable that I have little doubt people will finally believe her to be a classic. She sounds much more lively in real life.

Will you call up Dave Randall in the office and tell him I wrote that quotation the Library of Congress was asking about[1] all same I wrote the other fine medaeval one in the front of Martha's Stricken Field. I probably would have written pretty well in those times but unfortunately that's been written and these are these so try to write in these. Is far from easy.

. . . . .

. . . . .

. . . A woman ruined Scott. It wasn't just Scott ruining himself. But why couldn't he have told her to go to hell? Because she was sick. It's being sick that makes them act so bloody awful usually and it's because they're sick you can't treat them as you should. The first great gift for a man is to be healthy and the second, maybe greater, is to fall with healthy women. You can always trade one halthy woman in on another. But start with a sick woman and see where you get. Sick in the head or sick anywhere. But sick anhwhere and in a little while they are sick in the head. If they locked up all the women who were crazy— but why speculate I've known god-damned good ones; but take as good a woman as Pauline—as hell of a wonderful woman—and once she turns mean. Although, of course, it is your own actions that turn her mean. Mine I mean. Not yours. Anyway let's leave the subject. If you leave a woman, though, you probably ought to shoot her. It would save enough trouble in the end even if they hanged you. But you can't do it on account of the children and so there isn't any solution actually to anything except to get so nobody can hurt you and by the time you get to that you've usually been dead for some time.

. . . . .

How in hell will anybody who has been able to buy a book for $145 be expected to go back to paying $2.75 on it?[2] Why don't we ourselves have a proper cheaper edition or a gift edition r something to give more value. Bceuase when so ething has been 1.45 who the hell will pay 2.75 unless it is, say, good gin. Our only hope of ever selling another copy is that it is good gin. And next move is I suppose you won't even print any copies and it will be as hard to buy as Death In The Afternoon which I can't get a copy of anywhere in the world even when order it from the publishers. Don't tell me there's never going to be any more For Whom The Bells sold anywhere ever just because Marcia Davenport or Godilocks and the Seven Dwarfs or any other of your list leaders need so much paper. I mean paper to print on.

Best to you always,

---

[1]The epigraph for *WTN;* see EH's wire of 11 June 1933.
[2]The 1944 Grosset & Dunlap reprint of *FWTBT* was priced at $1.49.

*CC, 4 pp.*[1]

Feb. 17, 1944

Dear Ernest:

. . . . .

I was dead sure I would see you last Monday. All I found was your telegram about the Armed Forces edition. I had a message all ready from a letter from Martha. But it was chiefly to tell you to bring all the Kleenex you could, along with your pair of shoes.- By the way, "Liana" must by now have sold 14,000 copies, and although I wouldn't say it to her, and must not be quoted to that effect, I feel certain myself that it will at any rate reach 20,000. I hope you are getting the clippings.

. . . . .

Ernest, I have wonderful letters from Scott. Many long ones, about his own work and about other writers. Brilliant letters. I had no idea of it.In retrospect it had seemed as if all our correspondence was about money, and almost all by cable. I remember most of the things that I read, but I would have thought that I had got them in conversation. The reason I got the letters out was that Bunny is still fussing with that miscellaneous book in which I think he had meant to include letters from you. I never liked the idea of that book. It had things in it that I know Scott would not like himself, and that I did not think were right, and then it was <u>so</u> miscellaneous. Made up of so many scraps.- Bunny knew I disapproved of it. We declined it in fact, and he was mad at me on that account. But if it were to be done, I wanted it to be as good as it could be, and so had all Scott's correspondence got together, looked at it a little and saw its possiblities. Bunny wanted to take it away with him. I told him he could he could read it all here at any time during office hours. He said it was too noisy, and I said he could have a private room where it was completely silent.- But he thought I was most unreasonable,- though I don't see how anybody could think we could let a part of our records, the property of the House, be taken away from here. He wanted me to go through it, and I am trying to do it gradually, at odd moments. But a selection from it of four or five letters would be extremely difficult.

I don't think I told you that my other sister lost a boy in the war, shot down over Wake Island. I guess I showed more sense than anyone in the family after all, in choosing the sex of my children. It always seems as if the boy that was lost was the best one of the lot, too.

. . . . .

Always yours,
MAXWELL PERKINS

---

[1]183 words have been omitted from this letter.

*TLS, Finca Vigia stationery, 2 pp.*[1]
*Havana, Cuba*

February 25 1944

Dear Max:

Was glad to get the letter with the clipping about the noble Scribners author who returned the advance. Hope it wasn't meant as a hint. You'll get everything back from me in this same month I hope whenever the Dunlop payment comes in. Or if there isn't enough to pay everything and taxes and have some to live on too will stagger the payments. But remember they are not advances really; but loans against money to come in from reprints contracted for and while they pay a low rate of interest they are as good security as Govt. Bonds. They aren't on some future book I am to write but on reprints of a book already written. At least that is way I look at it. As far as I know I owe no one in the world a cent except Scribners and at the worst you could collect perfectly well out of my estate if I died.

I wish you would keep all the Scott letters for a definitive book instead of letting Bunny Wilson pee them away in his usual malicious driblets. He never asked me for any letters from Scott and I have very many; unfortunately all packed in Key West but available anytime I have something to do besides this war. Have letters from Gatsby period all through the Paris time and all the rest. All of them about writing and showing Scotts great strength and most of his weaknesses. I should suggest you save all of your letters; don't give permission for any of them to be used; until we could get out a good book n Scott and his letters. I know him, through some periods, better than anyone and would be glad to write a long, true, just, detailed (all of those I mean in the measure that anyone can do any such thing) account of the years I knew him. It might be better to wait and write it for my own memoirs but my memoir expectancy has been so slight these last years that might be good to write a good piece about Scott before I get too punchy to remember.[2] Would suggest that John Peale Bishop who knew, loved, and understood Scott much better than Wilson ever did edit the letters. John is unfailably kind, impersonal and disinterested while Wilson is usually twisting the facts to cover some expressed error of critical judgement he has made in the past or some prejudice or lack of knowlege or scholarship. He is also extremely dishonest; both about money and about his friends and other writers. I know no one who works so hard at being honest and less true inner honesty within himself. His criticism is like reading second rate gospels written by some one who is out on parole. He reads most interestingly on all the things one does not know about. On the things one knows about truly he is stupid, inaccurate, uninformative and pretentious. But because he is so pretentious his inaccuracies are accepted by all those with less knowlege of what

[1]134 words have been omitted from this letter.
[2]EH's recollections of Fitzgerald were posthumously published in *MF.*

he is writing about than he has. He is the great false-honest, false-craftsman, falsegreat-critic of our exceedingly sorry times which, if every one was honest in himself and what he writes, have no need to be sorry in any way. You can trace the moral decay of his criticism on a parrallel line with the decline in DosPassos's writing through their increasing dishonesty about money and other things, mostly their being dominated by women. But let us not attack that theme with limited time available. Anyway above is my suggestion with regard to Scott's letters. When I am through with this war will have to get in training and shape again to write and would be glad to help on the Scott book to warm up and get going.

I miss writing very much Max. You see, unlike the people who belaboured it as a dog's life <u>ce metier de chien</u> Conrad and old Ford were always suffering about I loved to write very much and was never happier than doing it. Charlie's ridiculing of my daily word count was because he did not understand me or writing especially well nor could know how happy one felt to have put down properly 422 words as you wanted them to be. And days of 1200 or 2700 were something that made you happier than you could believe. Since I found that 400 to 600 well done was a pace I could hold much better was always happy with that number. But if I only had 320 I felt good.

. . . . .
. . . . .
. . . . .
. . . . .

> Best Always to Charlie and your local mob,
> Ernest
> E. Hemingway

*CC, 4 pp.*[1]

March 10, 1944

Dear Ernest:

. . . . .
. . . . .
. . . . .

I fully agree with you about John Peale Bishop. He wrote about the best piece that ever was done on Tom Wolfe.- We are in hopes of soon publishing a collection of his essays and papers. Did you know that he had had a bad heart attack?- But now they think all may be right enough if he takes care. I always thought the trouble with him was a lack of physical vigor which prevented him from working long and hard.- On account of this I never dared to urge him much. He could have done so much more with the talents he has.

I know that Bunny is unscrupulous in financial matters, but I do not think

---

[1]268 words have been omitted from this letter.

330

that <u>he</u> knows it. Also he has an almost incredible and curious arrogance.- He has said things to me that could be only received with enraged counter abuse, or dead silence. I just barely managed the silence, and fortunately the talk was over the telephone. And then when I next saw him, I joked him somewhat about a Jehovah complex,- which puzzled him, I think. He is a queer case. I ought not to say all this, I suppose, and would not except to you, for he is still theoretically more or less our author. That is, we have a contract made long ago for a book that should have been published some years ago, but is not yet written.

. . . . .

Yours always,
MAXWELL PERKINS

*TLS, Finca Vigia stationery, 2 pp., JFK*[1]
*Havana, Cuba*

March 12 1944

Dear Max:

Thank you for the cable and for sending me the figures on what is due me, what I owe and Darrow's estimate.

I didn't like either the tone nor the content of Darrow's memorandum. Am I to take it that the paper (which has only been reduced 10% over the amount you were allowed or used in the 12 months preceeding Pearl Harbour an active year in publishing in which quite a lot of paper went into produceing my books) is to be so budgeted that my books are not to be reprinted? And that I am to be held down to a possible $4000 in earnings?

I don't care much for that type of budgeting.

Tell Mr. Darrow for me, please, that Cape, who is only allowed <u>40%</u> of the paper he used in the twelve months preceeding September 39 (a very bad year in publishing for him) is just printing another 7,000 copies of For Whom The Bell Tolls, 3,000 of a Farewell To Arms and 5,000 of the First Forty Nine Stories. Cape is a bastard in some ways but he does know goodwill is an asset Am sure the immediate advantages of dedicating paper to Archbishop Spellman and Monsignor Sheen[2] are obvious. And I have no new book that needs it.

If I had a new book do you suppose it would be able to compete with their needs for paper? I still hope and trust so although have seen some very odd things in my time and few of them any odder than that an old and honorable firm with the tradition that Scribners has should publish the unctuous lies the Archbishop wrote about Spain in Colliers.[3] I haven't seen the book so maybe

---

[1]125 words have been omitted from this letter.

[2]Francis Spellman, *Action This Day* (New York: Scribners, 1943), and Fulton J. Sheen, *Philosophies of War* (New York: Scribners, 1943).

[3]*Action This Day* first appeared as a five-part series in *Collier's* (16 October–20 November 1943); his letters from Spain were in the first installment.

you didn't publish them. And if Scribners did publish them have no doubt the Archbishop can square it with God for all concerned.

I am probably wrong about Darrow's memorandum, although I did not like the sound of it, and apologise if I am. But Max, if you published the Archbishop of Spain, as it appeared in Colliers, then it just makes me sick in my heart.

Just for my own education would you tell me when the church moved in on you guys and through whom? They must be very happy about it.

Now the obvious thing is to tell me not to be insulting, to get out, that I am a damned fool etc. But it doesn't work that way. At least I won't get out willingly. Because that is what they want.

I wish I could have gotten to New York to talk to you. We never quarrel when we can talk and I don't want to make bitterness and misunderstanding through letters. But I tell you that you are being used worse than the Communists used Ralph Ingersoll and PM when they packed his organization at the start.

. . . Probably see you in N.Y. some time in April. Had hope so to get up there and see you and Dawn[1] and my friend George Brown[2] and eat some cherrystones, and walk along the street and look in the windows and go to the Museum of Natural History and see the Breughel in the Metand the other good pictures and see what they have new at the Museum of Modern Art. Now when I get to N.Y. will probably have to be rushing around with shots and visas and appointments and not see a damned thing. Haven't done a damned I wanted to do now for well over two years, except shoot live pigeons occasionally, but then I guess no one else has either except Martha who does exactly what she wants to do as willfully as any spoiled child. And always for the noblest motives.

My god what a selfpitying last paragraph that one was. Actually I have been terrifically happy working and only thing wrong that did not have my wife. But once any goddamned woman gets into uniform with the assimilative rank of captain you can figure (when they are bossy anyway) they will never relinquish the rank (even when assimilative) willingly. Suppose will have to take a rank job eventually just to rank the bejeeses out of her so can say roll over captain a period of strenuous calistenics is about to begin. or something of that sort.

Too tired to write any more Max. Probably shouldn't have written this. But Whitney has a wonderful faculty to irritate me profoundly and probably he was only doing me a favour with my tax prospects. That just occurred to me at this moment.

As for the other citizens there is a lot goes on you don't know about and some of it I might be able to clear up some time when we talk. I have the greatest respect for the religion. It is when it mixes up in politics and in things outside of its province that it lays its-self open to examination and

[1]Novelist Dawn Powell (1897–1965).
[2]Brown was a boxing trainer.

criticism. The Spellman book, under guise of extreme simplicity and ingenu-ousness was one of the craftiest pieces of work I ever read. You are not sec-retary to the former papal secretary of state and present pope and write such simple, sweet and ingenuous letters to your dear old father. If you want to poison a coyote you put the strychnyne in a lump of meat. If you want to poison a child I suppose you put it in candy. In this book the poison was in a Baby Ruth Bar or a Milky Way: intended for all and sundry.

. . . . .

Yours always,
Ernest.
E. Hemingway

*ALS, 3 pp.*[1]
*Paris, France*

Oct 15 <u>1944</u>

Dear Max:

. . . . .

Weve had quite a hell of a time since I wrote you last. I was with the 4th Infantry division from the break through above St. Lo until they were tem-porarily in support on Aug 18 and I got mixed up with a Maquis outfit after some very interesting times, straight out of Mosby, we entered Paris with very first troops. Liberated the Travellers Club and the Ritz the first after-noon. Finest time ever had in my life. Then rejoined Division (Gen had loaned me a jeep for the Paris Campaign and we'd picked up the damndest lot of transport (mostly German) you've ever seen. I then made the rat race campaign in which we went way north, then pivoted East and ended up with the assault on the West Wall and then holding what we'd taken.

Have stuff for wonderful book Have been with every action of the Div. since just before the break through and if have good luck a little longer want to lay off and get to work on the book. Want to write novel—not war book. It should have the sea and the air and the ground in it. Had the sea ready to write when came over. Then had that time with R.A.F. Now have had the rest of this. Have written two long poems so there would be something around to cover what has happened up until now if had any bad luck.[2]

I got sort of cured of Marty flying Everything sort of took on its proper proportion. Then after we were on the ground I never thought of her at all. Funny how it should take one war to start a woman in your damn heart and another to finish her. Bad luck. But you find good people in a war. Never fails. Awful lot of things happen to them though.

Would like to talk to you Max but no good writing letters.

[1]30 words have been omitted from this letter.
[2]"To Mary in London" and "Second Poem to Mary."

Best to Charley and all the guys. If you get me back youve got a very valuable property because we hit very fine pay dirt on this last prospecting trip.[1]

Ernest

E. Hemingway, War Correspondent

c/o PRO COMZONE <u>Paris</u>

APO 887 c/o Postmaster

N Y.

*CC, 4 pp.*[2]

April 19, 1945

Dear Ernest:

I knew it would be mighty hard for you to get adjusted after all that. I
knew you knew it too, in your head, but I thought you probably would be
worried by feeling completely fit and yet not able to get going. I am dead
sure it will be all right, but I know it will be tough too.- But I think you
ought to take it easily. Get out into that old Gulf Stream where things always
seem to be all right,- not necessarily for you yourself, but in the big way.
Probably they are really all right that way too. When you say, "It is all done
with people," you touch on what is the great tragedy of life, I think.- That
nothing is ever in a condition of purity. I think that is the great surprise to a
boy who goes into anything,- that it is never the way he thought it would be.
It is all bitched up with other things that do not belong in it. That has always
been true in this business. It is true in everything, as you say about war. A
campaign is not conducted on pure military principles, but is all messed up
with political, financial, and otherwise foreign elements. Everything is that
way. Though in art, everything can be excluded. But not easily.- This is too
much to write about in a letter, but it really is the most shocking discovery a
boy makes when he gets into anything. Remember Prince Andrei looking up
at the stars after the artillery officer got the rough deal, and thinking, everything was so different from what he had thought it was going to be?

. . . . .

. . . . .

Always yours,

Maxwell Perkins

[1] In his 20 November 1944 letter to EH, MP responded: "I realize what you must have
accumulated,—or rather added to all the great store you have gathered up the last few
years.—But both Aeschylus and Goethe wrote masterpieces when they were eighty. It is
likely to take you that long to get everything said."

[2] 229 words have been omitted from this letter.

*TLS, 2 pp.*[1]
*Havana, Cuba*

July 23 1945

Dear Max:

. . . . .

. . . . .

. . . . .

. . . . .

He is Buck Lanham my pal and partner and former Col of 22nd Inf.Reg. now a B.G. and stuck all summer in Germany and very lonesome. He is asst. Divisional commander now in the 26th. We were sort of partners all through the rat race, the Schnee Eifel, Hurtgen and the defence of Luxembourg and if anything ever happens to me you could get hold of him to set straight any misconceptions about just what we were all doing in this last war that people like Bunny etc. would like to set going.

Buck thinks I am a much better guy than I am but his opinion, loaded in ones favour, might go in the balance against Max Eastman and Bunny W. and those of the guys who never fought and so denied us those simple stupid virtues that we have. (This subject bores me. But last year was a hard year. What we learned from it may not show for a long time. Very little of it was bought cheaply and really, Max, it probably isn't exactly what the dr. would order for a good writer, 45 years old, with what, when it is working right, is a good, delicate instrument. But I learned more while Buck and I were together than I had learned altogether up until then so I hope we will get some decent writing from it sometime. Will try very hard.

Will you have them send me Bunny's book on Scott?[2] I feel badly not to write anything about Scott when I knew him, possibly, the best of any of them. But you cannot write anything true as long as Zelda is alive anymore than I can write with my bitch of a mother still able to read. When I was liveing with Georgie Wertenbaker's P47 group there was a man named Jonah something or other (a preposterous name) maybe not even Jonah; who gave me all the Gen on Scott's last time. He was with him when he died etc. Also at the terrible thing with Sheilah. He never would have finished the book of course. It was more an outline to draw advances on; a mock-up of a project than a book. That was why the wonderful grandiloquence of it so impresses those people who are not in the secret of how writers are. The Epic, as we know, is usually false. And he pitched that at an Epic note that would be impossible for anyone to sustain. In wasn't by accident that the Gettysburg address was so short. The laws of prose writing are as immutable as those of flight, of mathematics, of physics. Scott was almost completely uneducated. He knew none of the laws. He did

---

[1] 614 words have been omitted from this letter.

[2] F. Scott Fitzgerald, *The Crack-Up,* ed. Edmund Wilson (New York: New Directions, 1945).

everything wrong; and it came out right. But geometry, always catches up with you. I always feel that you and I can talk truly about Scott because we both loved him and admired him and understood him Where other people were dazzled by him we saw the good, the weakness and the great flaw that was always there. The cowardice, the dream world that was not a late symptom as (reading the reviews Bunny seems to feel). He always had the dream of football greatness, war (which he knew <u>nothing</u> of) (The Sour Science) and when he couldn't walk across Fifth Avenue in traffic he thought 'with what I <u>know</u> now what a great broken field runner I would be.'

Next time I'll write what was good in him. But we take it for granted people should be good. And in a horse, a regiment, a good writer I look for what is wrong. Take it for granted they are good or would not be looking at them.

. . . . .

. . . . .

. . . . .

Ernest/

*TLS with holograph insert, Finca Vigía stationery, 3 pp.[1]*
*Havana, Cuba*

October 31 1945

Dear Max:

Am sorry to have been so remiss about writing but have been working so damned hard on the novel that when finish each day am too pooped to write anything else.[2] Please excuse me and ask Charley to excuse me for not haveing asnwered his letter. It is on the desk in the little house marked must be answered at once. Sorry it's been there so long.

Averaged 750 words a day all month which is high for me. It was hard to get going again after that last smash and all but am in very good shape now. Weigh 202 never take a drink after the wine at dinner, never take a drink in the night, nor in the morning until after my work is finished and never before noon. Cutting down on drinking after a war is the hardest part of training for me. Can remember what a bastard it was to get in shape for the last novel. It's a lonely damned job too. I guess trying to write a good book is about as lonely work as there is. But it makes you happier than anything else.

Charley sent me his Petain pamphlet.[3] It has much excellent sense in it but it also ignores many unpleasant things about the Marechal. Charley admired him so much he deliberately closed his eyes to much. It is good he wrote what he wrote though because the other side will be written and over-written. The French trials are obscenely awful. Wasn't the Laval trial and execution a

---

[1]531 words have been omitted from this letter.
[2]EH was working on a novel that was posthumously published as *Islands in the Stream*.
[3]Charles Sweeny, *Pétain* (Salt Lake City, Utah: Privately printed by Arrow Press, 1945).

shocking mess? I had F.T.P.F. under my command at their request, that's Franc Tireur Partizan Francaise the extreme left resistance group, and that is about as far from being a collaborationist as you can be I guess. But some of this last stuff has been shocking. And many of the most guilty and the greatest connivers with the Germans comparatively unpunished.

I don't mind at all the people being simply killed as Mussolini was. I think that is fitting and good. But any semblance of a trial should get some justice into it. What has been going on in France ever since the liberation is the phase of a war and a revolution that I hate worst of all.

. . . . .
. . . . .
. . . . .
. . . . .
. . . . .
. . . . .
. . . . .
. . . . .

Has Charley gone to England yet? I wish he would write me telling what the other books were in his projected pocket edition series and why, if he was a part owner of the reprint co. my royalties should be split 50-50 between myself and the Co. of which he a part owner?[1] I did not understand that at all. Nor agree.

Best always
    <u>Ernest</u>

*TLS, 2 pp.*[2]
*Sun Valley, Idaho.*

October 4 1946

Dear Max:

. . . . .

Thank you very much for writing to Casper. Mary[3] was very sick there and nearly died. She had a tubular pregnancy and the left falopian tube burst and there was great hemmorage. The tube had to be removed but the other tube and all other organs are o.k. It burst early in the morning while she was asleep and it was difficult to get a doctor but I got a good one finally and operated as soon as could build her up sufficiently from the hemmorage (or get at all ahead of it as it was still continuing). She had to have five bottles of plasma dureing the operation and later two transfusions but made it and is

---

[1]Charles Scribner's Sons had recently formed a partnership with other publishers to underwrite Bantam Books.
[2]580 words have been omitted from this letter.
[3]Mary Welsh, a war correspondent, married EH on 14 March 1946.

comeing along fine now. But I have not written you as I have been busy look-ing after her and with the boys. I missed nearly all of Gigi's[1] vacation. But Bumby was here until last week when he returned to Missoula to college and Patrick is still here.

. . . . .
. . . . .
. . . . .
. . . . .
. . . . .
. . . . .

We are very short of books here and have now read all Bantams. Tell Charley if he will give me the terms the Author's League says are O.K. he can publish Farewell To Arms in Bantams. They are attractive, well made books. He ought to publish some sort of edition of Farewell To Arms anyway. beside the Bantam deal. In the last royalty statement that I saw it seemed to be out of print. Maybe it was let go out of print to force me to accept the Bantam proposition. Let me know what its status is will you please and whether Scribners would be interested in publishing it in Bantam books on the basis that the Author's League says is fair. I do not remember what it is but I signed that pledge that they sent out not to publish any cheap reprints at less than the basis they approved. Chris LaFarge sent me the pledge. You could find out what the basis is from him. They made some sort of study of costs etc. and drew up what they considered to be a fair percentage. I know nothing about the two bit reprint business but think writers should certainly try to learn to stick together as they have been most unmercifully gypped by tax legislation because they have not been organized. I have tried to do what I can about the tax legislation by paying the costs of that appeal which was decided in favour of allowing work to be spread out over the years it takes to write it so far as income goes; even though it is not retroactive and I get nothing out of it.

From what I have seen of Bantam Books they are well put out and excel-lently distributed and are a first rate thing and am all for them if the writer receives a just percentage of the profits.

. . . . .
. . . . .

Best to you always,
Ernest

[1]Gregory Hemingway.

*TLS, Finca Vigía stationery, 2 pp.*[1]
*Havana, Cuba*

March 5 1947

Dear Max:

I have been very remiss about writing you. Please forgive me. It has been a combination of working very hard, then being interrupted, and haveing to work even harder to make up. Haven't been out in the boat in a month and three days and am getting stale so am going out tomorrow no matter what.

First when got here had to do taxes etc. Then Hellinger[2] came down on a movie deal which I have decided against. I do not want to be in a motion picture company even though it means plenty of money. Have all the work I can handle writing. I am going to give him an option (first option) on any stories written (short stories) for a fixed price and a share of the money they make. This way what he will do is entirely up to him and I have no more to do with it than I always have had: nothing. He wanted us to go into a partnership, form a company to acquire the stories, produce etc. Made it very very attractive financially. But I am a writer of novels, stories and an occasional journalist (never I hope to God again) and I do not want to be in picture business in any way. What I should do is to sell my stories, when I do sell them to pictures, in such a way that I participate in the profits instead of selling out-right and haveing taxes take the most of what the story brings and then it gone for good as property. This am trying to work out.

Then came Speiser: increasingly difficult for me to deal with or through. He's gone now.

Last night Cape got in. I haven't seen him yet as am putting him up at the Hotel. The son of a bitch first wrote from London for me to get him a visa. To do this I had to go to Dept. of Immigration and then to Minister of State and have him cable visa to N.Y. Consulate. Cape couldn't locate it so I had to take all steps again and send him the number of the cable that carried it. He then asked for a visa for his wife and I had to interrupt my work and go through the whole damned thing again. Asking favours and useing up credit with govt. people I could have well kept for myself. He cabled he needed a bed for four nights so have gotten him a room at the Nacional Hotel and told them I would pay for it and for their meals. That will be about $80 a day. So let's hope his limiting it to 4 days is accurate. But worth it not to have him here at the house so I can continue to work mornings I never have been able to like Cape and it is too late to make a great effort toward that now.

In spite of all that have been working steadily and well. But it leaves no time for anything else. Have been re-writing from the beginning that part I did before I left, and writing much of it new where I did not have it right. I had a hell of a time starting it originally and all that I have now redone so it

[1]377 words have been omitted from this letter.
[2]Mark Hellinger, a former Broadway columnist, was a Hollywood producer.

is about the way it ought to be. Have done 137 typed pages which, with the newly written part that has gone in, brings me to page 156 of the hand-written Mss. There is 907 pages of the hand-written mss altogether. But a lot of it will take very little re-writing as I was going much better after the start and in the middle. I wish these goddamned visiting firemen would not come and bother me as the cool winter days are the best of the year for working.

Well all of that is why I haven't written you. There have been other inter-ruptions of all sorts but I am fairly ruthless about them. Have a big sign on the gate that says in Spanish Mr. H. receives no one without a previous apointment. Save yourself the annoyance of not being received by not come-ing to the house. Then if they do come up I have the right to curse them off.

I will write to you in detail about the illustrating problem later. This much I do know: No Groth under any circumstances.[1] I like him very much but not his illustrations. Please do not make any definite commitment with Quin-tanilla. His work has gone down-grade (for me at least) and has degenerated into caricature. He <u>could</u> do it well if he would. But I would have to be sure he would. Hell I seem to be going into this in some detail in spite of haveing to get this off. I think Patrick might do a good A Farewell To Arms. Will not know for a while. If I can get to Europe think I might be able to get Picasso to do at least one of the books. He can illustrate beautifully you know and is a good friend of mine. I would like to have really good illustrations. The Marsh things in Dos's books were absolutely atrocious I thought.[2] I am not surprized Dos's didn't sell. None of the separate parts did. All of ours did and still do in some form. Am sorry not to be able to present something con-structive at this time but I have thought a lot about it and that is what <u>I know</u> so far.

. . . . .

. . . . .

Today I am cableing you to please deposit $3138.13 the amount of Feb royalty statement showed in the Guaranty trust. This I'd planned to use for liveing expenses but got cable from Speiser today that he needed $2100 for first installment of taxes. If I don't sell anything to pictures I will have a light income year. Have turned down $50,000 for Fifty Grand, and they would give $75,000, because do not want to sell anything for cash the way taxes are unless I can have some share in the profits.

When you get this letter will you please <u>loan</u> me, not advance me, $3000. and deposit it in my account in the guaranty. Just cable me $3000 deposited and I will know then I can draw on it. Will pay same interest as on other loans.

Am trying to live as economically as I can altho everything is expensive as hell. I think it is better for all of us concerned to borrow from you when I

[1] John Groth (1908–1988) had illustrated a reprint of *MWW* (Cleveland and New York: World, 1946), and EH had introduced Groth's *Studio: Europe* (New York: Vanguard, 1945).

[2] Reginald Marsh (1898–1954) drew the illustrations for the deluxe edition of John Dos Passos's *U.S.A.* trilogy.

need it than get mixed up in a big movie deal which could not help but distract from my one job which is to write good book. I do not want to ever have any thought of anything I write being made into motion picture.

The Snows of Kilimanjaro would make a wonderful picture and whenever I sell it I can pay back what I borrow if the book isn't done by then. I think I have enough assets and the book is far enough along so it is o.k. to borrow.

. . . . .

. . . . .

. . . . .

Ernest[1]

CC, 3 pp.[2]

March 19, 1947

Dear Ernest:

I know—although nobody does know who has not been through it—what you are involved in with the book, and I do not want you to write me any letters except about matters that have to be taken up. One trouble about the illustrated editions is that you are the kind of a writer—I have often said you wrote like a painter—who makes everything visible to the eye, and so an illustrator is likely to be repetitious,- if he could even be that. You have presented it so that the reader sees it. Dos did not do that. He told you what did happen. But still, I do think we'll have to have illustrations.

Then when you speak of such a man as Picasso, I fear that he would not do what he should as an illustrator, and subordinate himself to the writer. Maybe I am wrong, and you would be the better judge of that. Anyhow, I'll wait until you write me, or perhaps until Patrick makes a try at A FAREWELL. Dos's books never did sell since THREE SOLDIERS, but I think that in their way they are very remarkable.

Cape came in after he got here, but he did not tell me nearly as much as you did in your letter, though he seemed to have enjoyed himself.

. . . . .

I'll do my very best for Patrick at Harvard, and maybe could help him get references if he needs them from the really top boys. I don't think they think much of me up there, in so far as they think of me ever. But I know the crowd, and I hope Pat will go there for I think it is the place where a man can be most the way he wants to be.[3]

It seems to me that your attitude about the movies and movie deals, and all that, is just exactly right.

Always yours,

[1]EH's last letter to MP.
[2]28 words have been omitted from this letter.
[3]Patrick Hemingway was admitted to Harvard and graduated.

*CC, 1 pp.*

June 5, 1947

Dear Ernest:

This is just a line to tell you that after I telephoned you, though I could hardly hear, I gathered that things were going on well. I now have heard that although that seems to be true, you have had a very devil of a time.[1] I am mighty sorry about it. I know how horrifying such things are, but in my case they have been brief.- I could not have taken it for the length of time you have. But you are always good that way. There is no sense in my saying all this, but it is impossible not to say something. It has been mighty tough, and I do greatly hope the situation is now better.[2]

Yours always,

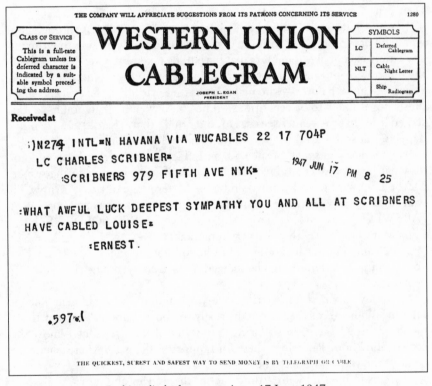

THE COMPANY WILL APPRECIATE SUGGESTIONS FROM ITS PATRONS CONCERNING ITS SERVICE 1280

# WESTERN UNION
# CABLEGRAM

JOSEPH L. EGAN
PRESIDENT

CLASS OF SERVICE

This is a full-rate Cablegram unless its deferred character is indicated by a suitable symbol preceding the address.

SYMBOLS

| LC | Deferred Cablegram |
| NLT | Cable Night Letter |
| | Ship Radiogram |

Received at

;)N274 INTL=N HAVANA VIA WUCABLES 22 17 704P

LC CHARLES SCRIBNER=

:SCRIBNERS 979 FIFTH AVE NYK=      1947 JUN 17 PM 8 25

:WHAT AWFUL LUCK DEEPEST SYMPATHY YOU AND ALL AT SCRIBNERS HAVE CABLED LOUISE=

:ERNEST.

.597•(

THE QUICKEST, SUREST AND SAFEST WAY TO SEND MONEY IS BY TELEGRAPH OR CABLE

Perkins died of pneumonia on 17 June 1947.

[1] Patrick had been dangerously ill in Cuba.
[2] MP's last letter to EH.

*From: Charles Scribner III*                                                                    *CC, 3 pp.*

June 25, 1947

Dear Ernest:

Max's death was naturally a great shock to me as I never had a better friend and at the same time I have to do all in my power in the next days to fill the void that he left in our organization.

I had lunched with him Thursday and, although he seemed at times physically and nervously exhausted, he would not do anything about it. Sunday evening they found he had a temperature of 103, but it was not until Monday that they suspected it was pneumonia. He was taken to the hospital Monday afternoon and his heart gave out at about five o'clock Tuesday morning. I have been swamped with letters from friends and from hysterical women. Fortunately, the best of the latter have decided that it is now up to them to go on writing and do their best, as that would be what Max would have wished. I suspected that some of my publishing friends would try to raid our list, but I have received assurances from most of the agents that they will stand one hundred per cent behind Scribner's in their advice to wayward authors. Fortunately, we have Meyer, Wheelock and Burroughs Mitchell, Max's latest choice, who is working out wonderfully well. I do need two younger men and I am thinking of taking Charlie upstairs, although he is doing a better job in our Advertising Department than anyone we have had in a long time. On the whole, things will work out, but it means double the amount of work for me for some time.

Max told me in confidence something of your son. You must have had a terribly anxious time. I would have written to you, but he did not seem to think I ought to, as I do not think he wanted you to know that he had told me, although it was naturally in strict confidence as far as I was concerned. I sincerely hope that his condition is now entirely satisfactory. It must have completely interrupted your own work.

Naturally, I am most concerned that the fact that Max is no longer here may affect your relationship with Charles Scribner's Sons. I have not seen you or written to you as much as I would like to have because I knew how close you were to Max and that you would rather hear from and see him which I could very well understand. You are not an author who needs inspiration from an editor or editorial work done on your books and if you entrust us with your novel, I believe that your friend, Wallace Meyer, can see it through the press as well as any man I know of. It would seem best, however, if you carried on any correspondence in the meantime directly with me. When we meet there are many things I would like to talk over with you. One matter that is very much on my mind is making a new edition of A FAREWELL TO ARMS about which Max and I were talking the last day he was here. I feel sure you will like Norman Snow who has taken Whitney

---

[1]Charles Scribner, Jr. (1921–1995), the son of Charles Scribner III.

Darrow's place and he is entirely in accord with me in believing that we should put far more pressure on the promotion of the older books that we publish. I think that Whitney Darrow was oversold on the importance of reprint houses. They can do a good job, but it is all-important for our authors, as well as the House, to maintain a strong backlog of seasoned books.

Next time I hope that I can write you a more cheerful letter. With every good wish to you and your son,

Sincerely yours,

*To: Charles Scribner III*                              TLS *with holograph postscript, Finca Vigía*
*stationery, 2 pp.*[1]

June 28 1947

Dear Charlie:

Don't worry about me kid. . You have troubles enough without that. I didn't write you after I cabled because what the hell can you say. We don't need to talk wet about Max to each other. The bad was for him to die. I hadn't figured on him dying; I'd just thought he might get so completely damn deaf we'd lose him that way Anyway for a long time I had been trying to be less of a nuisance to him and have all the fun with him possible. We had a hell of a good time this last time in New York and wasn't it lucky it was that way instead of a lot of problems and arguments. Anyway he doesn't have to worry about Tom Wolfe's chickesnhit estate anymore, or handle Louise's business, nor keep those women writers from building nests in his hat. Max had a lot of fun, anyway I know we had a lot of fun together, but useing up all his resistance that way by not takeing some lay offs to build up is a good lesson to us and don't you get to overworking now, at least until young Charlie gets to know the business for quite a long time because I want to be able to see your alcohol ravaged face when I come in the office for at least the next twenty two years to help me feel someone in N.Y. has a worse hangover than I have.

Charlie don't worry about me at all. I never liked that son of a bitch Darrow but he's out. Wallace and I like and understand each other very well. You and I get along damn well. A lot better than people know and you don't have to worry about writing me letters. I'd have to work and try to write well if I were in jail, or if I had 20 million dollars, or if I was broke and working at something else to keep going, or if I was going to die, or if I had word I was going to live forever. So don't worry about me. I'm not going to succomb to any temptations and I don't flatter easy any more. You've got enough dough to back me to extent that I have to ask for it while I write this book and I will borrow as little as I can and write as good as I can. Have been working out

---

[1]198 words have been omitted from this letter.

ways for my existant stories to be sold to pictures on a non-whoreing basis to keep me going while write, same as always, with no regard for whether it is to sell; but only on a basis of how well I can write it. At least have been working on that and if Speiser doesn't blow it up by over-extending his negociatory ability should be o.k. within this month. However things go I have dough now to last me until Sept. But if the deal with Hellinger goes through I am set for all the time I will need on the book and some afterwards.

If it would do any good you might let it be known that while Max was my best and oldest friend at Scribners and a great, great editor he never cut a paragraph of my stuff nor asked me to change one. One of my best and most loyal friends and wisest counsellors in life as well as in writing is dead. But Charles Scribners Sons are my publishers and I intend to publish with them for the rest of my life.

Malcom Cowley can tell you what he and Max and I and later he and Max were lineing up of getting out a three vol. edition of Farewell To Arms, Sun Also Rises, and For Whom The Bell Tolls showing the relationship between the three with illustrations and an introduction by Cowley. That might come after the new edition of A Farwell To Arms you said you and Max were talking about. I think it is g od policy to keep these books going in our own editions and the three comeing out together with the Cowley tie-up of them would insure g od reviews. Might do better hitting with all three than throwing in piecemeal.[1]

If only the boys hadn't done away with Ben Siegal[2] we might have put him in charge of getting me the Nobel prize. He asked me one time, "Ernie why don't you ever get any of these prizes? I see other writers getting prizes what's the trouble Ernie? There's certainly someway that can be rigged."

Won't bother you with any more of this with everything you have on your hands. If young Charlie is going good in the advertizing end why not leave him there for a while instead of yanking him?

. . . . .
. . . . .
. . . . .

We have real Gordon's gin at 50 bucks a case and real Noilly Prat and have found a way of makeing ice in the deep-freeze in tennis ball tubes that comes out 15 degrees below zero and with the glasses frozen too makes the coldest martini in theworld. Just enough vermouth to cover the bottom of the glass, ounce ¾ of gin, and the spanish cocktail onions very crisp and also 15 degrees below zero when they go in the glass.

This has been rugged as I said but there are better ways of sweating it out than putting your head on the wailing wall.

Did Max get the invitation to the Bronze Star thing? Gen.Lanham who I was with from Normandy on when he was commanding 22nd Inf.Regt. said

[1] This plan was never implemented.
[2] Ben "Bugsy" Siegel, a Las Vegas racketeer, was murdered in 1947.

I should have turned it down but I thought that would be rude and also imply I thought I should have something better which I thought sort of chickenshit. One time in the war got drunk at a dinner because was to get DSC but it got turned down at the top. So thought better take this before it got cancelled.

So long Charlie. Take care of yourself.

Best always

<u>Ernest</u>

Have you heard anything from Martha? I havent heard from her since Christmas. Have a new house-maid named Martha and certainly is a pleasure to give her orders. Marty was a lovely girl though. I wish she hadnt been quite so ambitious and war crazy. Think it must be sort of lonesome for her without a war.

# APPENDIX ONE

◆

*In the Hemingway Collection at the John F. Kennedy Library are the following fragments which may be drafts of his 7–10 December 1929 letter.*

[*Fragment One*]                                                                                    ALS, 3 pp.

What about this Morley business? Am I supposed to swallow all that? Referring to Isabel P's Colum of Nov 24—<u>Casts from a Book Worm</u> (It's the only thing people ever send me!)=I havent been at the Dome for 3 years— have never disparaged Morley's knowledge of boxing, boxed with him 5 different times last spring, ordinarily all rounds ended when Morley was winded, the one other time, after the big lunch, I wrote you about at the time—If he could hit he would have killed me as it was about 35 rounds boxed altogether he won one and he gave me a bad beating in one—but then was too light a hitter to put me on the floor or knock me out—

So now I read that I insulted him, he challenged me and knocked me cold! If Morley had anything to do with starting the story—(It may be just malicious gossip by Pierre Loving or some other kike rat who lies to appear in the know) I would like to know about it so I'll know what steps to take. After boxing with him five times, stopping every time he was winded, stopping and apologizing every time I'd happen to hit him with a right hand, always shooting them high up on his head so as <u>not</u> to get his jaw and having him once when I was tight and could hardly see punch me around for 2 1/2 extra minutes (given by Scott) hitting me wherever he wanted whenever he wanted and not be able to do any real damage—(He had about 20 free shots at my jaw and should have killed me) I know what he is worth as a boxer. He is an excellent <u>boxer,</u> but fat and short winded, a very light hitter and easily hurt. If he has told you any knocking cold story please tell him for me to use a little more imagination in his stories and a little less in his interviews (that should do as an insult) but if he wants it a little stronger tell him I consider his novel one of the worst cheap fakes I ever tried to read, that his fight story is another fake, that there is more to knowing the psychology of professional fighters than being a good amateur boxer yourself, that the reason I wrote about the war was to get somewhere he hadn't been and where it was too late for him to go so he couldnt imitate it and that I am always at his disposal

347

for him to knock me cold at any time he wishes. Also please add that if he should knock me cold (providing for every emergency) or if he should knock my young son Bumby cold that I doubt very much if it would make him a writer.

I havent been worth a damn as a boxer since about 1924—5—But still hope to god I know enough to beat that fat one. I hadnt had gloves on in two years when I boxed Morley—his wife told me he had been boxing 3 or 4 times a week with the Intercollegiate light heavy weight champion all through the winter Evidently preparing his big coup. It was Morley suggested boxing. So now having been unable to do what he wanted to do he claims to have done it instead.

I write this to you instead of to him so that it may be public—as in the story he says I insulted him publicly—All right I'll insult him once more—I hope when I see him to beat him up so badly that you'll have to get another Fake Hemingway to fill in on the seasons when I dont write books—

Please send him this letter. That is the part referring to him—

Yours always—<br>Ernest

[Fragment Two]                                                    AL, 1 p.

harm through malice. One in a very minor way would seem to be Isabel Patterson whom I've never even seen and the other is a Russian Jew with a name like Lipchtsky who calls himself Pierre Loving and hates and lies about everybody. He is a disappointed writer.

This is not the sort of thing that I care to write about in letters but since you wrote to Scott I I have no great choice, Scott is the soul of honor when sober and completely irresponsible when drunk and as he is sooner or later always drunk—anything you write him is liable to become a public issue. If it's all the same I would rather you wrote me when you hear stories about me—not Scott. Please do not write Scott reproaching him for a breach of confidence as he is not to blame. He is absolutely the soul of honor when sober and when drunk is no more responsible than an insane man. And he is drunk on 4 glasses of wine. He did not say you had written him any definite stories—but told me stories he had heard from Callaghan as the type of thing McAlmon had probably told you. When McAlmon told one of those stories in the presence of Evan Shipman—Evan called him a liar and fought him. When McAlmon told me Scott was a homosexual—(it is one of his manias)—I told him he was a liar and a damned fool. It was not till after he had left for N.Y. that I heard the story he was telling about Pauline. Frankly I think he is crazy. Callaghan has no such excuse. He is a cheap, small town gossip anxious to retail any filth, no matter how improbable.

[*Fragment Three*]                                                        *ALS, 2 pp.*

harm through malice. One would seem to be Isabel Patterson whom I've never even seen and the other is a Russian Jew with a name like Lipipsy who calls himself Pierre Loving. He imitated me, then hated me, have never spoken a dozen words to him but he is almost as great a starter of malicious lies as McAlmon.

Yes there is one more. Some of the damndest stories of all come from a woman named Kay Boyle that I have never even <u>seen</u> in my life. She is also a writer.

Have always stayed away from N.Y. in order not to make enemies there so that my work might be judged without personality coming in—but when I have this book out 4 of the 5 known enemies I have are concentrated there. And the system those people lie on is that if they tell something monstrous enough there will always be some people who will say "Well where is smoke there is fire!"

MacAlmons first theory about me being a homosexual was that I had a "suppressed desire" for him, McAlmon! He finally decided, though, and told freely that I was [*word obliterated*], who do you think? Waldo! I take the word out on acct. of this going through the mail.

Now I have no persecution mania—but this is all getting a little too strong. What the hell are they jealous of? I dont want the publicity, I dont get the money—All I want is to work and be left alone and by God you should have a right to be.

Wire yesterday that the sale was 57,000 plus—Thank you for sending it.

Dont make up that English press ad until you get the British clippings—I sent them off to Berlin—but they should be back in a day or two and will send them on. But may be you have them.

Anyway best to you always—I must apologize for having introduced McAlmon to you. Expect I'll live to hear more foul things about myself but doubt if many more foul from anyone that have written a letter of introduction for and was trying to get before a publisher.

Yours always—

Ernest

# BIBLIOGRAPHY

———◆———

Baker, Carlos. *Ernest Hemingway: A Life Story.* New York: Scribners, 1969.

———, ed. *Ernest Hemingway: Selected Letters, 1917–1961.* New York: Scribners, 1981.

Berg, A. Scott. *Maxwell Perkins: Editor of Genius.* New York: Congdon/Dutton, 1978.

Bruccoli, Matthew J. *Fitzgerald and Hemingway: A Dangerous Friendship.* New York: Carroll & Graf, 1994.

Caruthers, Clifford M., ed. *Ring Around Max: The Correspondence of Ring Lardner & Max Perkins.* De Kalb: Northern Illinois University Press, 1973.

Cowley, Malcolm. *Unshaken Friend.* Boulder, Colo.: Roberts Rinehart, 1985. Originally published as a two-part profile of Perkins in *The New Yorker* 20 (1 April 1944): 32–36, 39–42; and 20 (8 April 1944): 30–34, 36–43.

Kuehl, John and Jackson Bryer, eds. *Dear Scott/Dear Max.* New York: Scribners, 1971.

Raeburn, John. *Fame Became of Him: Hemingway as Public Writer.* Bloomington: Indiana University Press, 1984.

Reynolds, Michael S. *Hemingway: The American Homecoming.* Cambridge, Mass: Blackwell, 1992.

———. *Hemingway: An Annotated Chronology.* Detroit: Manly/Omnigraphics, 1991.

———. *Hemingway: The Paris Years.* Cambridge, Mass: Blackwell, 1989.

Scribner, Charles, Jr. *In the Company of Writers: A Life in Publishing.* New York: Scribners, 1991.

———. *In the Web of Ideas: The Education of a Publisher.* New York: Scribners, 1993.

Wheelock, John Hall, ed. *Editor to Author: The Letters of Maxwell E. Perkins.* New York: Scribners, 1950.

# INDEX

◆

Page numbers in *italics* refer to illustrations.

*Across the River and Into the Trees* (Hemingway), 304
*Action This Day* (Spellman), 331–32, 331*n*
Adams, C. L., 81*n*
Adams, J. Donald, 314
Adams, Truslow, 219
*Adventures of a Younger Son, The* (Trelawny), 43*n*
advertising:
  of *A Farewell to Arms*, 123–25, 126
  of *To Have and Have Not*, 254
  of *Winner Take Nothing*, 202
Aeschylus, 334*n*
Africa, 206, 215, 222
"After the Storm" (Hemingway), 187, 188, 191, 195, 199, 202
Aiken, Conrad, 47, 50, 68, 81, 97, 196
Alcázar, siege of (1936), 246–47
Aldington, Richard, 319
Allen, Hervey, 37*n*
Allen, Jay, 265
*All Good Americans* (Bahr), 248*n*
Allington, Floyd, 151*n*
*All Quiet on the Western Front* (Remarque), 101–2, 107, 122
*All the Brave* (Quintanilla), 265*n*
*All the Sad Young Men* (Fitzgerald), 71*n*
"Alpine Idyll, An" (Hemingway), 41
"American, An" (Kipling), 317
American Civil Liberties Union, 259
*American Earth* (Caldwell), 156*n*
American News, 300
American Writers' Congress, 250*n*
Anderson, Sherwood, 29, 35, 115, 309
*Appointment in Samarra* (O'Hara), 232*n*
Arlen, Michael, 49
Ashley, Brett, 48, 54, 73
Aswell, James, 125
*Atlantic Monthly*, 34*n*, 160, 193

Authors League, 165, 281, 338
*Autobiography of Alice B. Toklas, The* (Stein), 193*n*

Baer, Max, 140, 240
Bahr, Jerome, 248*n*
Bailey, Temple, 54
Baker, Carlos, 109*n*, 143
Baker & Taylor, 300
Balzac, Honoré de, 78, 97
"Banal Story" (Hemingway), 61*n*, 263
Bancroft, Caroline, 138
Bantam Books, 337*n*, 338
Barrie, James M., 65
Barth, Sidney, 174
Basso, Hamilton, 24
Bates, Ralph, 319
"Battler, The" (Hemingway), 149
bayonets, 37
B.B.C. (British Broadcasting Corporation), 136
*Beautiful and Damned, The* (Fitzgerald), 25, 29, 166
Beegel, Susan F., 158*n*
Beerbohm, Mary, 49
Belloc, Hillaire, 42, 44, 45, 48
Belmonte, Senora, 187
Benét, Bill, 48, 49, 85
Benét, Stephen, 300
Berg, A. Scott, 25*n*, 28*n*
Bergman, Ingrid, 299*n*, 316
Bessie, Alvah, 275, 276, 278, 280, 281
*Best Short Stories of 1923, The* (O'Brien, ed.), 128*n*
*Bibliography of the Works of Ernest Hemingway, A* (Cohn), 156*n*
Biggs, John, 67, 73, 301
Big Horn, Wyo., 202
"Big Two-Hearted River" (Hemingway), 64*n*, 215

Bilbao, 251
Billings, Mont., 151*n*
Bird, William, 29
Bishop, John Peale, 116, 150, 259, 329, 330
Black Sun Press, 156
*Blood and Sand* (Ibanez), 187
"Blood on the Snow" (Gellhorn), 278*n*
Bodenheim, Maxwell, 106*n*
*Bombs Away* (Steinbeck), 318
Boni and Boni, 73
Boni & Liveright, 24, 25, 29, 33, 34, 35–36, 62, 63, 69, 132, 146, 220
    see also *In Our Time* (story collection)
Book-of-the-Month Club, 123, 161, 162, 163, 289, 294, 299
Boston, Mass., censorship in, 58, 61, 106–7, 108, 110
boxing:
    by EH, 105, 116–17, 132, 137–38, 347–48
    Joe Louis-Max Baer fight (1935), 140, 240*n*
    Joe Louis-Max Schmeling fight (1938), 234
Boyd, James, 24
Boyd, Thomas, 37*n*
Boyle, Kay, 349
*Brentano's Book Chat,* 78, 78*n*
*Bridge of San Luis Rey, The* (Wilder), 73–74, 100, 124, 125
Bridges, Robert, 53, 55, 76, 81, 177
    *Farewell to Arms* serialization and, 88, 90, 92, 95–96, 127
Briffault, Robert, 231*n*
British Broadcasting Corporation (B.B.C.), 136
Bromfield, Louis, 51, 55, 64, 120, 129, 193, 197, 201
*Brooklyn Daily Eagle,* 68
Brooks, Cleanth, 313*n*
Brooks, Van Wyck, 42, 75*n*, 316
Brown, George, 332
Bruccoli, Matthew J., 23*n*, 40*n*, 116*n*
Bruce, Otto, 277
Bryer, Jackson R., 25*n*, 252
"Budding Friendship, A," see "Short Happy Life of Francis Macomber, The"
Bull, Harry, 277
bull fighting, 34, 38, 39, 52, 187
    see also *Death in the Afternoon*
"Bullfighting, Sport and Industry" (Hemingway), 136*n*

"Bull in the Afternoon" (Eastman), 190*n*, 233, 252
"Burial of the Guns" (Page), 321
*Burke's Peerage,* 73
Burne, Alfred H., 271*n*
Burnett, W. R., 151
Burt, Struthers, 24, 76
Burton, Harry, 280
"Butterfly and the Tank, The" (Hemingway), 266*n*, 273, 274, 275
"Byron of Our Day, The" (Benét & Benét), 300*n*

Caldwell, Erskine, 156
Caldwell, Taylor, 24
Callaghan, Morley, 58, 70, 75*n*, 76, 77, 105, 116–17, 143, 151, 261
    EH's feud with, 116*n*, 132–33, 137–38, 347–48
"Canary for One, A" (Hemingway), 53*n*, 55*n*, 57, 263
Canby, Henry Seidel, 203
Cantwell, Robert, 232
Cape, Jonathan, 36, 56, 63–64, 176, 241, 298, 323, 331, 339, 341
"Capital of the World, The" ("The Horns of the Bull") (Hemingway), 239, 244, 249, 263, 267
*Captains and the Kings Depart, The: The Journals and Letters of Reginald, Viscount Esher,* 271
Carnegie Hall, 250
Carney, W. P., 272
"Case to Be Tried On Its Merits," 260*n*
"Casts from a Book Worm" (EH's joke; Paterson's column is called "Turns with a Bookworm"), 347
"Cat in the Rain" (Hemingway), 149
censorship in Boston, 58, 61, 106–7, 108, 110
"Censorship and *A Farewell to Arms*" (Donaldson), 106*n*
Cerf, Bennett, 153–54, 155
Chamberlain, John, 202*n*, 298
Chambers, Esther, 277
Chamson, André, 75
Charles Scribner's Sons, 24–25, 26, 34, 139, 140, 337
    bookstore of, 186
    Depression and, 130, 182, 204
    EH's criticisms of, 309–10
    *For Whom the Bell Tolls* plagiarism suit and, 309
    Martha Gellhorn at, 303

New York offices of, *141*
paper shortage and, 326, 331
reprint rights and, 322–23, 325
rumors of EH's departure from, 120, 122
stockholders' meetings at, 152
Wolfe's departure from, 233, 253, 254–55, 257
*Charterhouse of Parma, The* (Stendhal), 89*n,* 319
"Chauffeurs of Madrid, The" (Hemingway), 249*n*
Chekhov, Anton, 90*n*
"Che Te Dice La Patria" (Hemingway), 115
*Chianti Flask, The* (Belloc Lowndes), 216
*Chicago Tribune,* 64
Christian Scientists, 135
Churchill, Winston, 204, 319
Civil War, U.S., 315, 319
"Clean, Well-Lighted Place, A" (Hemingway), 139, 191, 195, 199
CLEON (Cleonike Damianakes), 118
Cohn, Louis Henry, 145*n*, 156, 162, 192, 259, 262–63
Coleman, Emily Holmes, 68–69
*Collier's,* 276, 278, 331, 332
Colum, Molly, 78, 97, 107, 113, 255
Committee for the Defence of Political Prisoners, 162
Communism, 155, 332
*Complete Short Stories of Ernest Hemingway, The: The Finca Vigía Edition,* 273*n*
Conrad, Joseph, 330
Contact Press, 29
Cooper, Gary, 299, 316
*Cooperative Commonwealth,* 125*n*
Copeland, Charles Townsend, 24, 316
*Cosmopolitan,* 79, 81, 160, 176, 191, 203*n*, 204, 206, 221, 239, 240, 241, 243, 244*n*, 273, 274*n*, 280*n*
*Costumes by Eros* (Aiken), 81*n*
"Count of Darkness" stories (Fitzgerald), 223*n*
Cowley, Malcolm, 25*n*, 78, 242
*Crack-Up, The* (Fitzgerald), 335*n*
"Crack-Up, The" (Fitzgerald), 237*n*
Crane, Stephen, 321
Crichton, Kyle, 191
"Critic Lauds `A Farewell to Arms'—The Biography of a Virginal Mind" (Aswell), 125*n*

Crosby, Caresse, 156*n*
Crosby, Harry, 156*n*
"Cross-Country Snow" (Hemingway), 16
*Crowded Hours* (Longworth), 204*n*
Crowley, Aleister, 42*n*
Crowley, Michael H., 106*n*
Crown Publishers, 317
Cuba, 184, 188, 239, 240, 273
Cummings, E. E., 194–95
Cunard, Nancy, 49
*Currito de la Crus* (*Shadows of the Sun*) (Lugin), 187*n*
Curtis Brown agency, 36, 54

Dakin, Fraden, 135*n*
Damianakes, Cleonike (CLEON), 118
*Dance of the Machines, The* (O'Brien), 129*n*
"Dark in the Forest, Strange as Time" (Wolfe), 214*n*
*Dark Journey, The* (Green), 119*n*
Darrow, Whitney, 175, 181, 182, 189, 232, 241, 248, 249, 331, 332, 343–44
Dashiell, Alfred, 66, 81, 88, 90, 106–7, 112, 159–60, 162, 164, 172, 177, 184, 221
Davenport, Marcia, 24, 176, 327
Davis, Richard Harding, 319, 321
"Day's Wait, A" (Hemingway), 191, 192
Dean, Dizzy, 277
*Dear Scott/Dear Max* (Kuehl & Bryer, eds.), 25*n*, 252
*Death in the Afternoon* (Hemingway), 27, 139, 158–78, 184, 196, 200, 202, 238, 284, 327
  deluxe edition of, 162, 186
  EH's outlay for illustrations, 185–86
  final chapter of, 158*n*–59*n*
  galleys of, 161, 171, 172–73, 175
  illustrations for, 161, 162, 164–65, 166, 167–69, *168,* 185–86
  options on, 187
  proofs of, 161, 167, 171
  publisher's price for, 162, 164–65, 165*n*
  reviews of, 190*n*
  royalties on, 181, 182, 185, 188, 189
  sales of, 178
  Waldo Frank described in, 173
*Death of a Hero* (Aldington), 319
"Death of the Standard Oil Man" (Hemingway), 156*n*

*Debrett's Peerage,* 73
"Defense of Dirty Words: A Cuban Letter" (Hemingway), 217*n*
"Denunciation, The" (Hemingway), 266*n*, 273, 274
*Denver Post,* 138
Detroit, Mich., 259
*Devotions Upon Emergent Occasions* (Donne), 282*n*
"Diamond As Big as the Ritz, The" (Fitzgerald), 314
Dinamov (editor), 242
"Dog of Flanders, A" (Ouida), 313
Domingo, Roberto, 162, 177, 185
Donaldson, Scott, 106*n*
Donne, John, 282, 283
Dorrance, Ward Allison, 276*n*
Dos Passos, John, 55, 56, 71, 151*n*, 157, 166, 167, 170, 172, 177, 213, 223, 233, 340
*Dostoyevsky* (Yomolinsky), 216
*Dragon Murder Case, The* (Van Dine), 204*n*
*Drums Along the Mohawk* (Edmonds), 319
Dry Tortugas, 139, 152–53, 154, 155
*Dubliners* (Joyce), 16
Duell, Sloan and Pearce, 278

Eastman, Max, 190, 193, 196, 233, 252, 253, 255, 256, 335
Ecclesiastes, 36*n*, 45, 51, 52
Eddy, Mary Baker, 135
*Education Before Verdun* (Zweig), 101*n*
*Eimi* (Cummings), 195*n*
Eliot, T. S., 151
Ellerslie Mansion, 61, 66
Empey, Arthur Guy, 37, 319, 321
"Ernest Hemingway" (Perkins), 295–97
"Ernest Hemingway: A Publisher's Assessment" (C. Scribner, Jr.), 13–17
*Ernest Hemingway: Critiques of Four Major Novels* (Baker, ed.), 109*n*
*Ernest Hemingway: Selected Letters, 1917–1961* (Baker, ed.), 28*n*
"Ernest Hemingway and the Post-War Decade" (Stein), 193*n*
"Ernest Hemingway Has Put on Maturity" (Gregory), 202*n*
Esher, Reginald, Viscount, 271–72
*Esquire,* 16, 210*n*, 214, 215, 217, 218, 221, 223*n*, 229–30, 231, 244*n*, 266*n*

EH's stories for, 238, 239, 245, 270*n*
Fitzgerald's pieces for, 237, 237*n*
*Europa* (Briffault), 231, 231*n*

Fadiman, Clifton, 203, 203*n*
"Far Away and Long Ago" (Hudson), 115
*Farewell to Arms, A* (Hemingway), 26, 27, 57, 58, 59, 69*n*, 97, 149, 157, 202, 204, 219, 256, 291, 296, 297, 318, 338, 343
adaptations of, 121
book jacket of, 117–18, 120
Chapter 40, galleys of, 117, 117*n*
criticism and reviews of, 111–12, 111*n*, 120, 123
dedication of, 110
disclaimer for, 136*n*
editing of, for serial, 91–93, 94–96
editions of, 110
EH's advertising suggestions for, 123–25, 126
EH's ease with writing of, 69, 71, 74, 76
ending of, 108–9
Fitzgerald's suggestions for, 219
Fitzgerald's worries over, 123, 126, 134–35
Fredric Henry in, 104
German translation of, 121, 123, 127
illustrated edition of, 340, 341
Miss Van Campen in, 104*n*, 108, 109–10, 115
obscene words in, 90, 91, 102–4, 103, 105, 106–7, 109–10
Perkins's synopsis of, 88–90
Perkins's views on, 86, 98–99
royalties for, 122–23, 127, 129, 130, 134
Russian edition of, 242
sales of, 122, 123*n*, 126, 127–28, 129–30
serializing of, 56, 57, 58, 74–75, 77, 78, 80–81, 86, 91–93, 94–96, 106–7, 127
Wister's comments on, 97, 99–101, 104
"Farewell to the Nineties" (Canby), 203*n*
"Fascism Is a Lie" (Hemingway), 233, 250, 251
"Fathers and Sons" ("The Tomb of his Grandfather") (Hemingway), 192, 193, 199, 200, 203*n*

"Fatigue" (Hemingway), 273
*Feet First* (Finney), 281*n*
Fielding, Henry, 56, 78
*Fiesta* (Hemingway), 57*n*
  see also *Sun Also Rises, The*
*Fifth Column, The* (play) (Hemingway),
  234, 252*n*, 253, 256, 257, 258,
  259, 260–61, 263, 266, 273
  production of, 264–65
*Fifth Column and the First Forty-Nine*
  *Stories, The* (Hemingway), 234,
  239, 252*n*, 256–71, 322, 325
  order of stories in, 257–63, 266–68
"Fifty Grand" (Hemingway), 34, 47,
  48, 49, 52, 68, 81, 128, 160,
  188, 202, 220, 221, 240, 262,
  263
films of EH's works, 52, 169, 299, 316,
  320
Finca Vigía, La, 234
Finney, Ben, 281
"First Fifty-Seven, The" (Hemingway),
  212, 218
Fitzgerald, F. Scott, 15, 23, 36–37, 43,
  50, 57, 58, 83, 162, 184, 201,
  256
  alcoholism of, 78, 84, 97, 209, 222,
    246, 348
  death of, 234, 301–2, 327
  depressions of, 70–71
  EH's correspondence with, 36–37,
    53, 61
  EH's views on works of, 71, 208–9,
    275, 313–14
  *Esquire* pieces of, 237, 238, 240,
    307
  *Farewell to Arms* suggestions of,
    219
  *Farewell to Arms* worries of, 123,
    126, 134–35
  father's death and, 153
  financial difficulties of, 37, 62, 81,
    238, 241–42, 276
  health problems of, 66–67, 68, 175
  Hemingway-Callaghan feud and,
    116, 132, 137, 347, 348
  in Hollywood, 252, 259, 314
  letters of, 328, 329
  love affair of, 224, 227
  *New York Post* interview of, 246–47
  Perkins and, 24, 27, 62, 70–71, 78,
    82–83, 204–5, 210, 211, 223
  Perkins's correspondence with, 75,
    77, 182, 258

  posthumous works of, 307, 308–9,
    313–14, 335–36
  publishing business and, 118,
    122–23
  in "Snows of Kilimanjaro," 245,
    245*n*, 268–69
  sobriety of, 255
  Virginia battlefields trip with Perkins
    of, 173
  works of, 25, 64, 71, 204–5, 207,
    223*n*, 307, 308–9, 313–14,
    335–36
  writing difficulties of, 71, 73
  Zelda and, 81, 82, 144, 150, 166,
    170, 327
Fitzgerald, Scottie, 301, 307
Fitzgerald, Zelda, 61, 67, 70, 73, 153,
  174, 176, 205, 242, 301, 313
  EH's views on, 82, 175, 184, 327,
    335
  Fitzgerald and, 81, 82, 144, 150,1
    66, 170, 327
  novel of (*Save Me the Waltz*),
    166–67
*Fitzgerald and Hemingway* (Bruccoli),
  116*n*
*Fix Bayonets!* (Thomason), 37*n*
Florida, east coast of, 226
*Flowering of New England, The*
  (Brooks), 316
Ford, Ford Madox, 15, 149–50, 330
"Ford Madox Ford and the Devil's Dis-
  ciple" (Hemingway), 42*n*
Forsythe, Robert (Kyle Crichton), 191*n*
*Fortune,* 136
*For Whom the Bell Tolls* (film), 299,
  316, 320
*For Whom the Bell Tolls* (Hemingway),
  25, 27, 240, 274*n*, 277–95,
  298–300, 327
  award received by, 315*n*
  Chapter 4 of, 287*n*
  Chapter 18 of, 26
  dust jacket for, *235*
  EH's corrections in, 289–93
  EH's style sheet for, 292
  EH's taxes and, 315, 323
  El Sordo in, 284, 288–89
  epilogue of, 291–94
  Finney's reading of, 281
  Goltz in, 284, 285, 286, 291
  Karkov in, 285, 288, 291, 293
  last chapter of, 284, 285
  Perkins's editing of, 286–89

*For Whom the Bell Tolls* (*cont.*)
  Perkins's views on, 279, 283–84, 286
  plagiarism suit against, 309
  potential libel in, 288
  reprinting of, 327*n*
  reviews of, 298–99
  Robert Jordan in, 279, 284, 285,
    287–88, 291
  sales of, 299–300, 301, 307, 308,
    316, 320
  serialization of, 280–81, 283
  title of, 282–83
4th Infantry Division, U.S., 333
France, 274, 336–37
Franco, Francisco, 272
Franc Tireur Partizan Francaise
    (F.T.P.F.), 337
Frank, Waldo, 99, 173
Franklin, Sidney, 186, 187, 205, 207, 212
*F. Scott Fitzgerald: A Life in Letters*
    (Bruccoli, ed.), 25*n*, 40*n*

Galsworthy, John, 75, 204
"Gambler, the Nun and the Radio,
    The" ("Give Us a Prescription,
    Doctor) (Hemingway), 180,
    183*n*, 191, 202
*Game Fish of the Pacific* (Thomas and
    Thomas), 164*n*
*Garden Murder Case, The* (Van Dine),
    231*n*
*Garden of Eden, The* (Hemingway), 13
Gellhorn, Martha, *see* Hemingway,
    Martha Gellhorn
"Gift Horse, A" (Wister), 135
Gingrich, Arnold, 28, 214*n*, 219, 240,
    243, 244
"Give Us a Prescription, Doctor" (Hem-
    ingway), 139, 183*n*
*Glory Hunter* (Van De Water), 216
"God Rest You Merry, Gentlemen"
    (Hemingway), 191, 195
Goethe, Johann Wolfgang von, 334
Gordon, Caroline, 24, 25
Graham, Sheilah, 307, 335
*Great Gatsby, The* (Fitzgerald), 29, 71,
    211, 307, 316
*Great Modern Short Stories*, 312*n*
Greco-Turkish War (1922), 319*n*
Green, Julian, 74, 119
*Green Hat, The* (Arlen), 49*n*, 54
*Green Hills of Africa* (Hemingway), 27,
    140, 206*n*, 222, 224, 229–30,
    231, 241, 322

alternate titles for, 215–16, 217–18
photographs for, 222–23
Russian edition of, 242
sales of, 237–38
serialization of, 219–20, 221–22
Gregory, Horace, 202*n*
Gris, Juan, 162, 175
Grosset & Dunlap, 146, 153, 154, 155,
    169, 322, 326, 327*n*
Groth, John, 340
Gyzyka, Miss, 162

Haig, Douglas, 271
Hale, Nancy, 24, 240, 255
Hale, William Harlan, 167, 167*n*
Hamer (bookseller), 259
"Handle With Care" (Fitzgerald), 237*n*
Hansen, Harry, 106, 111–12, 113, 204
"Happy Ending, The," *see* "Snows of
    Kilimanjaro, The"
Harcourt Brace, 165, 166
Harper, 170, 254*n*
Harper Prize, 64, 119*n*
"Harry Morgan" (Hemingway), 249, 251
Hart, Henry (editor), 199
*Harvard Advocate*, 24
Hauser, Benjamin Gayelord, 171, 172
Havana, 240
Hearst magazines, 62*n*–63*n*, 63
    *see also Cosmopolitan*
*Heart of Another, The* (Gellhorn), 303
Heinemann, 54
Hellinger, Mark, 339, 345
Hellman, Lillian, 233
Hemingway, Carol, 167, 181
Hemingway, Dr. Clarence, suicide of,
    57, 83–84, 157
Hemingway, Ernest:
    accidents of, 68, 151*n*, 152
    ambition of, 15
    American writing as viewed by, 102
    anti-Scribners rumors about, 120,
        120*n*, 122
    anti-Semitism of, 50, 56, 273
    on being a writer, 278, 280
    as biographical subject, 23
    book clubs as viewed by, 163
    boxing by, 105, 116–17, 132, 137–38
    bull fighting and, 46, 52, 53
    Callaghan's feud with, 116*n*,
        132–33, 137–38
    careerism of, 208
    Charles Scribner, Jr.'s assessment of,
        13–17

Charles Scribner III's friendship
    with, 11–12, 344–45
Communism as viewed by, 155
competitiveness of, 76
as correspondent, 19–20, 23, 233,
    246, 258–59, 324
critics as viewed by, 190–91, 203–4,
    232, 242–43, 244, 264, 298–99
death of, 13, 304
defensiveness of, 202–3
discouragements of, 43–44
Eastman's scuffle with, 233, 252
education of, 14, 24
Far East trip of, 303, 308
finances of, 74, 79, 110–11, 129–30,
    203, 207–8, 323, 340
fishing by, 72, 85, 91, 169, 192–93,
    200, 244, 296–97
Fitzgerald's championing of, 25,
    33n, 34
Fitzgerald's correspondence with,
    36–37, 53, 61
Fitzgerald's crack-up and, 237, 240
Fitzgerald's writing as viewed by, 71,
    208–9, 275, 335–36
gambling of, 240
good writing as viewed by, 209–10,
    214
guns owned by, 206
Hadley's divorce of, 56n, 57
Hollywood spurned by, 314, 339
hunting by, 176, 178, 206
hurricane experienced by, 226–27
injuries of, 152, 157
journalism of, 14, 203, 241
at Kansas City Star, 14–15, 24
in Key West, 2
Last Tycoon as viewed by, 313–14
letters of, 13
marriages of, see Hemingway,
    Hadley Richardson; Hemingway,
    Martha Gellhorn; Hemingway,
    Mary Welsh Monks; Hemingway,
    Pauline Pfeiffer
meeting of Lardner and, 83n
Nairobi trip of, 139, 205–6
Napoleonic story idea of, 271
nicknames of, 14
Pauline's divorce of, 234
Perkins as viewed by, 325, 344–45
Perkins's article on, 295–97
Perkins's death and, 342–45
plagiarism suit against, 309–10,
    311–12

publicity hated by, 179, 295
Q-boat activities of, 324n
rages of, 27
reporter's eye of, 14–15, 230
rumors about, 119, 120, 122,
    132–33, 310, 347–49
self-image of, 14
sensitivity of, 16, 297
shooting of, 223
Spanish Civil War and, 233, 234,
    246, 258–59, 269, 271, 272, 274
Stein on, 193, 194–95
story ideas of, 273
superstition of, 171–72
weight of, 274
Wilson as viewed by, 231, 242,
    329–30
Wolfe's meeting with, 139, 182–83,
    297
women as viewed by, 327, 332
in World War I, 296
World War II as viewed by, 315, 318,
    323
writing business as viewed by, 5, 63,
    111, 118–19, 136, 154–55,
    205–6, 214
writing pace of, 69, 71, 74, 76, 186
writing tips of, 297
Zelda Fitzgerald as viewed by, 82,
    175, 184, 327, 335
see also Hemingway-Perkins rela-
    tionship
Hemingway, Ernest, works of:
abandoned novel, 57, 65n, 69n
adaptations of, 52, 121, 169, 234
advertising of, 47, 61, 66, 67, 74,
    75, 123–25, 126, 202
criticism of, 202–3; see also specific
    works
EH's advertising suggestions for,
    123–25, 126
Esquire "Letters," 210n, 214, 215,
    217, 218, 221, 223n, 229–30, 231
Fifth Column, The, 234, 252n, 253,
    256, 257, 258, 259, 260–61,
    263, 264–65, 266, 273
introductions and prefaces, 213,
    248, 317, 319, 340n
magazine articles, 159, 160, 249
notebooks, 167, 169
novels, see specific novels
obscene words in, 26–27, 42, 43, 90,
    91, 102–4, 103, 163, 169–70,
    179–80

Hemingway, Ernest, works of: (*cont.*)
   poetry, 333
   posthumous publications, 13, 324*n*,
      329*n*, 336*n*
   potential libel in, 145–46, 145*n*,
      147, 260–61, 262, 288
   reprinting of, 313, 322–23, 325,
      338, 344
   serial rights for, 62–64
   speeches, 233, 250, 251
   stories, 16, 24, 34–35, 41, 44, 46,
      47, 50, 52–53, 55, 61, 63*n*, 128,
      144–46, 187–89, 238–39,
      319–20, 322; *see also specific sto-*
      *ries*
   stories in chronological order, 262–63
   story collections of, *see Fifth Col-*
      *umn and the First Forty-Nine Sto-*
      *ries, The*; *In Our Time*; *Men*
      *Without Women*; *Winner Take*
      *Nothing*
   unfinished stories, 156*n*
   World War II propaganda for, 318
Hemingway, Gregory "Gigi," 277, 338
Hemingway, Hadley Richardson, 29,
      56, 57, 119, 127, 132, 169, 263
Hemingway, John Hadley Nicanor
      "Bumby," 55, 104, 119, 274,
      317, 338, 348
Hemingway, Madelaine "Sunny," 96–97
Hemingway, Martha Gellhorn "Marty,"
      233, 234, 258*n*, 277, 278, 303,
      314, 320, 324, 332, 346
   articles of, 278
   books by, 278, 327
   EH's divorce of, 303
   EH's war experience and, 333
Hemingway, Mary Welsh Monks, 16,
      303
   tubular pregnancy of, 337–38
Hemingway, Patrick, 74, 79, 157, 240,
      277, 338, 340, 341, 342, 343
Hemingway, Pauline Pfeiffer, 57, 77,
      96, 104, 112, 113, 116, 123,
      143, 157, 180, 188, 206, 243,
      249, 258, 263, 270, 271, 274,
      277, 327
   divorce settlement of, 310, 311, 324
   EH's divorce of, 234, 258*n*
   rumors about, 132–33, 348
"Hemingway and the Wars" (Wilson),
      272*n*
"Hemingway Legend, The" (Cowley),
      78*n*

Hemingway-Perkins relationship:
   chronology of, 29–30, 57–58,
      139–40, 233–34, 303–4
   Eastman article and, 252, 253, 255,
      256
   EH's rages and, 27
   EH's view of, 28
   EH's World War II experience and,
      334
   EH's writing encouraged, 5, 224–25
   epistolary nature of, 26, 324–25
   first meeting, 24
   fishing trips, 152–53, 155, 155*n*
   *For Whom the Bell Tolls* plagiarism
      suit, 309–10, 311–12
   *Green Hills of Africa* misunderstand-
      ing, 219–22
   lost letter, 29, 33
   meetings, 26, 30, 139, 233, 234,
      305
   reprint rights and, 322–24, 325
   Stein affair and, 193–97, 201
"Hemingway Reports Spain," 250*n*
"Hemingways in Sun Valley, The" 301*n*
"Hemingway Slaps Eastman in Face,"
      252
Henry, O. (William Sydney Porter),
      319, 321
Hergesheimer, Joseph, 42, 44, 45, 48
Herrick, Robert, 132
Hewlett, Maurice, 298
Hickock, Guy, 68, 78
"Hills Like White Elephants" (Heming-
      way), 188, 202, 203*n*, 262, 263
Hilton, James, 319, 321
Hollywood, Calif., 252, 259, 310, 314
"Homage to Switzerland" (Heming-
      way), 139, 177, 191
*Hommes de la route, Les* (Chamson),
      75
"Horns of the Bull, The," *see* "Capital
      of the World, The"
"Horse Thieves, The" (Chekhov), 90
Houghton Mifflin Fellowship, 239–40
House of Books Limited, 191
Howard, Sidney, 78
Huddleston, Sisley, 52, 93*n*
Hudson, W. H., 115
Hughes, Rupert, 113
hurricanes, 226–27

Ibanez, Carlos, 187
*Idiot's Delight* (Sherwood), 254
"'I'm Not an Old Fogey and You're Not

a Young Ass': Owen Wister and
Ernest Hemingway" (Price), 97*n*
"In Another Country" (Hemingway),
55, 57
"Indian Camp" (Hemingway), 267
"Indian Summer," *see* "Fathers and Sons"
*Indigo* (Weston), 326*n*
Ingersoll, Ralph, 332
*In Our Time* (story collection) (Heming-
way), 24, 29, 34, 35, 36, 53,
63–64, 69, 85, 132, 139,
144–45, 188, 197, 215, 239,
266, 267
"Introduction by the Author" ("On
the Quai at Smyrna") of, 150*n*
Wilson's introduction to Scribner's
edition of, 145, 147, 149, 150
*in our time* (vignettes) (Hemingway),
29, 258, 258*n*, 263
*International Literature*, 242
International Magazine Co., 79
International Writer's Convention, Sec-
ond, 233
*In the Company of Writers* (C. Scribner,
Jr.), 13
*In the Web of Ideas* (C. Scribner, Jr.), 12
"Introduction by the Author," *see* "On
the Quai at Smyrna"
"invincible, L'," *see* "Undefeated, The"
*Islands in the Stream* (Hemingway), 13,
324*n*, 336*n*
Italy, 296
"Italy—1927" ("Che Ti Dice La
Patria?") (Hemingway), 61, 61*n*
*I Thought of Daisy* (Wilson), 84
Ivens, Joris, 277

James, Henry, 38, 40–41, 48, 112
James, Will, 24
Jews, 50, 56, 273
Joe Louis-Max Baer fight (1935), 140,
240*n*
Joe Louis-Max Schmeling fight (1938),
234
John (Perkins's nephew), 324
Jonathan Cape, 36, 56, 63–64, 176,
241, 298, 323, 331, 339
Joyce, James, 15, 16, 49–50, 75, 128,
143, 151

*Kansas City Star*, 14, 24
*Ken*, 262
Key West, Fla., 2, 26, 57, 76, 136, 139
EH's stories about, 166

"Killers, The" (Hemingway), 44, 46,
55*n*, 57, 61, 65, 68, 128, 128*n*,
156, 202, 262, 263
Kipling, Rudyard, 97*n*, 100, 317
Komroff, Manuel, 49

LaFarge, Christopher, 277, 338
*Land of Plenty, The* (Cantwell), 232*n*
"Landscape with Figures" (Heming-
way), 273
Lanham, Gen. Buck, 335, 345–46
"Lantern Bearers, The" (Stevenson), 14
Lardner, Ring, 25, 54, 54*n*, 57, 67,
82*n*, 83, 162, 188, 188*n*, 217
*Last Tycoon, The* (Fitzgerald), 307,
313–14
Laval, Pierre, 336
*Lee, Grant and Sherman* (Burne), 271
Lengel, William, 162
*Letters of Thomas Wolfe, The* (Nowell,
ed.), 269*n*
"Letter to Mr. Hemingway, A" (Fadi-
man), 203*n*
"Letter to the Russians about Heming-
way" (Wilson), 229*n*
Lewis, Lloyd, 319
Lewis, Sinclair, 315
*Liberty*, 35
"*Life* Documents His New Novel with
War Shots," 301*n*
"Light of the World, The" (Heming-
way), 177, 191, 194, 199
*Literary Digest Book Review Magazine*,
54
*Little Caesar* (Burnett), 151*n*
*Little Review, The*, 61, 146
Liveright, Horace, 25
"Lone Star Preacher" (Sweeny), 319
Long, Ray, 62*n*, 79, 80, 81
"Long Time Ago Good," *see* "Fathers
and Sons"
Longworth, Alice Roosevelt, 204
*Look Homeward, Angel* (Wolfe), 58, 183
Loper, Richard H., 125
Lorimer, George Horace, 82
Losey, Joseph, 264
"lost generation, the," 39, 45
Louis, Joe, 140, 233, 240*n*
Loving, Pierre, 133, 347, 348, 349
Lowndes, Marie Adelaide Belloc, 216
Lugin, Alejandro Perez, 187

McAlmon, Robert, 29, 119, 129,
132–33, 137–38, 174, 348, 349

Mackenzie, Compton, 179
MacLeish, Archibald, 15, 50, 136, 157, 200, 233
Madrid, 233
"Maison Tellier, La," (Maupassant), 194
Malraux, André, 232
*Man's Fate* (Malraux), 232*n*
*Marlborough* (Churchill), 204
Marsh, Reginald, 340
Marshall, Margaret, 298*n*
Marvell, Andrew, 189*n*
Masefield, John, 216
Mathews, Elkin, 143*n*
Matisse, Pierre, 213
Maupassant, Guy de, 194*n*, 313
"Meditation XVII" (Donne), 282
*Men at War* (Hemingway, ed.), 303, 317
    EH's editing of, 318–19, 320, 323
    Perkins's views on contents of, 321–22
*Men Without Women* (Hemingway), 57, 61, 62, 65, 66, 67–68, 69, 74, 85, 127, 189, 239, 267, 340*n*
Mérimée, Prosper, 37
Metro-Goldwyn-Mayer, 158
Meyer, Wallace, 108, 199, 281, 286, 289, 343, 344
Miami Weather Bureau, 226
Millay, Edna St. Vincent, 151
"Million Dollar Fright" (Hemingway), 240*n*
*Mrs. Eddy* (Dakin), 135
Modern Age Books, 265
Modern Library, 153*n*, 154, 169, 172, 325
Mok, Michel, 246*n*
*Moment of Truth* (Sweeny), 324*n*
"Moment of Victory, The" (Henry), 319
Monks, Mary Welsh, *see* Hemingway, Mary Welsh Monks
Montijo, John Igual de, 309*n*, 325
Moorhead, Ethel, 174*n*, 175
Morgan, J. P., 170
Morgan, Pat, 82
"Mother of a Queen, The" (Hemingway), 177, 191, 202
*Moveable Feast, A* (Hemingway), 13, 329*n*
movies, of EH's works, 52, 169, 299, 316, 320
Murphy, Gerald, 208–9, 263, 301, 307*n*, 313

Murphy, Sara, 208, 209, 301, 313
Mussolini, Benito, 337
*My Life and Loves* (Harris), 50*n*
"My Old Man" (Hemingway), 128, 188, 262
"My Own Life" (Hemingway), 50*n*

Nairobi, 139
NANA (North American Newspaper Alliance), 233, 250
*Nation, The*, 63, 272*n*, 298
"Natural History of the Dead, A" (Hemingway), 156, 180, 191, 192, 199
*Navire D'Argent, La*, 37
"Necklace, The" (Maupassant), 313
*New England Indian Summer* (Brooks), 316
"New Kind of War, A" (Hemingway), 249*n*
*New Masses*, 250, 250*n*
*New Republic*, 50, 84, 190*n*, 229*n*, 242*n*, 249, 250, 251, 298*n*
"New Slain Knight, A" (Hemingway), 57, 65*n*, 69*n*
*New Statesman*, 132
New York, N.Y., 83, 139, 140, 233, 234, 243, 303, 332, 349
*New York Daily Mirror*, 122
*New Yorker, The*, 50*n*, 203*n*
*New York Herald Tribune*, 47, 138, 202, 298*n*, 300
*New York Post*, 246–47
New York State Society for the Suppression of Vice, 170*n*
*New York Times*, 47, 50, 107*n*, 202, 252, 314
*New York Times Book Review*, 132
*New York World-Telegram*, 106, 111–12
*Nigger to Nigger* (Adams), 81
"Night Before Battle" (Hemingway), 271, 273, 274, 275
*1919* (Dos Passos), 166, 170*n*
"Nobody Ever Dies" (Hemingway), 273, 274, 275
"No Door" (Wolfe), 312*n*
North American Newspaper Alliance (NANA), 233, 250
Nowell, Elizabeth, 269*n*

Oak Park and River Forest High School, 14, 24
Ober, Harold, 222, 301, 307*n*
O'Brien, Edward, 64–65, 128–29

obscenity, 77*n*
    in EH's works, 26–27, 42, 43, 90,
        91, 102–4, *103*, 163, 169–70,
        179–80
    *see also* censorship, in Boston
"Occurence at Owl Creek Bridge, An"
    (Bierce), 321
*Of Time and the River* (Wolfe), 183*n*,
    297
O'Hara, John, 232
*Old Man and the Sea, The* (Heming-
    way), 16–17, 273*n*, 304
"Old Man at a Bridge, The" (Heming-
    way), 262, 266
"Old Newsman Writes: A Letter from
    Cuba" (Hemingway), 218*n*
"Old Soldiers Never Die" (Richards),
    319
Old Testament, 56
"On Being Shot Again" (Hemingway),
    223*n*
*One More River* (Galsworthy), 204*n*
"One Reader Writes" (Hemingway),
    191, 202
"One Trip Across" (Hemingway), 203*n*,
    206*n*, 227, 238, 240, 243, 244
*On Literature Today* (Brooks), 316*n*
"On the Quai at Smyrna" (Heming-
    way), 150*n*, 263, 267
"The Other Side of Paradise, Scott
    Fitzgerald, 40, Engulfed in
    Despair," (Mok), 246*n*
*Our Times* (Sullivan), 231*n*
"Out of Season" (Hemingway), 149,
    262
*Over Here* (Sullivan), 204*n*
Overton, Grant, 119

Pamplona, 46, 52, 56
Paramount Studios, 299, 301
Paris, 15, 24, 29, 263
*Paris Salons, Cafés, Studios* (Huddle-
    ston), 93*n*
Parker, Dorothy, 151, 202
"Pasting It Together" (Fitzgerald), 237*n*
Paterson, Isabel, 120, 133, 347, 348,
    349
Paul, Elliot, 265
Pearl Harbor attack, 315
Peralto, Francisco "Facultades," 187
Percival, Philip, 206
Perkins, Louise, 140, 219, 224
Perkins, Maxwell Evarts:
    article on EH by, 295–97

author's responsibilities as viewed
    by, 24
background of, 24–25
book clubs as viewed by, 165
Brooks criticized by, 316
at Charles Scribner's Sons offices,
    *305*
death of, 303, 342, 343
discomfort in company of women,
    217
editorial technique of, 25
EH defended by, 200–201
EH's writing as viewed by, 33,
    34–35, 52, 280
*A Farewell to Arms* as viewed by,
    88–90, 98–99, 106–7
Fitzgerald's correspondence with,
    75, 77, 182, 258
Fitzgerald's deterioration and, 62,
    70–71, 78, 82–83, 206
on Fitzgerald's *Esquire* pieces, 238
Fitzgerald's writing as viewed by, 73,
    77, 204–5, 210, 211
*For Whom the Bell Tolls* as viewed
    by, 279, 283–84, 286
hay fever attacks of, 77, 78, 82–83
in Key West, 2, *88*, 90, *139*, 219
literary values of, 26
misogynistic reputation of, 24
*The Old Man and the Sea* dedicated
    to, 304
obscene words avoided by, 26–27
on publishing business, 122–23, 150
on Stein, 194–95
place in literary history, 135, 135*n*
*The Sun Also Rises* as viewed by,
    38–39, 52
superstition of, 172–73
Virginia battlefields trip with Fitzger-
    ald of, 173
Wilson as viewed by, 326, 330–31
Wolfe's writing habits and, 182–83,
    205, 211–12
writing as viewed by, 5
*see also* Hemingway-Perkins rela-
    tionship
Perkins, Peg, 294
*Pétain* (Sweeny), 336*n*
*Peter Pan* (Barrie), 65*n*
Pfeiffer, Gustavus Adolphus, 110,
    113–14
Pfeiffer, Pauline, *see* Hemingway,
    Pauline Pfeiffer
Phelps, William Lyon, 49, 100, 167

"Philippe" stories (Fitzgerald), 223n
Philosophies of War (Sheen), 331n
Philosophy Four (Wister), 135–36
Picasso, Pablo, 340, 341
"Piece of String, A" (Maupassant), 313
Peirce, Waldo, 71, 72, 73, 78, 82, 96, 97, 113, 135, 277, 310, 311, 312, 349
Pierre Matisse Gallery, 213
Piggott, Ark., 73
Pilar (EH's boat), 210n, 216, 324n
"Pilgrim on the Gila" (Wister), 135
plagiarism suit against EH, 309, 310, 312
Pocket Books, 325
Pound, Ezra, 15, 66, 143, 151
Powell, Dawn, 332, 332n
"Prescott, Roger," 41
Price, Alan, 97n
Publishers' Weekly, 260
"Pursuit Race, A" (Hemingway), 63n

Quintanilla, 213n
Quintanilla, Luis, 172, 177, 213, 265

Randall, David, 327
Random House, 312
Rawlings, Marjorie Kinnan, 24, 217, 233, 255
Red Badge of Courage, The (Crane), 51
Redbook, 223n
Re-Discovery of America, The (Frank), 99
Reglamento, 167
Replenishing Jessica (Bodenheim), 106n
Reynolds, Paul Revere, 50, 121
Richards, Frank, 319
Richardson, Hadley, see Hemingway, Hadley Richardson
"Rich Boy, The" (Fitzgerald), 314
Richmond Times-Dispatch, 125
"Right Honorable, the Strawberries, The" (Wister), 135
River War, The (Churchill), 319
Road, The (Chamson), 75
Roth, Samuel, 49–50, 54
Round-Up (Lardner), 188n
Rowohlt, Ernst, 85, 176

Sackville West, V., 136
St. Lo, 333
Saki (H. H. Munro), 319
San Francisco earthquake (1906), 316

Saturday Evening Post, The, 82n
Saturday Review of Literature, 202, 203n
Save Me the Waltz (Z. Fitzgerald), 167n
Scott, Peter, 272
Scribner, Charles, Jr., 12, 305
    Hemingway assessed by, 13–17
Scribner, Charles, III, 27, 81, 134, 182, 184, 189, 217, 224, 273, 277, 281, 305, 308, 320, 325, 330
    Boston censorship incident and, 108, 110
    EH's friendship with, 11–12, 344–45
    Perkins's death and, 343–44
    and plagiarism suit against EH, 310, 312
Scribners, see Charles Scribner's Sons
Scribner's Magazine, 34n, 41n, 56, 66, 150, 159n, 165, 214, 219–20
    EH's articles for, 159, 160
    EH's stories published in, 46n, 53n, 139, 191
    A Farewell to Arms serialized in, 56, 57, 58, 74–75, 77, 78, 80–81, 86, 91–93, 94–96, 106–7, 127
    Green Hills of Africa serialized in, 219–20, 221–22
    June 1929 issue of, 106
    publication ceased by, 280n
"Sea Change, The" (Hemingway), 188, 191, 202
"Second Poem to Mary" (Hemingway), 333n
Seldes, Gilbert, 70, 71
Selected Letters (Hemingway), 143
serialization:
    of A Farewell to Arms, 56, 57, 58, 74–75, 77, 78, 80–81, 86, 91–93, 94–96, 106–7, 127
    For Whom the Bell Tolls and, 280–81, 283
    of Green Hills of Africa, 219–20, 221–22
Shadows of the Sun (Curritos de la Crus) (Lugin), 187n
Shakespeare, William, 136
Sheen, Fulton J., 331
Shelley, Percy Bysshe, 24
Shenton, Edward, 224
Sheridan, Wyo., 202
Sherman, Fighting Prophet (Lewis), 319
Sherwood, Robert, 254
Shipman, Evan, 133, 192, 324, 348

*Shock of Recognition, The* (Wilson, ed.), 326

"Short Happy Life of Francis Macomber, The" ("A Budding Friendship") (Hemingway), 239, 240, 244, 249, 263, 265, 267, 322

*Shot-Gun Psychology* (Smith), 271

Siegal, Ben "Bugsy," 345

"Simple Enquiry, A" (Hemingway), 202

Simpson, Kenneth, 50

Smith, Chard Powers, 147*n*

Smith, Lawrence B., 271*n*

Snow, Norman, 343

"Snows of Kilimanjaro, The" ("The Happy Ending") (Hemingway), 239, 240, 241, 244, 245, 246, 249, 263, 265, 268–69, 322
movie rights to, 341

social realism, 26

*South Moon Under* (Rawlings), 217*n*

Soviet Union, 194–95, 223, 229, 242

Spain, 34, 39, 248, 250, 251
Civil War in, 233, 234, 246, 258–59, 269, 271, 272, 274
October Revolution in, 213
as setting for *For Whom the Bell Tolls*, 283–84

*Spanish Earth, The*, 233

Speiser, Maurice, 28, 248, 254, 259, 309, 325, 339

Spellman, Francis Cardinal, 331–32, 333

"Spring Freshets" (Turgenev), 218

"Square Egg, The" (Saki), 319

Stallings, Laurence, 121

Stearns, Harold, 46, 46*n*

Steffens, Lincoln, 165

Stein, Gertrude, 15, 45, 51, 196, 199, 201
on EH, 193, 194–95
EH on, 225, 227–28

Steinbeck, John, 318

Stendhal (Marie Henri Beyle), 89

Stevenson, Robert Louis, 14

Stewart, Donald Ogden, 46, 51, 52

Stock Market Crash (1929), 122, 130

*Strange Fugitive* (Callaghan), 75–76

Strater, Henry (Mike), 129, 132, 135, 169, 178

*Stricken Field, A* (Gellhorn), 278, 327

*Studio: Europe* (Groth), 340*n*

Sullivan, Mark, 204, 231

Sumner, John S., 170

Sumner, William, 200

*Sun Also Rises, The* (Hemingway), 26–27, 30, *31*, 36, 37, 54–55, 66, 69, 79, 97, 127, 157, 202, 253, 256
Barnes's emasculation in, 40–41
Brett in, 43, 46, 47, 48, 54, 73
British edition of, 57, 63–64
dedication of, 45
EH's revisions to, 44–45, 47
epigraphs in, 36, 45, 51, 52
German edition of, 85
Gorton in, 38, 40, 46
"Irony and Pity" passage of, 40, 42, 44, 45
movie rights to, 52, 169
obscene words in, 42, 43
Perkins's suggested prologue for, 47, 48
Perkins's views on, 38–39, 52
reviews of, 46–47, 48–49, 51, 55, 56
royalties of, 56
Russian success of, 242

Sun Valley Lodge, Idaho, 234

Sweeny, Charles, 315, 319, 322, 324
Pétain pamphlet of, 336–37

*Taking of the Guy* (Masefield), 216

*Tales from a Dugout* (Empey), 37*n*

Tate, Allen, 55, 56, 145

Temple, Mildred, 63

*Tender Is the Night* (Fitzgerald), 64*n*, 73*n*, 140, 207, 208–9, 275, 307, 313

Teruel, 253, 273

Thalberg, Irving, 313

*That Summer in Paris* (Callaghan), 116*n*

theater:
*A Farewell to Arms* adapted for, 121
*Fifth Column, The*, 234, 252*n*, 253, 256, 257, 258, 259, 260–61, 263, 264–65, 266, 273

*This Quarter*, 143, 191, 192

*This Side of Paradise* (Fitzgerald), 25, 29

"Thistle, The" (Tolstoy), 284, 321

Thomas, George Clifford, Jr., 164

Thomas, George Clifford, III, 164

Thomason, John W., 37, 276, 315, 319, 320, 322

Thompson, Charles, 206

Three Mountains Press, 29, 33, 35, 132, 258

*Three Soldiers* (Dos Passos), 341

*Three Stories and Ten Poems* (Hemingway), 29, 145*n*

*Through the Wheat* (Boyd), 37
Tinker, Frank, 318
*Tobacco Road* (Caldwell), 156*n*
"Today Is Friday" (Hemingway), 54,
    156, 262, 263
*To Have and Have Not* (Hemingway),
    27, 185*n*, 233, 257, 297
    advertising for, 254
    alternate titles for, 250
    Detroit suppression of, 259
    form of, 249–50, 251
    publication of, 245, 248
    reviews of, 266
    sales of, 253
"To His Coy Mistress" (Marvell),
    189*n*
Tolstoy, Leo, 24, 197, 284, 318, 321
"To Mary in London" (Hemingway),
    333*n*
"Tomb of His Grandfather, The"
    ("Fathers and Sons") (Heming-
    way), 192, 193, 199, 200, 203*n*
*Tom Jones* (Fielding), 69, 72
"Torero, The" (Gris), 175
Toronto *Star,* 15, 24, 70
*Torrents of Spring, The* (Hemingway), 29,
    30, *31,* 35–36, 41, 53, 56, 143
*Torrents of Spring, The* (Turgenev),
    218*n*
*Toward the Flame* (Allen), 37
*Town and Country,* 128, 277
"Tradesman's Return, The" (Heming-
    way), 238, 239, 243, 244
Train, Arthur, 24, 259
Trelawny, Edward John, 43*n*
Turgenev, Ivan, 218*n*
22nd Infantry Regiment, U.S., 303, 345
Twisden, Duff, 49
*Two Gentlemen of Verona* (Shake-
    speare), 136
*Two Worlds Monthly,* 49

*Ulysses* (Joyce), 49, 56
"Undefeated, The" (Hemingway), 37*n*,
    52, 68, 128, 128*n*, 202
*Understanding Fiction* (Brooks and War-
    ren, eds.), 313*n*
"Under the Ridge" (Hemingway), 274,
    275
*Unshaken Friend* (Cowley), 25*n*
"Up in Michigan" (Hemingway), 16,
    144–45, 145*n*, 241, 244, 257, 258,
    259, 260, 263, 266, 267, 270
*U.S.A.* (Dos Passos), 170*n*, 340*n*

Vanderbilt, Alfred, 206
Van Dine, S. S. (Willard Huntington
    Wright), 24, 42, 112, 205, 231
*Vanity Fair,* 115
Vassar College, 307*n*
"Very Short Story, A" (Hemingway),
    147
Villalta, Nicanor, 171
*Virginian, The* (Wister), 76*n*
*Virgin Spain* (Frank), 173*n*
*Viva Madero* (Montijo), 309
Von Kurowsky, Agnes, 147*n*

Walpole, Hugh, 63, 136
Walsh, Ernest, 143–44, 174*n*, 175
*War and Peace* (Tolstoy), 24, 37, 197,
    317, 321
Warren, Robert Penn, 313
Wartels, Nat, 317, 318, 319
"War Years, The" (Hilton), 319
Watkins, Ann, 158
Watson, Ark., 139, 178
"Way You'll Never Be, A" (Hemingway),
    189, 191, 192, 194*n*, 203*n*
Weber, William, 281
Welsh, Mary, *see* Hemingway, Mary
    Welsh Monks
Wertenbaker, George, 335
Wescott, Glenway, 41*n*, 64*n*, 65, 74
Weston, Christine, 24, 326–27
Wharton, Edith, 75, 130
Wheeler, John N., 250, 251
Wheelock, John Hall, 39, 99, 343
*Where the Rivers Meet* (Dorrance), 276,
    276*n*
Whitehead, 201
Whittier, John Greenleaf, 66
"Who Murdered the Vets?" (Heming-
    way), 227*n*, 249, 250, 251
*Wild Chorus* (Scott), 272
Wilder, Thornton, 73–74, 118, 124,
    125, 149
Wilson, Edmund "Bunny," 50, 55, 84,
    137, 326
    *The Last Tycoon* edited by, 307,
    308–9, 313–14
    Fitzgerald's letters and, 328,
    329–30
    *In Our Time* introduction by, 145,
    147, 149, 150–52
    literary criticism by, 311
    Perkins's views on, 330–31
    reviews of, 229, 231, 242, 272, 298,
    300

"Wine of Wyoming" (Hemingway), 139, 191, 202
"Wings Always Over Africa" (Hemingway), 229n, 230, 241
*Winner Take Nothing* (Hemingway), 139, 187–205, 232, 239, 267, 322
   advertising for, 202
   dedication of, 200
   order of stories in, 191, 194, 195
   proofs of, 195–96, 200
   reviews of, 201–3
   sales of, 204
*Winter's Tale, The* (Shakespeare), 295n
Wister, Owen, 76, 97, 98, 99–101, 104, 105–6, 111, 112, 121, 122, 135–36, 241, 280
Wolfe, Thomas, 24, 25–26, 27, 58, 156, 162, 180, 181, 184, 214, 218, 233, 234, 330
   death of, 269, 270, 271

   departure from Scribners of, 233, 253, 254–55, 257
   EH's meeting with, 139, 182–83, 297
   illness of, 265, 266, 268, 269
   libel case against, 311–12
   writing habits of, 182–83, 205, 211–12
Woolf, Virginia, 66
World War I, EH's service in, 296
   *see also Farewell to Arms, A*
World War II, 315, 316–17, 318, 323, 333
Wright, Willard Huntington, 24, 42
   *see also* Van Dine, S. S.
Wykoff, Irma, 90
Wylie, Elinor, 84–85

*Yearling, The* (Rawlings), 217n, 233

Zweig, Arnold, 101n